KŪKAI: MAJOR WORKS

Prepared for the Columbia College Program of Translations from the Oriental Classics   WM. THEODORE DE BARY, EDITOR

Number LXXXVII *of the Records of Civilization: Sources and Studies* EDITED UNDER THE AUSPICES OF THE DEPARTMENT OF HISTORY, COLUMBIA UNIVERSITY

KŪKAI

MAJOR WORKS

TRANSLATED, WITH AN
ACCOUNT OF HIS LIFE
AND A STUDY OF HIS
THOUGHT, BY

Yoshito S. Hakeda

COLUMBIA UNIVERSITY PRESS

NEW YORK

Yoshito S. Hakeda, Associate Professor of Japanese in the Department of East Asian Languages and Cultures and Associate Professor in the Department of Religion at Columbia University, is the translator of *The Awakening of Faith, attributed to Aśvaghosha* (1967), and one of the collaborators assisting Wm. Theodore de Bary in preparing *Buddhist Tradition in India, China, and Japan* (1969).

Portions of this work were prepared under a grant from the Carnegie Corporation of New York and under a contract with the U.S. Office of Education for the production of texts to be used in undergraduate education. The texts so produced have been used in the Columbia College Oriental Humanities program and have subsequently been revised and expanded for publication in the present form. Copyright is claimed only in these portions of the work not submitted in fulfillment of the contract with the U.S. Office of Education. Neither the Carnegie Corporation nor the U.S. Office of Education is the author, owner, publisher, or proprietor of this publication, and neither is to be understood as approving by virtue of its support any of the statements made or views expressed therein.

UNESCO COLLECTION OF REPRESENTATIVE WORKS
Japanese Series
This book
has been accepted
in the Japanese series
of the Translations Collection
of the United Nations
Educational, Scientific and Cultural Organis.·tion
(UNESCO)

TO YUJI

FOREWORD

Kūkai: Major Works, Translated, with an Account of His Life and a Study of His Thought is one of the Translations from the Oriental Classics by which the Committee on Oriental Studies has sought to transmit to Western readers representative works of the major Asian traditions in thought and literature. In most cases these are writings which in our judgment any educated man should have read. There is a difficulty, however, in making such a claim for the works of Kūkai. Though he is undoubtedly one of the great geniuses of Japanese religious and cultural history, it cannot be said that his works have been widely read in the original. Esoteric Buddhism, of which they are probably the most important expression in any language, does not itself place prime reliance on transmission by written texts. The very term "esoteric" suggests the inherent difficulty of communicating truth through words and concepts alone. And for the modern reader Kūkai's style in classical Chinese prose and poetry of the T'ang period is impenetrable by all but the initiated.

Fortunately one of the initiated, Professor Hakeda has undertaken to render these cryptic and highly allusive texts into modern English. That he has done so, fully aware of the odds against the translator, shows not his temerity but his humility. Someone, he feels, must be willing to run these risks, even though there can be no assurance of achieving a definitive result. It is that important for us to have some understanding of Kūkai's philosophy, which provided the spiritual and theoretical basis for much of Japanese classical culture, and especially the arts.

WM. THEODORE DE BARY

PREFACE

This book is offered to provide a comprehensive introduction to Kūkai, or Kōbō daishi. Kūkai is preeminent in Japanese cultural history, like a majestic watershed from which streams of culture run down through history. Because of his antiquity and popularity, he has been so veiled by myths and legends that only after years of study of his original works, of his historical background, and of the tradition he inherited did I feel sufficiently confident to write on his life and thought and to translate his representative works.

The writing of the first two parts of this book has been made possible by the Fulbright-Hays Fellowship, which I received from July 1, 1967, to July 1, 1968; the third part has been supported under a contract with the U.S. Office of Education under which the Committee on Oriental Studies at Columbia University has prepared texts for foreign area studies. I wish to acknowledge my indebtedness to Acharya Bokushō Kanayama, the late chief abbot of Mt. Kōya, who inspired my interest in Kūkai's religion; to the late Professor Shuntsū Kōjiro, who opened my eyes to the writings of Kūkai; to Acharya Ryūshun Soeda, abbot of Rengejōin monastery on Mt. Kōya, who initiated me into the practice of Shingon Esoteric Buddhist meditation; to Professor Toranosuke Utsumi, who guided me in religious philosophy; to Professor Gishō Nakano, director of the Research Institute of Esoteric Buddhist Culture on Mt. Kōya, who read part of my draft and furnished pertinent data; and to Acharya Seytsū Takahashi, head priest of the Koyasan Buddhist Temple of Los Angeles, California, who warmly encouraged me and contributed research materials. I would like to express my deep gratitude to Professor Wm. Theodore de Bary, who

recommended that I undertake this project for the Committee on
Oriental Studies when I came to Columbia University in 1961, and who
also read the manuscript, offering valuable suggestions; and to my col-
leagues Professors Donald Keene and Philip Yampolsky, who read
portions of the manuscript and gave me helpful advice. I would also
like to express my sincere appreciation to Mr. Royall Tyler of Columbia University, who critically read the manuscript and improved on
its style, and to Miss Elisabeth Shoemaker of Columbia University Press
for her editorial services.

YOSHITO S. HAKEDA

Columbia University
November 12, 1971

CONTENTS

KŪKAI: MAJOR WORKS

INTRODUCTION

Kūkai (774–835) is commonly known as Kōbō daishi, an honorific title given to him posthumously by the Heian court, *kōbō* meaning "to spread widely the Buddhist teachings" and *daishi*, "a great teacher." The lofty title of *daishi* was, in the course of history, conferred upon other eminent Buddhist masters, but as the popular saying goes, "Kōbō stole the title of daishi." Kūkai is, indeed, one of the most respected and popular Buddhist masters of Japan.

Legends about Kūkai are still being told all over the country, especially in the western part where he grew up and spent most of his life. In addition to the common belief that, as the inventor of the *kana* syllabary, he was the father of Japanese culture, he is remembered as the founder of Shingon or Esoteric Buddhism in Japan, the founder of the monastic center on Mt. Kōya, the originator of the pilgrimage circuit of eighty-eight temples on Shikoku, a builder of lakes, a wandering saint who engaged in severe ascetic practices, and a great calligrapher. Legendary accounts of his accomplishments were added to the numerous biographies of Kūkai written in medieval times. Attribution of these marvelous works to Kūkai owed much to the energetic propaganda activities of the Kōya-hijiri, wandering priests dispatched from Mt. Kōya. Nevertheless, the fountainhead of the legends is Kūkai himself.

This versatile man has often been depicted as a scholar-monk with three faces and six arms. Such a representation implies a mysterious entity whose entirety can be grasped only vaguely. Any student of Kūkai may wonder who Kūkai really was and what was the unifying principle, if any, behind the variety of the man's thought and action.

Outwardly, Kūkai's life may appear to be full of contradictions. He renounced the world, yet led a creative and constructive life within it. He was one of the most influential cultural leaders in the capital and participated in poetry meetings at the court, at the same time that he was a son of nature who wandered and meditated alone in remote forests. He began a new religious movement and critically evaluated established Buddhist teachings and practices, yet remained friendly with the leaders of the great Buddhist institutions. His life and works reveal in him the existence of certain polarities in a state of harmonious tension. In the same manner, the *kū* (sky) and *kai* (sea) of his name suggest two entities which are forever separate and yet conjoined. He combines rationality and a suprarational mind, fondness for both the abstract and the concrete, love both of simplicity and of variety, pragmatism and idealism, severity and gentleness.

Anyone studying ancient Japan, whether in the realm of religion, thought, literature, history, art, architecture, calligraphy, lexicography, linguistics, education, or civil engineering, sooner or later must encounter Kūkai, since his writings in those areas have been preserved and works done by him or carried out under his leadership identified. Thus, he has been admired in Japan as a culture hero and as an all-round creative genius. Although his popularity has declined in the last century, those of his works which recent research has proven genuine would compel anyone to recognize that his accomplishments were extraordinary and his influence far-reaching.

Contrary to the impression one may have of the word *esoteric*, Kūkai's Esoteric Buddhism was for a while perhaps the most international form of Buddhism in the East. Though it was short lived in China and in the Southeast Asian regions such as Ceylon and Indonesia, it survives to this day in Tibet and in the Himalayan kingdoms. Just as the Shingon sect Kūkai established in Japan was international in outlook, so Kūkai the man was one of the most international personalities among the cultural or religious leaders of pre-modern Japan, having studied under Japanese, Chinese, and Indian teachers. Other founders of major Japanese Buddhist sects visited China, but Kūkai alone studied in China's cultural center at Ch'ang-an, the T'ang capital and the most cosmopolitan city in the East. There Kūkai had an opportunity to observe the various races and cultures of the continent. He knew both

Chinese and Sanskrit. Kūkai did not actually invent the *kana* syllabary, but its emergence owed much to his introduction of Sanskrit studies, for the *kana* system is formed on the basis of the Sanskrit alphabet. Moreover, he introduced to Japan many aspects of Chinese culture. In this Kūkai's accomplishment is phenomenal, for his stay in China did not exceed two years. Instead of listing his contributions as an importer of Chinese culture, let me quote part of a letter he wrote to the governor of Yüeh, the region to the south of the Yangtze River. The year was 806, as Kūkai was waiting for the ship that would take him back to Japan. The letter asked the governor for assistance in collecting materials to be taken back to his native land. It shows how eager Kūkai was to import whatever he thought useful to his people.

I, Kūkai, was born on an island where reeds grow high and was raised on a tiny strip of land. My caliber is limited and my learning narrow. Yet, at the risk of my life, I have eagerly sought the truth; and to this end I have traveled to many places. Seeking for the sea of teachings in this great country, I hope to pour its waters over the dry land to the east. Entrusting my life to the perils of the ocean, I at last have come here in order to find a means to grasp the truth. Now I am in possession of about three hundred scrolls of Buddhist scriptures, treatises, and commentaries, and great mandalas of the Matrix (*garbha*) and Diamond (*vajra*) Realms, etc., which I managed to reproduce in the city of Ch'ang-an. I exhausted all my efforts and drained all my resources in seeking after and reproducing them. Owing to my inferior capacity and to the magnitude of the teachings, however, what I have gathered is no more than a strand of hair. Gone are all my reserves. Since I am no longer able to hire anyone, I have copied them myself, forgetting to eat and sleep. The chariot of the sun does not reverse its direction, and thus the time for my departure has neared. To whom should I open my heart so as to dispel my anxiety? . . . Humbly I beg you to reflect upon the will of the Buddha,[1] to have compassion on me who have come from afar, and to assist me in transmitting to my distant country, regardless of their quantity, whatever teachings might enlighten the darkness of the people and help save them materially, be these scriptures, ethical texts, philosophical treatises; biographical records pertaining to Confucianism, Taoism, and Buddhism; books of poetry or of rhyme-prose (*fu*); collections of inscriptions; or texts on divination, medicine, linguistics, arts, mathematics, logic. . . .[2]

---

[1] That one should make an effort to preserve correct teachings and to have compassion toward others.

[2] *Kōbō daishi zenshū* (henceforth abbreviated *K.Z.*), III, 459–60.

Judging from the collection Kūkai brought back from China, the governor must have been moved to extend generous aid to him and, through him, to Japan.

Along with these contributions, Kūkai is remembered for the way he assimilated foreign culture to the indigenous way of thinking. Independence and originality of mind can be detected, for example, in his works of poetry in Chinese and in his calligraphy. The ideal attitude for learning poetry and calligraphy was that "a poet should learn the styles of olden times but not imitate them; a calligrapher should absorb the spirit manifested in ancient works but not copy them." [3] This attitude was further demonstrated in his uniquely creative systematization of Esoteric Buddhism; his planning of the monastic center on Mt. Kōya; the artistic devices he applied to the Lecture Hall (*kōdō*) of the Tōji in Kyoto; his interpretation of the Buddhist scriptures; and his curriculum for a school for the children of the poor.

The Esoteric Buddhism which Kūkai systematized was an artistic religion of rich symbolism and it appealed to Heian Japan. As a result, one area of Kūkai's influence on Japanese culture was in the arts. Minutely regulated religious ceremonies; mysterious and exotic liturgies in Sanskrit; a rich iconography; abundant use of sound instruments; the symmetrical structure of the altar in squares, rectangles, and circles; colorful paintings, gorgeous costumes, and elaborate ritual implements —all these hallmarks of Esoteric Buddhism fascinated the Heian intellectuals, stimulating their imagination and refining their aesthetic sensitivity. The practices of Esoteric Buddhism contributed much to the spiritual and aesthetic foundations of Heian culture. In turn, it was the aesthetic standards of this culture which set the tone for all subsequent artistic expression in Japan.

For Kūkai, "the arts" covered a very wide area:

The arts were generally considered by Kūkai's school under four aspects: 1) painting and sculpture; 2) music and literature; 3) gestures and acts; and 4) the implements of civilization and religion. Ability in any or all of the arts may be achieved by a mastery of the Three Mysteries [of body, speech, and mind] and can result in the creation of flowers of civilization which are Buddhas in their own right. For Kūkai whatever was

[3] *K.Z.*, III, 427.

beautiful partook of the nature of Buddha. Nature, art, and religion were one. It is not difficult, then, to see why so aesthetic a religion found favor at a time when Japanese civilization was at the height of its flowering.[4]

In relation to the arts, the effect which Kūkai's Esoteric Buddhism had on the method of transmission of traditional culture in medieval Japan should be considered. Individualistic and international Esoteric Buddhism had a personal way of transmitting religious knowledge from master to disciple. Kūkai's introduction of this way of transmitting Esoteric Buddhist teachings had a far-reaching effect on Japanese culture, for almost all divisions of learning, art, and craftsmanship in medieval Japan came to follow this method. Indeed, some of the traditional arts are still not free of it. This aspect of Kūkai's influence may have been reinforced several centuries later by the arrival from Sung China of Zen Buddhism, which had a similar method of transmission.

The most conspicuous and immediate impact of Kūkai's religious thought and practice was on the existing Buddhist sects and, in particular, on the newly formed Tendai sect. Together with Kūkai's Shingon sect, Tendai became dominant and was the breeding ground for new sects in the following historical period. Saichō (767–822), the founder of Tendai, received instruction in Esoteric Buddhism from Kūkai. His successors increasingly stressed Esoteric Buddhism over the Tendai teachings proper, the system of thought of the Chinese T'ien-t'ai sect developed mainly on the basis of the *Lotus Sutra*. Under the impetus of Kūkai's Esoteric Buddhism, the most eminent successors of Saichō, such as Ennin (794–864), Enchin (814–91), and Annen (841–915), busied themselves adopting and assimilating Esoteric Buddhist elements into the Tendai teachings. Consequently, about a century after Kūkai, Mt. Hiei and Miidera, a temple near the shores of Lake Biwa, became centers of Esoteric Buddhism, and Taimitsu (Tendai Esotericism) came to contend with Tōmitsu (Shingon Esotericism, that of the Tōji) for supremacy in Japan.

The contest between Tendai and Shingon for recognition as the center of esotericism resulted in victory for the Hiei monks. Their success was due partially to the failure of Shingon to produce great leaders in the genera-

[4] Wm. Theodore de Bary, ed., *Sources of Japanese Tradition* (Columbia University Press, 1958), p. 142.

tions after Kūkai, and partially to the advantage which geographical prox-
imity to the capital gave to Hiei over the more distant Kōya.[5]

Paradoxically the triumph of the Tendai monks also meant their defeat,
for the Esoteric Buddhism advocated by Kūkai virtually overwhelmed
them. Hence, the Esoteric Buddhism shared by the Tendai and Shingon
sects exerted much religious influence on the Heian and medieval Japanese, molding to a great extent their views of life, nature, and the world
at large.

Kūkai stressed that his Esoteric Buddhism was on one hand of great
use in "pacifying and defending the nation (*chingo kokka*)," and, on
the other hand, would enable an individual to "attain enlightenment in
this very existence (*sokushin jōbutsu*)." He asserted that his religion
was, among all other teachings, the most efficacious in these two areas.
Certainly one of the reasons that Esoteric Buddhism may be considered
an international form of Mahayana Buddhism is its individualistic character. A sense of individual salvation was weak or absent in the Nara
period. Generally speaking, Nara Buddhism served the well-being of
the state or of communities; or it became an object of academic learning. Confucianism was less a religion than an ethico-political teaching,
one which every aspirant to an official post was obliged to study.
Taoism represented a way to lead a life of escape, or a means to prolong
one's life span. Shinto, which involved shamanistic practice, was the
binding spiritual force among Japan's clan-centered communities; hence,
it could hardly encourage the notion of individual salvation. Esoteric
Buddhism's message of individual salvation allowed the devotee to
develop a sense of religious hope and despair, for it encouraged an
aspiration toward salvation at the same time that it made plain the re-
moteness of the goal. This message prompted the Japanese to look
within, to develop a sense of individual moral and religious responsibility, and to become aware of the weight of personal karma.

Kūkai was the first in Japan to hold that man is originally enlightened
(*hongaku*). His insistence that one can attain enlightenment here and
now was grounded on this belief, a belief derived from the simple insight that unless a man is enlightened from the very beginning he has
no way to reach enlightenment. Kūkai could not have been innocent
enough to hold such an optimistic view without being aware of the

[5] *Ibid.,* p. 158.

darker aspect of man's mind. He was not a born optimist; in fact, it was only in his forties that he started to advocate this idea. He exhorted his followers to be aware of the bondage of evil karma but encouraged them to perceive the originally enlightened nature of man through the veils of evil karma. He believed that evil karma could be wiped away but not man's originally enlightened nature. "If one has faith and practices, then, whether one is male or female, or of high or low birth, one will qualify as having a great capacity." [6] The thought of original enlightenment appealed to the basically optimistic Shinto mentality of the Japanese. The Esoteric Buddhism of Kūkai, though incomparably more complex and sophisticated than Shinto, had many elements compatible with the latter. A few of these were the idea of the oneness of man and nature, a belief in the magical efficacy of the word (mantra in the former, *kotodama* in the latter), and the concept of a ritually consecrated realm. It was only natural that as time went by Esoteric Buddhism should come into close association with Shinto.

Kūkai's religion was a religion of both mountains and plains. His monastic center on Mt. Kōya, located in a remote forest of gigantic cedars, refused easy access to men and was until recently forbidden to women; while another center he established, the Tōji, was in Kyoto itself. The state- or clan-supported temples of Nara Buddhism represented the religion of the plains or of the city. Until the beginning of the Heian period, when Saichō and Kūkai opened their monastic centers, no major Buddhist institution existed on a mountain. For Kūkai Mt. Kōya was the sacred forest where he sat in meditation, freed himself from all secular concerns, and gave himself up to the beauty and mystery of unspoiled nature. It was in his headquarters in Kyoto, on the other hand, that he placed himself in relation to the world. The Tōji was the base from which Kūkai disseminated his religion; it was an institution designed to serve the well-being of the country. Kūkai officially named the temple "The Temple for Defense of the Nation by Means of the King of Doctrines (*kyōō gokoku ji*)." Here also he opened a school for the poor. His religion was, in other words, characterized simultaneously by seclusion from and participation in the world. In time Kūkai came to be regarded as a prototype of the holy ascetic of magical power who from time to time descended from the

[6] *K.Z.*, III, 551.

sacred mountain into the world to help save people. Mt. Kōya, located at several days' walking distance from the capital, was regarded as a locus of divine power. It was Esoteric Buddhism as a mountain religion that established an intimate relationship with Shinto.

In ancient Japan the mountains, where kami resided, were believed to be more sacred than the plains. In the Nara period many quasi-Buddhist ascetics, followers of an unsystematized Esoteric Buddhism (*zōmitsu*), disciplined themselves in the sacred mountains with the aim of obtaining occult power. The government frequently prohibited their activities but without success. Naturally, these mountain ascetics were not free from a Shinto mentality and prayed both to their Buddhist guardians and to the kami of their respective mountains for success in their endeavors and for protection from danger. These mountain ascetics made no differentiation between the Buddhist guardians and the Shinto kami as objects of prayer. Thus there arose, through practical necessity rather than through any theoretical speculation, a real fusion between Esoteric Buddhism and Shinto. This developed into Shugendō, an indigenous, ascetic mountain religion which greatly affected popular spiritual life up to the early Meiji period. Shingon and Tendai Esoteric Buddhism, as a religion of the mountains, had provided Shugendō with its theories and patterns of practice. Moreover, the influence of Esoteric Buddhism on Shinto did not stop at the systematization of Shugendō but penetrated in due course to the heart of Shinto. It was not Kūkai, as is popularly believed, who identified the kami with the Buddhas and Bodhisattvas of the Shingon mandalas on the theory that the former were incarnations of the latter. (This doctrine, known as *honji suijaku*, held, for example, that the Sun Goddess Amaterasu was the incarnation of Mahāvairocana, the central Buddha of the Shingon pantheon.) Yet I believe that the fusion of Buddhism and Shinto, a feature of Japanese religious life at large, owed much to Kūkai's establishment of Esoteric Buddhism as a system of thought, as a way of life, and as a religion congenial to the Japanese mental climate.

An effort has been made to examine Kūkai's actions, sentiments, and thought in Parts One and Two of this book. I present him as a historical person on the basis of primary sources. Necessarily, the discussion is limited to his own lifetime, for Kūkai lived on in faith, myth, and legend, and apocryphal stories about him alone could fill a whole vol-

ume. I have tried to understand his thought directly from his own
writings, although without disregarding such other evidence as his
design for the monastic center on Mt. Kōya, the altar layouts he advocated, and the actual course of his life.

Kūkai's writings are by no means easy to comprehend. To begin
with, his thought centers around the secrets of Esoteric Buddhism, and
his medium of expression is an extremely ornate style of classical Chinese interspersed with many Sanskrit terms. That he wrote in Chinese
was not extraordinary. In Kūkai's time Japan did not yet have a language or a writing system capable of expressing abstract ideas. In order
to express oneself in writing, one had to have mastered Chinese. Nor
was one accepted by court society unless one could compose Chinese
poetry and write ornate prose.

Despite Kūkai's fame, his thought is not widely known outside of a
restricted circle of Buddhist scholars and Shingon clergymen. On the
whole, Kūkai has been admired without his original works having been
read or his thought understood. This is partly because the closed community of Shingon clergymen has guarded his teachings for centuries
as a religious secret. In my opinion his major works command special
attention in that they are early expressions of the original, critical, and
synthetic mind of Japan. As to scope of vision, breadth of learning, and
tenacity in the pursuit of understanding, there are few Japanese think-
ers who can equal him.

Part Three consists of eight of Kūkai's works in translation. To
understand Kūkai's religious teachings, Shingon monks have since medieval times been required to study a book called the *Ten Fascicles* (*Jikkan
shō*). This includes *Aspiration to Enlightenment* (*Bodaishin ron*) attributed to Nāgārjuna [7] in one fascicle, and the following six works of
Kūkai in nine fascicles: *Attaining Enlightenment in This Very Existence* (*Sokushin jōbutsu gi*) in one fascicle; *The Meanings of Sound,
Word, and Reality* (*Shōji jissō gi*) in one fascicle; *The Meanings of the
Word Hūṃ* (*Unji gi*) in one fascicle; *The Difference between Exoteric
and Esoteric Buddhism* (*Benkenmitsu nikyō ron*) in two fascicles; *The*

---

[7] *Taishō Tripiṭaka* (henceforth abbreviated ᴛ) 1665. A work of disputed
authorship. It is certain that the author is not Nāgārjuna, the second-century
founder of the Mādhyamika school of Buddhism in India. Kūkai quotes extensively from it, especially in the concluding part of his *Precious Key to the
Secret Treasury*.

Precious Key to the Secret Treasury (*Hizō hōyaku*) in three fascicles;
and *The Secret Key to the Heart Sutra* (*Hannya shingyō hiken*) in
one fascicle. In addition to these six essential works, there are two more
which I regard as indispensable to an understanding of Kūkai's early
period and which initiate the development of his mature thought. One
is the *Indications of the Goals of the Three Teachings* (*Sangō shiki*),
Kūkai's first work and a product of his early twenties, and the other,
*A Memorial Presenting a List of Newly Imported Sutras and Other
Items* (*Shōrai mokuroku*), which was written and presented to the
Emperor Heizei (r. 806–9) immediately after Kūkai returned from
China.

   Among the famous works of Kūkai that are not included in my
selection are *The Ten Stages of the Development of Mind* (*Jūjūshin
ron*) in ten fascicles, *The Secret Treasure-house of the Mirrors of
Poetry* (*Bunkyō hifu ron*) in six fascicles, and *The Collected Works of
Prose and Poetry of Kūkai* (*Seirei shū*) in ten fascicles.[8] The *Ten
Stages*, consisting of about 75,000 Chinese characters, is a monumental
work of synthesis, the first of its kind in Japan. It is encyclopedic and
full of quotations from Chinese Buddhist sources. No sooner had
Kūkai finished the *Ten Stages* than he revised it, condensing the entire
work to one fifth of its former length, dropping most of the quotations,
and naming it *The Precious Key to the Secret Treasury*. This book is
translated in Part Three. For the specialist in Buddhism the *Ten Stages*
is an invaluable source of information, but for the general reader the
Precious Key is not only more easily accessible but its literary value is
greater. *The Secret Treasure-house of the Mirrors of Poetry* is the most
important extant book about the poetical theory and phonology of Six
Dynasties and Early T'ang China, but it, again, is too specialized to be
included here. Finally, *The Collected Works of Prose and Poetry* could
well be an independent book if translated in its entirety; the work is
quoted frequently in Parts One and Two of this book.

   The texts used for translation are those collected in *The Complete
Works of Kōbō daishi* (*Kōbō daishi zenshū*). The commentaries used
are those given in *The Complete Works of the Shingon Sect* (*Shingon-*

----

[8] Commonly known as the *Shōryō shū*, the full title given by Kūkai's disciple
Shinzei being *Henjō hakki seirei shū* (The collected works of the universally
illuminating, soul-inspiring one), K.Z., III, 385–560.

shū zensho), the *Taishō Tripiṭaka, The Complete Works of Buzan* (*Buzan zensho*), and *The Complete Works of Chizan* (*Chizan zensho*), in which the standard medieval Shingon commentaries on Kūkai's major works have been collected.

In translating Kūkai's major works I have often omitted lengthy quotations and parenthetical expressions when the omission does not affect the development of the theme; when there are more than two quotations aiming at the same effect, only one is kept. In the case of *The Difference between Exoteric and Esoteric Buddhism*, only the first and the concluding parts are translated and what lies between, a series of quotations amounting to about 85 percent of the work, has been deleted. Sanskrit words listed in Webster's Third International Dictionary are written as they are found there without diacritical marks.

PART ONE

LIFE OF KŪKAI

I

YOUTH

In 774 the future Kūkai was born to Lady Tamayori and Saeki Tagimi, members of a declining aristocracy, at Byōbugaura, the present-day Zentsūji, in the province of Sanuki on Shikoku.[1] The Saeki were a branch of the Ōtomo clan, whose history extends back into mythological times. They belonged to one of the noblest houses of ancient Japan.[2]

[1] There are two reliable sources for the year of Kūkai's birth. One is a statement by Kūkai appearing in the *Indications* (see p. 129) and another is a copy of a letter sent to China reporting Kūkai's death. *K.Z.*, V, 391.

[2] As far as the present writer knows, Kūkai's lineage is agreed upon by his biographers. The most reliable source on this is the material (see *Sandai jitsuroku* 5, entry on the eleventh day of the eleventh month, Jōgan 3 [861]) presented by Tomo Yoshio, a great-grandchild of Ōtomo Yakamochi, requesting that the offspring of Saeki Tagimi, Kūkai's father, be granted the title of *sukune*, a hereditary title usually given to nobles occupying high positions at court. The Saeki clan to which Kūkai belonged had the title of *atae* which was usually given to local governors (*kuninomiyatsuko*) and their descendants. Kūkai was aware that

The Ōtomo and the Saeki clans had already produced many celebrated generals, statesmen, poets, and scholars. Of these, perhaps the best known today is Ōtomo Yakamochi (d. 785), the compiler of that great poetic anthology, the *Man'yōshū*. As to the day and month of Kūkai's birth, nothing reliable is known. It was not until about four hundred years after his death that the Shingon sect designated June 15 as his official birthday to be celebrated by all believers.[3]

It is said that Kūkai in his childhood was called Tōtomono or Mao.[4] Little is known of his life up to the age of fifteen,[5] in 788, when he began to study the Chinese classics under the guidance of Atō Ōtari, his maternal uncle and the tutor of Crown Prince Iyo. Atō Ōtari, a distinguished Confucian scholar, apparently recognized the child's genius, took the fifteen-year-old Kūkai to the capital,[6] and educated him at his own home. Kūkai writes: "When young, I studied [Chinese] poetry a great deal with my maternal uncle." [7] The earliest biography of Kūkai, ascribed to his disciple Shinzei, confirms that "when he

he belonged to the old Saeki-Ōtomo clan. In one of the letters to a general of the Ōtomo clan, Kūkai states that "the men of Ōtomo and Saeki are brothers" (*K.Z.,* III, 432). There is also the opinion that the Saeki clan to which Kūkai belonged was different from the one which is known to be a branch of the Ōtomo clan. See Tsunoda Bunei, *Saeki Imaemishi* (Tokyo, 1963), pp. 7, 256. In ninth-century Japan, however, Kūkai was thought of as being of Ōtomo-Saeki lineage.

[3] Moriyama Shōshin, ed., *Bunkashijō yori mitaru Kōbō daishi den* (The life of Kōbō daishi seen from the standpoint of cultural history) (Tokyo, 1934), p. 42.

[4] The name Tōtomono (Precious One) appears in the *Twenty-Five Article Will* (*Nijūgokajō no goyuigō*) (*K.Z.,* II, 781). The name Mao (True Fish) is recorded in a document compiled much later in the *Baien kishō*, which contains collections of old paintings and documents in reproduction, published in 1828. See Katsuno Ryūshin, *Hieizan to Kōyasan* (Mt. Hiei and Mt. Kōya) (Tokyo, 1966), p. 122. Though the name Mao is popularly used in modern writings, its origin is not clear.

[5] Throughout this book Kūkai's age is given according to the old Japanese system of counting. A child was considered one year old at birth, then two years old on New Year's Day, regardless of the date of birth. "At fifteen" may mean thirteen or fourteen in the Western counting system, depending on the date of birth. In the case of Kūkai there is no way of converting his age to the Western system because of his uncertain birthdate.

[6] The capital was located at Nagaoka, a southwestern suburb of present Kyoto.

[7] The preface to his *Secret Treasure-house of Mirrors of Poetry* (*Bunkyō hifu ron*). *K.Z.,* III, 2.

reached the age of fifteen, he received instruction from his maternal uncle, Atō Ōtari, on poetry, and on the *Analects,* the *Classic of Filial Piety,* the *Historical Records,* etc." [8]

At the age of eighteen, Kūkai entered the college (*daigaku*) in the capital, which was the highest educational institution in Japan. Its curriculum was based on the standard Confucian curriculum of China, and its sole aim was to recruit and train officials. Enrollment was, with few exceptions, limited to the sons of the ruling aristocratic families. Presumably, Kūkai devoted himself wholeheartedly to his studies. Shinzei's biography describes them as follows: "He went to the capital to attend the college, where he studied the *Book of Odes* and the *Book of History* under Amasake Kiyonari, a lecturer; and the *Spring and Autumn Annals* under Doctor Okada. He read widely in the classics and in history." [9]

How long Kūkai stayed at the college or why he left is unknown. Some clues, however, can be gleaned from the style and content of the draft [10] of his *Indications of the Goals of the Three Teachings,* written in 797 when he was twenty-four, which will be discussed later. To return to Shinzei's narrative:

He read widely in the classics and in history, showing interest especially in Buddhist scriptures. He constantly told himself, however, that what he was learning was only dregs derived from the men of old. They benefited him little at that time; how much less would they benefit him after death when his body had decayed? He then thought it essential to learn the ultimate Truth.

This led Kūkai to compose the *Indications* (*Sangō shīki*) in three fascicles. He became a Buddhist layman and for some time went alone to engage in ascetic practices on the precipices of famous mountains and in the innermost recesses of lonely valleys surrounded by steep cliffs. Once, while he was meditating atop Mt. Tairyū in Awa, the great sword of

[8] *K.Z.,* Shukan, 1. This document, known as the *Biography of Kūkai Sōzu* (*Kūkai sōzu den*), is believed to have been written by Kūkai's immediate disciple Shinzei (780–860) several months after Kūkai's death. This version is the earliest among the biographies of Kūkai and its contents are the least exaggerated. However, it cannot be accepted as the work of Shinzei, for its style and content are quite impoverished when compared to his Introduction to *The Collected Works of Poetry and Prose of Kūkai* (*K.Z.,* III, 385–88).

[9] *K.Z.,* Shukan, 1.

[10] *K.Z.,* III, *The Indication of the Goal for the Deaf and Blind* (*Rōko shīki*), 287–323.

Ākāśagarbha Bodhisattva came flying toward him. Thus, the Bodhisattva showed his own mystical powers in response [to Kūkai's prayers]. Another time, while Kūkai was meditating with closed eyes, the planet Venus entered his mouth; the Bodhisattva had revealed to him the Buddha's supernatural power. In winter, when the snow fell heavily, Kūkai's hardships were great; he disciplined himself by exposing his body to the elements, clad in a cloth made of arrowroot fiber. In summer he practiced repentance day and night, all the while eating no grain at all. At twenty Kūkai shaved his head and received the Precepts, becoming a Buddhist novice.[11]

From this it can be gathered that while in the college Kūkai became dissatisfied with his Confucian studies and so turned to Buddhism in his search for higher spiritual values. The account of Kūkai in *The Twenty-Five Article Will* (*Nijūgokajō no goyuigō*),[12] traditionally believed to have been written by Kūkai six days before he breathed his last, tells us in almost identical phraseology [13] that he composed the *Indications* and went to practice asceticism. As to Kūkai's initiation, the *Will* is more specific: "At twenty, led by the abbot of Yuwabuchi, he went to the Makinōsan Temple and there he shaved his head and received the Ten Precepts." [14]

According to these descriptions, no sooner had the eighteen-year-old Kūkai entered the college than he gave up his studies, composed the *Indications*, engaged in a period of ascetic practice, and finally became a Buddhist novice at twenty. All this happened within three years, or possibly in less than two years. Because of the sanctity of the two texts involved, traditional scholars have accepted their statements uncritically. The draft of the *Indications* states, however, that the text was completed when the author was twenty-four. This date is crucial to a

[11] *K.Z.*, Shukan, 1–2.

[12] The first article consists of an autobiography or rather a historico-mythological account of Kūkai (*K.Z.*, II, 781–88). The article is spurious with respect both to authorship and to content. The anonymous writer, in an attempt to glorify Kūkai, presents him as a supernatural being. Some of the historical information may be true, but the lofty spirit and humility of Kūkai attested to in his own writings are absent. Still there seems to be no doubt that the *Will* existed not too long after Kūkai's death. A reliable copy of it dated 969, about 130 years after his death, is still extant. See Katsuno, *Hieizan to Kōyasan*, pp. 120–21.

[13] The fact that both the *Will* and Shinzei's biography use many identical or similar expressions indicates that one was influenced by the other, or that both were derived from a common source.

[14] *K.Z.*, II, 783.

critical account of Kūkai's youth. Hence, it will be necessary to examine its reliability and to consider the relationship between the draft
and its final version.

The draft is a manuscript preserved at the Kongōbuji on Mt. Kōya.
In 1910 it was published in *The Complete Works of Kōbō daishi* and
was for the first time made accessible to the general reader. The manuscript, classified as a national treasure by the Japanese government, is
believed by specialists to be in Kūkai's hand [15] and to be the original
version of the *Indications*, differing from the latter only by its title,
preface, and concluding poem, in addition to some minor matters of
phrasing in the body of the work. One can safely conclude that both
the draft and the body of the *Indications* were completed when Kūkai
was twenty-four. Presumably, Kūkai completed the draft when he was
twenty-four and changed the preface, concluding poem, and title later.
The date given in the preface to the *Indications*, however, was not
written at the same time as the date in the preface to the draft. This is
evident from the wording of the two dates, though in both cases the
meaning remains the same, that is, the first day of the twelfth month,
Enryaku 16. In the *Indications* the date is expressed in a sober, dignified
manner, while in the draft the impression is one of self-conscious elegance.[16] This feeling of greater maturity is corroborated by the preface
and the concluding poem themselves, for the change from the draft to
the *Indications* manifests the same trend. Both are, in the case of the
Indications, of far greater literary maturity and spiritual quality than
in the case of the draft. In all probability Kūkai was in his thirties or
forties when he performed the revision. In summary, one can only state
that Kūkai completed the draft of the *Indications* at twenty-four and
that his initiation took place some time between the ages of twenty-
four and thirty-one,[17] when he was sent to China by the court as a
student monk.

[15] Tsuji Zennosuke, *Nihon Bukkyōshi* (History of Japanese Buddhism), I (Tokyo, 1944), 305; Kawasaki Yasuyuki, *Nihon bunkashi taikei* (History of Japanese
culture), IV (Tokyo: Shōgakukan, 1958), 152.

[16] This difference was noted by Igarashi Tsutomu in *Heianchō bungakushi*
(History of Heian literature), I (Tokyo, 1937), 164–65. Igarashi classifies the
Indications as a work of didactic fiction, thus recognizing it as the earliest Jap-
anese fiction (*shōsetsu*) extant.

[17] The official history covering this period, the *Shoku Nihon kōki*, Vol. II, puts
the age of initiation at thirty-one. Cf. Emperor Nimmyō, Jōwa 2, 3–25.

2

DAYS OF CRISIS

The shifting of the capital from Nagaoka to Kyoto (Heian) officially took place in 794. Actually, the construction of the new capital and the tearing down of the old had both begun in the first month of the preceding year when Kūkai was twenty. Meanwhile, the court was receiving frequent reports of uprisings in northeastern Honshu. The period of Kūkai's education in the capital was an unsettled one.

Japan at the end of the eighth century was still young as a unified nation. Two hundred years had not yet passed since the tribal, decentralized Yamato kingdom had been converted into a unified state. Politically this was a period of intensive effort to build up a strong, centralized administrative power under the emperor. Society was aristocratic, and the gap between the well-to-do and the poor was wide. The public was exhausted by repeated tax levies, forced labor, and military conscription. Homeless people were everywhere, and unordained monks (*shidosō*), disguised in order to escape taxation and forced labor, filled the country. Officials rushed from one capital to another, moved by the capricious wishes of the powerful Emperor Kammu (r. 781–806). The court was rife with intrigue. The Buddhist temples were powerful at this time and owned much land. It is believed that the main reason why the Emperor Kammu had decided in 784 to move the capital from Nara to Nagaoka was to check the power of the Buddhist institutions and to start his nation building anew.

When Kūkai entered college, Kammu was planning to move his capital for the second time within a few years. Nagaoka had been cursed from the beginning. In 784 Kammu had appointed two trusted nobles, Fujiwara Tanetsugu and Saeki Imaemishi (the chief of the Saeki clan to which Kūkai belonged), to be in charge of the construction of the new capital. The anxious emperor moved to the new capital that same year. One night about ten months later, Fujiwara Tanetsugu was shot by an arrow while inspecting the construction site and died on the following day. Ōtomo Yakamochi, the head of the Ōtomo clan and an ardent opponent of the move, was thought to have been the main conspirator, though he had died less than a month previous to this incident. The dead man was deprived of his title and men of the Ōtomo and Saeki clans were exiled or executed. The heir apparent, Prince Sawara, who was said to have been on bad terms with Fujiwara Tanetsugu, was also considered a suspect and exiled, but he refused food and died on the way to Awaji Island.

Following these events, the empress died, Kammu's son contracted a prolonged illness, and various other disasters occurred. All were believed to be the work of Prince Sawara's vengeful spirit; it was to escape this baneful power that Kammu abandoned Nagaoka in favor of Kyoto. In order to clear his conscience, the emperor soon bestowed the title of emperor on the dead prince and in 806 restored their titles to the Ōtomo and Saeki men whom he had mercilessly punished. Saeki Imaemishi himself, however, had died in 790, and Kammu's action came too late to save the two clans from decline.

Thus it was that in 791, when Kūkai entered the college, he had no highly placed patron and his prospects for a government career were dim. It was only natural then that his ambition to be a statesman should wane and that he should lose interest in pursuing Confucian studies. Years later, in the preface to the *Indications*, Kūkai recalls those days of frustration and serious quest and says of himself:

At eighteen I entered the college in the capital and studied diligently. Meanwhile a Buddhist monk showed me a scripture called the *Kokūzō gumonji no hō*.[1] In that work it is stated that if one recites the mystic verse one million times according to the proper method, one will be able to memorize passages and understand the meaning of any scripture. Believing what the Buddha says to be true, I recited the verse incessantly, as if I were rubbing one piece of wood against another to make fire, all the while earnestly hoping to achieve this result. I climbed Mount Tairyū

[1] *Hsü-k'ung-tsang-ch'iu-wen-ch'ih-fa*, T1145. The text was translated into Chinese in 717 by Śubhākarasiṃha (637–735), the first patriarch of Esoteric Buddhism in China. A Japanese monk, Dōji (d. 744), who went to China in 701 and returned in 718, imported this newly translated text of Esoteric Buddhist meditation.

in Awa Province and meditated at Muroto Cape in Tosa. The valley reverberated to the sound of my voice as I recited, and the planet Venus appeared in the sky.

From that time on, I despised fame and wealth and longed for a life in the midst of nature. Whenever I saw articles of luxury—light furs, well-fed horses, swift vehicles—I felt sad, knowing that, being as transient as lightning, they too would fade away. Whenever I saw a cripple or a beggar, I lamented and wondered what had caused him to spend his days in such a miserable state. Seeing these piteous conditions encouraged me to renounce the world. Can anyone now break my determination? No, just as there is no one who can stop the wind.[2]

Considering Kūkai's background and the conditions under which he attended college, his intense perception of transiency (*mujō*) and of human misery is hardly surprising. He elaborated on these themes in the draft of the *Indications* and even included a lengthy rhyme-prose (*fu*) entitled "Transiency." [3] It was his perception of "transiency" that drove him to renounce the world.

In Japanese history Kūkai is usually identified as a man of the Heian period, though the capital was not moved to Kyoto until Kūkai was twenty-one. While Kūkai was busy at the college, Saichō, seven years his senior, was living obscurely on Mt. Hiei in a grass hut which he had built at the age of nineteen. The religious atmosphere up to the time Kūkai left the college was very much that of the Nara period; the legacy of Buddhist teachings and practices which he inherited was also that of Nara Buddhism. In fact, Kūkai's initial meditation practices can be identified with those of the Nara period mountain ascetics.

The history of Buddhism in Japan up to this time is brief, for it had been only 250 years or so since the official introduction of Buddhism from the Korean peninsula in 552. In the Nara period the fervor for temple building continued as one of the most important enterprises of the government. In 741 the government issued an order to all provincial governors that two state Buddhist temples should be built in each province. One was to be served by twenty monks, the other by ten nuns. Two years later a plan was announced to build the Tōdaiji in Nara and to install therein a huge Vairocana Buddha molded from over a million pounds of bronze. This temple was to be built to function as the headquarters of the provincial state temples.

[2] *K.Z.*, III, 324; see the *Indications*, p. 102.   [3] *K.Z.*, III, 312–15.

The state adopted Buddhism primarily in order to enhance its own authority and in particular to impress its cultural superiority upon the rebellious clans. The chief demands made on Buddhism were less spiritual than magico-religious—for example, preventing calamities, checking epidemics, stopping or inducing rains, and, at the utmost, praying for the well-being of the souls of the dead. The Buddhist establishments grew steadily in economic and political power, while corruption infiltrated the priesthood. The great temples in Nara performed their official functions in the most up-to-date, exotic Chinese style. Whereas these activities tended to be non-Buddhist, the monks officially studied the most advanced Buddhist philosophical texts. The highly sophisticated, extremely subtle doctrines of Kegon (Avataṃsaka), Sanron (Mādhyamika), and Hossō (Yogācāra) were no doubt accessible only to a chosen few. As is always the case, there were some priests who remained friends with the people, turning away from the activities of the great temples, but one can assume that the majority of the monks were engaged in a split life.

In this period there were two types of Buddhist priest: official and private. The former were those monks who had passed the qualifying examination administered by the monastic officials (sōgō) appointed by the government and who had been ordained at one of the three national ordination platforms (kaidan). They were bureaucrats clad in priestly robes and staffed the state-supported temples. Their official role was "the pacification and defense of the nation (chingo kokka)." The private priests, or unordained monks (shidosō), led a secular life while engaging in such activities as ascetic practice, healing, divination, preaching tales of reward in heaven and punishment in hell, encouraging repentance and accumulation of merit.[4] The number of this latter group had become astonishingly high by the end of the eighth century. The spread of temple estates and the growing number of priests caused a serious decline in state income. From 771 on and all during Kūkai's stay in the capital, a stream of decrees was issued in the hope of reducing the powers of the Buddhist institutions. These prohibited the erection of clan temples and discouraged individuals from becoming

[4] Vivid descriptions of the religious atmosphere of the time can be found in the *Nihon ryōiki* (Miraculous stories of Japan) written and compiled in 824 by a lowly married clergyman named Gyōkai who belonged to the Yakushiji in Nara.

priests. Strong measures were taken against the so-called private priests, forcing the unqualified to return to their secular status.

In the latter half of the eighth century certain Nara monks, dissatisfied with the vain, pompous affairs of the urban Buddhist establishments, built temples in secluded mountains for the practice of meditation. Examples of these are the Murōji in Yamato Province and Hisosanji in Yoshino Province. The group associated with the Hisosanji was called the Natural Wisdom school (*jinenchi shū*).[5] It was this group that advocated meditation accompanied by recitation of the mantra of Ākāśagarbha (*Kokūzō gumonji no hō*). At the start of his spiritual quest, Kūkai most likely joined this group as a private priest and for a time devoted himself to recitation of the mantra. This practice, related to Esoteric Buddhism, apparently enabled him to recover his psychic equilibrium. Thus his interest in Buddhism arose not so much from book learning as from the actual experience of meditation. This point is important to an understanding of his religion as a whole.

Kūkai left no statement about why he withdrew from the college, but the decision was no doubt seriously taken. By withdrawing, Kūkai became free to act and think as his inner voice prompted. He gave up future security as a bureaucrat, the most envied profession of the time, in favor of a life of trial and quest. Not only did he resign from the college but he left the capital and returned to nature. The mode of life he chose was that of a wandering hermit. Perhaps Kūkai's description of a wandering ascetic in his draft of the *Indications* will convey something of his own mood during this period:

The blue sky was the ceiling of his hut and the clouds hanging over the mountains were his curtains; he did not need to worry about where he lived or where he slept. In summer he opened his neck band in a relaxed mood and delighted in the gentle breezes as though he were a great king, but in winter he watched the fire with his neck drawn into his shoulders. If he had enough horse chestnuts and bitter vegetables to last ten days, he was lucky. His bare shoulders showed through his paper robe and clothes padded with grass cloth. . . . Though his appearance was laughable, his deep-rooted will could not be taken away from him.[6] . . . Not being obliged to his father or elder brothers and having no contact with his rela-

[5] Ienaga Saburō, ed., *Nihon Bukkyō shisō no tenkai* (Development of Japanese Buddhist thought) (Kyoto, 1956), pp. 36–37; Sonoda Kōyū, *Nanto Bukkyō*, IV, (1957), 45–60.

[6] *K.Z.*, III, 305.

tives, he wandered throughout the country like duckweed floating on water or dry grass blown by the wind.[7]

When traveling and begging for food, Kūkai came face to face with ancient native ways of life and with the native gods, or kami. Shinto references are not explicitly to be found in Kūkai's early writings, but Shinto beliefs must have pervaded his upbringing. No one born and raised in the Japanese countryside, as Kūkai was, would have escaped their influence. Kūkai's return to nature meant his reinstatement into the Shinto way of life. He often expressed in his poems joy or contentment over the sweetness, the vitality, and the mystery of nature; he felt a close affinity between nature and man. It was such predilections as these, no doubt, which in the end prompted him to build his monastic center on remote Mt. Kōya.

Nevertheless, Kūkai did not spend all his time as a hermit. Occasionally he returned to the world and studied intensively, for the draft of the *Indications* contains ample evidence of wide reading. Exactly where Kūkai went is not known, but it probably was Nara, for only there or in the capital itself were books easily accessible. Thus early in his life Kūkai set a pattern of alternating between seclusion and participation in the world, the same pattern that is visible in his later travels between Mt. Kōya and Kyoto. Given his taste for participation and for seclusion, writing the draft of the *Indications* may have been for Kūkai a necessary exercise by which to reassure himself as well as his family and relatives that he did not err in choosing the Buddhist way of life.

Attention will now be turned to the kind of books Kūkai read in his early twenties. On the basis of quotations and allusions found in the draft of the *Indications*, he had been exposed to more than ninety books in hundreds of fascicles, though some of the quotations and allusions may have been taken from anthologies. These books include twenty-six texts on Buddhism: the major Mahayana sutras, such as the *Lotus Sutra* and the *Avataṃsaka Sutra*, and treatises such as *The Awakening of Faith;* several Taoist texts, such as *Chuang Tzu, Tao-te Ching,* and *Pao-p'u Tzu;* and many other Chinese works besides Confucian texts, including an erotic story that happened to be popular in Japan at the

[7] *K.Z.,* III, 308.

time. The introduction to the draft of the *Indications* reveals that Kūkai was familiar with Japanese literary works. After he resigned from college, therefore, one can assume that Kūkai read widely in works other than the Confucian classics, historical records, and collections of poetry and that his interest lay in Taoism and, even more so, in Mahayana Buddhism.

3
RENUNCIATION AND QUEST

After spending some time as a wandering ascetic, Kūkai at twenty-four committed himself to Buddhism. He wrote the draft of the *Indications* to show the superiority of Buddhism over both Confucianism and Taoism. The exact position of Taoism in Japan at this time is not certain, but it seems to have been despised and its study and practice discouraged.[1] It was excluded from the educational curriculum and was considered a threat to society. Nonetheless, Kūkai was so bold as to rank it higher than Confucianism, the intellectual orthodoxy of the time. Kūkai's aim in the draft of the *Indications* is to prove that entering the Buddhist priesthood does not necessarily mean repudiating loyalty and filial piety. He attempts to persuade the reader that by becoming a Buddhist monk one can practice these virtues in the broadest and highest possible manner and that Buddhism alone can satisfy man's spiritual aspirations. In short, Kūkai justifies his own determination to choose Buddhism.

The draft of the *Indications* can very well be called an epoch-making

[1] Ōya Tokujō, "Sangō shiki sakusei no haikei toshite no Narachō no shisō (Nara period thought as background for the composition of the *Indications*)," *Mikkyō Kenkyū*, LI (1934); 265–89; Yoshioka Yoshitoyo, "Sangō shiki no seiritsu ni tsuite (On the organization of the Introduction to the Three Teachings [sic])," *Indogaku Bukkyōgaku Kenkyū*, XV (1960), 114–18.

work in the history of Japanese literature and thought. When comparing it to Kūkai's later works, however, one cannot fail to detect in it a certain immaturity. In his preface Kūkai remarks:

Chang Wen-ch'eng in China wrote a book to dispel gloom.[2] Its style is beautiful and imaginative. Unfortunately, it is filled with lasciviousness and is totally devoid of decency. Even Liu Hsia [-hui] would have deplored the book on reading it,[3] and a Buddhist monk cannot remain unaffected by it. A Japanese named Hi no Obito composed the *Suikaku ki*,[4] which is extremely comical and witty. At the mention of this author's name, even a man [as solemn as] the image of a god will clap his hands and burst into laughter, and even a deaf man, on dipping into it, will open his mouth wide and raise his voice. Both works are excellent, but they cannot serve as examples to guide later generations.[5]

With youthful temerity, Kūkai announces an ambition to surpass his popular predecessors both in style and in value of content. Also such words as "a Buddhist monk cannot remain unaffected by it" are not those expected of a man who really has matured in Buddhist training. It was only natural that Kūkai should later replace this preface with the more dignified one. Such lightness of tone is not found elsewhere in Kūkai's works. One is obliged to conclude, despite innumerable biographical accounts to the contrary, that Kūkai wrote his draft of the *Indications* during a period of prolonged spiritual crisis and that his final version represents a more stable, mature viewpoint.

In the draft of the *Indications* Kūkai's embellished, literary interpretation of Buddhism lacks originality. His treatment of the Dharmakaya, his central concern in later years, is too intellectual and impersonal to convey the impression that it moved his entire being. His commitment to Buddhism was yet provisional; only after he made his draft public did he become a Buddhist layman (*ubasoku*).

Yet the draft of the *Indications* demonstrates Kūkai's critical spirit and his drive to be honest with himself. It also reveals two of his basic

[2] This book, entitled *Yu-hsien-k'u*, was lost in China but preserved in Japan and reintroduced to China in modern times. It deals with a traveler who stumbles upon a house of fairy sisters and enjoys an overnight stay with them.

[3] Liu Hsia-hui warmed with his body a girl trembling from cold, yet remained unmoved.

[4] This book is lost and the mention here is the only information about it that we have. It may well have been the first fiction written in Japan.

[5] *K.Z.*, III, 287–88.

attitudes: that a man is capable of improving himself, no matter how wicked and biased he may be, provided he is given suitable surroundings and proper instruction; that a man can develop himself spiritually through awareness of a higher spiritual realm obtained by means of self-examination and stimulation from others. Kūkai explored these approaches more fully in his later works, *The Ten Stages of the Development of Mind* and *The Precious Key to the Secret Treasury*.

Kūkai has left no account of his life from the age of twenty-four, when he wrote the draft of the *Indications*, to the age of thirty-one, when he set out for China. His biographers have filled the gap with stories of miracles performed by him in various places. One can only assume that he wandered widely and energetically in pursuit of the Buddha Dharma. Being free from all secular ties, Kūkai seems to have lived as a traveling ascetic, sometimes meditating in deep forests and at other times studying Buddhist texts extensively at one temple or another, all the while seeking after something higher and more comprehensive. Innumerable legends concerning Kūkai remain scattered throughout Japan; they probably date from this period. Later, in 816, when Kūkai requested that the Emperor Saga (r. 809–23) grant him Mt. Kōya as the site for a monastic center, he mentioned that he had been there while young.[6] Kūkai's first visit to Mt. Kōya could have taken place during this period of silence.

Having become a student of Buddhism, Kūkai seems to have followed his earlier pattern; dissatisfied with existing Buddhist doctrine and practice, he sought the highest, this time within Buddhism itself. The first biography gives a vivid account of his seriousness:

He prayed before the image of Buddha: "Since being initiated into Buddhism, I have been eager to realize the essence of Buddhism. I have studied all Buddhist doctrines, but I still have doubts and have been unable to solve them. I earnestly hope that the Buddha will reveal to me the higher truth." He prayed ardently. Then, in a dream, a man appeared before him and said: "The *Mahāvairocana Sutra*[7] is [the scripture which contains] the doctrine you have been searching for." He awakened in delight. Soon he

[6] *K.Z.*, III, 524.

[7] T848; one of the two basic sutras of Shingon Buddhism. Chapter One is theoretical but the rest are practical, containing methods of Esoteric meditation, construction of the sacred ground, etc. The sutra reveals the Matrix Realm (*garbhadhātu*) of Mahāvairocana, represented by the Matrix Mandala.

obtained the sutra and read it through, only to find difficult passages which no teacher could interpret for him.[8]

In 821, at forty-eight, Kūkai reminisced:

I, disciple Kūkai, being driven by an inner urge, had all the while thought of returning to the Source. Not knowing the way to it, I cried many a time standing at the crossroad. My sincere wish was rewarded, however; I found this, the Esoteric Buddhist approach. I started reading [the *Mahāvairocana Sutra*] only to find that I was unable to understand it; I wished to visit China.[9]

A comment may be needed on the phrase "returning to the Source (*gengen*)," the realization of which was Kūkai's final goal, and the discovery of "the way to it," Kūkai's immediate objective. Briefly, *gengen* is a synonym for "attaining enlightenment." It means to return to, or to reinstate oneself in, the original order, or the world of enlightenment, to which one belongs intrinsically but from which one has in actuality fallen. Such a concept requires belief in the original or intrinsic enlightenment (*hongaku*) of all beings as taught in *The Awakening of Faith*.[10] By using this expression, Kūkai indicated his intention to find the main stream of Buddhism and to work his way up to its fountainhead without being led astray by tributaries. He was eager to realize the essence of Buddhism.

All accounts agree that Kūkai went to China in order to answer his questions on the *Mahāvairocana Sutra*. This reason is plausible enough, for understanding of the *Mahāvairocana Sutra* requires a knowledge of Sanskrit, oral instruction on the methods of meditation it prescribes, and other esoteric knowledge. It was the basic text of Esoteric Buddhism representing the most recent phase of seventh-century Indian Buddhism. The amazing fact is that a sutra still relatively new in India and in China should already have been available in Japan. A reliable early document records that a copy of this sutra was made in Japan in 736.[11] It had been translated from Sanskrit into Chinese by an Indian master

---

[8] *K.Z.*, Shukan, 2.   [9] *K.Z.*, III, 476.

[10] Yoshito Hakeda, trans., *The Awakening of Faith* (Columbia University Press, 1967), pp. 37–43.

[11] *Dainihon komonjo* (Ancient documents of great Japan), (Tokyo, 1907), VII, 75. The exact year is not certain, but it is classified under the 28th of the third month, Tempyō 8 (763).

of Esoteric Buddhism, Śubhākarasiṃha (637–735), in 726. Therefore, it was only ten years later that a copy was made in Japan.

In any event, study of the *Mahāvairocana Sutra* was probably the reason Kūkai gave in his official request for permission to travel to China. Kūkai's desire to further his quest thus resulted in an adventurous voyage to the continent. He must have been well aware that Esoteric Buddhism was flourishing in Ch'ang-an, the T'ang capital. Before his departure Kūkai intended to stay for twenty years.[12] No doubt study of the sutra was not Kūkai's sole object in visiting China. Perhaps, well versed as he was in all areas of Chinese letters, Kūkai simply wished to immerse himself in the country itself, so as eventually to transmit to Japan a living understanding of the achievements of Chinese civilization.

What is more puzzling is why this nameless wandering ascetic was finally sent to China as a government-sponsored student. Was this Emperor Kammu's compensation for his own harsh treatment of the men of the Saeki clan? Or was it Kūkai's maternal uncle Atō Ōtari, the imperial tutor, who recommended him to Prince Iyo, who in turn informed the emperor about Kūkai's potential and suggested that he be sent to China? Or was it the envoy, Fujiwara Kadonomaro, who desired Kūkai's company on the journey and so recommended him? A questionable document states that he was recommended by a leading clergyman of the period, Gonzō (758–827).[13] Be that as it may, Kūkai was selected and sailed for China in 804, at the age of thirty-one.

[12] This information is found in a letter Kūkai wrote to an official in Fukien soon after he reached China in 804. *K.Z.*, III, 456.

[13] *K.Z.*, V, 423. It has also been suggested that Kūkai went to China as an interpreter to the envoy. Though he wrote a letter to a Chinese official on behalf of the envoy (*K.Z.*, III, 454–56), there seems to be no evidence for this conjecture.

4

ENCOUNTER WITH
MASTER HUI-KUO

On the sixth day of the seventh month of Enryaku 23 (804), a fleet of four government ships set sail for China from the port of Tanoura in Kyushu. Kūkai was on Ship One in the company of the envoy to the T'ang court, Fujiwara Kadonomaro. On Ship Two was Saichō, who was bound for Mt. T'ien-t'ai, the center of the T'ien-t'ai (Jap. Tendai) school of Buddhism, situated not too far from the coast, south of the Yangtze River. The day after sailing, the four ships were driven apart by a storm. After drifting for over a month, Ship One arrived at a small port in the province of Fukien; Ship Two arrived at Ningpo after about two months at sea. Ship Three turned back to Japan and left again the following year, only to be shipwrecked on an island in the South Seas. Ship Four was lost with only one survivor.

A voyage to China in those days was extremely dangerous. Whenever the government announced plans to send an envoy to the Chinese court, officials of the middle or lower ranks were thrown into a state of frenzy for fear that they might be sent. Some had to be punished for evading government orders, and others became exhausted from mental strain even before embarking. Japanese shipbuilding at that time was much inferior to that of Korea or China, and navigators were not able to take full advantage of the seasonal winds.

The party aboard Kūkai's ship was greeted coldly by the Chinese officials. Not only was the province undergoing a change of administration but no Japanese envoy had ever anchored at their port. Hence, they refused permission to land and advised the envoy to proceed to the port of Fukien, the seat of the local governor. All negotiations failed, the ship was impounded, and the party lived miserably on swampland for about two months. In the meantime, Kūkai wrote a letter to the governor on behalf of the envoy explaining why the ship had come.[1] The governor was apparently impressed by this letter. He immediately trusted the party and, pending the arrival from Ch'ang-an of a reply to his report on the Japanese envoy, provided them with fifteen houses equipped with all the necessary comforts. The party left Fukien on the third day of the eleventh month and headed north by land to the capital, reaching there on the twenty-third day of the twelfth month, approximately six months after they had left their native country.

Chinese civilization attained its peak of glory in the T'ang period (618–907). When Kūkai reached Ch'ang-an, the city was the cultural center both of China and of Central and Eastern Asia. Many races, religions, and customs could be seen there, and the atmosphere was liberal and cosmopolitan. Foreigners were proud to serve the T'ang court, for apparently there was no discrimination against government employees of foreign origin as long as they passed the civil examinations. Indian cultural influence was easily visible. In the mid-eighth century there existed in Ch'ang-an sixty-four Buddhist temples for monks and twenty-seven for nuns; ten Taoist temples for men and six for women; and three foreign temples.[2] Of the three foreign temples it is certain that one was Nestorian Christian and one was Zoroastrian or Manichaean. Moreover, the number of Moslems in Ch'ang-an was increasing. All these must have attracted Kūkai's curiosity. Among the Buddhist schools Esoteric Buddhism, which had recently been imported from India, was especially fashionable in court circles.

A first-hand account of Kūkai's activities in Ch'ang-an is available. It is *A Memorial Presenting a List of Newly Imported Sutras and Other Items* [3] written by Kūkai immediately after his return from China in 806 and presented to the Emperor Heizei. There survive in addition some letters Kūkai wrote in China [4] and the poems dedicated to him at his departure by his Chinese friends.[5]

---

[1] A copy of the letter has been preserved: *K.Z.*, III, 454–56.

[2] Toganoo Mitsudō, ed., *Kōbō daishi to Nihon bunka* (Kōbō daishi and Japanese culture) (Kyoto: Rokudai shimpōsha, 1929), pp. 501–3.

[3] *K.Z.*, I, 69–102; see translation.   [4] *K.Z.*, III, 454–63.

[5] *K.Z.*, V, 357–58.

According to the *Memorial*, Kūkai and the envoy stayed at an official residence provided by the T'ang court from the twenty-third day of the twelfth month to the eleventh day of the third month of the following year (805) when the envoy returned to Japan. That very day, Kūkai moved to the Hsi-ming Temple. This famous temple built in 658 was one of four temples in the capital that escaped destruction when, forty years later, the Emperor Wu-tsung undertook mass persecution of Buddhism.

While residing here, Kūkai visited many Buddhist teachers. Finally he met Master Hui-kuo (746–805), the patriarch of Esoteric Buddhism in China, who lived in the East Pagoda Hall of the Ch'ing-lung Temple. Master Hui-kuo (Keika in Japanese) had inherited the Dharma of the Esoteric tradition from the famed master Pu-k'ung, or Amoghavajra (705–74). This Buddhist school was transmitted to China in 716 when an Indian master, Śubhākarasiṃha (637–735), came to China by invitation of the Emperor Hsüan-tsung (r. 713–55). The Indian master was highly reputed in China and on his arrival was honored with the title of National Teacher. With the assistance of I-hsing (683–727), he translated the *Mahāvairocana Sutra*. Four years later, in 720, another great master of Esoteric Buddhism, Vajrabodhi (d. 741), arrived in Canton by sea and also undertook the translation of Esoteric Buddhist texts under the patronage of the imperial household. Pu-k'ung became the chosen disciple of Vajrabodhi and one of the most respected Buddhist teachers. He is regarded as one of the four greatest translators of Buddhist texts in China, having served three successive emperors, Hsüan-tsung, Su-tsung (r. 756–62), and Tai-tsung (r. 763–79). When Pu-k'ung died, the Emperor Tai-tsung ordered all court activities stopped for three days in mourning for this great master. Hui-kuo, under whom Kūkai studied, was the legitimate successor of Pu-k'ung.

The encounter with Hui-kuo, described by Kūkai a year later, was dramatic:

I called on the abbot in the company of five or six monks from the Hsi-ming Temple. As soon as he saw me he smiled with pleasure and joyfully said, "I knew that you would come! I have waited for such a long time. What pleasure it gives me to look upon you today at last! My life is drawing to an end, and until you came there was no one to whom I could transmit the teachings. Go without delay to the altar of *abhiṣeka* [6] with incense and a flower." I returned to the temple where I had been staying and got the things which were necessary for the ceremony. It was early in the sixth month then that I entered the altar of *abhiṣeka* for primary initiation.[7]

Hui-kuo, at sixty, was living on solely to transmit his whole teachings to Kūkai. Kūkai received all the master had to offer, as one would "pour water from one jar into another." [8] In the early part of the eighth month, within three months after his first meeting with Hui-Kuo, Kūkai was permitted the final *abhiṣeka* and ordained master of Esoteric Buddhism, thus becoming the eighth patriarch at the age of thirty-two. The speed of Kūkai's achievement is astonishing. Less than two years before he had been meditating and studying somewhere in Japan, a nameless ascetic. Presumably, his understanding of Esoteric Buddhism had already reached a high level even during the period of lonely quest in Japan. The dying Hui-kuo summoned up his last energy to guide Kūkai, joyful that he had at last found the man to inherit his whole teachings. For this honor, Kūkai throughout his life remained deeply grateful.

One day, near death, Hui-kuo gave Kūkai his final instructions:

Now my existence on earth approaches its term, and I cannot long remain. I urge you, therefore, to take the mandalas of both realms and the hundred volumes of the teachings of the Diamond Vehicle, together with the ritual implements and these objects which were left to me by my master. Return to your country and propagate the teachings there.

When you first arrived, I feared I did not have enough time left to teach you everything, but now I have completed teaching you, and the work of copying the sutras and making the images has also been finished. Hasten back to your country, offer these things to the court, and spread the teachings throughout your country to increase the happiness of the people. Then the land will know peace, and people everywhere will be content. In that way you will return thanks to the Buddha and to your teacher. That is also the way to show your devotion to your country and

---

[6] *Abhiṣeka* (Jap. *kanjō*) is a Sanskrit word meaning literally "sprinkling water." Here it is an initiation ritual requiring sprinkling holy water on the forehead of the one who is to be initiated.

[7] *K.Z.,* I, 99.

[8] This expression was used by Master Hui-kuo to describe his relationship with Kūkai. *The Transmission of the Shingon Dharma* (*Shingon fuhō den*), *K.Z.,* I, 61.

to your family. My disciple I-ming will carry on the teachings here. Your task is to transmit them to the Eastern Land. Do your best! Do your best! [9]

On the night of the full moon in the twelfth month of the same year Hui-kuo purified himself in a ritual bath, lay on his right side and, making the mudra (hand gesture) of Mahāvairocana Buddha, breathed his last. Kūkai, representing the disciples and followers of Hui-kuo, wrote the epitaph for his late master's tomb.[10] The epitaph was written under the eye of his fellow disciples, of the faithful, and of the men of letters of Ch'ang-an. This composition proved Kūkai worthy of the title Eighth Patriarch of Esoteric Buddhism. It was probably around this time that Kūkai decided to return home as instructed by Hui-kuo.

Fortunately, another group from Japan soon arrived. Kūkai sent a letter to its leader, Takashina Tōnari, asking permission to return to Japan with him.[11] Kūkai's original plan to stay in China for twenty years was therefore reduced drastically. His accomplishments, however, were phenomenal: not only did he become the Eighth Patriarch of Esoteric Buddhism but he also learned Sanskrit and Indian Buddhism from the Indian masters Prajñā and Muniśrī, calligraphy from Han Fang-ming, poetry, and such a minor thing as how to make a brush out of badger's hair. Carrying voluminous sutras, huge mandalas, and books of poetry, among other items, Kūkai left Ch'ang-an probably in the early part of 806. By the fourth month he was somewhere south of the lower Yangtze area. It is not clear when Kūkai left the continent nor when he again set foot on his native soil. Back in Kyushu on the twenty-second day of the tenth month of Daidō 1 (806), Kūkai wrote *A Memorial Presenting a List of Newly Imported Sutras and Other Items* and gave it to Takashina to present to the emperor. Takashina reported the completion of his mission to the court on the thirteenth day of the twelfth month of the same year. Kūkai's trip to China had lasted thirty months. He was thirty-three years old.

[9] *K.Z.*, I, 100–1.   [10] *K.Z.*, III, 420–25.   [11] *K.Z.*, III, 461.

5

PERIOD OF TRIAL

Kūkai's *Memorial Presenting a List of Newly Imported Sutras and Other Items* consists of the memorial proper and of lists of 142 Buddhist sutras in 217 fascicles, 42 Sanskrit texts in 44 fascicles, 32 commentaries in 170 fascicles, 5 mandalas, 5 portraits of the patriarchs, 9 ritual implements, and 13 different objects given to Kūkai by his master Hui-kuo. Between the lists and also in his conclusion Kūkai explains the significance of all these items, summarizes the Esoteric Buddhist tradition, and narrates how he succeeded to Hui-kuo's teachings. This clearly dated *Memorial* is essential to an understanding of Kūkai and his thought. It was also vital to Kūkai's own career, for it had to impress the court with the value and importance of Kūkai's Buddhism. The court's permission was required even to reside in a Buddhist temple, and state support for a new school of Buddhism was mandatory. Legally, private religious activity was almost impossible. The state maintained strong administrative control over religious matters through an institution known as *sōgō*. The court based its policy toward Buddhism on this institution's recommendations. Therefore, Kūkai's *Memorial* was a report of his achievements as a government-sponsored student in China, an inventory of the books and objects he had brought back with him, and a statement of what he could do for Japan. At the same time it was a petition for state support in establishing the new religion. The court, first of all, had to be convinced that the highest authority on Esoteric Buddhism and the authentic transmitter of its tradition was Kūkai himself.

The court did not reply to the *Memorial* until three years later, in 809, a silence longer than Kūkai's entire trip to China. In fact, Kūkai did not even receive permission to proceed to the capital and so was obliged to await the court's reply in Kyushu. Since in his surviving writings Kūkai does not comment upon the court's silence, it is necessary, in order to attempt an explanation, to examine the historical context of Kūkai's return from China.

The Emperor Kammu, who had authorized Kūkai's journey, was no longer alive; he had died while Kūkai was in the lower Yangtze area waiting for the ship to set sail for Japan. Heizei, Kammu's successor, is said to have shown at this time no great enthusiasm for Buddhism, though later misfortunes prompted him to take orders and to receive religious instruction from Kūkai. Moreover, Heizei seems to have favored Saichō. While still heir apparent, Heizei had sent Saichō an admiring note when the latter lectured at the Takaosanji in 802 and had also supported him generously on his trip to China. In any case, Saichō was famous as the master of Tendai Buddhism even before he went to China. When Kūkai returned to Japan, Saichō was active as the great authority on Esoteric Buddhism. Upon receiving Kūkai's *Memorial*, the court presumably hesitated to credit his claim to authentic mastery of the Esoteric tradition, and the court-appointed monastic officials no doubt remained noncommittal.

Since from this time on Kūkai's career cannot be divorced from that of his rival Saichō, a brief sketch of Saichō's life up to 806 may not be out of place.

Saichō was born in 767 into a wealthy family of Chinese origin that had been settled for generations near Lake Biwa on the other side of Mt. Hiei from Kyoto. At twelve he left his family to study under Gyōhyō (722–97), the head priest of the provincial state temple in Ōmi. At fourteen he took Buddhist orders, and at nineteen he was ordained at the Tōdaiji in Nara. One hundred days after being ordained, Saichō built a grass hut on Mt. Hiei and lived there alone to pursue meditation and study. His reason for choosing this course, it is said, was a strong sense of the transiency of the world and frustration at the decline of true Buddhism. While living on Mt. Hiei he became particularly attracted to the teachings of Tendai Buddhism. At twenty-two he built a temple on the mountain and named it Hieizanji, which was later changed to Enryakuji. This remained the center of the Japanese Tendai sect. In 797, the same year that Kūkai wrote his draft of the

Indications, Saichō was appointed one of ten leading clergymen to serve in the palace. At thirty-six, in 802, he lectured on basic Tendai doctrine at the Takaosanji near Kyoto. The lecture was a great success and Emperor Kammu sent Saichō a message expressing his admiration. Encouraged, Saichō requested permission to visit China in order to obtain accurate copies of Tendai texts and to receive instruction in their meaning directly from the Chinese masters. As an accomplished monk-scholar, Saichō was given an ample allowance to make an inspection tour for a limited period of time. Kūkai, on the other hand, was a student and so was given a minimum allowance for an indefinite period of time. Saichō stayed on Mt. T'ien-t'ai for thirty days receiving instruction from the master Hsing-man. Then he spent altogether about 140 days studying under the master Tao-sui in the vicinity of Mt. T'ien-t'ai.

On the twenty-fifth day of the third month of 805, Saichō arrived at the port of Ming-chou to await his return ship but found that the ship would not leave for another six weeks or so. Not to waste time, he decided to make copies of certain texts which were still missing from his collection. With the permission of the local government office, he visited the Buddhist temples near the port, accompanied by his interpreter, servant, and copyists. At the Lung-hsing Temple in the Yüeh region he happened to meet Shun-hsiao, an Esoteric Buddhist master, who initiated Saichō into Esoteric Buddhism. Saichō made copies of 102 Esoteric Buddhist texts in 115 fascicles and obtained seven Esoteric Buddhist ritual implements. This rather fortuitous encounter was responsible for the introduction of the Esoteric Buddhist tradition into Japanese Tendai.

Saichō returned safely after a total of nine and a half months, and on the fourth day of the seventh month he presented his report to the emperor. The ailing Kammu was pleased; he invited Saichō to the palace and asked him to pray for his health. The emperor issued an order to hold the *abhiṣeka* ritual at the Takaosanji under the auspices of the state, declaring:

Esoteric Buddhism had not yet been transmitted to this land, but fortunately Saichō has obtained it. It will be fitting to select from among the clergymen in the great temples those who are endowed with both knowledge and virtue and to have them go through the *abhiṣeka* ritual. . . . All necessary funds for the performance of the ritual, regardless of amount, are to be provided as Saichō shall direct.[1]

The leading clergymen of the period received *abhiṣeka* from Saichō on the first day of the ninth month in 805. This was the first Esoteric Buddhist ritual performed in Japan. On the third of the first month of 806, Saichō presented a memorial requesting official recognition of the Tendai sect, recommending that henceforth the court should limit the number of Buddhist clergymen to be newly ordained. He proposed that twelve clergymen be ordained yearly as follows: Kegon, 2; Tendai, 2; Ritsu, 2; Sanron and Jōjitsu together, 3; Hossō and Kusha, 3. The leading clergymen of Nara yielded to Saichō's pressure and accepted this recommendation. Of the two allotted to the Tendai sect, Saichō specified that one should concentrate on the study of Tendai proper and another on Esoteric Buddhism, namely, the study of the *Mahāvairocana Sutra*.

Thus, even before Kūkai's return, Esoteric Buddhism had been recognized officially as an integral part of the Tendai sect. It is no wonder then that the court took no immediate action when Kūkai presented his *Memorial*. Later in life Kūkai writes: "For many years after I returned from China, I was unable to propagate the teachings widely, for the time was not yet opportune." [2] It was only in 835, the year Kūkai died, that the Shingon sect was finally permitted to ordain three clergymen yearly. For Saichō, the last year of the Emperor Kammu's reign (806) was the peak of his career, and after that his popularity steadily declined.

Little is known of Kūkai's life between the presentation of the *Memorial* and the year 809. The traditional biographies are hardly to be taken seriously, and there is only one reliable clue to his whereabouts. That is, he was still in Kyushu on the twenty-first day of the second month of 807, for on that day he officiated at a memorial service and the prayer he wrote for the occasion still survives.[3] Certain other events are generally accepted but, given the nature of their sources, the accounts do not seem completely trustworthy. They are that Kūkai received an order from the court to stay in the Kanzeonji in Kyushu on

---

[1] *Dengyō daishi zenshū* (The complete works of Dengyō daishi—Saichō), V (*Bekkan*—Supplementary volume), 92–93.

[2] *K.Z.*, III, 529.   [3] *K.Z.*, III, 489–90.

the twenty-ninth day of the fourth month of 807; [4] that on the eighth day of the eleventh month of the same year he made his first public appearance and lectured on a commentary on the *Mahāvairocana Sutra* [5] at the Kumedera in Yamato; [6] that from 807 to the sixteenth day of the seventh month of Daidō 4 (809) he stayed at the Makinōsanji in the province of Izumi; [7] that on the same day the governor of the province of Izumi was ordered to have Kūkai proceed to a Buddhist temple in Kyoto. [8]

6

RISE TO EMINENCE

In the latter half of 809 Kūkai received an order from the court to reside at the Takaosanji in the suburbs of Kyoto. This temple later came to be known as the Jingoji. It was the headquarters of Kūkai's activities from 809 until 823 when he moved to the Tōji, also in Kyoto. At the Takaosanji, Kūkai began to establish himself as the religious and cultural leader of early Heian society. The Emperor Heizei had recently retired because of illness, and the new Emperor Saga had succeeded him at twenty-four. The change in reign brought forth a new climate favorable to Kūkai. In religious circles, as well, the tide had turned. As Kūkai rose to eminence, the glory that Saichō had once enjoyed under the Emperor Kammu waned. The positions of these two celebrated religious leaders were soon to be reversed.

[4] *K.Z.*, V, 423.

[5] *Ta-jih-ching su,* T1796. The standard commentary expounded by Śubhākara-siṃha and written down by his disciple I-hsing (683–727) who is also known for his work on astronomy adopted by the T'ang court.

[6] This has often been regarded as the date of the founding of the Shingon sect by Kūkai. Its unreliability is discussed by Moriyama, *Bunkashijō*, pp. 263–64.

[7] This is probable but not proven. Tsuji (*Nihon Bukkyōshi*, p. 301) and Moriyama (*Bunkashijō*, p. 265) accept it as a historical fact.

[8] *K.Z.*, V, 424.

The Emperor Saga had been brought up among the most promising young scholars of Chinese classics and poetry. He grew up to be a leading poet in the T'ang style and, with Kūkai and Tachibana Hayanari (d. 842), one of the three great calligraphers of Japan (*sampitsu*). During his lifetime Saga sponsored three anthologies of poetry composed in Chinese by leading Japanese poets. His reign from 809 to 823 spans a period of great cultural excellence known as the "Kōnin Period." Artistic as he was, Saga retired at thirty-nine simply to escape from the burdens of ruling and to enjoy a life of elegance. He outlived Kūkai by seven years.

Emperor Saga turned out to be the promoter of Kūkai just as the Emperor Kammu had been of Saichō. One day in 809 he sent a messenger to Kūkai requesting that Kūkai write Chinese calligraphy on two folding screens.[1] Though Kūkai remained inactive socially, he must have been well known as a poet, calligrapher, writer, and master of Esoteric Buddhism. From this time on the emperor often invited Kūkai to the palace, and many a time Kūkai wrote letters on behalf of the emperor, exchanged poems with him, and presented to him, often on imperial request, his calligraphy, books of poetry, and Sanskrit writings and writing brushes.[2] With this imperial patronage in addition to his talent, Kūkai could not have failed to attract the powerful nobles surrounding the throne and the men of letters who were enthusiastic admirers of Chinese culture.

It was in 810 that Kūkai emerged as a public figure. The significant events of that year were Kūkai's appointment as administrative head (*bettō*) of the Tōdaiji in Nara;[3] his memorial to the Emperor Saga requesting permission to perform an Esoteric Buddhist ceremony at the Takaosanji; and his formation of a personal group of students and disciples.

The Tōdaiji, the central temple in Nara, was the most imposing Buddhist institution in Japan at that time. Kūkai's appointment had to be issued by the government on the recommendation of the monastic offi-

[1] *K.Z.*, III, 435.

[2] Sections 3 and 4 of *The Collected Works of Prose and Poetry of Kūkai* (*Seirei shū*) contain the materials that describe the close relationship between the emperor and Kūkai. *K.Z.*, III, 426–53.

[3] This appointment has been traditionally regarded as fact on the basis of an ancient document at the Tōdaiji, but there is also an opinion that the document is questionable. See Katsuno, *Hieizan to Kōyasan*, pp. 169–71.

cials, the heads of the powerful Nara temples. There is no way to tell whether it was initiated by the monastic officials or by Saga himself. At any rate, Kūkai's later success in superimposing his own Esotericism on Nara Buddhism had its inception in this appointment. He seems to have stayed in this office from 810 to 813, though his headquarters continued to be the Takaosanji.

Concerning Kūkai's memorial to the Emperor Saga dated the twenty-seventh of the tenth month, it is not clear whether this memorial was presented on Kūkai's own initiative or at the request of the court. There is also no reliable record to prove that the ceremony was actually performed. But on the fourteenth of the next month the emperor asked Kūkai to write for him one personal letter to a pious monk and one imperial reply to one of the monastic officials.[4] This implies a friendly relationship between the emperor and Kūkai, a relationship unlikely if the emperor had just thwarted Kūkai over the memorial. Another reason to believe Kūkai's request was granted is that Saga was in the midst of a serious political crisis and would have needed Kūkai's spiritual support.

The Emperor Saga apparently fell ill several months after his enthronement in 809 and again about the middle of the following year.[5] On the sixth day of the ninth month, during Saga's convalescence, the retired Emperor Heizei suddenly announced his wish to transfer the capital from Kyoto to Nara. His obvious intention was to recover the throne, and his act constituted revolt. The rebellion was quickly suppressed by the action of the imperial army under Sakanoue Tamuramaro. Fujiwara Kusuko, Heizei's favorite and an instigator of the plot, committed suicide; her brother Fujiwara Nakanari, a coconspirator, was killed; Heizei shaved his head and became a monk; and Heizei's son, the Crown Prince Takaoka, was deposed. Takaoka later became one of Kūkai's ten greatest disciples and died in his late sixties somewhere in the Malay peninsula on the way to India. To the ailing Saga, this must have been an extremely painful period.

The revolt came to an end after much bloodshed on both sides. Kūkai's ceremony would have helped to appease the souls of the dead and to calm the minds of those who, though still alive, had been de-

[4] Tsuji, Nihon Bukkyōshi, p. 302. K.Z., III, 519–20, 522–23.
[5] Kitayama Shigeo, Nihon no rekishi (History of Japan), IV, 117–18.

prived of their ranks and titles. The revenge of both living and dead was, according to the understanding of the times, much to be feared, and Buddhist institutions were expected to deal with such matters.

Kūkai's entire memorial reads as follows:

I, monk Kūkai, having been so fortunate as to receive the favor of the former emperor [Kammu], have had an opportunity to study far away in China. By luck I was able to enter a monastery where *abhiṣeka* was practiced and to receive the teachings of the Diamond Vehicle contained in more than one hundred texts. These sutras are the essentials of the teachings of the Buddha and are sacred treasures of the nation. Therefore, since the K'ai-yüan era (713–41) in China, each emperor and his three highest ministers have received *abhiṣeka* and have recited and meditated on the mantras. Thus they have maintained the land in peace and sought after enlightenment. In the palace they converted the Chung-shen Hall into a building to perform Buddhist services, and experts in meditation and in mantra recitation were made to meditate and practice their rituals there every seventh day of the month. Within and without the capital they built monasteries where mantras are recited in order to pacify the nation. There are such examples in the Buddha's own country as well.

The imported sutras consist of the *Jen-wang ching*,[6] *Shou-hu-kuo-chieh-chu ching*,[7] *Fo-mu-ming-wang ching*,[8] and the like, which are concerned with the teaching of mantra recitation. The Buddha preached these sutras especially for the benefit of kings. They enable a king to vanquish the seven calamities,[9] to maintain the four seasons in harmony, to protect the nation and family, and to give comfort to himself and others. For these matters these texts are sacred and excellent. Though I have received the transmission from my master, I have been unable to perform [the rituals prescribed in these sutras]. For the good of the state I sincerely desire to initiate my disciples and, beginning on the first day of next month, to perform the rituals at the Takaosanji until the dharma takes visible effect. Also, I wish that throughout this period I might not have to leave my residence and that I might suffer no interruption. I may be an insignificant and inferior man, but this thought and this wish move my heart.

That which covers me and that which bears me are the sky and the earth of Your Benevolent Majesty. It was, indeed, the noble emperor, the King of Medicine [the Emperor Kammu], who opened my eyes and ears [to Esoteric Buddhism, permitting me to study in China]. My desire to repay the favor that I have received is boundless. May Heaven [the Emperor Saga] understand my sincere heart! This is all that I devoutly hope for. Respectfully I submit this memorial to the court. I am overwhelmed by

6 T994.   7 T997.   8 T982.

9 Eclipse, disorder in constellations, fire, flood, windstorm, drought, brigands.

a sense of awe and with an apprehension that by this hasty action I may disgrace the dignity of Your Majesty.

> Most respectfully,
> Monk Kūkai
> Written on the twenty-seventh day
> of the tenth month, Kōnin 1 (810).[10]

Boldly Kūkai voiced his wish to stay at the temple for an extended period and to remain uninterrupted. The memorial implies that the emperor must have frequently ordered Kūkai to leave the temple. Kūkai's other letters to the emperor written during his stay at the temple suggest that the emperor's calls were little related to the religious activities with which Kūkai was primarily concerned. One may suppose that the emperor's recognition of Kūkai as principally a cultural leader may have disappointed Kūkai. Had he not indicated to the emperor that there was a world above and beyond the secular world—the religious world—with which even the emperor could not interfere? It may be that in the memorial Kūkai was asserting himself as a religious rather than as a cultural leader. Unfortunately, the emperor's immediate reaction is not known, but it is certain that henceforth his friendship with Kūkai grew.

7

ABHIṢEKA CEREMONIES
AT THE TAKAOSANJI

Not only the sovereign but Saichō as well sent messages to Kūkai. On the twenty-fourth day of the eighth month in the year of Kūkai's entry into the Takaosanji (809), Saichō asked to borrow twelve books, consisting mainly of the Esoteric Buddhist texts which Kūkai had

[10] K.Z., III, 435–36.

brought back from China.[1] He humbly signed his letter "The lowly monk Saichō." The conciseness of the letter suggests that this was not the first communication between Saichō and Kūkai, but there is no surviving evidence of any previous contact.[2] Henceforth, they maintained a cordial relationship that foundered several years later when Kūkai refused to lend a book to Saichō and when Saichō's leading disciple almost went over to Kūkai.

One can imagine that Saichō was most sensitive to Kūkai's movements as Kūkai approached the capital and prepared to participate in its cultural and religious life. Tendai Buddhism proper, based as it was on the *Lotus Sutra,* theoretically held Esoteric Buddhism to be of secondary importance. For Kūkai, on the other hand, it was paramount. Furthermore, Saichō's Tendai sect included not only Tendai proper and Esoteric Buddhism but also Zen and Ritsu. Inherent in Tendai was the tendency to become syncretic at best, or, at worst, to adopt different traditions at random. Ironically, what made Saichō famous after his return from China was not Tendai Buddhism but Esoteric Buddhism.

Of the two novices permitted by the state to be ordained as Tendai monks, Saichō required that one should specialize in Esoteric Buddhism, or in the study of the *Mahāvairocana Sutra.* Because of this official commitment, Saichō, the hitherto publicly recognized authority on Esoteric Buddhism, had to augment his knowledge. Among the collection of documents containing some forty letters written by Saichō,[3] nearly half are addressed to Kūkai and ask to borrow texts which Kūkai had brought back from China. In fact, Kūkai eventually turned down such a request with the severe remark that "the essence of Esoteric Buddhism

---

[1] *K.Z.,* V, 361–62.

[2] Many biographers of both Kūkai and Saichō believe that the two met for the first time when they left for China. Strictly speaking, there is some room for doubt in this, for Kūkai embarked on Ship One from the port of Naniwa (Osaka), and Saichō, on Ship Two from the port of Tanoura in Kyushu, though both ships set sail for China on the same day from Tanoura. Regarding their first meeting after returning from China, the Tendai scholars say that Kūkai paid his respects to Saichō by visiting Mt. Hiei on the third day of the second month of Daidō 4 (809). As evidence, they adduce Kūkai's visiting card which is included in a document called *Enryakuji gokoku engi (Dainihon Bukkyō zensho* No. 126). On the other hand, the Shingon scholars insist that this item is a fabrication (for example, see Moriyama, *Bunkashijō,* p. 274).

[3] *Zoku gunsho ruijū,* Shakuka Section, *Dengyō daishi shōsoku.*

is not to be obtained from written words but to be transmitted from mind to mind; the written words are mere lees and dregs; they are bricks and pebbles." [4]

On the twenty-seventh day of the ninth month of Kōnin 3 (812) Saichō and his disciple Kōjō were returning from Nara and visited Kūkai at the Otokunidera in the southwestern suburbs of Kyoto. Saichō stayed there overnight. At this time Saichō requested Kūkai to perform *abhiṣeka* for him, received his consent, and returned to Mt. Hiei for preparation. Kūkai then headed for the Takaosanji on the twenty-ninth day of the same month.

In order to fulfill his promise, Kūkai on the fifteenth of the eleventh month conducted the introductory *abhiṣeka* (*kechien kanjō*) of the Diamond Realm (*vajra-dhātu*). A memorandum entitled *List of the Recipients of Abhiṣeka* (*Kanjō rekimyō*) [5] (written in Kūkai's hand and preserved in the Takaosanji) gives us the details of that and the following two *abhiṣeka* which took place at the temple. On the fourteenth of the following month Kūkai held the introductory *abhiṣeka* of the Matrix Realm (*garbha-dhātu*) for Saichō and his disciples, Nara priests, nobles, etc. These two *abhiṣeka* are the simplest of their kind and are given to clergymen and laymen alike regardless of their qualifications. The aim is to initiate an individual into Esoteric Buddhist practice, that is, to let him establish a personal relationship (*kechien*) with a Buddha, Bodhisattva, or guardian. The seeker throws a flower onto a mandala. The flower falls upon a certain deity, and the master gives the seeker the mantra and the mudra which correspond to that deity.

The first *abhiṣeka* initiated only four persons: Saichō, the Wake brothers (the supporters of the temple), and a certain Mino Tanehito. This ceremony was obviously intended for Saichō and was rather private in character. In contrast, the second *abhiṣeka* was truly public. Saichō's name is recorded first for this ceremony in the *List*, but Kūkai had clearly taken this opportunity to spread his influence widely. More than 190 candidates assembled at the Takaosanji. The leading priests of the great Nara temples were present, as were many figures from the

---

[4] *K.Z.*, III, 550.

[5] This is one of the few surviving documents undoubtedly by Kūkai himself. It has been studied by Japanese calligraphers as one of Kūkai's finest works. See *K.Z.*, III, 620–28.

nobility. There is no doubt that Kūkai's reputation as the master of Esoteric Buddhism had become firmly established.

After the completion of the second *abhiṣeka*, Saichō asked Kūkai to perform for him the highest *abhiṣeka*, the initiation as a master of Esoteric Buddhism. Kūkai refused, saying that three years' study would be necessary in order to qualify. Saichō, who had hoped to receive this *abhiṣeka* in only a few months, left his disciples Enchō, Taihan, and Ken'ei under Kūkai's guidance and returned to Mt. Hiei. The following spring, Saichō's seventeen disciples received from Kūkai at the same temple the *abhiṣeka* of the Transmission of the Dharma (*dembō kanjō*) of the Diamond Realm. The names of these disciples are noted by Kūkai in the *List*, but the name of Saichō is not among them. Saichō was on Mt. Hiei while his disciples received the *abhiṣeka* of the Transmission of the Dharma. Saichō himself, as an authority on Esoteric Buddhism, had performed the ceremony at the same temple only a few years previously, immediately after his return from China. The *abhiṣeka* ceremonies at the Takaosanji had come to be performed on Saichō's initiative. Now, however, he was forced to relinquish the position of master. Nevertheless, the friendly association between Kūkai and Saichō was not yet at an end.

As a result of these successive *abhiṣeka* ceremonies, Kūkai not only distinguished himself as the master of Esoteric Buddhism in Japan but was able to educate his disciples and to organize his order. With respect to the monastic community at the Takaosanji, he made his leading disciples responsible for administration, monastic discipline, and maintenance and construction.[6] In 813 Kūkai outlined the aim and practices of his order in a document called *The Admonishments of Kōnin* (*Kōnin no goyuikai*).[7] Under Kūkai's strong leadership, the Takaosanji became identified as the center of Esoteric Buddhism in Japan. Kūkai's activities were to be based at this temple for the next ten years.

Kūkai already enjoyed the patronage of the Emperor Saga and of the leading nobles and was popular at court and among the people. As his own writings show, he became busier than ever exchanging poems with the emperor, providing new scriptures, holding memorial services, and writing epitaphs and petitions on request. Yet Kūkai's true creative genius, nurtured by the practice of meditation, found expression in religious treatises. It was during this early period at the Takaosanji that

[6] K.Z., III, 532–33.   [7] K.Z., II, 861–62; see translation in Part Two, pp. 94–95.

Kūkai wrote *The Difference between Esoteric and Exoteric Buddhism*,[8] in which he proclaims the independence of Shingon Buddhism and its superiority over all other existing Buddhist doctrines in China and Japan. Furthermore, he completed the basic texts of his religion, *Attaining Enlightenment in This Very Existence*,[9] *The Meanings of Sound, Word, and Reality*,[10] and *The Meanings of the Word Hūṃ*.[11] Here, too, he drafted *The Secret Treasure-house of the Mirrors of Poetry*.[12] Close to the end of this period Kūkai conceived the basic ideas and structure of his *Ten Stages of the Development of Mind*,[13] the actual writing of which was done much later.

The more Kūkai committed his teaching to writing, the more his disciples multiplied and the more he wished to build a genuine monastic center where students might concentrate on the practice of Shingon meditation. He required a site free from the encumbrances of custom and tradition and isolated from the political and social influences of the capital. The Takaosanji was too close to the capital and too small in area to allow the realization of his vision. Kūkai was ready to undertake his life work.

8

FOUNDING OF MT. KŌYA

On the nineteenth of the fifth month of Kōnin 7 (816), Kūkai asked the Emperor Saga to grant him Mt. Kōya. Numerous legends have developed around the opening of Mt. Kōya, regarded as one of the holy mountains of Japan, but Kūkai's memorial is the most authentic document. The entire text reads as follows:

[8] *K.Z.*, I, 474–505; see translation.   [9] *K.Z.*, I, 506–18; see translation.
[10] *K.Z.*, I, 521–34; see translation.   [11] *K.Z.*, I, 535–53; see translation.
[12] *K.Z.*, III, 1–206. This work was completed later on Mt. Kōya.
[13] *K.Z.*, I, 125–414. The basic pattern of Kūkai's thought can be seen in a work written in 822 and given to the ex-emperor Heizei when the latter received *abhiṣeka* from Kūkai (*Heizei tennō kanjō bun, K.Z.*, II, 154–72).

I, Kūkai, have heard that where the mountains are high the clouds let fall much rain, thus nourishing vegetation, and that where drops of water accumulate fishes and dragons breed and multiply. Thus it was that the Buddha preached on steep Mount Gridhakūṭa [in North India] and that Avalokiteśvara manifested himself on Mount Potalaka [in South India], whose strange peaks and precipices face the shores. Indeed, these mountains had evoked their presence. Students of meditation fill the five Buddhist temples on Mount Wu-t'ai [in North China], and friends of concentration crowd the temple on Mount T'ien-t'ai. They are treasures of the nation; they are like bridges for the people.

At our imperial court, each generation of emperors has paid special attention to the teachings of the Buddha. Many temples and monasteries, both government and private, have been built, and a number of excellent priests who preach the profound meaning of the Dharma reside in each temple. Buddhism appears to be at its height, and as many temples as could be have been built. It is regrettable, however, that only a few priests practice meditation in high mountains, in deep forests, in wide canyons, and in secluded caves. This is because the teaching of meditation has not been transmitted, nor has a suitable place been allocated for the practice of meditation.

According to the meditation sutras, meditation should be practiced preferably on a flat area deep in the mountains. When young, I, Kūkai, often walked through mountainous areas and crossed many rivers. There is a quiet, open place called Kōya located two days' walk to the west from a point that is one day's walk south from Yoshino. I estimate the area to be south of Ito-no-kōri in Kinokuni [Wakayama-ken]. High peaks surround Kōya in all four directions; no human tracks, still less trails, are to be seen there. I should like to clear the wilderness in order to build a monastery there for the practice of meditation, for the benefit of the nation and of those who desire to discipline themselves.

The sutras say, however, that a mendicant who avails himself of anything without permission is a thief. The rise or fall of the Dharma, indeed, depends on the mind of the emperor. Whether the object is small or large, I dare not make it mine until I have been granted your permission. I earnestly wish that the empty land be granted me so that I may fulfill my humble desire. If permitted, I shall respond to your generous offer by practicing meditation four times a day. Should His Majesty decide to grant me permission, I should appreciate his forwarding the imperial order to the court. I am afraid that I have taken up this matter in haste, causing your Imperial Majesty inconvenience. I, Kūkai, present this memorial to the emperor, reverently and with awe.

> Written on the nineteenth day
> of the sixth month, Kōnin 7 (816) [1]

[1] *K.Z.*, III, 523–24.

There is nothing of the legendary or of the marvelous here. Kūkai's aims and his methods were ambitious but perfectly practical. He had known Mt. Kōya ever since the days of his wandering as an ascetic, and he had long cherished the desire to build a monastery far from human habitation. In a letter to a layman dating from this period, Kūkai states that while at sea on the way back from China his ship was in danger and that he vowed to build a monastery if he reached Japan in safety. Now, Kūkai added, he wished to fulfill that vow, for twelve years had gone by without his doing so.[2]

As for the legends pertaining to the opening of Mt. Kōya, the commonest one concerns a three-pronged *vajra*. When Kūkai was about to return from China, he stood on the shore and threw this *vajra* toward Japan, while praying that it might indicate the place most suitable to be the center of Esoteric Buddhism. The *vajra* disappeared into the sky. Then in 816, when Kūkai went to search for the *vajra*, he met a hunter accompanied by a white dog and a black dog in Uchi County in Yamato Province. The hunter told Kūkai that the *vajra* was on Mt. Kōya. Guided by the hunter, Kūkai climbed Mt. Kōya and there found the *vajra* hanging in a three-needled pine tree. (Ordinary pines in Japan have twin needles.) Thereupon, a kami appeared and declared that he, the lord of the mountain, would give the mountain to Kūkai.[3]

At that time Mt. Kōya was a forest wilderness, visited only occasionally by hunters. Mt. Kōya, located several days' walking distance southeast of Kyoto, is the highest mountain in this area. Surrounded by eight peaks, the highest of which is 3,230 feet above sea level, Mt. Kōya is characterized by a central plateau covered by giant evergreens. The plateau is approximately three and a half miles long and one and a half miles wide. Abundant water is available from many streams. Kūkai was convinced that this was the ideal place to build his monastic center.

The emperor officially granted Kūkai's request on the eighth day of the seventh month of the same year. Kūkai immediately sent his disciples to the mountain to build a few crude huts there. It was in the eleventh month of the following year (818), more than a year later, that Kūkai himself climbed Mt. Kōya. He had to perfect his archi-

[2] *K.Z.*, III, 574–75.

[3] Since the story appears in the *Heike monogatari* and elsewhere, it must have been widely circulated.

tectural planning so that it would be in harmony with the topography of Mt. Kōya as well as with Shingon teaching. Besides, he had to make financial preparations, for the opening of Mt. Kōya was his responsibility alone. The mountain had been granted personally to Kūkai and was henceforth free from all state control.

On the third day of the fifth month of the next year (819), Kūkai officiated at the formal consecration of Mt. Kōya. The rituals continued seven days and nights, in the course of which the sacred boundary was drawn around an area seven *ri* on each side.[4] The ground was broken at the center of the plateau where Kūkai planned to erect the great pagoda, the lecture hall, etc. Soon after the groundbreaking ceremony, Kūkai entrusted the construction work to his disciples Jichie, Taihan, and others, and returned unwillingly to the capital. He had received an imperial order to act as an adviser to the secretary of state (*nakatsukasa-shō*). How often he climbed Mt. Kōya to supervise the work and how long he stayed there on each visit are not known. From the several letters he wrote during this period, it is certain that he went to Mt. Kōya whenever he could. These letters describe the difficulties he met in the task of opening the mountain. For example, a letter whose address is missing states:

I came to this peak last month on the sixteenth day in order to practice silent meditation. The mountain is high, the snow is deep, and walking is painful. I am sorry that I have not written to you for a long time, but I have been concentrating on this matter. I have just received rice and oil from you, at which I leap with joy. It is snowing here and cold. I am wondering how you are getting along. . . .[5]

At times Kūkai sent to his personal supporters such letters as this: "We are out of nails; the carpenters cannot finish their work. I sincerely wish that you would send me some nails as soon as possible." [6] All the materials, except wood and water, had to be packed in by bearers from a considerable distance. The manpower requirements must have been enormous, but no details on this subject are available. Despite all difficulties, the project gradually took shape under Kūkai's direction and with the heartfelt cooperation of his disciples and of the local people. Financial difficulties, however, plagued the work up to the very end of

---

[4] *K.Z.*, III, 530. One *ri* equals 2.44 miles. [5] *K.Z.*, III, 603.
[6] *K.Z.*, III, 595.

Kūkai's life. In a document Kūkai wrote six months before his death, he assures the general public that "even a penny or a grain of rice will be welcome." [7]

Kūkai saw Mt. Kōya as the Matrix Realm, whose symbol is a lotus flower: the eight peaks surrounding the central plateau were the eight petals of the lotus. He named the temple complex in the center of the consecrated ground Kongōbuji, Vajra or Diamond Peak Temple, representing the *Vajra-dhātu*, the Diamond Realm of eternity and of infinite activity and wisdom. Thus Mt. Kōya consists of two circles, the circle of the Diamond Realm within the circle of the Matrix Realm. Within the Diamond Realm, that is, within the Diamond Peak Temple, Kūkai laid out the Grand Pagoda (*daitō*) representing the Diamond Realm. Seated in the center of the pagoda is the ultimate Reality, the Mahāvairocana of the Diamond Realm, surrounded by the four Buddhas of the Matrix Realm placed to the east, south, west, and north. The entire mountain with the central pagoda symbolizes the nonduality of both Realms, which is, according to Kūkai, the order of the World of Dharma. To the south, Kūkai placed the Lecture Hall (*kōdō*; presently called *kondō*, the Golden Hall) where the monks practice meditation and study the teachings. Behind the Lecture Hall, to the north, still on consecrated ground, Kūkai situated the monks' quarters.

Kūkai did not live to see all his ideas transformed into buildings on Mt. Kōya. Not even the Grand Pagoda, for whose central pillar the timbers were cut in 819, was completed while he was alive. This suggests the difficulties he encountered in carrying out his project. But the mountain was already his spiritual home. The poems apparently composed during one of his stays there reveal how he loved his life, and nature, on the mountain, an ideal place for his retreat. The following is an example: [8]

> I have neither family nor country to which I belong;
> I am completely free from the ties of kinsmen. . . .
> Mountain birds call on me and warble from time to time;
> Monkeys exhibit before my eyes their superb leaps from tree to tree.
> Spring flowers and autumn chrysanthemums smile upon me;
> The moon at dawn and the breezes at morn cleanse my heart.

In the midst of nature, surrounded by his devoted disciples and witnessing the construction of his temple, Kūkai must have found life most

[7] *K.Z.*, III, 517.   [8] *K.Z.*, III, 408.

congenial and stimulating. While on the mountain he received invitations from friends in the capital and responded with poems announcing his intention to remain on Mt. Kōya forever. He sent this poem to a nobleman in Kyoto: [9]

You ask me why I entered the mountain deep and cold,
Awesome, surrounded by steep peaks and grotesque rocks,
A place that is painful to climb and difficult to descend,
Wherein reside the gods of the mountain and the spirits of trees.

Have you not seen, O have you not seen,
The peach and plum blossoms in the royal garden?
They must be in full bloom, pink and fragrant,
Now opening in the April showers, now falling in the spring gales;
Flying high and low, all over the garden the petals scatter.
Some sprigs may be plucked by the strolling spring maidens,
And the flying petals picked by the flittering spring orioles.

Have you not seen, O have you not seen,
The water gushing up in the divine spring of the garden?
No sooner does it arise than it flows away forever:
Thousands of shining lines flow as they come forth,
Flowing, flowing, flowing into an unfathomable abyss;
Turning, whirling again, they flow on forever,
And no one knows where they will stop.

Have you not seen, O have you not seen,
That billions have lived in China, in Japan?
None have been immortal, from time immemorial:
Ancient sage kings or tyrants, good subjects or bad,
Fair ladies or homely—who could enjoy eternal youth?
Noble men and lowly alike, without exception, die away;
They have all died, reduced to dust and ashes;
The singing halls and dancing stages have become the abodes of foxes.
Transient as dreams, bubbles or lightning, all are perpetual travelers.

Have you not seen, O have you not seen,
This has been man's fate; how can you alone live forever?
Thinking of this, my heart always feels torn;
You, too, are like the sun going down in the western mountains,
Or a living corpse whose span of life is nearly over.
Futile would be my stay in the capital;
Away, away, I must go, I must not stay there.
Release me, for I shall be master of the great void;
A child of Shingon must not stay there.

[9] K.Z., III, 406–7.

> I have never tired of watching the pine trees and the rocks at Mt.
>   Kōya;
> The limpid stream of the mountain is the source of my inexhaustible
>   joy.
> Discard pride in earthly gains;
> Do not be scorched in the burning house, the triple world!
> Discipline in the woods alone lets us soon enter the eternal Realm.

In spite of Kūkai's inclination to live a pious, meditative life secluded from the outer world, imperial orders and the requests of powerful clerics compelled him to come down from Mt. Kōya and to participate in agricultural rites, prayers for rain, and the like, in and around the capital. In any case, Kūkai could not remain forever on Mt. Kōya absorbed in meditation and writing. He needed wider support from the court, from clerical circles, and from the general public.

At this point Kūkai's significant achievements up to the year 822 which are reliably attested will be listed.

In the summer of 820 Kūkai completed *The Essentials of Poetry and Prose (Bumpitsu ganshin shō)*,[10] a condensed edition of his former work, *The Secret Treasure-house of the Mirrors of Poetry*. In the following year, acting upon the order of the court, he directed the reconstruction of a reservoir (Mannō no ike) for irrigation in his native province Sanuki. The reservoir had originally been constructed in the early part of the eighth century. After several minor failures, it finally broke down in 818. The court decided to rebuild it and sent a director to take charge of the work, but he was unsuccessful. The desperate governor of Sanuki requested that the court appoint Kūkai as director. Here is part of the official letter sent by the governor to the court:

Since last year, the officers responsible for building the reservoir have been trying to repair it. The lake is large and the workers are few so that there is as yet no prospect of completing the work. Now the head of the county office tells me that the monk Kūkai is a native of Tado County. He is a man of exemplary conduct and his fame, like that of Mount Sumeru, is unsurpassed. They say that, when he sits in meditation in the mountains, the birds build nests on him and animals grow tame. He studied abroad to seek the Way; he went empty-handed and returned fully equipped. Clergymen and laymen alike are delighted to receive his good influence, and the people look forward to seeing him. If he stays, a crowd of students assem-

10 *K.Z.*, III, 207–86.

bles around him; if he goes, a multitude follows him. He has long been away from his native place and lives in Kyoto. Farmers yearn for him as they do for their parents. If they hear that the master is coming, they will run out in haste to welcome him. I sincerely request that he be appointed the director.[11]

In view of the purpose and the style of the document, one does not need to take this description of Kūkai literally. Nevertheless, it gives a glimpse of Kūkai as a popular and highly respected monk with a magnetic personality. Kūkai seems to have arrived at the construction site in the early summer and returned to Kyoto about three months later, after successfully completing the project with which the previous director had struggled in vain. His success was probably due to his advanced knowledge of civil engineering and to the willing cooperation of the local people under his leadership. The lake is still remembered as having been constructed by Kūkai and, though it has needed repair from time to time, serves the local people to this day.

In the same year Kūkai completed *The Transmission of the Shingon Dharma (Shingon fuhō den)*,[12] a simplified edition of his *Transmission of the Dharma (Fuhō den)*.[13] He also directed, at the Takaosanji, the reproduction of twenty-six religious paintings brought back from China. This project was supported by the emperor, the empress, the heir apparent, the court ministers, and the general public. In a prayer at the ceremony performed before undertaking the project, Kūkai remarked that "the silk has been torn and discolored, and the images are about to disappear." [14] Hardly fifteen years had passed since the paintings were done in China; therefore, it seems unlikely that they should have been so mutilated. Yet, considering the difficulty of transporting the huge paintings from China in a small boat, Kūkai's several years of wandering after his return, and his frequent use of these paintings for *abhiṣeka* ceremonies, it is possible that they might have been considerably damaged. The project of reproducing them proved to be one of Kūkai's contributions to the history of Japanese art.

In 822 Kūkai performed the *abhiṣeka* ceremony for the ex-emperor Heizei, who had retired to Nara. Early in the year Kūkai completed the Abhiṣeka Hall in the Tōdaiji in Nara and performed services there.

---

[11] *K.Z.*, V, 433–34.   [12] *K.Z.*, I, 50–66.   [13] *K.Z.*, I, 1–49.
[14] *K.Z.*, III, 476.

By then, apparently, his impact on Nara was pervasive, for, as previously stated, this temple functioned as headquarters of Nara Buddhism.

9

THE TŌJI PERIOD

At the Takaosanji, on the nineteenth day of the first month of Kōnin 14 (823), Kūkai unexpectedly received a messenger from the Emperor Saga informing him that the emperor would present him with the Tōji. Kūkai promptly moved into the Tōji, leaving the Takaosanji in the hands of some of his disciples.

At that time the Buddhist temples in Kyoto were few compared to those in Nara. The Emperor Kammu did not permit the powerful Nara temples to encroach upon the new capital. Soon after the move to Kyoto from Nagaoka, Kammu had decided to build two state temples, the Tōji (Eastern Temple) and the Saiji (Western Temple). They were to stand on either side of the main avenue at the southern entrance to the capital. The original purpose of this plan was mainly magical, that is, to defend the new capital from evil influences of all kinds, although an aesthetic effect was also clearly intended. Since no such structures existed in the T'ang capital, one can assume that the plan followed the pattern of Nara, which had the Tōdaiji (Great Temple in the East) and the Saidaiji (Great Temple in the West). Nearly thirty years had elapsed since the removal of the capital, but the construction of the new temples in Kyoto progressed slowly with frequent changes of director. The unfinished buildings at the entrance to the city must have been unsightly, and quick completion of the work was called for.

Finally, just three months prior to his retirement, the Emperor Saga entrusted the completion of the Tōji to Kūkai, allowing him to continue it at his discretion so that it could become the Esoteric Buddhist center of Kyoto. The administrative skill, artistic talent, and technical knowledge that Kūkai had demonstrated at the Takaosanji, at the Tōdaiji, and in the reservoir project must have made him an obvious choice.[1] None the less, this last favor bestowed by Saga upon Kūkai was outstanding, a fitting culmination to Saga's many acts of patronage toward Shingon Buddhism.

On the twenty-fourth day of the fourth month (823), Kūkai from the Tōji presented a letter of congratulation to the new Emperor Jun'na (r. 823–33) on the occasion of his enthronement. Like the retired emperor, the new emperor was well disposed toward Kūkai. A little later, Kūkai asked Jun'na to approve his *List of Texts, Consisting of the Three Divisions of Study (Sangaku roku)*.[2] It listed 424 fascicles of texts including sutras, shastras, vinaya texts, and materials for the study of Sanskrit, the whole constituting a course of study for Shingon students. Kūkai's presentation of the *List* can be understood as a request for the recognition of Shingon, on a doctrinal basis, as an independent sect. The new emperor graciously approved the proposal on the tenth day of the tenth month of the same year. His imperial decree [3] used the term "Shingon sect (*Shingon shū*)" for the first time in an official document. It authorized Kūkai to retain fifty Shingon monks regularly at the Tōji and to educate them according to the requirements defined in the *List*. The decree also permitted Kūkai to use the temple exclusively for Shingon students and forbade monks of other sects to reside there. This was revolutionary. In the great temples of Nara students belonging to many sects were allowed to stay in the same temple and study together, and on Mt. Hiei, where all monks belonged to the Tendai sect, there were students of both Exoteric and Esoteric practices. Kūkai, who had selected Esoteric Buddhism as the most effective approach to attaining enlightenment, had now succeeded in establishing his religion on a solid institutional basis by state authorization. His entry into the Tōji, therefore, was the final step toward the independence of Shingon Buddhism.

The ten years between 823 and Kūkai's retirement to Mt. Kōya in

[1] One possible reason why Saga gave Kūkai the Tōji is that about six months earlier, seven days after Saichō's death, Saga had permitted the Tendai sect to build an independent initiation platform on Mt. Hiei. He might have felt compelled, in all fairness, to do a favor for Kūkai also.

[2] *K.Z.*, I, 105–22.   [3] *K.Z.*, V, 435.

832, at the age of fifty-nine, embraced his most colorful period. Kūkai's rival Saichō had died in 822 and the monks at Mt. Hiei were eager to adopt Esoteric Buddhist practices into Tendai Buddhism. Kūkai had a Shingon institution in the Tōdaiji in Nara, and among the Nara leaders there were none who could equal Kūkai in breadth of learning, religious authority, leadership, and popularity among all classes of society.

At fifty, Kūkai was at the peak of maturity, and his career was at its height. He was ready to turn his genius to the construction of the Tōji. When he entered the temple, the Golden Hall (*kondō*) and certain other buildings were already standing. In 824 he was officially appointed administrative head in charge of the maintenance and construction of the temple. In the following year, he received permission from the government to build the Lecture Hall (*kōdō*). This hall was designed by Kūkai to contain an altar, or rather a sacred stage; art was used to manifest fully the essential truth of Shingon. Thus the entire setting was transformed into a spiritual vision. The carving of the images to be installed in the hall was also undertaken under Kūkai's guidance and supervision. Among the twenty-one images standing in the hall today, fourteen date from then. In 826 Kūkai initiated the construction of a pagoda within the temple precinct. An old document states that for the pillars of the pagoda 3,490 workers were mobilized to haul the timber from nearby Mt. Higashiyama.[4] Nevertheless, the pagoda was not completed during Kūkai's lifetime. The present pagoda, towering conspicuously in the southern part of Kyoto, was rebuilt in 1644 by the third Tokugawa shōgun, Iemitsu.

Meanwhile, the construction of the monastic center on Mt. Kōya continued under Kūkai's supervision. As if he did not have enough to do, the court and people often asked Kūkai to perform services, and the leading clergymen of Nara invited him to participate in their religious activities. His position as a monastic official steadily advanced: in 824 he was appointed junior director (*shōsōzu*) and in 827, senior director (*daisōzu*). In each case Kūkai tried to decline, but the court insisted. In the interval, in 825, he was invited to act as tutor to the crown prince.

There are other activities of this period that are noteworthy. Kūkai opened the School of Arts and Sciences (*Shugei shuchi-in*) in 828 near

---

[4] *K.Z.*, III, 522; Watanabe Shōkō and Miyasaka Yūshō, *Shamon Kūkai* (Monk Kūkai) (Tokyo: Chikuma shobō, 1967), p. 164.

the Tōji. In 830 he completed his life work in thought and religion, *The Ten Stages of the Development of Mind* and, soon afterward, a simplified edition of this book, entitled *The Precious Key to the Secret Treasury*. Here the discussion will be confined to the school; the two major works will be taken up later.

The School of Arts and Sciences was a private school open to all students, regardless of their social status or economic means. It was the first school in Japan to provide for universal education. Behind it was Kūkai's conviction of the oneness of humanity, his ideal of equal opportunity in education, and his belief in the intrinsic value of each individual. Affirming the importance of both religious and secular studies, Kūkai included in his curriculum Buddhism, Taoism, and Confucianism. Unfortunately, there is no information on Kūkai's success, for only two documents on the school exist: *The Regulations of the School of Arts and Sciences (Shugei shuchi-in shiki)* [5] written by Kūkai at the opening of the school; and an official document issued by the government in 847, permitting the Tōji to sell the school.[6]

In the *Regulations*, Kūkai states the need to open a school for the general public:

In the capital of our country, there is only one government college and no other institution of learning. As a result, the sons of the poor have no opportunity to seek knowledge. . . . Would it not be well to establish a school which might give broad assistance to uneducated children? [7]

The government college admitted almost none but the sons of nobles; therefore, educational opportunity for the children of commoners was totally denied. In order to realize his ideal of educating the sons of the poor and ignorant, Kūkai first of all had to educate his teachers. Kūkai explained to lay teachers, who might be more inclined than monks to prejudice:

If young, uneducated children wish to learn how to read and write, teachers, if genuine, should instruct them in a spirit of deep compassion, emphasizing filial piety and loyalty. Whether students are high- or low-born, rich or poor, they should be given appropriate instruction and unremitting admonishment from their teachers. "The beings in the triple

---

[5] *K.Z.*, III, 535–39; Wm. Theodore de Bary, ed., *The Buddhist Tradition* (New York: Modern Library, 1969), pp. 309–13.
[6] *K.Z.*, V, 474.   [7] *K.Z.*, III, 537.

world are my children," announced the Buddha [in the *Lotus Sutra*]. And there is a beautiful saying of Confucius that "all within the four seas are brothers" [in *Analects*, VII, 5]. Do honor to these teachings! [8]

Kūkai expressed the need for wide learning in this manner: "There has never been anything that produced a delicious dish out of one flavor or a beautiful melody out of one tone." [9] He also announced in the *Regulations* the distribution of free meals to both teachers and students. Providing meals must have been a necessary condition for gathering poor students and for attracting humble teachers who might be willing to cooperate with Kūkai. It may well be in this period that Kūkai compiled for his school children a dictionary (*Tenrei banshō myōgi*),[10] the oldest extant in Japan.

Kūkai's work toward education for all was shattered only too quickly when the school was closed a short ten years after his death. It was sold by Kūkai's successor at the Tōji for the purchase of some rice paddies, the yield of which was to provide funds to train monks. These monks, in turn, would only divert the thrust of Shingon activity from the universalistic and egalitarian spirit fostered by Kūkai.

IO

RETURN TO MT. KŌYA

Toward the end of the fifth month of Tenchō 8 (831), Kūkai fell seriously ill and was obliged to retire from his official duties. He wished to return to Mt. Kōya to spend his remaining days and to devote his time to the construction project which had been lagging for years. The emperor, however, did not accept his resignation, ordering him to remain in office while caring for his health.[1] It is not certain when he

---

[8] *K.Z.*, III, 538.   [9] *K.Z.*, III, 535–56.   [10] *K.Z.*, VI, 1–723.
[1] *K.Z.*, III, 520–21.

became free, but Kūkai was on Mt. Kōya on the twenty-fourth of the eighth month of the following year, officiating at the Offering Ceremony of Ten Thousand Lights and Flowers.[2] Thereafter, he spent almost all his time on the mountain.

Although physically retired to Mt. Kōya, Kūkai still had a few more requests to make to the court for the sake of his religious establishment. In order to reward the ailing monk, the court generously complied with each. On the nineteenth day of the twelfth month of Jōwa 1 (834), he was given authorization to establish a Shingon chapel in the palace (Shingon-in) and to perform Shingon rituals there for a week, starting with the eighth of the first month of each year. A similar practice already existed at the Chinese court. This week of services became part of the annual rites performed by Shingon priests at court.[3] Also, on the twenty-second day of the first month of Jōwa 2 (835), two months prior to Kūkai's death, the court permitted him to ordain annually on Mt. Kōya three monks under state sponsorship. This meant that the hitherto private monastic center on Mt. Kōya had been officially recognized as a state-supported Buddhist institution.

As his last days approached, Kūkai sat absorbed in meditation and refused food. According to the Will, he prophesied that his death would come on the twenty-first day of the third month.[4] Shinzei's biography gives this account:

On the last day of the fifth month of Jōwa 1 (834), he asked his disciples to gather around him and said: "My life will not last much longer. Live harmoniously and preserve with care the teaching of the Buddha. I am returning to the mountain to remain there forever."[5]

In the early part of the ninth month, the master chose his burial place. From the first month of the second year (835), he drank no water. Someone advised him to take certain herbs as the human body is readily subject to decay, and a celestial cook came day after day and offered him nectar, but he declined even these, saying that he had no use for human food.

At midnight on the twenty-first day of the third month (835), Master Kūkai, lying on his right side, breathed his last. One or two of his disciples

---

[2] The prayer is still extant. K.Z., III, 516.

[3] K.Z., III, 518–19. This is the origin of the annual ritual in the palace called mishuhō, mishiho, or misuho, often mentioned in the works of Heian literature.

[4] K.Z., II, 787.

[5] These words seem to have been spoken by Kūkai to his disciples at the Tōji on his last visit there.

knew that he had been suffering from a carbuncle. In accordance with his will, Kūkai, clad in his robes, was interred on the Eastern Peak. He was sixty-two years of age.[6]

A document that conveys the feelings of the people about his death is the report sent to the Ch'ing-lung Temple in Ch'ang-an where Kūkai had met his master Hui-kuo. It was prepared by one of his leading disciples, Jitsue (d. 847). A portion of this report, written about a year after Kūkai's death, reads as follows:

In the third month of Jōwa 2 (835), his fuel became exhausted and his fire was extinguished. He was sixty-two years old. Alas! Mt. Kōya turned gray; the clouds and trees appeared sad. The emperor in sorrow hastily sent a messenger to convey his condolences. The disciples wept as if they had lost their parents. Alas! We feel in our hearts as if we had swallowed fire, and our tears gush forth like fountains. Being unable to die, we are guarding the place where he passed away. . . .[7]

At the report of Kūkai's death, the Emperor Nimmyō (r. 833–50) sent to Mt. Kōya a message dated the twenty-fifth of the same month:

I can hardly believe that the master of Shingon, the foremost teacher of Esoteric Buddhism, on whose protection the state depended, and to whose prayers animals and plants owed their prosperity, has passed away. Alas! Because of the great distance, the mournful report has arrived here too late; I regret that I cannot send my representative in time for the cremation. . . .[8]

A great transformation, ordinarily called death, happened to Kūkai on the twenty-first day of the third month of Jōwa 2 (835). Unusual as his last moments may seem according to these early sources, they were not supernatural. Nonetheless, in legend and in the memory of the faithful, the image of his death remained unearthly. Kūkai had not died but had merely entered into eternal samadhi and was still quite alive on Mt. Kōya as a savior to all suffering people; for Kūkai had specially descended to earth between the appearances of the Buddha Shakyamuni and the future Buddha Maitreya.

[6] *K.Z.*, Shukan, 4.   [7] *K.Z.*, V, 391–92.
[8] *K.Z.*, V, 389. The message, written in Kyoto four days after Kūkai's death, assumes that Kūkai was cremated as was the custom for Buddhist monks. Shinzei writes that Kūkai was interred.

PART TWO

THOUGHT OF KŪKAI

I

EXOTERIC BUDDHISM
AND ESOTERIC BUDDHISM

Between his return from China and his last years, Kūkai wrote roughly fifty religious works. These disclose the two main themes of his writing. First, they demonstrate the superiority of Esoteric Buddhism over all the other systems of thought and religions that Kūkai knew, particularly over the Buddhism then current in China and Japan; second, they reveal the essential doctrines of Esoteric Buddhism. The first theme appears in Kūkai's discussions of the relationship between Exoteric and Esoteric Buddhism. The second, treated in the next chapter, can be summed up as his assertion that by practicing Esoteric Buddhism one can attain enlightenment here and now.

It was from Hui-kuo that Kūkai had inherited these two basic attitudes. Kūkai's intention was to hold strictly to the Esoteric Buddhist tradition and to carry on the Dharma in a manner completely faithful to his master's teachings. As a result Kūkai came to systematize Esoteric Buddhism to an extent hitherto unknown in China. He lived up to his maxim, "To seek the Way is to forget oneself in the teachings leading to the Way." [1]

To prove the superiority of Esoteric Buddhism, Kūkai starts by assuming antagonism and incompatibility between it and all other Buddhist schools. Next, in order to demonstrate the universality of Esoteric Buddhism, he shows that the Exoteric sutras contain Esoteric elements which have previously gone unnoticed. These two viewpoints stand out clearly in the writings of his early forties. Then finally in 830, at the age of fifty-seven, Kūkai reaches the third viewpoint in *The Ten Stages of the Development of Mind* and its abridged edition, *The Precious Key to the Secret Treasury*. That is, that Esoteric Buddhism contains in itself all Exoteric teachings and, without losing its own identity, synthesizes them from a higher and more comprehensive standpoint. Kūkai's ideas on this subject go from recognition of differences to discovery of common ground and, finally, to the establishment of a synthetic point of view that allows the coexistence of a variety of particulars without isolating one from the other: in this case, mainly, the contending schools of Exoteric Buddhism.

EXOTERIC VERSUS ESOTERIC BUDDHISM

Kūkai first declared the superiority of Esoteric over Exoteric Buddhism, taking Hui-kuo as his authority, in the epitaph he wrote for Hui-kuo's tomb.[2] His most representative work on the subject, as the title indicates, is *The Difference between Exoteric and Esoteric Buddhism*, written in 814 or 815. The points which he discusses in this and in numerous other works are mainly: the difference between the revealers of the two teachings; the qualitative difference in the contents of the teachings; the great disparity in the speed with which each leads to enlightenment; the benefits to be derived from each; and the wide difference in methods of practice.

As to the first and second points, Kūkai expresses himself concisely in the opening paragraph of the *Difference*:

[1] *K.Z.*, III, 550.   [2] *K.Z.*, III, 423.

The doctrine revealed by the Nirmanakaya Buddha [Shakyamuni Buddha] is called Exoteric; it is apparent, simplified, and adapted to the needs of the time and to the capacity of the listeners. The doctrine expounded by the Dharmakaya Buddha [Mahāvairocana] is called Esoteric; it is secret and profound and contains the final truth.[3]

His assertion that Esoteric Buddhism was not the doctrine expounded by the historical Buddha was a radical one: everyone believed that literally all the Buddhist sutras had been preached by him. According to Kūkai, the historical Buddha is but one manifestation of Mahāvairo-cana, who exists in history and yet at the same time transcends it. Mahāvairocana in his samadhi is timeless and eternally present in a state of bliss. The Esoteric teachings contained in the *Mahāvairocana* and *Vajraśekhara Sutras*,[4] Kūkai says, unconditionally reveal the inner-most secrets of that eternal samadhi of Mahāvairocana; and by practic-ing Esoteric Buddhist methods of meditation, one can quickly experi-ence the samadhi of Mahāvairocana. In other words, one can attain enlightenment.

Kūkai further discusses enlightenment in his *Attaining Enlightenment in This Very Existence*, among other works. He says that the Esoteric approach is the "sudden approach" in contrast to the "gradual ap-proach" of Exoteric Buddhism. Nor is this the only advantage of the Esoteric approach. Those who have been denied a chance of salvation by the Exoteric teachings—such as the cursed ones (*icchantika*) and those guilty of serious crimes—can be saved by the most rudimentary Esoteric practice of reciting a mantra. Kūkai untiringly explains the mystical power inherent in mantras, saying that they are impregnated with Mahāvairocana's saving power. Hence, the recitation of a mantra unites the reciter directly with Mahāvairocana, or reaches Mahāvairo-cana indirectly through lesser Buddhas, Bodhisattvas, and others. Kūkai employed the magic of words, or the common belief in the mystical

[3] *K.Z.,* I, 474.

[4] Two translations of the *Vajraśekhara* (or *Tattva-saṃgraha*) *Sutra* were known to Kūkai: one (T865) done by Vajrabodhi and another (T866), by Pu-k'ung (Amoghavajra). The framework of Kūkai's Esoteric Buddhist thought was furnished by the Esoteric Buddhist teachings of sixth- or seventh-century India contained in the *Vajraśekhara Sutra* as well as in the *Mahāvairocana Sutra*. Both sutras were written in the later phase of development of Buddhist thought. As a result Kūkai's thought, though systematized thousands of miles away from India, retained much of what was new there.

power of sound, for the spiritual discipline of all, be it learned monks or humble folk.

Kūkai's last point concerning the supremacy of Esoteric Buddhism is that only Esoteric Buddhism has systematic methods of meditation aiming at enlightenment, as well as magico-religious rituals to be performed for secular purposes. He criticizes as ineffective the practice of reciting or expounding sutras which was common among the Buddhist sects of his time. He was convinced that the study of Buddhism without the practice of meditation was fruitless and that meditation not grounded in the synthetic view was rash.[5]

ESOTERIC BUDDHISM WITHIN EXOTERIC BUDDHISM

Kūkai's belief that, though approaches may differ, Buddhism is in reality one appears already in the writings of his early thirties, such as *A Memorial Presenting a List of Newly Imported Sutras and Other Items*:

The sea of Dharma is of one flavor but has deep and shallow aspects in accordance with the capacity of the believer. Five Vehicles can be distinguished, sudden and gradual according to the vessel. Among the teachings of sudden enlightenment, some are Exoteric and some, Esoteric. In Esoteric Buddhism itself, some aspects represent the source, others, the tributary. The teachers of the Dharma of former times swam in the waters of the tributary and hung on to the leaves, but the teaching transmitted to me now uproots the enclosure which blocks the source and penetrates it through and through.[6]

According to Kūkai, the historical Buddha was, after all, but one manifestation of Mahāvairocana. It was only natural then that the Exoteric Buddhist doctrine preached by the historical Buddha should contain Esoteric Buddhist elements, no matter how imperfect they might be and no matter how they might be disguised. Specifically, Kūkai regarded two elements as Esoteric: passages in Exoteric texts to the effect that the Dharmakaya Buddha preached or expressed himself; and the appearance in Exoteric texts of mantra and dharani. Kūkai takes

[5] *K.Z.*, I, 554. In the opening poem of *The Secret Key to the Heart Sutra*, Kūkai states: "How can we be freed from the endless cycle of samsara? The only way is to practice meditation and correct thinking." See also *K.Z.*, I, 102.
[6] *K.Z.*, I, 83.

up the first element in *The Difference between Exoteric and Esoteric Buddhism*. Before quoting a number of passages to prove that the Dharmakaya Buddha preached in Exoteric texts, Kūkai writes a section in a conversational style expressing his own opinions on the subject. In the following quotation, from an argument in the opening section of the work, "Question" represents the consensus of the Exoteric teachers and "Answer," Kūkai's opinion:

QUESTION: The fact that the Nirmanakaya Buddha preached is agreed upon by all schools. As to the Dharmakaya Buddha, however, we understand that he is formless and imageless, that he is totally beyond verbalization and conceptualization, and that therefore there is no way of explaining him or showing him. Sutras and commentaries describe him in this way. Why do you now assert that the Dharmakaya Buddha preaches? What is your evidence for this?

ANSWER: Now and again the sutras and commentaries refer to this preaching. Misled by their biased preconceptions, people overlook these pertinent passages. Indeed, their meanings will be revealed only in accordance with the capacity of the reader: the same water may be seen as emerald by heavenly beings and as burning fire by hungry ghosts; the same darkness may be seen as light by nocturnal birds and as darkness by men. . . . The masters of the Dharma who transmitted the Exoteric Buddhist teachings interpreted the [passages of] profound significance [appearing in the Exoteric Buddhist texts] in the light of their shallow doctrines and failed to find any Esoteric import in them. Faithfully transmitting the Exoteric Buddhist teachings from master to disciple, they discussed Buddhism according to the tenets of their particular schools. They so eagerly supported their beliefs that they found no time to meditate on those [passages] which might have been disadvantageous to their doctrines.[7]

On the second element just mentioned, the most representative of Kūkai's numerous writings is *The Secret Key to the Heart Sutra*, written in his last years. The sutra, the shortest of all popular Mahayana sutras, ends with the mantra *gate gate paragate pārasaṃgate bodhi svāhā*. Kūkai's method of interpreting the sutra with special emphasis on the mantra is unique. Elsewhere Kūkai goes so far as to regard the Sanskrit title of a sutra as a mantra. For example, he considered the title of the *Lotus Sutra sad-dhar-ma-pun-ḍa-rī-ka sū-traṃ* as a mantra and as a Dharma-mandala.[8] As he remarks, "The eyes of the King of Medi-

---

[7] K.Z., I, 475–76.

[8] Kūkai's five introductions to the *Lotus Sutra*, written on different occasions, are collected in K.Z., I, 756–808. He defines the Sanskrit title of the sutra as a

cine never allow a medicinal herb on the roadside to pass unnoticed.
An expert on gems detects a gem in ore. Who is to be blamed if one
fails to see [the herb or the gem]?" [9]

SHINGON BUDDHISM, THE SYNTHESIS
OF EXOTERIC BUDDHISM

Although Kūkai found Esoteric elements in many so-called Exoteric
texts, some of the latter naturally had a more Esoteric flavor than others.
The stronger this flavor, the higher Kūkai ranked the text in question.
Those doctrines which came closest to the Esoteric teachings were, in
his judgment, more profound and more integrated. Shingon Buddhism,
the most profound teaching of all, embraced all others, however imperfect, as integral parts of itself. Kūkai's final viewpoint was that
the other varieties of Buddhism were as steps ascending toward the
final, exalted level of Shingon, which, though including all within its
ample scope, remained aloof and independent. Shingon, in other words,
was the goal of all Buddhist schools and the highest expression of Buddhist teaching. Anyone who practiced any form of Exoteric Buddhism
should necessarily, as his religious mind developed, come to Shingon
itself.

It is not certain exactly when Kūkai began explicitly to state such
views. In a short work written in 822,[10] several years after the *Difference*, Kūkai evaluates according to his criteria the Buddhist sects then
active in Japan. He categorizes the eight sects from the lowest to the
highest in the following order: Ritsu, Kusha, Jōjitsu, Hossō, Sanron,
Tendai, Kegon, and Shingon; and he makes a striking effort to include
other doctrines in the Shingon system. Thus, he states that the doctrines
of the Exoteric sects render explicit the samadhi of certain Bodhisattvas

---

Dharma-mandala, a mandala expressed by means of letters, and regards it as a
seed mantra with the idea that by reciting the title and meditating upon it one
can attain enlightenment. For example, see *K.Z.*, I, 762 ff.

[9] *K.Z.*, I, 562.

[10] *K.Z.*, II, 154–72. This work was written by Kūkai as an introduction to
Shingon Buddhism for the ex-emperor Heizei, when Kūkai performed the
abhiṣeka ceremony for Heizei. The pattern of the ten stages of development of
mind is also evident in Kūkai's poem in *The Meanings of the Word Hūṃ* written most probably in his late forties. *K.Z.*, I, 543–45.

who also play a role in the Shingon pantheon. For Kūkai, these are all manifestations of Mahāvairocana, manifestations especially prepared to meet the spiritual needs of sentient beings in differing stages of religious development. For instance, Hossō teaches the samadhi of Maitreya; Sanron, that of Mañjuśrī; Tendai, that of Avalokiteśvara; and Kegon, that of Samantabhadra. Each doctrine, therefore, is a part of Shingon Buddhism, "like a ministry of the Dharma-King (Shingon) or one of his one hundred offices." [11]

It is noteworthy that Kūkai's classification of the Japanese sects corresponds to the order he gave them in *The Ten Stages of the Development of Mind* and in *The Precious Key to the Secret Treasury.* No doubt the ten stages of the development of mind had long occupied Kūkai's thoughts. By 822 he was well prepared to attempt a grand synthesis of "the sea of Dharma," as well as of existing non-Buddhist religion and philosophy, in the light of Shingon Buddhism. He needed only a suitable occasion to give coherent expression to such a synthesis.

It was in 830, five years before his death, that Kūkai produced his most ambitious work, the *Ten Stages,* perhaps the most comprehensive religious work that has come down to us in Japan. In that year, the Emperor Jun'na (r. 823–33) had ordered each of the six sects of Buddhism—Ritsu, Hossō, Sanron, Tendai, Kegon, and Shingon—to present a treatise on the essentials of its teaching. Thus it was that Kūkai wrote the *Ten Stages,* which was followed by a simplified version, the *Precious Key.*[12] Both mention that they were written by imperial order. The *Ten Stages,* it appears, was so complex and difficult that the emperor had Kūkai condense it and make its gist more accessible. Whether or not this is true, the *Precious Key* was to be the last of Kūkai's works on the problem of Exoteric and Esoteric Buddhism.

At the core of both the *Ten Stages* and the *Precious Key* is the

[11] *K.Z.,* II, 161.

[12] One of the characteristics of the *Ten Stages* is the use of extensive quotations from sutras, commentaries, and treatises. It impresses me as being the first draft of a dissertation on thought and religion in which source materials are abundantly collected under the ten categories, with brief remarks. Kūkai quotes most extensively, in his presentation of the first to the sixth stages, from a book called *Fan-chang-chieh-ti-chang* (*Bonshōkaijishō*) by Liang-pi (d. 777) which he brought back from China. See Katsumata Shunkyo, ed., *Kōbō daishi chosaku zenshū* I (Tokyo, 1968), p. 221, n. 2; p. 589.

following passage from the *Mahāvairocana Sutra,* quoted in the introductory section of the *Ten Stages:* "To attain enlightenment is to know one's own mind as it really is." Kūkai continues:

Now, on the basis of this sutra, I am going to reveal the stages of development of the mind of one who practices Shingon and the distinctions between the Exoteric and Esoteric teachings contained therein. There are innumerable stages in the development of mind, but, for the moment, I shall present ten categories into which they will be combined.[13]

These ten categories are the ten levels of mind from the lowest to the highest. The development of the religious mind is a process of spiritual awakening or of discovery of one's mind, a full actualization of the intrinsically enlightened mind contained in the lowest stage. As Kūkai writes in the *Ten Stages* in the opening lines of the discussion of the tenth stage: "These are the stages of development of mind through which the dark goatish mind [which thinks of satisfying the instincts only] advances higher, leaving darkness behind and seeking after light." [14] The ten stages of development of mind outlined in the introduction to the *Precious Key* [15] will be quoted below and commented upon briefly in order to facilitate understanding them as a whole.

"*The First Stage: The Mind of Lowly Man, Goatish in Its Desires.* The ignorant, ordinary man, in his madness, does not realize his faults. He thinks only of lust and hunger like a goat." Kūkai describes the mind of one who lives in the realms of hell, hungry ghosts, and beasts—realms that are within the man himself—who fails to distinguish between good and evil and who refuses to believe in the law of karma. In the *Ten Stages,* Kūkai discusses at length those who dwell in these hells. He shows that man may at any moment and in any place sink into a nonhuman existence. That is, without being aware of doing wrong, he breaks the Ten Precepts and thus kills, steals, commits adultery, lies, exaggerates, utters slander, equivocates, and entertains greed, hatred, and biased views. Nevertheless, Kūkai allows even this lowest state of mind the potentiality for full awakening—Buddha nature. On the other hand, Kūkai senses the same crisis to be inherent in the more advanced levels of mind. The process of development of mind, starting at this lowest stage, is a gradual rise from a lower level to a higher, brighter one.

[13] *K.Z.,* I, 129–30.   [14] *K.Z.,* I, 397.   [15] *K.Z.,* I, 420.

"The Second Stage: The Mind That Is Ignorant and Childlike, Yet Abstemious. Influenced by external causes, a man suddenly thinks of moderation in eating. The will to perform charity sprouts, like a seed of grain which has encountered the proper conditions." In the second stage Kūkai describes the world of ethics, in which the observance of individual and social ethics is the requirement for man to be called a human being. For Kūkai, the observance of the Buddhist precepts— non-killing, non-stealing, non-adultery, and so forth—and of the Con- fucian ethical code—the practice of benevolence, righteousness, and the like—is necessary for man. Kūkai equates this level of mind with that of a Confucianist:

The withered trees of winter are not always to be leafless; once spring ar- rives, they bloom and flourish. Thick ice does not remain frozen forever; when summer comes, it melts and flows. Given ample moisture, seeds of grain sprout, and when the time comes, plants bear fruit. . . . As there is no immutable nature in things, how can a man remain bad always? When favorable conditions are provided, even a fool aspires to the great Way, and while he follows the teachings faithfully, he aspires to be equal to a sage. A goatish man has no immutable nature; an ignorant child likewise does not remain ignorant. When his intrinsically enlightened nature begins to permeate him within and when the light of the Buddha shines upon him from without, there suddenly emerges in him an instantaneous thought that he should moderate his intake of food and practice acts of charity.[16]

"The Third Stage: The Mind That Is Infantlike and Fearless. A non-Buddhist hopes for rebirth in heaven, in order to gain peace there for a while. He is like an infant or a calf that follows its mother." Kūkai grades aspiration to rebirth in heaven or to immortality one step higher than mere observance of ethical precepts, but he calls such an aspiration "infantlike" and severely criticizes it as being egoistic. Kūkai does recognize that this approach is valuable as a device to accommo- date sentient beings with a certain limited capacity. From a higher viewpoint, however, he rejects it as being similar to "phantoms, dreams, or threads of gossamer." Kūkai assigns to this level of mind Taoism, the sixteen Hindu schools such as Saṃkhya and Vaiśeṣika, the various types of Yogic practices, and the Buddhist groups that emphasize re- birth in heaven. From this stage on to the ninth, Kūkai in the *Ten Stages* adds an Esoteric interpretation to the end of the discussion of each

16 *K.Z.,* I, 423.

stage, identifying each stage as corresponding to the levels of development of the religious mind in Shingon.

"*The Fourth Stage: The Mind That Recognizes the Existence of Psychophysical Constituents* [17] *Only, Not That of a Permanent Ego.* This mind recognizes the existence of components only and denies a permanent ego. The Tripiṭaka of the Goat-cart of Hinayana [18] is entirely included herein." In the third stage Kūkai's central criticism is directed at the religious egoism behind the practices of asceticism, yoga, merit accumulation, and devotion, and at escapism involved in a pessimistic view of the world. These fundamental ills, Kūkai holds, originate in a false belief in the existence of a permanent individual soul or ego which isolates one man from another. Kūkai identifies the fourth stage, the mind freed from this way of thinking, with the śrāvakayāna of Hinayana Buddhism, the followers of the teachings of the historical Buddha.[19] He summarizes the basic Buddhist doctrines, such as the Four Noble Truths, and the meditation practices of this school and its subschools. In his description of this stage in the *Precious Key*, Kūkai inserts a lengthy discussion on the relationship of Buddhism to the state, which is of interest in understanding Kūkai in a historical context (see translation).

"*The Fifth Stage: The Mind Freed from the Seed of the Cause of Karma.* Having mastered the Twelve Links of Causation,[20] the mind extirpates the seed of ignorance. Rebirth necessitated by karma comes to an end; even though one does not preach, the fruit is obtained." Kūkai identifies this level of mind with the pratyekabuddhas of Hinayana Buddhism. There may actually never have been any, but they are referred to in many Mahayana sutras as ranking slightly higher than the śrāvakas but lower than the lowest of the bodhisattvas. This mind stands free from the seed of the cause of karma, that is, basic blindness, but has fallen into self-complacency. Kūkai criticizes the pratyekabuddhas'

[17] There are five: form, sensation, perception, volition, and consciousness.
[18] Three vehicles are identified in the *Lotus Sutra*. Among them the goat-cart stands for the śrāvakayāna of Hinayana Buddhism.
[19] Literally, "the vehicle of listeners," which designates the Buddhism practiced by the direct disciples of the Buddha.
[20] Ignorance, volition, consciousness, name and form, sense organs, contact, sensation, craving, grasping, formation of being, birth, old age and death; these together make up the Wheel of Life, or Cycle of Causation and Becoming.

apathetic attitude toward fellow beings, their narrowness of vision, and their otherworldliness. In the concluding verses of this stage in the *Precious Key*, Kūkai suggests the want of altruism in this and in the preceding stage: [21]

> To fall into the two stages of Hinayana
> Is called the death of a bodhisattva;
> He loses all of his gains.
> The fear he must experience in falling into hell
> Is no greater than this;
> To fall into these Two Vehicles is
> The greatest fear, indeed.
> Even if he falls into hell,
> He may in the end become a Buddha;
> But if he falls into the Two Vehicles,
> The path to Buddhahood is completely obstructed.

Kūkai warns that those who are deeply committed to a religious cause should be alert to the dangers on the way to the development of the religious mind, such as inertia of the spirit, self-complacency, and lack of sympathy for suffering fellow beings.

"*The Sixth Stage: The Mahayana Mind with Sympathetic Concern for Others.* Compassion arises unconditionally; this is the first instance of great compassion. Recognizing phenomena as illusory shadows of mind, [a student of Yogācāra who believes that] what exists is mind only negates the validity of the world of objects." The doctrine of subjective idealism characteristic of Hossō, or Yogācāra, discusses the mind in terms of five sense perceptions, mind (mental faculty), ego-consciousness, and *ālaya*-consciousness (the subconsciousness).[22] Kūkai summarizes this mind in the following manner: [23]

> The sea of Mind is forever tranquil
> Without even a single ripple;
> Stirred by the storm of discriminations,
> Billows rage to and fro.
>
> Men in the street are deluded;
> They are fascinated by phantomlike men and women.

[21] *K.Z.*, I, 449.

[22] *Ālaya* means an abode, receptacle, etc. The Himalaya is in Sanskrit *Hima-ālaya*, i.e., the abode of snow or depository of snow. *Ālaya-vijñāna* is often translated as "Storehouse-consciousness."

[23] *K.Z.*, I, 451.

Heretics are crazed;
They adhere to the grand tower of mirage.

They do not know
That heaven and hell are fabricated by their own minds.
Do they come to realize
That "mind-only" will free them from their tragedies?

Be that as it may,
By practicing the Six Paramitas for three aeons,
By practicing the fifty-two stages of enlightenment,
They will uncover One Mind.

When they become purehearted,
Cutting off their emotional and mental obstacles,
They will find their own Treasury—
Enlightenment, or Nirvana.

Kūkai situates this level of mind at the primary stage to the development of the Mahayana mind and links it to the doctrines of Hossō, which explain the samadhi of Maitreya.

"The Seventh Stage: The Mind That Realizes that the Mind Is Unborn. By means of the Eightfold Negation, useless arguments are ended. When an insight into the truth of emptiness is gained in a moment of thought, the mind becomes serene and undefinably blissful." Kūkai identifies his seventh stage with the Mādhyamika (Sanron) philosophy of Nāgārjuna. "Unborn" is not diametrically opposed to "born" but belongs to a higher order transcending the dichotomy of being and nonbeing, birth and death. In order to suggest emptiness, or voidness (*śūnyatā*), Nāgārjuna had denied all possible qualities by means of the Eightfold Negation: unborn, imperishable, unceasing, nonconstant, nonidentical, not different, not going away, and not coming. Hence, at this seventh level, the mind discovers unity in diversity, voidness manifesting itself through phenomena. Kūkai opens his discussion as if he were trying to verbalize an almost aesthetic experience of the samadhi of voidness:

The great space, being vast and tranquil, embraces all phenomena within itself; the great ocean, being deep and serene, contains in a single drop of water a thousand beings. As the cardinal number one is the mother of one hundred and one thousand, so is voidness the root of all relative beings. . . .[24]

[24] *K.Z.,* I, 452.

To the question whether this mind—peaceful and free, transcending senseless speculations—could be called the height of enlightenment, Kūkai replies in the negative. On the other hand, he regards this level of mind as that to be attained by practicing the samadhi taught by Mañjuśrī and concludes that Mañjuśrī represents an aspect of the wisdom of Mahāvairocana.

"*The Eighth Stage: The Mind That Is Truly in Harmony with the One Way.* He who knows that the nature of mind is one and originally pure and that both subject and object interpenetrate is called Vairocana." Under this heading Kūkai summarizes the goal, doctrines, and methods of meditation of the Chinese T'ien-t'ai school of Buddhism established on the basis of the *Lotus Sutra* and the works of Nāgārjuna. One of the reasons why Kūkai breaks the order of historical development of Buddhism here and places the school of Mādhyamika (the seventh) a step higher than Yogācāra (the sixth), reversing the sequence of their origins in India, is the inseparable relationship that exists between Mādhyamika and the formation of the T'ien-t'ai doctrines. In the section of Esoteric Buddhist interpretation at the end of the discussion of the eighth stage in the *Ten Stages*, Kūkai identifies this mind as corresponding to the samadhi experience of the Avalokiteśvara, an aspect of Mahāvairocana. He sums up in verse the attainment of this mind and also shows the direction for further development: [25]

> The bodhisattvas in the former stages engage in groundless speculations.
> The experience of enlightenment of this mind is not yet genuine.
> The One Way, unconditioned and signless, is spotless;
> It unfolds the teaching of nonduality of neither being nor nonbeing.
> When both the seeing and the seen are negated, the eternal ground of quiescence will be found;
> When all thought determinations are exhausted, one will meet with Mahāvairocana.
> He, like vast space, knows no duality of body and mind.
> Adapting himself freely to all beings, He manifests himself forever and ever.

"*The Ninth Stage: The Profoundest Exoteric Buddhist Mind That Is Aware of Its Nonimmutable Nature.* Water has no immutable nature of its own. When it meets with the wind, waves appear. The World of

[25] *K.Z.,* I, 459.

Dharma (*dharma-dhātu*) is not yet ultimate. One must proceed further by receiving revelation." Kūkai pronounces the doctrines of Hua-yen Buddhism to be the culmination of Exoteric Buddhism, explaining the import of the *Avataṃsaka Sutra* as well as that of works by such Chinese Hua-yen masters as Tu-shun (557–640) and Fa-tsang (643–712). Kūkai explains the doctrine of interpenetration of the *Avataṃsaka Sutra*, which he deeply admired, as follows:

As the sun first shines upon the high peaks while the world is still lying in darkness, so He [the Buddha] illumined those whose aptitude was high with the doctrine of the nonduality of the mind and the Buddha. He taught that infinite time is in one moment and that one moment is in infinite time; that one is in many and that many is in one, that is, that the universal is in the particulars and that the particulars are in the universal. He illustrated this infinitely interdependent relationship of time and space with the simile of Indra's net and with that of the interfusion of the rays of lighted lamps.[26]

This level of mind, Kūkai holds, is attainable through the experience of the samadhi of the Samantabhadra. Despite his admiration for Hua-yen, Kūkai criticizes it for lacking the elements of direct and personal religious experience as quoted above: "One must proceed further by receiving revelation."

"*The Tenth Stage: The Glorious Mind, the Most Secret and Sacred.* When the medicines of Exoteric Buddhism have cleared away the dust, Shingon opens the Treasury. Then the secret treasures are at once manifested and one realizes all values." In the *Ten Stages* Kūkai begins his presentation of this mind with the following definition: "The glorious mind, the most secret and sacred is, ultimately, to realize one's own mind in its fountainhead and to have insight into the nature of one's own existence." [27] He conceives man as "body-mind," not as mind or body, nor body and mind, and holds that this "body-mind" is grounded in the "Body-Mind," the secret and sacred living Body-Mind of all, the Dharmakaya Mahāvairocana. His premise is that our mind in its essence is united with the Mind of Mahāvairocana and that our body, so long as it is in the universe, is part of the Body of Mahāvairocana; all men as well as all other sentient beings are particular "body-mind" beings participating in the "Body-Mind." It is this "Body-Mind" that is represented in the Shingon mandalas, which describe various aspects of Mahāvairocana. Kūkai explains the world of the mandala in the *Ten*

26 *K.Z.*, I, 461.   27 *K.Z.*, I, 397.

Stages but not in the *Precious Key;* instead, in the latter he quotes extensively from *Aspiration to Enlightenment,* attributed to Nāgārjuna, which deals with Shingon methods of meditation.

Kūkai, aware of his approaching death—symptoms of his fatal illness soon appeared—was direct in expressing what he believed to be essential for the development of the religious mind. In the introduction to the *Precious Key,* he emphasizes the importance of putting the teachings into practice:

Alas! Men, unaware of the treasures they possess, regard their deluded state of madness to be the state of enlightenment. How foolish they are! The Father's compassion is penetrating; if it were not for these teachings, how could they be saved? If they refuse to take the medicines that have been offered, how can they be cured? If they merely talk about them or recite them emptily, the King of Medicine [the Buddha] will certainly reprimand them for it.[28]

The opening poem of the *Precious Key* best expresses Kūkai's criticism of the currents of his time and his despair at men's deep-rooted proclivity to remain spiritually unawakened, endlessly repeating the cycle of samsara.[29]

From the dim, remote, and immemorial past,
Texts are transmitted in a thousand and ten thousand tomes,
Elucidating Buddhist and non-Buddhist teachings.
Abstruse, obscure, and indistinct
Are a hundred opinions and theories,
Each claiming to be the final way.

Copying and reciting until one's death,
How can one penetrate into the ultimate Source? [30]

I do not know, however I ponder.
The Buddha, I believe, had no mind for this.
He took pity on diseased minds
And taught them to take medicinal herbs as Shen Nung [31] did.
Out of compassion, he showed the direction to the lost,
As did the Duke of Chou by making the compass-cart.[32]

[28] *K.Z.,* I, 419.   [29] *K.Z.,* I, 417–18.

[30] The common interpretation of this line is: "Had the books been lost and had there been none to recite them, what should we do about the essentials?"

[31] Shen Nung, the early Chinese God of Agriculture.

[32] The Duke of Chou, a statesman instrumental in founding the Chou Dynasty of Ancient China, was said to have provided a "south-pointing chariot" for some foreign emissaries who could not find their way back home.

But deranged men do not perceive their madness;
The blind are unaware of their blindness.
Born, reborn, and still born again,
Whence they have come they do not know.
Dying, dying, and dying yet again,
Where they go in the end they do not know.

2

ESSENTIALS OF KŪKAI'S ESOTERIC BUDDHIST THOUGHT AND PRACTICE

Kūkai's Esoteric Buddhism has traditionally been divided into two categories: the theoretical aspect (*kyōsō*) and the practical aspect (*jisō*). These have been compared to the two wheels of a cart or the two wings of a bird. The theoretical aspect refers to Kūkai's written expositions of doctrine. These also are of two kinds. The first kind deals with the superiority of Esoteric over Exoteric Buddhism and includes the works discussed in the preceding chapter, namely, the *Difference*, the *Ten Stages*, the *Precious Key*, and *The Secret Key to the Heart Sutra*. The second kind aims to demonstrate the validity of Kūkai's Esoteric doctrine and to persuade the reader of the effectiveness of his approach. This group is represented by what is commonly known as Kūkai's trilogy (*sambu no sho*), consisting of *Attaining Enlightenment in This Very Existence*, *The Meanings of Sound, Word, and Reality*, and *The Meanings of the Word Hūṃ*.

The practical aspect, on the other hand, refers to Kūkai's expositions of his method of meditation. Kūkai is known to have written numerous works on Esoteric Buddhist meditation, but most of them seem to have

been marred by later interpolations and emendations, and many of
those collected in *The Complete Works of Kōbō daishi* are of doubtful
authenticity.[1] Though it is difficult to determine which are genuine,
this vital aspect of Kūkai's thought cannot be ignored. Therefore, his
meditation method will be outlined in the concluding part of this chapter. First, the general characteristics of his thought will be described,
followed by a discussion of the central problem of his religion, the
nature of the Dharmakaya Mahāvairocana Buddha. One can pursue
Kūkai's Esoteric Buddhism by raising the following three questions: 1)
what is the aim of his religious approach; 2) why did he think that
realization of that aim was possible; and 3) how did he believe that aim
could be achieved.

GENERAL CHARACTERISTICS OF KŪKAI'S
ESOTERIC BUDDHIST THOUGHT

In advancing his answers to the perennial and central problems of
Buddhism—who is the Buddha, what is enlightenment, and how can
one attain it—Kūkai demonstrated considerable originality. He interpreted the Buddha as the Dharmakaya Mahāvairocana; the attainment
of enlightenment as the realization of the "glorious mind, the most
secret and sacred"; he taught that man is intrinsically capable, through
the grace (*kaji: adhiṣṭhāna*) of Mahāvairocana and through his own
efforts, of participating here and now in the Real, Mahāvairocana himself. Kūkai adopted the motto, "attaining enlightenment in this very
existence." His work that goes by that title is the most important systematic exposition of his thought. In time, this motto became the best-
known characterization of Kūkai's Buddhism.

What makes the motto unique is the phrase "in this very existence,"
for "attaining enlightenment" is the common parlance of all Buddhists.
By joining the two, Kūkai meant that the practice of Shingon Buddhism
enables the devotee to attain enlightenment here and now without
having to wait for rebirth in this or in another world. This motto
reflects both Kūkai's affirmative attitude toward this phenomenal world
as the very realm in which the highest enlightenment is to be attained
and his basic belief in man's potential for enlightenment. Indeed, Kūkai

[1] *K.Z.*, III, 188–716. Thirty-eight works are collected therein.

held that, even in the lowest level of mind, the highest "glorious mind, the most secret and sacred" is fully present. For this reason he did not share the pessimistic belief in universal degeneration which greatly influenced many Japanese Buddhists.[2] Accordingly, his religious orientation differed from that of the great Buddhist leaders of the Kamakura period, such as Hōnen (1133–1212), Shinran (1173–1262), and Nichiren (1222–82), although Dōgen (1200–53) on this point agreed with Kūkai.[3]

Translated literally, Kūkai's motto reads "attaining enlightenment in this very body." Judging from the contents of the work by this title, the word "body (*shin*)" clearly does not mean the body as opposed to the mind but stands for "existence" or "body-mind-being." The choice of the word "body " over the normally expected "mind" underscores the basic character of Kūkai's religion: emphasis on direct religious experience through one's total being and not merely through the intellect. Kūkai required that any religious teaching withstand the test of actual meditation and of daily life.

Centering around the theme of attaining enlightenment in this very existence, Kūkai in due time unfolded the idea of the "preaching of the Dharmakaya (*hosshin seppō*)." In the *Difference*, Kūkai for the first time used this expression as a criterion by which to distinguish Esoteric from Exoteric Buddhism. He insisted that Esoteric Buddhism was superior to Exoteric Buddhism in that the former was preached by the Dharmakaya Buddha, whereas the latter was preached by the Nirmanakaya Buddha, Shakyamuni, a temporal incarnation of the timeless Dharmakaya Mahāvairocana.[4] He used the word "preaching" literally and, as the years passed, developed the meaning of the "preaching of the Dharmakaya" in two directions. On one hand, Kūkai discussed the nature and value of the mantra, the shortest verbal form of the Dharma-

[2] There are three periods in Buddhist eschatology. Views differ as to the duration of the first and the second periods after Shakyamuni Buddha's death. According to Kūkai, the first period lasts one thousand years after the founding of Buddhism. During this time, Buddhist doctrines, practices, and the attainment of enlightenment flourish. During the second period, the following one thousand years, both doctrines and practices exist but there is no enlightenment. In the third period, which lasts ten thousand years, only doctrines exist but neither practices nor enlightenment. *K.Z.*, I, 434. On Kūkai's rejection of the theory, see *K.Z.*, I, 809.

[3] Dōgen, *Shōbō genzō*, I (Iwanami edition), 72.

[4] *K.Z.*, I, 474. The opening part of the *Difference;* see translation, p. 151.

kaya's preaching. On the other hand he expanded the meaning of the "preaching of the Dharmakaya" to include all phenomena.

He reasoned as follows: The sutras of Esoteric Buddhism, such as the *Mahāvairocana Sutra* and the *Vajraśekhara Sutra,* are records of the preaching of the Dharmakaya Buddha and exist because of his compassion and wisdom. Therefore, it is the mantras, conveying as they do the essential meaning of these sutras, which are most thoroughly impregnated with the preacher's spirit, compassion, wisdom, and saving power. Kūkai praises the efficacy of mantra recitation as follows:

> A mantra is suprarational;
> It eliminates ignorance when meditated upon and recited.
> A single word contains a thousand truths;
> One can realize Suchness here and now.
> Walk on and on until perfect quiescence is reached;
> Go on and on until the primordial Source is penetrated.[5]

At the same time that he linked the nature and value of the mantra to the preaching of the Dharmakaya Buddha, Kūkai expanded the meaning of the word "preaching." He interpreted it as the acts of communication of the Dharmakaya Mahāvairocana. Oral preaching is only one means of communication; preaching may sometimes be pursued by non-oral means, such as silence, gesture, color, or form. Kūkai's speculation along this line culminated in his work, *The Meanings of Sound, Word, and Reality,* one of the trilogy written after *Attaining Enlightenment in This Very Existence.* In *The Meanings of Sound, Word, and Reality,* Kūkai asserts that the Dharmakaya Mahāvairocana is Reality and reveals himself through all objects of sense and thought. In other words, all things in the universe reveal the presence of Mahāvairocana. All phenomena point to the underlying Reality, Mahāvairocana, and at the same time are expressions of that Reality. Mahayana Buddhism states that "Samsara is Nirvana and Nirvana is Samsara," [6] and Kūkai's conception of the preaching of Mahāvairocana represents his own explanation of that famous and perplexing dictum.

The source of the ideas Kūkai expressed in his trilogy was, in the final analysis, his direct and personal experience of samadhi—awareness of union with Mahāvairocana. One can hardly explain why Kūkai was so optimistic about man's potential for enlightenment here and

[5] *K.Z.,* I, 561.   [6] *Mādhyamika-kārikās,* chap. 25, verse 20.

now if one ignores the fulfillment he himself derived from such experiences. Kūkai's life and poetry leave little room for doubt about his basic honesty and sincerity. All the religious writings of his mature period were the products of his effort to translate the experience of samadhi into words. Kūkai, writing in classical Chinese, used all available texts, both Buddhist and non-Buddhist, in this endeavor. Apparent in his works, besides Indo-Chinese Esoteric Buddhism itself, are the influences of Yogācāra, of Mādhyamika, of T'ien-t'ai, and in particular of Hua-yen Buddhism. Nevertheless, Kūkai knew he could not give full verbal expression to experience itself. Because of the very nature of samadhi in which it is said both the seer and the seen are unknown, it is beyond any discursive description. On his return from China Kūkai said: "Since the Esoteric Buddhist teachings are so profound as to defy expression in writing, they are revealed through the medium of painting." [7] Nevertheless, one can find a greater vividness in Kūkai's poems when they are compared to his prose. The following poem was sent to a friend as an invitation to the practice of Esoteric Buddhist meditation: [8]

All beings as individuals are appearances only, like illusions:
They are composites of forever changing constituents.
Our blind desires, which are neither within nor without,
With their ensuing actions, delude us more and more.

The world is at once the creating and the created;
It is the Lotus Realm,[9] the infinite continuum of Reality.
Neither empty nor non-empty, nor the oneness of the two,
It is void, temporal, and yet real, beyond name and form.

Flowers in spring, though transient, are bright to our eyes;
The autumnal moon reflected in serene water delights us.
Swift summer clouds appear and disappear in deep dales.
Heavy snow in wind—dancing maidens—seems light to the streams.

Inflamed is the world when we are greedy and deranged;
The sublime Universe emerges if we with insight are egoless.
Alas! Wretched are those who in delusion refuse to meditate.
Let us transcend and reintegrate ourselves in the Realm Eternal—A.[10]

---

[7] *K.Z.*, I, 95.   [8] *K.Z.*, III, 553.

[9] The Lotus stands for Mahāvairocana in terms of the Matrix Realm, the source of potentiality and creativity.

[10] The letter *A*, the first letter of the Sanskrit alphabet, is one of the seed mantras of Mahāvairocana, standing for *anutpāda* or *ādi-anutpāda*, which among other things means "uncreated," "unoriginated," i.e., the World of Mahāvairocana.

DHARMAKAYA MAHĀVAIROCANA TATHAGATA

Mahāvairocana (Dainichi) means "Great Sun." It is understandable that Kūkai, when he discovered the *Mahāvairocana Sutra*, should have felt a special affinity with the Great Sun Buddha. The Great Sun Goddess (Amaterasu) is the central figure in the Shinto pantheon, and the parallel between the two is too obvious to need stressing. Later, with the development of Ryōbu Shinto, Amaterasu came widely to be recognized as an avatar of Dainichi Nyorai (Tathagata), and Kūkai could hardly fail to reach a comparable conclusion.

Mahāvairocana had not always been clearly recognized as the central Buddha in the Esoteric tradition. It was Śubhākarasiṃha who introduced Esoteric Buddhism into China and who translated the *Mahāvairocana Sutra*. Until the time of Hui-kuo, however, Mahāvairocana was apparently not rigorously upheld as the Dharmakaya Buddha. Pu-k'ung, Hui-kuo's teacher, might have believed him to be a Sambhogakaya Buddha, one who had become a Buddha only after long training as a bodhisattva.[11] The assertion that Mahāvairocana is the Dharmakaya appears first in the commentary on the *Mahāvairocana Sutra*[12] expounded by Śubhākarasiṃha and written down by his disciple I-hsing, but the same commentary also identifies Mahāvairocana with the Sambhogakaya.[13] Thus it was probably Hui-kuo who stressed the identity of Mahāvairocana with the timeless Dharmakaya Buddha and who also taught that the *Mahāvairocana Sutra* and *Vajraśekhara Sutra* were preached by the Dharmakaya Mahāvairocana himself rather than by the historical Buddha, as Buddhists had always held.[14] These two ideas,

[11] *Chin-kang-ting-yü-ch'ieh-lüeh-san-shih-ch'i-tsun hsin-yao*, T18, p. 292a; *Li-ch'ü-shih*, T19, p. 610b (though this text is listed as having been translated by Pu-k'ung, it seems to have been written by him).

[12] *Ta-jih-ching su*, T39, p. 580a.

[13] T39, p. 580c. There is a passage which in effect explains that Mahāvairocana was thought to be a Sambhogakaya Buddha: "When Vairocana was practicing in the beginning the Path of Bodhisattva. . . ."

[14] Kūkai in a document written on the first day of the fourth month of Kōnin 6 (815) repeats Hui-kuo's statement that the *Mahāvairocana Sutra* and the *Vajraśekhara Sutra* were preached by the "Pure and Exquisite Dharmakaya Mahāvairocana (*jōmyō hosshin Daibirushana Butsu*)." It is evident from this document that Hui-kuo taught that Mahāvairocana was the Dharmakaya and that these Esoteric Buddhist sutras were preached by the Dharmakaya Buddha. K.Z., III, 528.

breaking as they do with tradition, may represent the start of the Sinicization of Esoteric Buddhism, an understanding of Esoteric Buddhism based not on the original Sanskrit texts but on Chinese translations and on individual religious experience. Hui-kuo, in fact, was the first native Chinese in the line of transmission, all preceding patriarchs having been non-Chinese. Hui-kuo left no written exposition of his views, so that it was actually Kūkai who undertook the first systematic treatment of his master's ideas and of Chinese Esoteric Buddhism in general. However, Kūkai says nothing about the identity of Mahāvairocana and the Dharmakaya in his earlier writings. Even *A Memorial Presenting a List of Newly Imported Sutras and Other Items*, in which Kūkai summarizes the essentials of what he had learned abroad, makes no mention of it. It was not until nearly ten years later, in the *Difference*, that Kūkai defined Mahāvairocana as the Dharmakaya.

The identification of Mahāvairocana with the Dharmakaya was a great leap in Buddhist speculation, for the Dharmakaya hitherto had generally been regarded as formless, imageless, voiceless, and totally beyond conceptualization. How this shift affects the relationship of Mahāvairocana to the other Buddhas and how it bears on Kūkai's assertion of "attaining enlightenment in this very existence" will be analyzed. By defining Mahāvairocana as the Dharmakaya, Kūkai identified Mahāvairocana with the eternal Dharma, the uncreated, imperishable, beginningless, and endless Truth. It is the realization of this truth which made Gautama the Enlightened One and which makes all bodhisattvas into Buddhas. The sun is the source of light and warmth, the source of life. Similarly, Mahāvairocana is the Great Luminous One at the center of a multitude of Buddhas, bodhisattvas, and powers; He is the source of enlightenment and the unity underlying all variety. To attain enlightenment means to realize Mahāvairocana, the implication being that Mahāvairocana is originally within man. Hence Kūkai called Mahāvairocana the "enlightened mind (*bodhicitta*)," a synonym for Suchness, or the element of "original enlightenment" within man. On this immanence of the Dharmakaya Kūkai says: "Where is the Dharmakaya? It is not far away; it is in our body. The source of wisdom? In our mind; indeed, it is close to us!" [15] Thus it is that Kūkai speaks of "attaining enlightenment in this very existence."

[15] *K.Z.*, III, 483–84.

In discussing Mahāvairocana Kūkai frequently speaks of the Dharmakaya in Four Forms (*shishu hosshin*). The term itself comes from the *Vajraśekhara Sutra*.[16] The Four Forms are:

1. The Dharmakaya in the absolute state (*jishō hosshin*). This is the absolute aspect of Mahāvairocana, the true Body of gnosis of all the Buddhas, revealing itself to its own emanations—all sentient and non-sentient beings, the universe—and engaging eternally in a monologue which reveals the Dharma in the state of samadhi.

2. The Dharmakaya in Bliss or Participation (*juyō hosshin*). This has two aspects. One is the Dharmakaya in Bliss, the aspect of Bliss in the state of absolute samadhi just described; it is called the Self-oriented Body (*jijuyōshin*). The other is the Dharmakaya in Participation, which appears in the form of Buddhas to guide those who are in the advanced stages of Bodhisattvahood; it is called the Other-oriented Body (*tajuyōshin*).

3. The Dharmakaya in Transformation (*henge hosshin*). The Buddha appears in history to teach bodhisattvas who have not reached the final stages: śrāvakas, pratyekabuddhas, and ordinary people. The Dharmakaya in Transformation is equivalent to the historical Buddha.

4. The Dharmakaya in Emanation (*tōru hosshin*). The bodies emanating or issuing forth from Mahāvairocana in a variety of forms such as nonhuman beings, or dwellers in hells. They are expressions of the impartial compassion and wisdom in skillful means of Mahāvairocana to help develop the original enlightenment of all beings.

Mahāvairocana discussed above in terms of the eternal Dharma is identified in Kūkai's system as the Body of Wisdom (*chishin*), consisting of Fivefold Wisdom symbolized by the Five Buddhas in the Diamond Realm:

1. Wisdom That Perceives the Essential Nature of the World of Dharma (*hokkai taishō chi*): the eternal Source of gnosis, the Radiant, whose rays are to be differentiated in terms of the following four kinds of wisdom. This wisdom, represented by Mahāvairocana, is located in the center of the Diamond Mandala.

2. Mirrorlike Wisdom (*daienkyō chi*): the wisdom that reflects reality as it is without distortion. This wisdom is represented by Akṣobhya (Ashuku), the Unshakable, located in the east.

16 T18, pp. 253c, 287b.

3. Wisdom of Equality (*byōdōshō chi*): the wisdom that perceives the fundamental identity of all phenomena as issuing forth from the One Reality and that recognizes the absolute equality of all beings as to their intrinsic value. It is represented by Ratnasambhava (*Hōshō*), the Jewel Born, located in the south.

4. Wisdom of Observation (*myōkanzatchi*): the wisdom that observes the objects of mind free from discriminations and subjective calculations. It is represented by Amitābha (Amida), the Infinite Light, located in the west.

5. Wisdom of Action (*jōsosa chi*): the wisdom that is manifested as actions to help bring all sentient beings to spiritual maturity and, finally, to enlightenment. It is represented by Amoghasiddhi (Fukū-jōju), the Infallible Realization, located in the north.

Just as the theory of the Dharmakaya in Four Forms is a reworking of the theory of the Three Bodies of Buddha (*trikāya*) of Mahayana,[17] so the Fivefold Wisdom of Mahāvairocana is based on the Fourfold Wisdom taught by the Yogācāra school of Mahayana. The *Vajraśe-khara Sutra*, which contains the elements of the theory of Fivefold Wisdom, was closely related to the Yogācāra teachings. For the students of Yogācāra, who advocated the subjective idealism of consciousness-only, consciousness could be broken down into the following categories:

1. The five sensory consciousnesses (perceptions)—eye-consciousness, ear-consciousness, nose-consciousness, tongue-consciousness, and body-consciousness.

2. Consciousness—the total function of mind, characterized by subjectivity and discrimination, which conditions the five sensory consciousnesses.

3. Ego-consciousness—attachment to an ego which gives the data of mind egocentric coloring and which is derived from the wrong belief that an individual self, ego, or soul is absolutely real.

[17] Nirmanakaya (Body of Manifestation): the historical Buddha, a temporal manifestation of the eternal Dharma in this world. Sambhogakaya (Body of Reward or Bliss): those Buddhas appearing in the Mahayana texts, such as the Buddha Amitābha, who attained enlightenment and became Buddhas in time as a result of having fulfilled their vows and reside in their respective Buddha lands. Dharmakaya (Body of Dharma): Suchness (*tathatā*), the Nature of Dharma (*dharmatā*), etc. Because of the Dharmakaya's impersonal nature and transcendence of conceptualization, it is not identified with any Buddha.

4. The *ālaya*-consciousness—the subconsciousness in which all the impressions of the data of mind are stored.

According to the teachings of the Yogācāra school, when the unenlightened conscious being attains enlightenment, these four categories of consciousness are transformed into the Fourfold Wisdom of Buddha. Thus, the *ālaya*-consciousness becomes the mirrorlike wisdom; the ego-consciousness, the wisdom of equality; the consciousness, the wisdom of observation; and the five sensory consciousnesses, the wisdom of action. In short, the theory of the Fivefold Wisdom of Mahāvairocana demonstrates that there is an essential unity between the unenlightened individual and Mahāvairocana with regard to the nature of wisdom. It teaches that the microcosmic world of the unenlightened consciousness can be integrated into the macrocosmic enlightenment of Mahāvairocana.

The foregoing is only part of Kūkai's interpretation of Mahāvairocana. To complete the picture, two more aspects must be examined. One is Mahāvairocana as the Body of Principle (*rishin*) interpreted by Kūkai on the basis of the doctrines given in the *Mahāvairocana Sutra*. The other and the most important one is Kūkai's own theory of Mahāvairocana called the Body of Six Great Elements (*rokudaishin*).

The Mahāvairocana of the *Vajraśekhara Sutra*, the Body of Wisdom, is symbolized by the *vajra* (diamond, thunderbolt, or adamantine weapon, single-pointed, three-pointed, or sometimes five-pointed). The *vajra* stands for the power of illumination, for penetrating insight that breaks through the darkness of ignorance, for infallibility, dynamic function, and actualization. In the *Mahāvairocana Sutra*, on the other hand, Mahāvairocana appears as the Body of Principle and is represented by a lotus which stands for Principle yet unrealized, compassion, potentiality, growth, and creativity. Hence, the Body of Wisdom is represented by the Diamond Mandala; the Body of Principle, by the Matrix Mandala. Kūkai interpreted these two aspects of Mahāvairocana as being inseparably related and asserted that both Bodies are nondual (*richi funi*). He said: "That which realizes is Wisdom (*chi*) and that which is to be realized is Principle (*ri*). The names differ but they are one in their essential nature." [18] Kūkai in his mature writings frequently speaks of the "One of Principle and Wisdom (*richi*)" or the "One of *vajra* and lotus (*konren*)."

[18] *K.Z.*, I, 816.

Such a way of thinking was unknown in India, because the two sutras, though composed as part of a generally rising trend toward Tantric Buddhism, came into existence independently in time and place. Furthermore, the term *principle*, in Chinese *li* and in Japanese *ri*, is Chinese in origin and has no exact counterpart in Sanskrit. "Body of Principle" is therefore a Chinese concept. Yet it is not certain whether the thought of nonduality of the two originated in China or whether it is Kūkai's own. There is no conclusive evidence that Hui-kuo taught anything similar.[19] Kūkai, who was greatly influenced by Hua-yen teachings, might have adopted the term *li* from Hua-yen vocabulary. *Li* is one of the key words in Hua-yen Buddhism and means the universal principle underlying the multiplicity of particulars (*shih*).

Some of Kūkai's comments on the *Mahāvairocana Sutra* will serve to show why Kūkai regarded Mahāvairocana as the Body of Principle. The theme expounded in the first chapter of the *Mahāvairocana Sutra* is the enlightened mind of all sentient beings, and the rest deals with methods for making the originally enlightened mind manifest. Kūkai defines Mahāvairocana in his *Introduction to the Mahāvairocana Sutra* (*Dainichikyō kaidai*) as follows: "Mahāvairocana is the One whose own nature is the Dharmakaya, that is, the Body of Principle, which is intrinsic and original enlightenment (*honnu hongaku*)." [20] Mahāvairocana as the Body of Principle, therefore, is the element of original enlightenment in all sentient beings. Unmanifest, self-contained like a lotus seed whose potential is yet to be realized, it is universal because all particulars share it equally.

[19] The idea of Mahāvairocana in terms of *ri* appears in a book known as the *Record of the Secret Treasury* (*Hizō ki: K.Z.*, II, 1–71), which has traditionally been believed to be notes of instruction taken by Kūkai from his master Hui-kuo. If we believe this tradition, it was Hui-kuo who advocated this concept. Some elements in this book may well have been the words of Hui-kuo, but one hesitates to accept unquestioningly the traditional account. The book is in the form of questions and answers. Some questions asked sound too elementary for Kūkai, who had written the draft of the *Indications* nearly ten years before this and had a thorough mastery of the fundamentals of Buddhism long before he went to China. For example: "QUESTION: What are the Psychophysical Constituents? ANSWER: They are form, sensation, perception, volition, and consciousness." See *K.Z.*, II, 45. It is difficult to believe that Kūkai asked Hui-kuo such an elementary question and noted it down as secret knowledge. However controversial it may be, I am inclined to think that this book is a record of dialogues between Kūkai and his disciples.

[20] *K.Z.*, I, 640.

The *Mahāvairocana Sutra* begins, after setting the scene for the Buddha's preaching, by asking how it is that the Buddha Wisdom can be developed, what is the basic character of that Wisdom, and what is the criterion of its perfection. Mahāvairocana replies: "The enlightened mind is the cause, great compassion is the root, and [the use of] skillful means is the ultimate." [21] In other words, enlightenment is attainable because of the originally enlightened mind; the basic character of Buddha Wisdom is its capacity for compassionate acts; and the perfection of the wisdom can be judged by whether or not it works freely to help others grow spiritually. The key statement immediately following the above-quoted passage is that "enlightenment is to know your own mind as it really is. . . . Seek in your own mind enlightenment and all-embracing wisdom. Why? Because it is originally pure and bright." [22] Kūkai took this passage as the core of the sutra, writing in his introduction to the sutra that "the purport of the sutra is that the mind of any sentient being is no other than all-embracing wisdom; he who knows it as it really is, is to be called one with all-embracing wisdom [perfectly enlightened one]." [23] The originally enlightened mind is "that which is to be realized (*ri*)," and the Body of Principle of Mahāvairocana is the unmanifested state of original enlightenment in all sentient beings, in contrast to the fully manifested state of the Body of Wisdom. This is the meaning of the nonduality of the Body of Wisdom and that of Principle. Thus it is that the Matrix Mandala (Body of Principle) is hung on the east wall of the meditation hall, representing the young stage of the Great Luminous One, Mahāvairocana; and that the Diamond Mandala (Body of Wisdom) is hung on the west wall, signifying the final realization of Mahāvairocana, attaining enlightenment.

It was in his middle forties that Kūkai wrote *Attaining Enlightenment in This Very Existence*, in which he explains his conception of Mahāvairocana as the Body of Six Great Elements. Kūkai was not developing theory for theory's sake; his aim was the very practical one of proving the possibility of enlightenment here and now. The Body of Six Great Elements consists of three constituents: the Six Great Elements, the Four Mandalas, and the Three Mysteries. These three correspond respectively to the essence (*tai*), the attributes (*sō*), and the functions (*yū*) of the Dharmakaya Mahāvairocana.[24]

[21] T18, p. 1b.   [22] T18, p. 1c.   [23] *K.Z.*, I, 654–55.   [24] *K.Z.*, I, 508.

The essence of *Attaining Enlightenment in This Very Existence* is expressed by the following two stanzas, the rest of the work except for the introduction being a commentary on each line: [25]

> The Six Great Elements are interfused and are in a state of eternal harmony;
> The Four Mandalas are inseparably related to one another:
> When the grace of the Three Mysteries is retained, [our inborn three mysteries will] quickly be manifested.
> Infinitely interrelated like the meshes of Indra's net are those which we call existences.
>
> There is the One who is naturally equipped with all-embracing wisdom.
> More numerous than particles of sand are those who have the King of Mind and the consciousnesses;
> Each of them is endowed with the Fivefold Wisdom, with infinite wisdom.
> All beings can truly attain enlightenment because of the force of mirrorlike wisdom.

Unfortunately, such a translation, literal as it is, cannot begin to suggest the full effect of these eight terse, seven-character lines. According to Kūkai, the first stanza stands for "in this very existence" and the second, for "attaining enlightenment." The first stanza is the most original and the most difficult to understand. The second stanza, on the other hand, presents no serious problem, since it is a summary of the theory of nonduality of the Bodies of Wisdom and of Principle in all sentient beings. As Kūkai explains, the first line of the second stanza stands for the eternally enlightened state of the Dharmakaya Mahā-vairocana, that is, the Body of Wisdom; the second, for the infinity of his attributes, beginning with those Buddhas who surround him and including all sentient beings; the third, for the state of possessing perfectly the capacity to manifest the innate Fivefold Wisdom of all sentient beings, that is, the Body of Principle; and the fourth, for the reason why all sentient beings can attain enlightenment, which is the omnipresence of the mirrorlike wisdom of Mahāvairocana.

In the first line of the first stanza, "The Six Great Elements are interfused and are in a state of eternal harmony," Kūkai states two propositions: that Mahāvairocana consists of the Six Great Elements interfused

[25] *K.Z.*, I, 507–8.

and that Mahāvairocana is in a state of eternal harmony. The Six Great
Elements are earth, water, fire, wind, space, and consciousness. The
adjective "great" signifies the universality of each element. The first
five stand for all material elements and the last, for the spiritual element; or for the Body and the Mind of Mahāvairocana, which is the
Fivefold Wisdom. These Six Great Elements create all Buddhas, all
sentient beings, and all material worlds. There is no creator other than
the Six Great Elements, which are at once the creating and the created;
the Six Great Elements are in a state of perpetual interfusion. Mahāvairocana, consisting of the Six Great Elements, is one without a second
and the totality of all existences and movements in the universe. Thus,
all diverse phenomena are identical as to their constituents; all are in a
state of constant transformation; no absolute difference exists between
man and nature; body and mind are nondual; and, therefore, the value
of mind is not necessarily higher than that of body. Kūkai writes:

In Exoteric Buddhist teachings, the four great elements [earth, water, fire,
and wind] are considered to be nonsentient beings, but in Esoteric Buddhist teaching they are regarded as the *samaya*-body of the Tathagata.
The four great elements are not independent of the mind. Differences exist
between matter and mind, but in their essential nature they remain the
same. Matter is no other than mind; mind, no other than matter. Without
any obstruction, they are interrelated.[26]

Explained in this way, the theory of the Six Great Elements of
Mahāvairocana must have been accessible to the intellectuals of Kūkai's
time, familiar as they were with Shinto and with nonindigenous schools
of thought. Through this theory Kūkai succeeded dramatically in
rendering concrete the abstract world of Mahayana Buddhism. The
Six Great Elements are clearly analogous to the well-known five natural
elements—fire, wood, earth, metal, and water; the Body of Wisdom and
that of Principle, symbolized by the *vajra* and the lotus, or by the

---

[26] In Kūkai's writings the Sanskrit word *samaya* is used in the senses of "symbol," "equality," "promise," or "vow." Here "*samaya*-body" means "symbolic
body." For Kūkai any physical symbol has a double structure in that it is an
object standing for X and at the same time it is part of X; e.g., a flower or a
vajra is a symbol of Mahāvairocana Buddha but at the same time an integral part
of Mahāvairocana in terms of the totality of existence. Thus, the four great
elements cannot be regarded as "nonsentient beings" which have nothing to do
with Mahāvairocana. *K.Z.*, I, 511–12.

Diamond and the Matrix Mandalas, resemble yin and yang; and Mahāvairocana, the Great Sun Buddha, recalls the Great Sun Goddess.

In the proposition that Mahāvairocana is in a state of eternal harmony, the word "harmony" is a translation of *yuga*, which in turn is a transliteration of yoga. The word *yuga* in Kūkai's writings is interchangeable with dhyana (*zen*), samadhi (*jō*), or dhyana-samadhi (*zenjō*). That the universe is in a state of eternal harmony is the fundamental premise of Kūkai's Esoteric Buddhist thought and practice. To what degree he appreciated this basic intuition far more than he did intellectual devices can be seen in the following:

What kind of intellectual determinations can be made of the eternal Order that is naturally so (*hōni no dōri*)? Such terms as the creating and the created are symbolic expressions of Esoteric Buddhism, and we should not indulge in senseless speculation while clinging to the ordinary and superficial meanings of these words. The Existence consisting of the Six Great Elements, the essence of the World of Dharma, is free without any obstacle and is in a state of eternal harmony.[27]

Since the macrocosmos is in a state of eternal harmony, it follows that any microcosmos homogeneous in its elements with the macrocosmos —men as well as all other beings—is not outside of the harmony of the macrocosmos. The problem on the part of the microcosmos is how to become aware of that eternal harmony and to attune itself to it. To practice samadhi is to imitate the macrocosmic samadhi. The principle of Kūkai's Esoteric Buddhist meditation comes ultimately from this basic intuition that the universe is in a state of eternal harmony.

In the second line of Kūkai's poem, "The Four Mandalas are inseparably related to one another," the Four Mandalas stand for the attributes of Mahāvairocana. They are the Mahā-mandala, Samaya-mandala, Dharma-mandala, and Karma-mandala. These represent Mahāvairocana seen from four different perspectives. The word "mandala" can, in the context, be understood as a circle, sphere, or range. The Mahā-mandala is the great (*mahā*) circle, the universe, Mahāvairocana seen in his physical extension. The Samaya-mandala is the same circle seen from the viewpoint of the omnipresence of Mahāvairocana's intention (*sa-*

[27] *K.Z.*, I, 512.

maya). The Dharma-mandala is the same circle viewed as being the sphere where the revelation of truth (*dharma*) takes place continually, that is, Mahāvairocana's range of communication. Finally, the Karma-mandala is the same circle seen from the viewpoint of his action (*karma*).

The Four Mandalas, therefore, stand for the Mahāvairocana's extension, intention, communication, and action. His extension is the totality of the five great elements; his intention is affinity—love or compassion; his communication is the revelation of himself known as the "preaching of the Dharmakaya"; and his action, all the movements in the universe. That they are "inseparably related to one another" means that in any one of these four the remaining three are present.

The third line, "When the grace of the Three Mysteries is retained, [our inborn three mysteries will] quickly be manifested," proves the principle of practice of Kūkai's Esoteric Buddhism. The Three Mysteries are the suprarational activities or functions of the Body, Speech, and Mind of Mahāvairocana. The mystery of the activities of Body is manifest universally through forms or patterns of phenomena; the mystery of the activities of Mind, through aesthetic and ecstatic experiences of samadhi. The following symbolic lines, part of a lengthy poem, shed further light on Kūkai's conception of the Three Mysteries of Mahāvairocana: [28]

> The Three Mysteries pervade the entire universe,
> Adorning gloriously the mandala of infinite space.
> Being painted by brushes of mountains, by ink of oceans,
> Heaven and earth are the bindings of a sutra revealing the Truth.
> Reflected in a dot are all things in the universe;
> Contained in the data of senses and mind is the sacred book.
> It is open or closed depending on how we look at it;
> Both His silence and His eloquence make incisive tongues numb. . . .
>
> The sun and the moon shine forth in space and on the water,
> Undisturbed by gales in the atmosphere.
> Both good and evil are relative in His preachings;
> The notion of I and thou will be erased and lost.
> When the sea of our mind becomes serene through samadhi and
>   insight,
> He reveals himself unconditionally as water overflows.

[28] *K.Z.*, III, 402.

To return to the first stanza on *Attaining Enlightenment*, the expression "the grace . . . is retained" is a translation of the word *kaji* (*adhiṣṭhāna*), based on Kūkai's comments that *kaji*

indicates great compassion on the part of the Tathagata and faith (*shinjin*) on the part of sentient beings. The compassion of the Buddha pouring forth on the heart of sentient beings, like the rays of the sun on water, is called *ka* [adding], and the heart of sentient beings which keeps hold of the compassion of the Buddha, as water retains the rays of the sun, is called *ji* [retaining].[29]

Kūkai interprets the Three Mysteries as expressions of the compassion of Mahāvairocana toward sentient beings. He holds that faith comes through the grace of the Buddha: it is not acquired by the individual but given. To the question of how a man is capable of this "retaining" —how he can have faith at all—Kūkai answers that the three mysteries inborn in men (*honnu sammitsu*) are united with the Three Mysteries of Mahāvairocana. In other words, it is the basic homogeneity of man with Mahāvairocana which makes faith possible. Because of Kūkai's emphasis on the grace of the Three Mysteries, his religion has also been identified as the religion of "the three mysteries and grace (*sammitsu kaji*)." The theory of the grace of the Three Mysteries is one of the basic principles of the practice of Esoteric Buddhist meditation.

Finally, the fourth line, "Infinitely interrelated like the meshes of Indra's net are those which we call existences," means that Existence is Mahāvairocana, that seemingly discrete existences are the existences of Mahāvairocana, and that therefore they are real. Indra's net is a simile used to show the relationship that exists between the whole and its parts and between the parts themselves. It is derived from a myth that the celestial palace of Indra is covered by a cosmic net bearing a gem at the intersection of each mesh. These gems reflect each other, producing an infinite continuum of radiance. Individual existence is like a gem, an integral part of the net which is Mahāvairocana. Each is like a gem in the net, infinitely related with all other parts; thus, any one can be the center of the whole. Such is the meaning of "Reflected in a dot are all things in the universe," as commented upon by Kūkai:

Existence is my existence, the existences of the Buddhas, and the existences of all sentient beings. . . . All of these existences are interrelated hori-

[29] *K.Z.*, I, 516.

zontally and vertically without end, like images in mirrors, or like the rays of lamps. This existence is in that one, and that one is in this. The Existence of the Buddha [Mahāvairocana] is the existences of the sentient beings and vice versa. They are not identical but are nevertheless identical; they are not different but are nevertheless different.[30]

As far as the constituents are concerned, no difference can be recognized between existences and existences, or between existences and the Existence; the difference lies in the sixth great element, consciousness, or the difference in the degree of realization of the intrinsically enlightened mind. How effectively and quickly to transform unenlightened consciousness into the Buddha Wisdom is the problem of praxis.

In his attempt to prove his claim that a man can attain enlightenment here and now, Kūkai brings forth the theory of the Six Great Elements of Mahāvairocana, making it a whole with the theory of the Bodies of Wisdom and of Principle. Within the four lines of the first stanza just examined, Kūkai condenses the essentials of his Esoteric Buddhist thought and shows simultaneously the fundamentals of Esoteric Buddhist meditation. The vision of the world he presents therein is cosmic and aesthetic; the view of man, extremely affirmative and optimistic. Mahāvairocana, an abstract postulation conceived by the religious genius of India, became less abstract when interpreted by the Chinese mind, and turned concrete when transmitted by Kūkai to Japan. When reinterpreted, Mahāvairocana became congenial to the indigenous mentality, having been defined as the Existence of all existences, a pantheistic-monotheistic Supreme Being with personality—wisdom and compassion—who could be found here and now in nature and in our mind. The following quotation may best explain Kūkai's stand: "The Buddha Dharma is nowhere remote. It is in our mind; it is close to us. Suchness is nowhere external. If not within our body, where can it be found?"[31]

KŪKAI'S ESOTERIC BUDDHIST PRACTICE

The practical side of Kūkai's Esoteric Buddhism has two aspects: observance of precepts (*kai*) and sitting in meditation (*jō*). Along with the mastery of both Exoteric and Esoteric Buddhist doctrines (*e:* wis-

[30] *K.Z.,* I, 516.   [31] *K.Z.,* I, 554.

dom), Kūkai stressed these two as integral parts of his religion. These were the three guiding principles of his newly formed order.

With respect to the observance of precepts, Kūkai was uncompromising in his view that "it should be no different from the days when the Buddha Shakyamuni was in this world." [32] Kūkai stressed observance of the precepts not only because it was necessary for meditation but also because, for him, it was a way of life in harmony with man's essential nature. He held that violation of the precepts was self-defeating in the attempt to bring out the originally enlightened mind, for it created discord.

Kūkai urged his disciples to observe strictly both Exoteric and Esoteric Buddhist precepts if they wished to stay with him. The Exoteric Buddhist precepts, being derived from the words of the historical Buddha, were those common to all Buddhist sects. The Esoteric Buddhist precepts, on the other hand, were peculiar to Kūkai's Esoteric Buddhist order. There were, of course, more moderate rules for lay followers. The discussion below will be confined to those given to initiated disciples leading a monastic life.

On the last day of the fifth month of Kōnin 4 (813) Kūkai outlined the aim and the spirit of the observance of precepts and the principle of the practice of meditation in his order:

The aim of joining the order and practicing the Way is to attain Buddhahood and not to seek the power of the Universal Monarch, Brahmā, or Indra. It goes without saying that we are not aiming at getting petty worldly success and reward. If we aspire to go far, unless we depend on our feet, we cannot advance; if we wish to walk the Way of Buddha, unless we observe the precepts, we cannot reach the goal. Never violate either Exoteric or Esoteric Buddhist precepts; firmly observe them and maintain yourselves clean and pure. . . . All of these precepts have their foundation in the Ten Precepts. The Ten Precepts consist of the three items pertaining to body [non-killing, non-stealing, non-adultery], the four items pertaining to speech [no lying, exaggerated speech, slander, or equivocation], and the three items pertaining to mind [not to entertain greed, hatred, or biased views]. These ten can be reduced to one mind. The essential nature of our mind is not distinct from that of the Buddha; no difference exists between our mind, the mind of all sentient beings, and that of the Buddha. To abide in this mind is to practice the Way of the Buddha. . . . Unless we observe all these precepts, our eye of wisdom will be dark and blind.

[32] *K.Z.*, II, 152.

Knowing this, carefully guard them as you protect your eyes. Forsake your lives rather than violate them. Should there be those who violate them, they are not disciples of the Buddha, of the Vajra [the Mahāvairocana of the Diamond Mandala], of the Lotus [the Mahāvairocana of the Matrix Mandala], of the bodhisattvas, or the śrāvakas, nor are they my disciples, and I shall not be their teacher. Observe these precepts sincerely and practice the samadhi of Mahāvairocana.[33] Having been freed quickly from the three fetters [greed, anger, and blindness], realize enlightenment. Improve yourselves, help others, and fulfill your four obligations.[34] If you do all of these, you are no other than bodhisattvas. Those who behave differently are those who offend the teachings of the Buddhas. They are called *icchantikas* [cursed ones] and will sink forever into the sea of suffering, nor will they ever escape. I shall not live or talk with them—go, go, do not stay! [35]

So stern a tone is rare in Kūkai's writings, but he stressed these points repeatedly in his prayers and essays from this time, just after the formation of his order, until his last days. That Kūkai was severe with himself in living up to the standard that he imposed upon his disciples but was nevertheless a warm person can be imagined from the account left by his immediate disciple Shinzei: "When I visited him for the first time, I felt as if he had been very close to me for a long time. I served him as an attendant for years. Yet I have never seen him act without integrity." [36]

The so-called Esoteric Buddhist precepts are the vows (*samaya*) that a disciple takes just before he receives the ritual of initiation known as *abhiṣeka*. Beginning with the words, "These are the life and root of the correct Dharma of Mahayana," Kūkai summarizes the Esoteric Buddhist precepts as follows: [37]

Not to abandon the correct Dharma or to develop any incorrect behavior. All the correct teachings of the Tathagata should, without exception, be mastered, maintained, and recited, as the ocean swallowing the waters of a hundred rivers never tires. If anyone, thinking that some are perfect and others are imperfect, forsakes even so much as one teaching and develops

---

[33] Literally, "the samadhi of the principal Noble One (*honzon*)." The principal Noble One in Kūkai's Buddhism is the Dharmakaya Mahāvairocana, but *honzon* can mean any of Mahāvairocana's manifestations, such as Shakyamuni, Amitābha, or Acala. *Honzon* may also mean any of the Buddhas, Bodhisattvas, etc., enshrined in a temple.

[34] Obligations to parents, to all sentient beings, to the ruler, and to the Three Treasures (Buddha, Dharma, and Sangha).

[35] *K.Z.*, II, 861–62.   [36] *K.Z.*, III, 387.   [37] *K.Z.*, II, 150–51.

a wicked frame of mind, he is to be called a destroyer. He is to be expelled.

Not to give up the aspiration to attain enlightenment. From this, all acts of a bodhisattva issue forth. It is like the general's banner; if it is lost, the whole army will be defeated. Therefore, never abandon the aspiration to attain enlightenment. If one loses it, he is to be expelled.

Not to be tight-fisted about any of the teachings. All these excellent teachings resulted from the Tathagata's efforts, which were painful to the point that he sacrificed his own life. They are his legacy left to all sentient beings, just as parents leave all property to their children. They are not meant for one person. Any miserly person that will not share them with others is guilty of stealing the Three Treasures. He is to be expelled.

Not to go without benefiting all sentient beings. To violate this is to go against the spirit of the Four Embracing Acts.[38] A bodhisattva should practice the Four Embracing Acts and universally embrace all sentient beings, providing them with the conditions which will interest them in the Way. How can anyone give up the thought of benefiting sentient beings, discourage them, and behave contrary to the spirit of the Four Embracing Acts? If he does so, he is to be expelled.

Among these four, Kūkai emphasized the second item. He often called the Esoteric Buddhist precepts "the vow of keeping the aspiration to attain enlightenment (*bodaishin kai*)." Aspiring to attain enlightenment meant to make a wholehearted effort to uncover one's originally enlightened mind (*bodhicitta*). This resulted from Kūkai's interpretation of the word *bodaishin* or *bodhicitta* in two senses: the aspiration to attain enlightenment, and the potentially enlightened mind. These two meanings in turn were derived from two ways of analyzing the word in question: first, as "the mind (*shin* or *citta*) of enlightenment (*bodai* or *bodhi*)," that is, "the enlightened mind"; and second, as "the mind for enlightenment," that is, "the aspiration to attain enlightenment." Both were thought to be nondual, as though one were the beginning and the other the end of the same circle. In his *Introduction to the Samaya-Precepts (Sammayakaijo)*,[39] Kūkai distinguishes the two meanings of the word *bodhicitta*. One is the subjective *bodhicitta* and the other, the objective *bodhicitta;* the former is the aspiration to attain enlightenment and the latter, the "infinitely and gloriously adorned Body of the Diamond Realm, the Four Forms of Mahāvairocana, and the Four Mandalas." The latter then is the

[38] Charity, kind speech, beneficial acts, and adapting oneself to others.
[39] *K.Z.,* II, 136–37.

perfectly enlightened Body of Wisdom of Mahāvairocana. Kūkai named the perfect integration of the subjective *bodhicitta* with the objective *bodhicitta* the Esoteric samadhi (*himitsu sammaji*), the goal of his religious practice.

The essential point of Kūkai's declaration of 813 quoted above lies in the line, "Observe these precepts sincerely and practice the samadhi of Mahāvairocana." This brief sentence states the conditions under which his disciples were allowed to stay in his order. To practice the samadhi of Mahāvairocana was, indeed, the beginning and the end of Kūkai's Esoteric Buddhist meditation (*himitsu zen*). In what follows the way in which his Esoteric Buddhist doctrine is related to his method of Esoteric Buddhist meditation will be discussed.

Kūkai's practice of Esoteric Buddhist meditation is no more than a systematic effort to experience what the doctrines suggest. Accordingly, to practice Esoteric Buddhist meditation is to try to participate in the yoga or samadhi of Mahāvairocana, with the faith that a student of meditation is essentially identical with Mahāvairocana. Kūkai recommended that the practice of the samadhi of Mahāvairocana be repeated as a way of life and demanded that his disciples sit in meditation three times a day. To deepen the experience of the samadhi day after day is the process by which an individual—a finite existence estranged from others—relates himself with compassionate thoughts to other existences and acts and participates in the infinity of Mahāvairocana.

> By removing the mist we see the Light;
> And we find the inexhaustible Treasury open to all to enjoy,
> Shining forth ever more fresh day by day.[40]

Kūkai believed that there was no end to the experience of samadhi.

The doctrine of the Four Mandalas offers a concrete way by which the student can relate himself to Mahāvairocana, who otherwise remains an undifferentiated whole: that is, by differentiating Mahāvairocana into Body (*mahā-mandala*), Speech (*dharma-*), Mind (*samaya-*), and Action (*karma-*), each of which is inherent in the other three. The doctrine of the grace of the Three Mysteries further specifies the state of samadhi of Mahāvairocana in terms of his Action (*karma-mandala*) in which He perpetually unfolds himself for self-enjoyment. The basic

---

[40] *K.Z.*, I, 419.

principle of the practice of Esoteric Buddhist meditation is to integrate the microcosmic activities of body, speech, and mind of the individual existence into the macrocosmic activities of Body, Speech, and Mind, the contents of the samadhi of Mahāvairocana. This is done by the student through symbolic ritual acts of body: the pose of sitting in meditation and hand gestures; of speech: recitation of mantras, the symbols of the essence of the speech of Mahāvairocana; and of mind: activities of thinking, feeling, imagining, visualizing, listening, and ceasing the activities of mind itself.

In a word, the essence of Kūkai's Esoteric Buddhist meditation is simply "imitating." This is technically called the practice of "entering self into Self so that the Self enters into the self (*nyūga ga'nyū*)." The self is the individual existence and the Self, Mahāvairocana. To practice the samadhi of Mahāvairocana is to imitate it through one's total being —physical, mental, moral, intellectual, and emotional—like an actor acting alone on stage. The stage is the sacred ground (*mandala; dōjō*). This can be anywhere as long as it is ritualistically consecrated, but it is usually the main hall of a temple where a principal Buddha or bodhisattva or any other manifestation of Mahāvairocana is enshrined. Here the eternal and cosmic drama of the samadhi of self-enjoyment (*jijuyō sammai*) of Mahāvairocana is performed through rigidly prescribed activities of body, speech, and mind, every step exactly as prescribed: how to move one's fingers (mudra); what to think or visualize or feel; and which mantra to recite at what moment and how many times. On performing the rituals of purification and consecration of the ground and of the ten directions, the circle where the student meditates is transformed into the center of the universe. Then begins the invocation of the presence of Mahāvairocana, or of any of his manifestations, as the object of meditation confronting the subject, followed by a conscious effort to imitate the object through symbolic activities of body, speech, and mind. The climax is reached when the subject, while performing the acts of imitating, loses the awareness that he is imitating—the subject is transformed into the object, and the separation between the subject and the object disappears. In the end, as the actor withdraws from the stage, the subject returns to the imitating self, and the object, to where it came from, by means of ritual acts. The entire process is regulated by rules, that is, the process

of time is punctuated by prescribed activities so that the student will
not lose himself in timelessness; step by step he returns from uncon-
scious imitating to his conscious self by counting beats, striking a hand
bell, and so forth.

There is a variety of methods of meditation, as there are many
manifestations of Mahāvairocana shown in the paintings of the Dia-
mond and Matrix mandalas. A few of these methods are meditation on
Avalokiteśvara, on the Diamond Realm, on the Matrix Realm, on the
Moon (symbol of *bodhicitta*), on the letter *A* (Mahāvairocana in the
Matrix Realm), and on Acala (Fudō). All can be regarded as the practice of the samadhi of Mahāvairocana, because the object invoked in
each meditation is no other than a manifestation of Mahāvairocana.
Some are extremely simple, consisting of one mantra and one mudra.
The merit of Esoteric Buddhist meditation is in the method of meditation in action, for it mobilizes the student's total energy, preventing
him from falling into drowsiness and stagnation. On the other hand,
if the student loses the aspiration to attain enlightenment, his practice
will turn into dead formalism or into a reinforcement of mere superstition. Kūkai's awareness that his method of meditation might foster
superstition or produce misleading visions is suggested in the following
poem: [41]

> Full of strange things is the world of yoga in which manifold images
>   appear.
> There is a moment when we are drawn into a luminous world of
>   reality.
> Do not be proud of or deceived by it;
> Such a vision is yet provisional.
> Away with all images;
> The great samadhi of void is to be our companion.

Certainly, Kūkai was profoundly experienced in meditation and
appreciated direct samadhi over all other experiences. Life unaccom-
panied by aesthetic and ecstatic experiences of samadhi seemed to him
devoid of real value and purpose. In conclusion, here is another poem
which Kūkai probably composed on Mt. Kōya one summer morning
immediately after sitting in meditation: [42]

[41] *K.Z.*, III, 554.   [42] *K.Z.*, III, 552.

In a quiet forest, sitting alone
    in a grass hut at dawn,
"Bup pō sō!" [43] I thought
    I heard a bird cry.
Was it a bird's cry?
    I heard it in my mind.
The sound, stream, clouds, and mind
    diffuse brightly in the morning rays.

[43] A migrating bird found in the remote mountains of Japan during the warm season. It is popularly known, most likely because of this poem, as Buppōsō, the word for the Three Treasures of Buddhism. The bird's cry resembles the sound, "Bup pō sō."

PART THREE

MAJOR WORKS OF KŪKAI

I

INDICATIONS OF THE GOALS OF THE THREE TEACHINGS

(Sangō shīki)

PREFACE

For any natural phenomenon or literary work there exists a cause. The sun, the moon, and the stars appear when the sky is clear. A man writes when moved. So the Eight Trigrams of Fu Hsi, the *Tao-te Ching*, the *Book of Odes*, the *Elegies of Ch'u* were written down by men who were inspired from within. Of course, there can be no comparison between these sages of the past and a common man of the present such as I, yet somehow I feel compelled to express my innermost feelings.

At fifteen I began my studies [of Chinese classics] under the guidance of Atō Ōtari, the teacher of a prince and an uncle on my mother's side. At eighteen I entered the college in the capital [1] and studied diligently. Meanwhile a Buddhist monk showed me a scripture called the *Kokūzō gumonji no hō*.[2] In that work it is stated that if one recites the mantra one million times according to the proper method, one will be able to memorize passages and understand the meaning of any scripture. Believing what the Buddha says to be true, I recited the mantra incessantly, as if I were rubbing one piece of wood against another to make fire, all the while earnestly hoping to achieve this result. I climbed up Mount Tairyū in Awa Province and meditated at Cape Muroto in Tosa. The valley reverberated to the sound of my voice as I recited, and the planet Venus appeared in the sky.[3]

From that time on, I despised fame and wealth and longed for a life in the midst of nature. Whenever I saw articles of luxury—light furs, well-fed horses, swift vehicles—I felt sad, knowing that, being transient as lightning, they too would fade away. Whenever I saw a cripple or a beggar, I lamented and wondered what had caused him to spend his days in such a miserable state. Seeing these piteous conditions encouraged me to renounce the world. Can anyone now break my determination? No, just as there is no one who can stop the wind.

My relatives and teachers opposed my entering the priesthood, saying that by doing so I would be unable to fulfill the Five Cardinal Virtues[4] or to accomplish the duties of loyalty or of filial piety. I thought then: living beings are not of the same nature—there are birds which fly high in the sky and fish which sink low in the water. To guide different types of people, there are three teachings: Buddhism, Taoism, and Confucianism. Although their profoundness varies, they are still the teachings of the sages. If an individual chooses one, he does not necessarily repudiate loyalty and filial piety by doing so.

---

[1] The capital was located at Nagaoka.   [2] See Part One, p. 19, n. 1.

[3] The planet Venus is thought to be one of the manifestations of Kokūzō Bosatsu (Ākāśagarbha Bodhisattva).

[4] They are the Five Confucian Virtues: benevolence, righteousness, propriety, wisdom, and sincerity.

Now I have a nephew who is depraved and indulges in hunting, wine, and women, and whose usual way of life consists of gambling and dissipation. It is obvious that an unfavorable environment has caused him to lead this kind of life. What has induced me to write [this story] are the opposition of my relatives [to my becoming a Buddhist] and the behavior of this nephew.

Here in my writing I should like to propose Tokaku (Hare's Horn) as host, with Kimō (Tortoise Hair) as guest speaker for Confucianism, Kyobu (Nothingness) as spokesman for Taoism, and Kamei-kotsuji (Mendicant X) as representative of Buddhism. These speakers will debate over Shitsuga (Leech's Tusk), the nephew, and admonish him. The work will consist of three parts and be called the *Indications of the Goals of the Three Teachings*. Of course, I am writing just to express my own unsuppressible feelings and not in order to be read by others.

First Day of the Twelfth Month
Enryaku 16 (797)

PART ONE: THE ARGUMENT
OF KIMŌ [CONFUCIANIST]

There was a man called Kimō (Tortoise Hair). He was eloquent by nature and stately in appearance and had memorized completely the Nine Classics,[5] the Three Dynastic Histories,[6] the sayings of the three ancient kings, and the theories of divination. Once he opened his mouth, his speech could bring back to life a dead tree or revivify a skeleton. It has been said that the famous eloquent orators of old, such as Su Ch'in and Yen P'ing, became tongue-tied before him, and Chang I and Kuo Hsiang became silent even when they saw him at a distance.

As it was his day off, Kimō visited Tokaku (Hare's Horn). Tokaku welcomed him with a feast and they drank heartily together. After exchanging the customary three cups, they started to talk.

[5] The *Book of Changes*, the *Book of Odes*, the *Book of History*, the *Book of Rites*, the *Rites of Chou*, the *Book of Ritual*, the *Tso chuan*, the *Kung-yang chuan*, and the *Ku-liang chuan*.

[6] The *Historical Records* of Ssu-ma Ch'ien, the *History of the Former Han* of Pan Ku, and the *History of the Later Han* of Fan Yeh.

The topic of their conversation turned to the subject of Tokaku's nephew, Shitsuga (Leech's Tusk). He was dishonest by nature; he would not heed others' advice, nor pay attention to the proprieties. He indulged in gambling and hunting, was a profligate idler, and was arrogant and untrustworthy. One reaps as one has sown, but Shitsuga did not believe in the law of karma. Indulging in drinking, eating, and fleshly pleasures, he slept at irregular hours and did not worry about the sick even among his own relatives. He never greeted others when he met them, disgraced his father and elder brothers, and in his arrogance humiliated well-learned elders.

Tokaku said to Kimō: "I have heard that, in ancient times, Wang Pao was an expert in singing, and so the people of Kao-t'ang followed his singing; that Tsung-chih [Wen Weng of Former Han] liked learning, and so the people of Pa-shu came to like learning. An orange tree, when transplanted [from Huai-nan to Huai-pei], grows thick-skinned oranges; some crooked grasses, when grown side by side with hemp, straighten up of their own accord. By revealing the key to your inner wisdom, please enlighten this dull-minded one with your mystical eloquence so that he will awaken from his folly."

Kimō replied: "I have heard that a wise man will not become a fool even if he is not taught, but a fool will not become wise even if he is taught.[7] Since even an ancient sage has in grief spoken in this way, I have no other words to add."

The host, Tokaku, said: "Ancient wise men have talked of writing compositions to describe things and of composing poetry to express their feelings; since ancient times the writing of essays concerning problems which arise has been a highly esteemed occupation. Therefore, Wei Chao wrote a treatise condemning gambling, and Yüan-shu [Chao I], an essay attacking injustice; these have been recorded in books and preserved generation after generation as examples and admonitions. A dull knife, to cut through the bone, requires the help of a whetstone; a heavy wagon, to run well, needs oil. Even iron and wood which are devoid of intelligence depend on others; why should not man? If you clear the mist covering Shitsuga's mind and point out to him the errors of his conduct, remove the film that covers his eyes, and bring him back to the right path, how wonderful it will be!"

[7] The *Analects* of Confucius, XVIII, 3.

Thereupon, Kimō sank deep into thought and sighed. For some time he contemplated, looking first up at the sky and then down at the earth. Finally he smiled and said: "You have asked me cordially three times; therefore, I cannot refuse your request. I shall explain my humble views and judgments, relate my experience, and recount what I believe to be an outline of the method for controlling one's mind. I am, however, neither eloquent nor wise. My writing lacks the power to cure another's disease,[8] nor can my letters cause an enemy general to commit suicide.[9] If I desire to express my thoughts, I cannot speak smoothly; nevertheless, if I do not speak out, my heart will be oppressed. As I cannot bear to keep silent, I shall speak, using examples both modern and ancient. Now I shall explain to you [as Confucius said] one quarter of the whole and ask you to guess the remainder.

"This is what I think: In the beginning there was chaos—what was pure and light became heaven and what was turbid and heavy became earth. Human beings then came into existence. All men born inherit something of both heaven and earth, being endowed with four limbs and a head, but there are very few who are wise and good and many who are stupid and wicked. Their deeds vary as stars one from another, and their minds differ as do their faces. As there is a distinction between a gem and a pebble, so there is a distinction between one man and another. The difference is great between a wise man and a fool. If a man is allowed to do what he likes, he can do it as easily as he can drop a stone in the water; but if he is forced to do what he hates, then he cannot accomplish anything, just as oil cannot mix with water. Just as a foul odor remains in a fishstore, so he remains subject to bad influences; and yet, his original good nature is not apparent, as the straight furrows of hemp cannot be seen until the plants sprout. Just as the lice on the head [change their color according to the color of the hair] and the teeth of the people of Chin [who eat yellow Chinese dates, turn yellow], so one's mind is conditioned by environment. It is as if one covers one's self with a tiger skin, but within is nothing but

[8] Ch'en Lin of Wei was known for his good writing. It has been said that Emperor Wu's headache disappeared when he read a letter from Ch'en Lin.
[9] This is based on the story in the *Historical Records* of Ssu-ma Ch'ien. The General of Yen cried for three days and then committed suicide after having read the letter written by Lu Chung-lien, which had been tied to an arrow and shot into the castle.

a mass of excrement bundled in silk brocade. Such a person would be disdained all his life as if he were a beast, and even after his death he would be known for generations as the foolish one who tried to see the sky while carrying a tray on his head. What a shame! What a pity!

"I think that the uncut jade of Ch'u became lustrous only as a result of polishing, and that the brocade of Chen-tu became bright only after a rinse in the Yangtze River; Tai Yüan [10] changed his heart and rose to the rank of general; Chou Ch'u [11] also changed and made himself known for his loyalty and filial piety. A gem when polished may illumine darkness; a man by his effort may become intelligent. Even the son of a commoner, if he follows the teaching faithfully, will be able to rise to the three highest positions in the government. Even a descendant of the emperor, if he stubbornly resists advice, may become a common man. I have heard that a tree can be straightened with the help of a rope. It is equally valid that by accepting advice one can become a sage. From the emperor down to the most humble man, there has never been a case in which a man has realized [a truth] by himself without studying, or has understood [it] by going against the teachings. That the states of Hsia and Yin perished and those of Chou and Han arose are good examples of this; the fall of earlier dynasties serves to warn later generations. One should be cautious; one should be prudent.

"Therefore, Shitsuga (Leech's Tusk), listen to me with the attentive ears of Ling Lun [12] and look at me with the penetrating eyes of Li Chu; [13] listen carefully to my admonishments and reexamine the path along which you have come. Now let us look at your own nature:

"You look down on your parents; you do not greet them when you leave or return home. You insult the people in the world and have no compassion for them.

"Seeking pleasure in hunting birds and animals, you wander across fields and mountains; at other times, you row your boat out to the sea to fish.

[10] He was the head of a band of thieves when young.

[11] A notorious villain who is said to have killed a dragon and a tiger that had a white forehead.

[12] A famous musician who discovered the twelve standard tones during the reign of the Yellow Emperor.

[13] A man of old, well known for his keen vision.

"All day long you indulge in amusements so that your bad deeds will soon exceed those of Chou Hsü.[14] All night long you play and gamble, even more than Ssu-tsung [15] did. You even forget to eat and sleep, paying no attention to wise counsels. You do nothing whatsoever good and your greed becomes stronger and stronger. You hunger for the flesh of animals as if you were a lion or tiger, and for fish as if you were a whale. You never think of them as your beloved children or of their flesh as your own. When you are drunk, you put even an orangutan [16] to shame. Your greed for food is worse than that of a leech that sucks blood. When intoxicated you are as noisy as a cicada, having no regard for the admonitions against drinking. You make no distinction between day and night. No one would even care to criticize your behavior, as Ma-tzu did.[17] Your lasciviousness surpasses that of Teng T'u-tzu.[18] Even on seeing an ugly disheveled woman you are stirred; how much more so when you see a charming one! You would die of yearning for her as Śūrpaka [19] did. Like a horse in the spring and a dog in the summer, you have a heart that burns with lust. How can a fellow like you learn anything from such meaningful stories as those of the aged monkey and the poisonous snake? [20]

"You go on a spree in the gay quarters and behave like an ape playing in the treetops. Then at school you yawn and doze off like a crafty rabbit who takes a nap in the shade. It must be difficult for you to imagine that one [Sun Ching] studied hard [and kept himself from

[14] He became the ruler of the state of Wei after killing his stepbrother but was later assassinated.

[15] He was playing a game of chess at the time of his mother's death.

[16] An orangutan is said to be very fond of drinking.

[17] Three different remarks on Ma-tzu are found in the commentaries to the *Indications:* 1) the source is unknown; 2) Ma-tzu is taken as a sesame seed, implying the ascetic practice of the Buddha who is said to have subsisted on a sesame seed a day while concentrating on his ascetic practice; 3) Ma-tzu is interpreted as Wang Ma-tzu, who criticized Pai I and Shu Ch'i in Chou, causing them to starve to death (cf. *Shingonshū zensho,* XL, 21, 54). Since this appears as part of the speech of Kimō, a Confucianist, it seems appropriate to take the third interpretation here.

[18] He was scorned for having five children by his ugly, shaggy-haired wife.

[19] An Indian fisherman who yearned for a queen.

[20] Nanda, the Buddha's cousin and disciple, had a beautiful wife. She, however, looked like an aged monkey beside the celestial nymphs. It is better for a man to insert his penis into the mouth of a poisonous snake than to have intercourse with a woman.

sleep] by constricting his neck with a rope, or that another [Su Ch'in] did so by holding a gimlet against his thigh. Your mind is filled with thoughts of holding a glass of wine in one hand and a piece of crab in the other. You pay no heed to the story of the man in ancient times [Ch'e Yin] who studied by the light of fifty or sixty fireflies gathered in a bag. Instead you are like the man who carried a hundred coins tied to the tip of his cane [so that he might be able to drink wherever he found a wineshop]. Should you by chance step inside a Buddhist temple, you neither confess nor repent but instead your mind turns toward evil. You are ignorant of the fact that to recite even once the name of the Buddha and to meditate on him may result in your attaining enlightenment, or that to spend a penny to offer a candle may result in your becoming an Enlightened One in the future.

"Instead of blaming your own faults, you resent it when you receive instructions from your father. It is impossible for you to understand the feelings of your teacher, who instructs you with more patience than he does his own son.

"You criticize others' faults and disregard the ten maxims.[21] You are voluble and do not heed the admonitions about refraining from excessive talk. You know full well that to speak badly about others can be injurious, yet you are not cautious when what you say may well determine your own promotion or demotion.

"You have so many faults that it is impossible to describe them all. Even if you live a hundred years, if you indulge only in feasting, your life will have been spent like that of an animal. Even if you wear beautiful clothes throughout the year, you will still be like a dog or a pig. It is said in the *Book of Rites* that when a parent is sick the young son should not comb his hair, should abstain from frivolous behavior, should play no musical instruments, should drink only in moderation, and although merry should not reveal it by laughter. This is because the young son is so concerned about his sick parent that he cannot be bothered about his own deportment or appearance. Also in the same book it is said: 'When there is mourning next door, you should abstain from singing while pounding grain. Should there be a house in the neighborhood where a funeral has not yet been held, you should not sing in the streets.' This means that you should share the sufferings

---

[21] Ts'ui Tzu-yü's ten maxims, the first of which is, "Do not talk of others' faults, nor praise your own strong points."

of others, without making a distinction between relatives and strangers. Toward those to whom you are not related, you should act according to the above teaching; to those to whom you are closely related, you should act in the same way. Therefore, when a relative is sick, you must show your sincerity by calling a physician and then try the medicine first yourself. Otherwise, a wise man might look askance at you and be embarrassed by your behavior. When there is trouble in the neighborhood and you do not sympathize with or console those who suffer, relatives and intelligent people will be shocked. Your physical appearance differs from that of a bird or an animal; how can you remain [unaffected] like wood or stone? You have a human body, so why are you so much like a parrot or monkey?

"Shitsuga, if you change your heart and devote yourself to filial piety, you could be among those who are well known for this virtue. Think of the man who shed tears of blood; [22] of the man who struck a jar of gold; [23] of Meng Tsung; [24] of the man who caught carp; [25] or of Ting Lan.[26] You can readily surpass such well-known examples as these.

"If you have a change of heart and devote yourself to loyalty, you could be among those who are highly esteemed for this virtue: think of the man who broke the railing; [27] of the man who broke a window; [28] of the man who exchanged his liver; [29] of the man who was stabbed through the heart.[30] Some day you may well excel these paragons in giving straightforward advice.

[22] Kao Chai shed tears of blood for three years while mourning the death of his father.

[23] Kuo Chü, while digging a hole to bury his child alive so that he might save food for his mother.

[24] He miraculously found bamboo shoots in the winter because of his earnest wish to please his mother.

[25] Wang Hsiang caught two carp in an ice-covered pond while fishing at his stepmother's unreasonable command.

[26] He made a wooden image of his mother, who had passed away while he was still young, and served it as if it were alive.

[27] Chu Yün of Han, while being dragged away by an official to be put to death, broke the railing of the imperial palace in his earnest effort to give final advice to Emperor Ch'eng.

[28] Shih Ching of Wei, when he tried to hit Marquis Wen with a harp in order to correct the marquis's fault of not listening to another's advice.

[29] Hung Yen exchanged his liver with that of his lord, Duke I of Wei.

[30] Pi Kan, for remonstrating with King Chou of Yin.

"If you gave lectures on the classics, [great scholars like] Pao Hsien and Tzu Hsia would falter and withdraw. If you studied historical texts extensively, even Ch'ü Yüan and Yang Hsiung would hold their tongues in respect. If you devoted yourself to calligraphy, you would be able to write characters comparable to a bird flying or a tiger in repose. Chung Yao, Chang Chih, Wang Hsi-chih, the Ou-yangs [Ou-yang Hsün and his filial son Ou-yang T'ung] would throw away their brushes in shame. If you concentrated on archery, you could master the art to such an extent that you could hit the sun, and the monkeys would cry out in terror just seeing you put an arrow to the bowstring. [Masters of archery such as] I Yu-ch'iung, Yang Yu-chi, Keng Ying, and P'u Ch'ieh-tzu would break their strings in admiration of you. If you entered into battle, [geniuses of war tactics such as] Chang Liang and Sun Tzu would lament their lack of strategy. If you engaged in trade and agriculture, [successful businessmen such as] T'ao Chu and I Tun would bewail the fact that your grains exceeded theirs in variety. In politics your fame would transcend [Yang Chen's, who refused to be bribed, saying,] 'Heaven knows, the gods know, I know, and you know.' As a judge, you could win a reputation excelling that of the one [Liu Hsia-hui] who was discharged three times from his position [because of his honesty]. For prudence and purity, you might be compared to Mencius' mother or to Hsiao-wei;[31] for honesty and lack of greed, you could be compared to Po I and Hsü Yu.[32] If you concentrated on the study of medicine, you would be an expert surgeon, more skillful than the one [Pien Ch'üeh] who exchanged the hearts of patients, or the one [Hua T'a] who washed out the patient's stomach. As an artist, your technique could excel that of Chiang Shih [in *Chuang Tzu*] who [with a chisel] could remove from the nose a piece of plaster as thin as the wing of a fly [without so much as scratching the nose], or of Shu [Lu Pan] who carved a wooden kite.[33] If you became such an expert, you would be as broad-minded and wise as

[31] The mother of Mencius is famous for her prudence in educating her young son. Hsiao-wei of the Later Han, living in a cave in Mount Wu-an and enjoying his life of purity, declined an invitation to be a government official.

[32] Po I and Hsü Yu were famous men of old who are known for their reluctance to ascend the throne. Po I retired to the mountains, leaving the throne to his brother. Emperor Yao is said to have offered Hsü Yu the throne, but he declined the offer and then washed out the ears with which he had heard the emperor's offer. He lived content with poverty.

[33] A bird so real that it flew on high and did not return for three days.

Shu-tu [34] and as dignified and capable as Sou Sung.[35] Those who saw you would be unable to measure your greatness.

"A suitable place must be chosen for your residence. Bear in mind that proper human conduct is the floor of your house, virtue the bed on which you lie, benevolence the cushion on which you sit, righteousness the pillow on which you rest, propriety the bedding in which you sleep, and trust the clothing which you wear. Being careful not to waste even a minute's time, study the sages' teachings, choose only what is good, and try to understand it. Study diligently, and never for a moment lay aside your book or paper and brush.

"Through such practices, your eloquence could pour forth ceaselessly like a spring, inexhaustible as the ocean; you could be like the one [Chu Yün] who won the argument with Wu-lu [in front of Emperor Yüan of the Former Han], or like the one [Tai Ping] who defeated fifty scholars. The excellent style of your writing and its content could be as impressive as a range of tall green trees in a deep forest. Then, surpassing Sung Ch'o and Ssu-ma Hsiang-ju, your sentences could sound as if bells were tinkling; surpassing the beautiful sentences of Yang Hsiung and Pan Ku, they could resound like the clanking of gold and could be praised for being as beautiful as a garland of flowers. Just as the one [Liu An] who was able to compose immediately his interpretation of [Ch'ü Yüan's] "Solitude," or the one [Ni Heng] whose rhyme-prose (*fu*) on a parrot was so perfect that it needed no later revision, you could fly freely in the garden of poetry and rest at ease in the fields of prose.

"Should this happen, many people will come from afar to visit you, their wagons loaded with gifts of silk and jade as they crowd the front gate. You would be like the ancient wise man whom Wen Kung of Wei saluted from his royal coach while passing in front of his humble door; then you would not need to make yourself known by beating the horns.[36] Lü Shang was discovered by King Wen of Chou while he was fishing; Chu-ko Liang received three visits from Liu Pei.[37] Self-

---

[34] Huang Hsien. He was noted for his wisdom.

[35] Sou Sung (Sou Tzu-sung) may be an error for Wen Chiao. Cf. *Shingonshū zensho*, XL, 196, 328.

[36] Ning Ch'i, in order to get a position, drew the attention of Marquis Huai by beating the horns of an ox and singing.

[37] Literal translation: "The royal coach of the King of Chou passes by a grass hut on the way to the hunt." "The royal coach of the King of Chou" refers to

display in order to gain a promotion by striking the hilt of your sword would be unnecessary.[38] You could obtain a high position in government without depending on luck and could ascend to the ranks of a high official without deliberately exhibiting your talents. To get a position as a high governmental official is as easy as picking a speck of dust from the ground; it can be had readily. If you studied hard [like Su Ch'in who fought sleep] by pricking your thighs with a gimlet, you would quickly acquire the garment and sash of a high official.

"Being devoted to your parents, you would be loyal to your lord and sincere in your association with friends. A sword of rank would compliment your waist, and in your hands would rest the jade tablet of authority and the wooden tablet of command.

"By participating in politics, your name and glory would extend everywhere, and by governing with benevolence, you would receive censure from no one. Your name would remain in history and your descendants would prosper. While alive you would reach a high rank and, after death, you would be given a beautiful posthumous name. Is this not a grand and hallowed prospect? What more could one hope for?

"The worldly pleasures should be enjoyed while you are yet alive; after death there will be no one with whom to share these pleasures. The male star Altair laments his loneliness in the sky and looks forward to seeing Vega [a female star] once a year on the seventh day of the seventh month; a couple of mandarin ducks always rejoice at being able to live together. Therefore, there is in the *Book of Odes* a poem comparing a girl who is anxious to marry but has already passed the marriageable age to an overripe plum dropping wasted to the ground. And in the *Book of History* there is the story of Emperor Yao giving his two daughters to Shun. Not everyone can be like Liu Hsia-hui.[39] Who does not want to marry? Most people are unlike Tzu-teng [Sun Teng] who lived alone in a mountain cave. How can one sleep

King Wen's hunting trip in the royal coach during which he discovered Lü Shang, and "a grass hut" suggests three visits made by Liu Pei, the founder of the Former Han Dynasty, to the grass hut of Chu-ko Liang.

[38] Refers to Feng Huan, who sang while striking the hilt of his sword and asked Meng Ch'ang-chün for a promotion.

[39] He warmed with his body a girl trembling from cold, yet remained unaffected.

alone? Should one find a beautiful girl, one should arrange to marry her. Then on the wedding day the carriage in which the groom takes the bride home rolls merrily through the town—speeding wagons drawn by dashing horses pass through the city, and the retinue of the bride follows behind, with sleeves flying in the air. The sedan carriers and charioteers follow on foot, their sweat dropping to the ground like a light rain. The purple canopies resemble flying clouds, and the embroidered dresses sound like the wind as they swish along the ground. After the wedding and the ceremony of the bride returning to her parents' home have been completed, the bride and groom become true husband and wife and eat, drink, and sleep together without any obstacle between them. They arrange their home fittingly and live together in harmony; they stay fast together as though held by glue or plaster. Living together more harmoniously than the one-eyed fish of the East [40] or the one-winged bird of the South,[41] they will enjoy life without worry for a hundred years.

"Sometimes they may invite relatives and friends, drink excellent liquor, eat rare delicious foods, fill their glasses again and again, and drink endlessly as if they were walking around a circle. The guests perhaps will play the eight kinds of musical instruments and recite the poem: 'I am drunk, I had better go home.' The host will then say: 'I have removed the linchpins from your wagon and have thrown them into a well; you cannot go home.' Or, perhaps he will recite the poem: 'On your way home the dew will be dense; wait until it has dried.' The guests may then forget to go home for days and will dance night after night; they will thus exhaust the pleasures of the world. Could there be pleasure beyond this?

"Shitsuga! Give up quickly your foolish attachments and follow my admonitions. You can then perfect filial piety and loyalty, widen your friendships, and extend prosperity down through your family line. What I have told you are the essential things you need to advance in this world and to gain fame. Confucius has said, 'In farming one sometimes has to suffer a shortage of food, but for study a stipend is usually provided.' [42] This saying is indeed true. Let this truth sink into your mind."

[40] The one-eyed fish which cannot move unless two swim side by side.
[41] These birds can fly only in pairs.   [42] *Analects*, XV, 31.

On hearing this, Shitsuga prostrated himself and said:

"Yes, I have understood your advice well. Hereafter I shall concentrate on learning."

Thereupon, Tokaku descended from his seat, bowed twice, and said: "How excellent! Before, when I used to hear that a sparrow changes into a clam, I doubted the truth of the statement, but now that I have witnessed the dove-mind of Shitsuga change into that of a hawk, I do not doubt any more. I have heard the story of Ko Hsien-kung transforming the grains of cooked rice in his mouth into bees, and that of Tso Tz'u disguising himself as a sheep [in order to escape danger]; but the fact that your fine speech has changed this mad one into a fine person is superior to these miracles. This is indeed more than I had expected; it is like asking for vinegar and getting liquor, or aiming at a hare and shooting a beautiful fawn. For a student of Confucianism who learns the *Book of Odes* and the *Book of Rites*, there is no better instruction than what you have given today. It has been a lesson not only for Shitsuga but also for me; I shall treasure it in my mind as long as I live."

PART TWO: THE ARGUMENT
OF KYOBU [TAOIST]

Kyobu (Nothingness) had been beside them listening for some time. He was a person who concealed his wisdom by pretending to be a fool; he mingled with the people in the streets, acting as if he were mad. His hair was disheveled, more so than that of Teng T'u-tzu's wife,[43] and his ragged garment seemed shabbier than that of Tung Wei.[44] He had been listening, squatting with his legs far apart, and smiling arrogantly. But now he opened wide his eyes and spoke:

"How strange is your therapeutic medicine! When you started I thought your speech would be as valuable as a priceless fox coat; I was struck with awe as if I were facing a dragon or a tiger. But

[43] She was well known for her ugliness. See above, n. 18.
[44] He was reputed to care nothing about his clothes.

toward the end I felt as if I were watching a tiny snake or a rat. You are unable to cure your own dread disease, but still you have the nerve to speak about another's swollen legs; it is better not to cure at all than to cure by such a therapy."

Thereupon, Kimō turned around in astonishment. Quite embarrassed, he drew near to Kyobu and said:

"If you know of any other teaching, please share it with us. I may have spoken carelessly, being unable to ignore Tokaku's request. Please instruct us with your teaching, which is like the thunder in spring." [45]

Kyobu said: "The sun is bright, but a blind man is unable to see the glittering rays. Though thunder roars violently, a deaf man does not know the sound. The secret doctrines of Emperor Huang do not reach the ears of ordinary people. Why should I teach indiscriminately the divine founder's secret doctrines? In olden times people drank the blood of a sacrificial animal and made a vow before they heard the doctrines; these teachings can seldom be heard. They engraved an oath on the bones vowing that they would keep the secret. These doctrines cannot be easily transmitted. Why is this so? Ordinary people assume that the well is dry, when in actuality the bucket they lower has too short a rope and cannot reach the water; or they try to measure the depth of the ocean by dipping a finger into it and imagine that they have touched the bottom. To an unfit person, we do not open our mouths; unless a man be a proper vessel, we hide our book in a wooden box deep down in the earth. When the occasion comes, we open the box and transmit the secret to those who have been selected."

Thereupon, Kimō and the others consulted together:

"Long ago when Emperor Wu of Han went searching for the secret of longevity, he came upon Hsi Wang Mu [Queen of the West] and with her he pleaded earnestly in a most polite manner for the revelation of the secret; Fei Ch'ang-fang learned the secret formula from an old man in a jar. Now we have unexpectedly met this teacher; from him we can learn the method of attaining longevity. We need not exert ourselves as Ping Yüan [46] did. We may be able to live as long as P'eng Tsu [47] did. Will it not be marvelous! How fortunate we are!"

---

[45] The thunder in spring awakens beings from their hibernation.
[46] He wandered over one thousand *ri* in search of a teacher.
[47] He lived eight hundred and some odd years.

Thus they approached Kyobu, courteously prostrated themselves again, and said, "We earnestly entreat you once more to favor us with your instruction."

Then Kyobu said, "If you build an altar and make a vow, I shall teach you."

They did as they had been told. They constructed an altar and made a vow; they also drank the blood of a sacrificial animal and read an oath in front of the hole they dug in which to bury the animal. After completing the ceremony, they asked for instruction.

"Fine," said Kyobu. "Listen with sincerity. I shall bestow upon you the divine techniques for prolonging your life and attaining immortality. You, whose term of life is as short as that of the mayflies, will be able to live as long as a tortoise or a crane; you, whose speed compares to that of a lame donkey walking, will be as fast as a flying dragon. You will be everlasting like the sun, the moon, and the stars! You will be able to meet the Eight Immortals who ascended to the sky. You will climb the three mystical mountains [in the Eastern Sea] in the morning, enjoy yourselves in the silver palaces all day long, and in the evening reach the five mountains [in the East] and wander on the golden platform all night. I will make all these miracles possible for you."

Kimō and the others replied, "Yes, yes, we should like to hear."

"A potter's wheel when it shapes does not discriminate between earthen vessels; a large furnace, when melting metals, has neither affection nor hatred for the metals it melts. That Ch'ih Sung-tzu [48] and Wang Tzu-ch'iao [49] had long lives was not because they had any unusual good fortune; that Hsiang T'o [50] and Yen Hui [51] died young does not mean that they were unfortunate. The difference is determined by how well they maintained their given nature. The methods of nourishing nature and of maintaining longevity are many; therefore, I cannot explain them all to you. I shall teach you a little by describing things in outline.

[48] A magician famed for his ability to bring about rainfall during the legendary age of Shen Nung. He went to the residence of Hsi Wang Mu and became immortal.

[49] A magician of the sixth century B.C., the eldest son of King Ling of Chou. Riding through the air on a white crane, he ascended to heaven and became immortal.

[50] At seven he was a teacher of Confucius.   [51] A disciple of Confucius.

"In olden times, Emperor Shih Huang of Ch'in and Emperor Wu of Han longed for the art of becoming immortal, but their way of life had been the same as that of everyone else in the world. The functions of their ears were weakened by hearing music and their eyesight was dulled by the brightness of brocade and embroidery. They were unable, even for a short while, to be away from beautiful women, with their pink-colored eyelids and red lips. Dishes of fresh fish, birds, and animals appeared on their table without fail, even for the simplest meal. In battle they piled up corpses as high as a tall building, causing blood to flow like a river. Stories such as these are too numerous to tell in detail. In short, they exhausted their energies in vain; there was a gap between their aspirations and their achievements. They hoped that a round cover would fit a square container, or that fire would come from ice. How stupid they were! People in the world, however, say that, since even the noblest emperors were unable to attain immortality, how can it be possible for commoners like us to attain it. They therefore consider Taoism a fraud and call it nonsense. How confused they are! Luan T'ai [52] and both the emperors I have mentioned were but the lowest scum among all those who have been attracted to Taoism; they were abominable. Since people such as they exist, when we transmit the teaching, we must choose proper persons, regardless of their social standing. You had better apply yourselves diligently to learning so that you will not be blamed by later generations. Those who study well are different from the men I have mentioned. Refrain from killing the insects that come near you and do not let sperm or saliva escape from your body. Physically, abstain from worldly pollutions; mentally, get rid of your greediness. Stop looking into the distance and cease listening continuously. Avoid talking nonsense; give up eating delicious food. It goes without saying, however, that you should be dutiful to your parents, faithful to your friends, benevolent and compassionate. You must surrender wealth as if it were a thorn, and an emperor's position as if you were casting off your [worn-out] straw sandals. When you see a beautiful girl with a slender waist, think of her as a devil or a ghost. Consider peerage and fiefdom as if they were dead rats. Remain quiet, doing nothing intentionally; with pride reduce your worldly affairs. Thereafter, if you study, it [to master this art] will be as easy as pointing at your own palm. What the worldly people like

[52] He cheated Emperor Wu of the Former Han and was killed.

most, that the followers of Taoism most detest. To realize Taoism is not difficult if one stands apart from what people are fond of. Grains are poisonous to the internal organs. Spices are like a poisonous bird with a black body and red eyes—they damage your eyes. Liquors are swords that slice your intestines; pork and fish are halberds that cut your life; beautiful women are axes that chop you down; singing and dancing shorten your allotted period of time. To laugh heartily, to be overly delighted, to be extremely angry, and to be exceedingly sad all do great harm to your body. Even within our bodies are numerous enemies. Unless you overcome them, you cannot expect to have a long life. In everyday living it is extremely difficult to relinquish these enemies, but once rid of them it is very easy to realize Taoism. You should first understand the essence of it and apply the following prescriptions to yourselves:

"Medicines that cure inner diseases are *Atractylis ovata*,[53] *Polygonatum stenophyllum*,[54] pine resin, the seed of paper mulberry, etc. The arrow of Rubus, the halberd of reed, charms and spells, etc., prevent external difficulties. You must practice the methods for regulating your breath according to the time of day and the season. Inhale air through the nostrils and swallow your saliva. Dig the ground and drink minerals. Satisfy your hunger in the morning with *ts'ao-chih* [55] and *ju-chih*; [56] take *fu-ling* [57] and *wei-hsi* [58] for evening fatigue. After you have followed these practices, you will be able to make your shadow vanish, even when out under the sun, and to write in darkness during the night; you will be able to see through the earth and walk on water. You will be able to make demons your slaves, dragons and one of the excellent steeds [of Mu Wang of Chou] your vehicles. You will be able to swallow swords and fire, stir winds, and produce clouds. In this way there is no magic that cannot be practiced; there are no desires which cannot be fulfilled.

[53] A medicinal herb which promotes urination and perspiration and is good for stomach troubles. The herb is known among the Taoists for its effect in making the body light and in prolonging life.

[54] A medicinal herb which is supposed by the Taoists to prolong one's life by improving the functions of the internal organs.

[55] A species of fungus.   [56] A dried frog.

[57] A species of fungus that grows on the stump of a pine three or four years after the tree has been cut.

[58] A little plant that grows on old *fu-ling*.

"Silver and gold are the essence of heaven and earth. Divine pills and refined pills [59] are the most miraculous of all the medicines. Certain procedures in taking them and certain techniques in compounding them must be followed. If one becomes an expert, the other members of his family will also be able to fly into the sky; by drinking only a small quantity of the elixir, one can fly to the Milky Way during the day-time. There are yet many other methods—techniques of swallowing divine amulets and inhaling air; the technique of traveling swiftly, and the magic of changing one's form—so many that I cannot enumerate them all here.

"When you realize the Way and master this art, your aged body and gray hair will be rejuvenated and life prolonged. Death will be postponed and you will live long in this world. Freely you will fly up to the sky and wander in the regions where the sun sets. Whipping the horse of your mind, you will run to the ends of the eight directions; oiling the wagon of your will, you will gambol throughout the nine skies.[60] You may roam about the palace of the sun, wander in the mansion where the Emperor of Heaven lives; you may see the weaving girl [Vega] or seek Heng-e [61] in the moon. Visiting the Yellow Emperor,[62] you can stay in his company; seeking Wang Tzu-ch'iao,[63] you can make him your friend. You may investigate the whereabouts of the roc (*p'eng*) depicted in *Chuang Tzu* and see for yourself the footprints of Huai's dog.[64] You may examine the stables of the horse constellation and the residence of the star Altair. You can lie down at will anywhere and ascend and descend freely. You will be indifferent, free from de-sires, and at peace in solitude. You will live as long as the heaven and earth; enjoy life for an eternity together with the sun and moon. How excellent! How great! The existence of the immortal married couple, Tung Wang Kung [King of the East] and Hsi Wang Mu [Queen of the West], is not a fabrication; what I have spoken of is the most mysterious art that I have ever heard of or learned.

[59] Elixirs of life.   [60] The center and the eight directions of the sky.

[61] A man named I had received elixirs of life from Hsi Wang Mu, but his wife Heng-e drank them before he could and flew to the moon.

[62] The third king among the most ancient five kings of China, who is said to have flown to the sky on a dragon.

[63] An ancient man who is said to have attained immortality. Cf. n. 49, above.

[64] After Huai-nan Tzu had flown to the sky, his dog licked the remainder of the divine medicine left in a container in the garden and also went up to the sky.

"Now let us examine the worldly life. People are restrained by avarice and suffer bitterly. Chained by passion, their hearts burn. They are compelled to work for their morning and evening meals; they must exhaust themselves for the necessary summer and winter clothing. With the hope of gaining a wealth that is as unstable as floating clouds, they gather property that is just as foamlike. Seeking after unmerited luck, they cherish their bodies, which indeed are as transient as lightning. Given a little pleasure in the morning, they scorn the delights of heaven; but given a little worry in the evening, they agonize as if they have fallen into filthy mire, or onto a bed of burning charcoal. Before the merry music has ended, a sad tone creeps in. A prime minister today is a servant tomorrow. In the beginning men are like the cat on top of a rat, but in the end they are like the sparrow under a hawk. They rely on the dew on the grass and forget that the sun rises at dawn; they trust the leaves at the end of a branch and forget that the frost may come. What a pity! They are not different from the tailorbirds.[65] They are indeed not worthy to be mentioned. Which is better, my teacher's instruction, or what you believe in? Which is superior, what you enjoy, or the life we Taoists admire?"

At this point Kimō, Shitsuga, and Tokaku knelt in a row and said, "We have been fortunate to meet you and to hear a good speech. Now we realize the difference that exists between the foul smell of a fish store and the exquisite fragrance of mystical Mount Fang-hu, between the homeliness of Ch'ou Mi [appearing in the *Spring and Autumn of Mr. Lü*] and the fairness of Tzu Tu [in the *Book of Odes*]. Gold is different from stone; a fragrant grass cannot be compared with an ill-smelling one. From now on we shall concentrate on refining our spirits and for a long time savor your teaching."

PART THREE: THE ARGUMENT OF KAMEI-KOTSUJI [BUDDHIST]

There was a man called Kamei-kotsuji (Mendicant X). Though the place of his birth remains obscure, it is certain that he was born and

---

[65] The little birds that build nests by stitching leaves together and find that when the strong wind blows their eggs fall out and break.

grew up in a dilapidated, thatched house. He kept himself aloof from the hustle and bustle of the world and applied himself diligently to the realization of Buddhism. His shaven head was like a round tray of copper, and his ashen face, like an earthenware pot. He was haggard and small; his legs were long like those of a heron standing near a pond; and his sinewy short neck resembled that of a turtle in the mud. The often-mended begging bowl on his left arm was like a cow's feeding bag, and the rosary in his right hand with its 108 beads hung like a horse's girth. He wore sandals made of straw, not of leather; and his waist was bound, not by a sash adorned with rhinoceros horn, but by the rope used for a donkey's bridle. As he always carried a reed mat, even the beggars around the market place covered their faces in shame on seeing him. The thieves in prison, on seeing him carry a chair made of straw rope on his back, pressed their knees tightly together and sighed in disgust. He carried a broken water jug so that he looked like a poor oil-seller; like a firewood-seller, he carried in his hand a pilgrim's staff with the ring at the top missing. He had a crooked nose, deep eye sockets, pointed chin, square eyes, and a distorted mouth without a moustache, which resembled a strange seashell.[66] His irregular front teeth showed between his deformed lips like those of a rabbit. If by chance he entered the market place, people showered him with pieces of tile and pebbles; if he passed a harbor, people cast horse's dung upon him. Abishido,[67] however, was his fast friend and shared his aspirations, and the layman Kōmyō was his benefactor. Sometimes he climbed the mountain called Kingan and encountered difficulty because of the snow; sometimes he climbed Mount Seki and experienced hardship because of the shortage of food. Once he was attracted by a beautiful girl, Undō, and his determination was somewhat relaxed, but on meeting the nun Kobe he was encouraged and his loathing for the world was intensified. He had hardships as Tzu Ssu [68] had, gathering frost-withered vegetables to eat; yet he enjoyed life in nature, brushing aside the snow to sleep,

[66] The word given in the text is *kujakugai* (a peacock shell). According to a commentary (*Shingonshū zensho*, XL, 351a), this shell is oval and the upper shell does not exactly fit the lower shell.

[67] Of Abishido nothing is known. Abishido may well mean "an unordained monk (*shido*) Abi." From this point on, the scene shifts to Japan; Kūkai seems to have utilized his personal experiences as the basis for his description of Kamei-kotsuji, Mendicant X.

[68] K'ung Chi, the grandson of Confucius.

using his arms for a pillow. The blue sky was the ceiling of his hut and the clouds hanging over the mountains were his curtains; he did not need to worry about where he lived or where he slept. In summer he opened his neck band in a relaxed mood and delighted in the gentle breezes as though he were a great king, but in winter he watched the fire with his neck drawn into his shoulders. If he had enough horse chestnuts and bitter vegetables to last ten days, he was lucky. His bare shoulders showed through his paper robe and clothes padded with grass cloth. He was, however, quite satisfied with what was given him, like a bird that perches on a single branch, or like the one who subsisted on half a grain a day.[69] He did not ask for delicious foods like Ho Ts'eng [the gourmet], or warm furs like those of T'ien Tzu-fang.[70] He put the poor old man of three pleasures to shame,[71] and he could not be compared to the four old men with gray hair.[72] Though his appearance was laughable, his deep-rooted will could not be taken away from him.

A certain man said to him: "My teacher has told me: Man is the lord of all that is created. The most excellent virtues of man are filial piety and loyalty; among the infinite variety of virtues, those two are the most important. One should, therefore, not harm the body one has received from his parents; but, in time of crisis, one should know how to sacrifice one's life when duty calls for it. One should not neglect either to attain fame in the world or to enhance the name of one's ancestors. The pleasures of life are to seize wealth and position. As companions none are superior to one's own wife and children. Tzu Lu and Ts'eng Tzu, the disciples of Confucius, lamented that when they finally had obtained a high position, their parents had already passed away. In your case, however, your parents are still living and there is also a lord in the country whom you can serve. Why do you not serve your parents and your lord? You have meaninglessly sunk

[69] While practicing asceticism in the woods, Prince Siddhārtha, who became Buddha upon attaining Enlightenment, is said to have subsisted on half a grain a day.

[70] Having heard that Tzu Szu was leading a life of poverty, T'ien Tzu-fang sent him a white fox fur, but Tzu Szu declined it.

[71] The old man of three pleasures is a hermit who met Confucius and said that he had three pleasures: the pleasure of being born a human being, the pleasure of being born a male, and the pleasure of being able to live long. The story appears in Lieh Tzu.

[72] They are hermits who gave advice to the son of Emperor Kao-tsu of Han.

into the ranks of beggars, and associate with those who have failed to discharge their official duties. You put your ancestors to shame; your name will remain noxious to later generations. Your conduct deserves severe punishment, and any gentleman would be highly ashamed of behavior such as yours. Your relatives, out of embarrassment, will feel like crawling into the earth because of you. Even strangers, on seeing you, pretend that they have not seen you. You should change your heart and practice filial piety and loyalty."

The mendicant countered: "What is filial piety and what is loyalty?"

The man answered: "When you are at home, you must keep smiling, studying the moods of your parents so that you may do what they want done before you are asked. Greet them when you go out or return. Make sure that they live comfortably and are cool in the summer and warm in the winter. Arrange their bedding in such a way that they can sleep well, and always inquire after their health in the morning. Reading their faces, provide the things they need and give them satisfaction. Such is filial piety. Emperor Shun and King Wen of Chou, by practicing filial piety, ascended the throne; Tung Yung [73] and Po-chieh,[74] also by following filial piety, left their fame to succeeding generations. When the time comes to serve your master, transfer your devotion from the practice of filial piety to loyalty; exert yourself to the fullest extent, and give advice to your master when he is wrong, even if, by offending him, you lose your life. Know well both astronomy and geography. Think of past events and compare them to the present situation; pacify the people in distant areas and control well the people nearby. Govern the world with order and assist your king to be righteous. Then your fame and success will be transmitted to posterity. Such is loyalty. I Yin, the Duke of Chou, Chi Tzu, and Pi Kan [75] indeed fall into this category."

---

[73] A man of the Han period known for his practice of filial piety. He had lost his mother when he was young. When he lost his father, he wanted to sell himself as a slave to pay the funeral expenses, because of his poverty. A celestial weaver recognized his act of filial piety and helped him.

[74] A man noted for his devotion to his mother. He served his sick mother for three years without even taking off his sash. When she died, he made a hut near her grave and lived there.

[75] Men who were noted for their loyalty to their masters in giving straight-forward advice.

The mendicant said: "I understand your meaning well. To comfort parents and to correct the mistakes of the king are, indeed, marks of filial piety and loyalty. Though unworthy, I am nevertheless different from birds and animals; therefore, my heart is about to burst from being unable to forget these duties. My parents have reared me with the utmost care. When I reflect upon them, I feel that their merits are as high as the five mountains, and my obligation toward them deeper than the four [main] rivers [of China]. This thought penetrates my skin and bone. Who can forget his obligation to his parents? It is difficult to return the favors that I have received from them, for their extent is boundless. When I read such poems as *Nan-kai* and *Liao-e*,[76] I feel ashamed and sad. At the sight of a crow I am touched;[77] at the thought of an otter my heart is broken.[78] What I am afraid of is that, before I am ready, my parents may pass away. [As is said in *Chuang Tzu*,] a carp lying in a wheel rut needs water at once if it is to survive; it is too late to bring the waters of a great river to a fish once it has been exposed in a fish store. Because [Li Li of] Wu did not give the ruler of Hsü his sword, he was required to stand before his tomb.[79] With graying hair, my parents approach the grave. I am at a loss to know what to do in return for their favors. Time flies like an arrow and their lives get shorter and shorter. We do not have any savings, the walls are collapsing, the roof is falling in. My two elder brothers have already died and, to my sorrow, the fortunes of all our relatives are in decline. From morning till night, month after month, I have had no other recourse than to weep and to lament. Should I look for a position, I would find no master who would recognize me. And while I ponder over my difficul-

[76] The title *Nan-kai* is given in the *Odes*, but the poem itself is missing. A *Nan-kai* composed later appears in *Wen hsüan* XIX; it is a poem which emphasizes the filial duties of sons toward their parents. *Liao-e* is a poem which occurs in the *Odes*; its theme is the lamentation of a filial son who cannot serve his parents.

[77] It is said that a crow feeds its parents.

[78] An otter is said to offer fish to its ancestors.

[79] On his mission to the north, Li Li of Wu passed the country of Hsü and met its ruler. At that time the ruler was attracted by Li's sword but did not verbally express his desire. Li, however, understood the ruler's mind, but as he was on duty did not give him his sword. On the way back from his mission, Li again passed by the country of Hsü only to find that the ruler had already passed away. He offered the sword to the tomb of the ruler. The account appears in the *Historical Records* of Ssu-ma Ch'ien.

ties, my parents wait for my support. I mourn the inescapable situation in which I find myself; I can neither advance nor retreat. No matter how I struggle to wriggle out of my predicament, I cannot. I am at a loss. Therefore, to convey my feelings I have composed this poem:

> Even if I wish to plow, I lack the physical strength;
> In seeking for a master, I lack the wit of Ning.[80]
> If lacking talent I assume a job, then I insult the office;
> If I get a stipend without virtue, I do harm.
> To be paid for blowing the flute when I do not know how to play
>   is not right; [81]
> Only in Chou indeed were proper music and teaching known.
> Even Confucius, while seeking employment, spent no peaceful days;
> What rule should such an ignorant person as I follow?
> The desire to advance is hampered by lack of talent,
> Yet retreat is made an impossible circumstance.
> So caught between advancing and retreating,
> What else can I do but lament?"

After having written down the poem, he recited it slowly in a low voice. Then he said:

"I have heard that with great effort a small amount of filial piety is possible, but that great filial piety is almost unattainable. Think of T'ai-po who joined a group of barbarians after shaving his hair,[82] and the bodhisattva who stripped himself of his clothing and offered his body to a hungry tiger. Both of them caused their parents to fall to the ground in sorrow, and their relatives to cry to the skies in lamentation. Who can surpass these two in having harmed the bodies which were given them by their parents and in causing their relatives to mourn? According to what you have said, neither was filial to his parents. T'ai-po, however, is called the most virtuous of men, and the bodhisattva, the Enlightened Noble One. Therefore, as long as one conforms to the right way, it is not necessary to demand of him minor things. Was it not an act of great filial piety that Maudgalyāyana [a disciple of the Buddha] saved his mother from the world of hungry

---

[80] See above, n. 36.

[81] King Hsüan of Ch'i retained several hundred flute players at his court, as he liked to hear flute concerts. The next king liked flute solos, however, and asked the players to play singly; many of the players then fled.

[82] It is said that Wu T'ai-po of Chou did this in order to hand over the sovereignty to his younger brother.

ghosts, or that rich Naśa helped to remove the torments of his father
who was suffering in hell? Are they not good examples from which
to learn? Though I am a fool, I have been studying the right teaching
and at the same time appreciate and long for the good influences transmitted from olden times. I pray for the prosperity of the country and
endeavor to make my parents happy. All my efforts to bring about
success and to give happiness to my parents are no more than acts of
filial piety and loyalty. You, however, know only how to exert physical
labor to serve others and how to bow low to render homage; you do
not know that good deeds, like those of Yü Kung,[83] will bring success
to one's posterity, and that bad deeds, like those of Yen Yen-nien,[84]
even if one climbs to a high position, will end in the reverse of filial
piety. Your idea is inferior, indeed! I shall tell you in more detail later,
as what I have just said is not sufficient.'

The Buddhist mendicant lived up to his principles. Not being obliged
to his father or elder brothers and having no contact with his relatives,
he wandered throughout the country like duckweed floating on water
or dry grass blown by the wind. At dawn, when the brightness of the
Milky Way began to fade, he suffered from unbearable hunger as the
provisions in his cave ran out. His pots and pans were filled with dust
and covered by mold. Finally he thought it best to go to a village
where food was abundant; for it is written in Buddhist texts that living
beings depend on food, and a non-Buddhist book says that it is of
primary importance to get food and of secondary importance to study.
Therefore, he left his cave in the pine grove for the city. Following the
custom of Buddhist mendicants, he immediately started to beg. As he
had no novice accompanying him, he stood alone in front of the gate
of Tokaku's house with the scriptures in his hand. He happened to
hear the arguments of Confucianist Kimō and Taoist Kyobu. He
thought to himself:

"What they are thinking of is nothing but worldly gain, fame, and at
most the extension of the span of their own lives. They are fighting
with bodies that are as momentary as lightning; bound in the prison of

[83] Because Yü Kung of Han was a fair official at a provincial prison, his good
deeds were rewarded by the prosperity enjoyed by later generations of his family.
[84] Yen Yen-nien was a merciless governor of Ho-nang. His mother in sorrow
anticipated the retribution which might result from her son's misconduct.

the four types of birth,[85] they cherish dreamlike ideas and sensations.[86] They try to build castles of the imagination in the psychophysical domain [87] and to rally their bubblelike forces in the transitory material world.[88] Their soldiers wear helmets of cobwebs, ride on horses that are really insects that subsist on a diet of mosquitoes' eyebrows, and rally their forces by beating drums which are covered with the skins of lice. They indicate the whereabouts of their troops with flags made of mosquitoes' wings. Waving the halberds of egoism and the swords of little learning, held aloft by arms that are as fragile as a column of frost, they fight on a ghostly battlefield. In short, theirs is a fight of greedy stories, using arguments that are entirely secular."

Thus, with his eyes wide open, he listened attentively to their arguments. Kimō and Kyobu each claimed that he was in the right and that the other was wrong.

The mendicant then thought: "Their arguments are indeed miserable; they have no more strength in them than a drop of water. Their imaginations are like a tiny torch which illumines only a small area. Yet, they argue enthusiastically. But how much more qualified am I, the son of Buddha, to discuss these things. I am able to crush their idiocies, even though they pretend to be armed with sharp battle-axes that have the awesome power of a fierce tiger or panther. I know their attempts are as futile as a grasshopper's leap to the sun."

Thereupon, sharpening the sword of wisdom, letting flow the springs of eloquence, donning the armor of patience, riding the horse of compassion, the mendicant neither too hastily nor too slowly stepped into the discussion. He was neither overwhelmed by his opponents nor afraid of them. Sometimes he discreetly stayed out of the argument; at other times he was extremely active in it. At last he sent an envoy urging his opponents to surrender. Their generals were frightened and their soldiers had lost their morale. They yielded to unconditional sur-

[85] Born out of 1) the uterus; 2) an egg; 3) humidity; 4) by transformation.

[86] "Ideas and sensations" is literally "eighteen inns" in the text. "Eighteen inns" refer to the eighteen realms (*dhātu*) of Buddhism: the six senses; the six sense objects; and the awareness corresponding to the six sense organs.

[87] This is a free translation of five *skhanda*, the constituents of a sentient being —form, sensation, conception, volition, and consciousness.

[88] "Material world" is a free translation of the Four Great Elements, the components of the material world—earth, water, fire, and wind.

render and thus avoided unnecessary bloodshed. However, they were reluctant really to change their views, whereupon the mendicant patted them on the head, and with tears in his eyes, said to them in a sympathetic tone:

"The small fish in a puddle does not know the great fish that is thousands of miles long; the little bird flying around a fence does not know the roc that can fly 90,000 miles.[89] Likewise, the stupid people living by the sea believe that there could not possibly be a tree as large as a fish, and the fools living in the mountains wonder whether there could be a fish as large as a tree. Unless one is as sharp-eyed as Li Chu, one cannot distinguish an object as minute as the tip of a hair; unless one is as keen-eared as Tzu Yeh [depicted in the *Spring and Autumn of Mr. Lü*], one cannot distinguish the subtle differences in the sounds of various bells. What a difference there is between those who can see and those who cannot see, between a fool and a wise man! While I was listening to your arguments, I had the impression that you were trying to chisel a statue out of ice or to draw a picture upon water. Your efforts are futile; how meaningless they are! Here the question is not whether Kimō's legs are as short as those of a duck, or whether Kyobu's legs are as long as those of a crane; such arguments are completely beside the point.

"You have not yet heard the teaching of the Buddha, the King of the Enlightened Ones! Let me summarize his teaching for you. But first I should like you to reflect upon the mirror of Emperor [Shih Huang] of Ch'in which reveals falsehood in people. You must recognize the errors of your beliefs. With courage, face the true teaching directly; do not be like Yeh Kung who liked to paint dragons but ran away when he saw a real dragon. Do not be subjective as were the blind men who described an elephant. Now you should study the teaching of the Buddha, whose voice is as powerful as a lion's roar. Mānavaka and Kāśyapa[90] are both my friends. With pity for your ignorance, my teacher sent them; however, considering your inferior capacities, only the superficial aspects of the doctrine of yin and yang were revealed

[89] The great fish and huge bird refer to those mentioned in *Chuang Tzu*.

[90] It is said that Buddha sent his disciples Mānavaka and Kāśyapa to the East and that they became Confucius and Lao Tzu respectively. This is a popular story created by Chinese Buddhists in order to show the superiority of Buddhism over Confucianism and Taoism.

by the Buddha through these two disciples. He did not explain the principles of the time distinction of the past, present, and future and their interdependent relations. But each of you clings to his particular way and argues in support of it; yours is all an illusion."

Hearing this, Kyobu said: "Your appearance differs from that of other people: you have not a single hair on your head, and are carrying many things with you. Whose disciple and whose son are you, and from what country and state do you come?"

The mendicant laughed and said: "In the triple world [91] there is no permanent residence; there is no fixed place in the world of transmigration. Sometimes my home is in heaven; sometimes, in hell. Sometimes I may be your wife or your son; at other times, your father or your mother. Sometimes the Tempter King is my teacher and heretics, my friends. Ghosts, birds, and animals may be our parents, children, or wives. From the beginning to the present, there has been no such thing as first and second. How can there be a fixed state of existence from the present back to the very beginning! Turning like a circle or a wheel, beings transmigrate by changing their forms and states of being. Your hair may be completely gray, but it does not necessarily mean that you are my elder brother. My sidelocks may resemble a [dark] cloud, but this does not necessarily indicate that I am the younger brother. From the beginningless beginning, you and I have been transmigrating continuously without stopping in any fixed life. Therefore, essentially speaking, I have no permanently fixed birthplace or parents. However, in this present temporal existence, the visionlike being you see before you is residing at a bay in Japan, where a huge camphor tree spreads its shadow.[92] Having yet to attain what I am searching for, I have already reached the age of twenty-four." [93]

Kyobu was surprised when he heard these words and asked: "What is heaven and what is hell? Why do you carry so many objects with you?"

The mendicant replied: "If you do evil, the ox- and horse-headed demons of hell appear as a matter of course and punish you; if you do

[91] The world of desire, form, and non-form.

[92] This may well be the birthplace of Kūkai.

[93] The age at which Kūkai wrote the major part of the *Indications*. It is evident that it was written when Kūkai was twenty-four and not eighteen as some sources claim.

good, golden and silver pavilions immediately gather and you are offered ambrosial nectars. The thing that is difficult is to change your heart. There are no fixed heavens or hells. At first I, too, was perplexed and had doubts just as you do now. However, recently I met a good teacher who awakened me from the illusions which had continued from my previous existences.

"The original vows of Shakyamuni Buddha, who is my teacher, were profound. He manifested himself on this earth for eighty years; with boundless compassion, he began the work of salvation of others when he was about thirty years old. Those who were fortunate, not only humans but also serpent gods and others, received his nectarlike instructions and the promise that they would be enlightened in the future. Those who were unfortunate, on the other hand, regardless of their social standing, were unable to realize the taste of this excellent teaching, as they never could awaken from their conditioning under false doctrines. Therefore, the compassionate Buddha, on his last day on earth, instructed Maitreya, the virtuous Mañjuśrī, and others, saying that Maitreya would be the Buddha of the future, and that other disciples should assist him and devote themselves to the salvation of sentient beings. Thereupon, the Bodhisattva Mañjuśrī, the great Kāśyapa, and the others sent a message to all countries, declaring that Maitreya would assume the throne of the kingdom of the true teaching. When I heard this message, I made all necessary preparations and started out at once for the Tuṣita Heaven where Maitreya resides. But the path is far from human habitations and is filled with difficulties; there are many crossroads and the way is not well defined. Some followers of the teaching sink in the mud along the way and cannot free themselves from it. Others go ahead riding on a horse or wagon. This is the reason why I keep many small articles with me so that they may help me in my progress. My provisions, however, have run out and I have lost my way; that is why I am standing at your gate begging help to continue my trip."

At this point the mendicant resolutely composed a rhyme-prose entitled "Transiency," in which he illustrated the principle that one gains retribution according to one's deeds. He recited it for Kimō in a voice as beautiful as the sound of a small golden bell tinkling at the end of a stick, or of two golden balls striking gently together:

Towering Mount Sumeru,[94] which reaches almost to the Milky Way, will be reduced to ashes by the fires of the last day of earth. The oceans which reach as far as the distant skyline will also disappear when exposed to the seven suns at the end of this epoch. The infinite heaven and earth will be liquidated and the round firmament will likewise be burned and destroyed. Existence even in heaven is as transient as lightning, and the period on earth of a Taoist immortal even with his extended span is as short as a clap of thunder. How much shorter, then, for human beings who are not endowed with diamondlike bodies but whose flesh is as insubstantial as tiles or pebbles! The Five Psychophysical Constituents [95] which form us are illusions like the image of the moon reflected on water; the Four Great Elements [96] that constitute the natural world are as transitory as vapors of hot air. Man runs about within the circle of the Twelve Links of Causation,[97] which characterizes this life of ignorance, like a monkey leaping from branch to branch. The Eight Sufferings [98] bring forth anxiety and give pain to the innermost heart. The flames of greed, hatred, and stupidity burn day and night, and the thicket of the 108 defilements [99] flourishes throughout the four seasons.

Our fragile body is easily dispersed, like particles of dust in the wind or flower petals in the spring. When the time comes, our temporal life passes away like leaves carried off by the winds of autumn. A beautiful girl soon sinks into the world of the underground; even an emperor rises to the sky like smoke. The slender eyebrows of a beautiful lady vanish into the clouds like mist; her white teeth decay and disappear as if they were dew. The pretty eyes of an exquisite girl become two small swamps on which the moss floats. The ears, adorned by jewels, become a valley where the wind blows through the pine trees. Her pink cheeks become a resting place for flies and her red lips, food for crows. A coaxing smile can no longer be seen on a skeleton exposed to the wind and rain. Who would approach a decayed body, even though while alive it had been the most coquettish of maidens? Her rich black hair is scattered and tangled among flood-swept thickets, and deep in the grass her slender white arms rot. Her fragrance has vanished with the wind. From the openings of her body, stinking fluids pour forth. Your dearest wife

[94] The center of the universe in Indian myth.   [95] See above, n. 87.

[96] Earth, water, fire, and wind. Cf. above, n. 88.

[97] See Part Two, p. 70, n. 20.

[98] Suffering derived from birth, old age, disease, death, separation from loved ones, meeting with hated ones, not being able to obtain what one wants, and passion.

[99] In Buddhism, it is thought that a man has a hundred and eight defilements.

and your children are as unreal as the nymph whom King Sung of
Ch'u met in his dream;[100] a treasure house filled with jewels may
disappear in an instant, like the jade that Cheng Chiao-fu received
from the two celestial girls.[101] The pleasant wind blowing through
the pine groves strikes against the collar of the dead man; but where
are the ears that once enjoyed its sounds? The bright moon shines
on the once beautiful face, but the awareness that in the past took
delight in the glory of the moon is gone. Seen in this manner, we
cannot appreciate a graceful thin dress; our usual adornments are no
more than vines twisting in the fields. Palaces with red and white
walls will not remain unchanged. The tombs on which the plants
grow—these are our lasting abodes. Beloved wives and children
cannot see each other once they are in the quiet graves. Intimate
friends cannot chat together joyously once they are buried in the
desolate graveyard. Alone one must lie beneath the shade of the
tall pine trees in a remote grave deep under the grass; the only voices
that can be heard are the chatterings of birds. Then many thousands
of worms will crawl upon the body and wild dogs will rush in to
devour it. Even a man's wife and children will not be able to bear
the smell and will leave; his relatives will cover their faces and escape.
Alas! Even the body of the charming girl, who enjoyed eating all
kinds of delicious dishes, will turn into the urine and feces of dogs
and birds. The body of the beautiful girl adorned in fashionable
attire in various colors is burned by the fire at cremation. No longer
can one roam in the garden in spring and forget about the troubles of
the world; no longer can one feast beside the pond in autumn. Alas!
Whenever I read P'an An-jen's poem,[102] or hear the sad melody of
the song about Princess Po,[103] I feel depressed.

The storm of impermanence does not overlook even the Taoist.
The demon which deprives men of their lives does not discriminate
between noble and base. One cannot buy eternal life with wealth or
be kept alive by secular power. No matter how much of the elixir
of life one may drink, nor how deeply one may inhale the exquisite
incense that recalls the departed soul, one cannot prolong one's
life even for a second. Who can escape from going to that land that
lies deep underground?

Once a corpse rots in the grass, it can no longer be restored to its

[100] King Sung composed a rhyme-prose about his encounter with a celestial
girl.

[101] Cheng met two celestial girls and received from them a piece of jade. When
he had walked sixty or seventy steps away, he found that the jade had disappeared; when he looked back, the girls had also disappeared.

[102] P'an An-jen composed a moving poem lamenting his wife's death.

[103] The widow Princess Po of Lu threw herself into the flames.

original state. The departed spirit cannot escape from being boiled in an iron pot. Once in hell, the departed one may at times be thrown on a steep mountain of swords and shed much blood; at times he may suffer from the excruciating pain of a high mountain of spears piercing his breast. Sometimes he is run over by a flaming wagon wheel which bears the weight of many thousands of stones; and at other times he is made to sink into a bottomless river of ice. Sometimes he is forced to drink boiling water, or to swallow molten iron, or he is roasted in roaring flames. In these circumstances he can obtain nothing to drink, let alone even hear drink mentioned. He has no way of getting even the tiniest morsel of food. Lions, tigers, wolves open wide their mouths and leap at him with watering lips; the horse-headed devils, eyes wide in anticipation, come seeking him out. Though he may raise desperate cries for help to heaven, he finds no response and his chances for pardon decrease each night. An appeal to the King of Hell is useless; the king has no sympathy at all. Even if he wants to call his wife and children, he has no means of doing so. Even if he wants to redeem his wrong doings by the payment of riches, he has not a single gem in his possession. Even if he wants to escape, the walls are too high to climb. How terribly painful it is! Where may one find a man skilled in imitating the cry of a rooster so that he can help open the gate of hell? Where may one find a man who is good at stealing so that one can escape from the swords of punishment in hell? [104] However much one tries, there is no way of escaping. Once you fall into hell, repentance is of no value; you will forever repeat your cries in vain. Alas! If you do not make an effort to emancipate yourselves now, and if you once fall into the hell of suffering, however much you may lament and be tormented, there will be no one to help you. Exert yourselves; do your best while you are on this earth.

Kimō and the others were filled with anguish and their hearts were about to burst with terror. Their stomachs burned, although they had swallowed no fire, and their breasts felt as if pierced, although no swords had been thrust through them. They beat their breasts, cried, and rolled on the ground. Looking up, they appealed to heaven in their sorrow. They acted as if bereft of their parents or wives. One fainted out of dread, the other, out of grief. Thereupon, the mendicant

---

[104] Meng Ch'ang-chün bribed his way out of a predicament with a white fox fur, stolen by a retainer who was a skilled thief. When he came to a barrier, he found that the gate was closed. Among his retainers was a man who was good at imitating a rooster's cry. He crowed, so that the guards thought it was time to open the gate. Thus Meng Ch'ang-chün was able to escape.

took up a jar and sprinkled water on their faces after he had purified it with a sacred formula. In a little while they recovered consciousness but, as though drugged, they spoke no words. They were like Liu Hsüan-shih who lay in a grave,[105] or like Kao-tsung in mourning.[106]

Some while later, they knelt on the ground with tears in their eyes, bowing low with reverence, and said:

"We have been playing with worthless tiles and pebbles and have been absorbed in petty pleasures. We were like insects that eat bitter leaves but are unaware of their bitterness, or like the worms in the privy that do not notice the foul smell. We were like blind men crossing a dangerous road, or riders of a lame donkey in the dark. We did not know where we were going and to where we might fall. Because of your compassionate instruction, we now realize that our ways have been shallow and worthless. We deeply regret our past and shall try to do our best to enter the right path. O merciful and venerable one, please show us the right way!"

The mendicant replied: "Indeed it is fortunate that you have repented before you went too far. Now I will tell you of the origins of suffering in this life of transmigration and of the bliss of Nirvana. On these points the Duke of Chou and Confucius did not speak, nor did Lao Tzu and Chuang Tzu preach. Even the followers of Hinayana do not know about the attainment of bliss. Only the bodhisattvas who are destined to be Buddhas in the next stage can obtain and enjoy it. Listen well. I will summarize the essential points and show them to you."

Kimō and the others came down from their seats and said: "Yes, we will compose ourselves and listen to you attentively."

The mendicant opened his innermost heart, and with flowing eloquence narrated the essence in a rhyme-prose entitled "The Ocean of Transmigration," and, in addition, showed them how to attain great enlightenment:

> The ocean of transmigration is limitless, surrounding the furthermost limits of the triple world. It is without end, encompassing all the four continents. It gives breath to all and regulates all. By

[105] He stayed in a grave for three years without speaking after he had drunk strong wine.

[106] Kao-tsung of Yin is said to have remained silent for three years after his father had died.

emptying its enormous stomach, it absorbs many rivers; with its huge mouth, it sucks in many lakes and ponds. Huge waves strike incessantly with relentless force against the hills, and billows roar constantly against the capes. The sound of stones crushing against each other in the sea rumbles day and night like thunder. Within its waters grotesque objects are produced, monstrous creatures grow, and strange beings abound.

Among them are scaly fishes filled with hatred, stupidity, and extreme greed. Their heads and tails are endlessly long, and they seek constantly after food, with their fins raised, tails striking, and their mouths open. When they swallow a billow, the boat of nongreed is smashed, and its sail vanishes from sight. When they spew forth spray, the rudder of the boat of compassion is broken and all the people on it killed. Swimming and diving haphazardly, they are filled with avarice and dishonesty. Their greed being as deep as a valley, they fail to consider the inevitable later harms. Like mice or silkworms, they gnaw at everything, having no sympathy or regard for others. They forget completely the retribution that will afflict them for endless aeons in the future; they look forward only to acquiring honor and prosperity while alive.

Then again there are some birds that by nature indulge in flattery, crookedness, abuse, rudeness, talkativeness, inquisitiveness, adulation, and bad behavior. They fly far away from the right path and rush to seek pleasure. On the beach of the Four Erroneous Views,[107] they scream imprecations; they flap their wings in the lake of the Ten Evils,[108] picking at innocent water chestnuts and clean greens. Looking up, they try to ward off *feng* and *luan* [109] by shouting at them, fearing that their food may be stolen. Yet they are entirely ignorant of the minds of these great birds. Looking down, they catch rats and dogs, crying loudly all the while. Sometimes they fly about and sometimes they screech hideously, always hunting for immediate gain. They feel pain at times and some of them die, but they never think of the awful pains of the future. They do not stop to think that on the slope of Mount Yen-men [110] the nets are set, and that in the lake of K'un-ming [111] the sticky snares are hidden. Nor do they consider that they might be shot at, their necks broken, and their blood shed.

Also in the ocean of transmigration, there live various animals

[107] Consideration of transiency as eternity, anxiety as bliss, nonsubstantiality as substantiality, and impurity as purity.

[108] Killing, stealing, committing adultery, lying, using exaggerated speech, slandering, equivocating, coveting, giving way to anger, and holding biased views.

[109] Mythical auspicious birds, in Chinese belief.   [110] In northern China.

[111] Southwest of Ch'ang-an.

that are arrogant and ill-tempered, abusive and jealous. Praising
themselves and criticizing others, they are dissipated and
undisciplined, arbitrary, shameless, unfaithful, compassionless, and
adulterous. Having wrong views, they go to extremes of hatred
and attachment; filled with passion, they engage in killing and
quarreling. Some of these animals may have similar shapes but
differing minds; there are numerous kinds with a variety of
names. Some have sawlike nails and chisel-like teeth and eat grain,
always looking around with the glittering eyes of a tiger. Roaring
like a lion, they roam day and night in the mountains and valleys.
Other creatures that encounter them fall into a faint and their
brains and intestines are crushed. Those who see them from a
distance cover their eyes in horror. These creatures gather from
the topmost heaven to the lowest hell. In certain areas they line up
like the teeth of a comb or like houses ranged side by side along
the seashore. No matter how skilled a man might be in describing,
he would fail completely should he attempt to depict such scenes.

Therefore, the small boat bearing the Five Precepts [112] must be
made to float to the shore where the demons abide, and the wagon
carrying the Ten Precepts [113] must be drawn to the regions where
the devils dwell. Unless a man gives rise to the excellent aspiration
to attain enlightenment in the evening and seek after the result of
enlightenment in the morning, he cannot approach the grand
Dharmakaya [114] and break through the vast ocean of transmigration.
Borne on the raft of the Six Paramitas,[115] he should cross to the
other side. He should cross the waves of passion on the ship of the
Noble Eightfold Path,[116] using the mast of effort and the sail of
meditation, with the armor of patience for protection from thieves,
and the sword of wisdom for defense against enemies. Whipping
the horse of the Seven Means [117] to attain enlightenment, he should
gallop away from the ocean of transmigration and transcend the
clamorous dust-filled world. Then as a token of predicted future
enlightenment, he will receive the gem hidden in the topknot of the
Universal Monarch, as did Śāriputra and the Nāga girl, who offered

[112] Non-killing, non-stealing, not committing adultery, not telling lies, and
abstinence from intoxicating beverages.

[113] Opposite of the Ten Evils; see above, n. 108.

[114] The ultimate Reality, the unconditioned Absolute, personified.

[115] Charity, morality, patience, effort, meditation, and wisdom.

[116] One of the basic doctrines of Buddhism by which one can approach final
deliverance: right views, right thinking, right speech, right action, right livelihood,
right effort, right mindfulness, and right concentration.

[117] Contemplation, choosing the correct doctrine, effort, joy, repose, samadhi,
and equanimity.

her necklace to the Buddha.[118] Soon he will pass through the ten stages of attaining enlightenment. The stages may be many, but the required disciplines are not difficult to fulfill. Meanwhile, he will overcome all obstacles and attain Suchness (*tathatā*) and upon reaching enlightenment will be called the Lord, the Buddha. Then he will abide in the principle of unity, with his mind freed from discriminations; by virtue of his wisdom shining like four mirrors,[119] he will be detached from both the abuse and the praise of the world. Transcending the phenomenal world, he will be immutable. Knowing neither increase nor decrease, he will be tranquil and serene, rising above the three divisions of time.[120] How magnificent and splendid will he be! Not even the Yellow Emperor, the sage king Yao, and Fu Hsi will be worthy of tending his footgear, nor will the Universal Monarch, Indra, Brahmā, and the rest be worthy to serve as his footmen. No matter how much abuse the devils and heretics may heap on him, it will be in vain, and no matter how much praise the disciples of the Buddha and those who have attained enlightenment by themselves may offer him, it will still be inadequate.

Nevertheless, the Four Vows [121] have not been realized as yet; the beloved, only son [mankind] is sunk deep in the trough. When [the Dharmakaya Buddha] thinks of his only son, he is downhearted, but in his benevolence he thinks of a means to save his son. Thereupon, manifesting himself in numberless forms in countless places, he reveals himself as a man [Shakyamuni Buddha] who follows the path to enlightenment and leads people to Nirvana. Showing his majestic dignity, appearing on the paths which people frequent, and exhibiting countless miracles, he sends his message all over the world.

Then he waits for all beings to come to him. Riding on the wind or the clouds they come, as numerous as the raindrops from heaven or the particles of spray from a fountain on earth. They come from filthy places and clean places, like clouds and like smoke. Gods, demons, monks, nuns, and lay followers come continually. Hymns,

[118] Predictions that Śāriputra and the Nāga (serpent) girl would be the future Buddhas appear in the *Lotus Sutra*. After the Nāga girl had offered the Buddha a priceless necklace, she was transformed into a man and later attained Buddhahood. т9, p. 35c.

[119] In *The Awakening of Faith* the characteristics of enlightenment are discussed with analogies to four types of mirror. See *The Awakening of Faith*, pp. 42–43.

[120] Past, present, and future.

[121] Salvation of all beings, cessation of all defilements, mastery of the doctrines, and attainment of enlightenment.

drums, and bells resound, and heaven and earth are filled with
fluttering flowers, the luster of gems, and the sound of horses and
wagons. They throng so closely together that they step on each
other's feet, and are obliged to draw in their arms and shoulders to
make enough room, yet they never fail to be courteous to each
other. With reverence and sincerity, they concentrate their minds.

Then the Buddha, preaching in a language which can be
understood by all, crushes their illusions. He throws the entire
world into another universe and reduces Mount Sumeru to a poppy
seed. Pouring a rain of nectar, he admonishes and guides them; he
gives them the food of joy, the doctrine that contains wisdom,
and the method of moral discipline. They celebrate peace on earth,
saying that the Emperor of Truth will come and all will be
awakened. They enjoy themselves so much that they forget the
existence of the Emperor, the Buddha. This is the place where all
sentient beings from innumerable worlds gather in reverence. This
is the noblest and the best capital, the source of ultimate value. Who
can match the Buddha, the grandest and the loftiest of all!

"Though what I have said is but the smallest part of the teachings
of my master the Buddha, now it should be evident to you that the
petty seeking for longevity of Taoism and that dusty breeze of the
secular world, Confucianism, are not worthy of comparison. They are
not worthy to be spoken of in the same breath with Buddhism."

Kimō and the others were, while listening, at times frightened,
ashamed, sorrowful, or filled with laughter. Along with the development of the story, they changed their expressions—sometimes they
dropped their heads, and then again they lifted their faces. Finally they
said approvingly:

"We are fortunate to have met this great authority and to have
learned the supreme teaching which transcends the mundane world.
We had not heard this doctrine before, and perhaps we would not
again have had the opportunity to listen to it. If we had not met you,
we would still be occupied in greedy activities and would have fallen
into hell, the world of ghosts, or the world of beasts. Your instructions
have made us feel much relieved in both body and mind. We feel that
we are awakened, like worms stirred by thunder in the spring after the
long sleep of winter, or like the ice in the shade that starts to melt when
the sun rises. How superficial the teachings of Confucius and Lao Tzu

are! From now on we will observe faithfully your teaching with our whole beings—by writing it on the paper of our skins, with pens of bone, ink of blood, and the inkstone of the skull. Thus your teaching will be the boat and the wagon by which we may cross over the ocean of transmigration."

The mendicant said: "Please go back to your seats. I will compose a poem of ten rhymes clarifying the three teachings; recite it instead of singing popular songs." Then he made this poem:

> The light of the sun and moon breaks through darkness,
> And the three teachings illumine ignorance.
> Nature and desire vary from person to person,
> Treatment differs with each physician.
> Human duties were preached by Confucius;
> On learning them one becomes a high government official.
> Lao Tzu taught the creation by yin and yang;
> On receiving his instructions one can observe the world from the
>   tower of a Taoist temple.
> Most significant and profound is the teaching of the ultimate path
>   of Mahayana.
> It teaches the salvation of oneself and of others;
> It does not exclude even animals or birds.
> The flowers in the spring fall beneath the branches;
> Dew in autumn vanishes before the withered grass.
> Flowing water can never be stopped;
> Whirling winds howl constantly.
> The world of senses is a sea in which one well may drown;
> Eternity, Bliss, the Self, and Purity are the summits on which we
>   ultimately belong.
> I know the fetters that bind me in the triple world;
> Why should I not give up the thought of serving the court?

2

A MEMORIAL PRESENTING A LIST OF NEWLY IMPORTED SUTRAS AND OTHER ITEMS

(Shōrai mokuroku)

The report of Kūkai, a monk who studied the Dharma in T'ang China:

In the twenty-third year of Enryaku (804), I, Kūkai, as one of a number of students sent to study abroad by imperial order, sailed far away to a port tens of thousands of *ri* distant. In the last month of the same year, we arrived at Ch'ang-an. On the tenth day of the second month of the following year, in obedience to an imperial edict, I took up residence at the Hsi-ming Temple.

Thereafter, I visited Buddhist temples everywhere, calling on Buddhist teachers. I was fortunate enough to meet the acharya [master] of *abhiṣeka,* whose Buddhist name was Hui-kuo, of the Ch'ing-lung Temple. I regarded him as my main preceptor. This great priest was the disciple chosen to transmit the Dharma of the Master of the Tripiṭaka of Broad Wisdom, Pu-k'ung, of the Ta-hsing-shan Temple. He was well versed in the sutras and in the rules of discipline and had a thorough knowledge of the Esoteric Buddhist teachings. He was a defender of the Dharma and was esteemed the teacher of the nation. This great teacher eagerly desired to spread Buddhism and was deeply concerned about uprooting the sufferings of people.

This master granted me the privilege of receiving the Esoteric Buddhist precepts [1] and permitted me to enter the altar of *abhiṣeka*. Three times I was bathed in the *abhiṣeka* in order to receive the mantras and once to inherit the mastership. I learned directly from him whatever was left untaught and heard reverently from him whatever was new to me. I was fortunate enough, thanks to the compassion of the great master, a national teacher of distinguished merit, to learn the great twofold Dharma [2] and the yogic practices which use various sacred objects of concentration. This Dharma is the gist of the Buddhas and the quickest path by which to attain enlightenment. This teaching is as useful to the nation as walls are to a city, and as fertile soil is to the people. Thus, it is known that unfortunate ones are deprived of a chance even to hear the name of this teaching mentioned; the heavily defiled ones are unable to approach it. In India the Tripiṭaka Master Śubhākarasiṃha renounced his throne in order to practice it; in China the Emperor Hsüan-tsung (r. 713–55) forgot the savor of other things in the excess of his appreciation and admiration for it. Henceforth, in China, each successive emperor and his three highest ministers devoted themselves to it one after another; the four classes of believers [3] and tens of thousands of people respectfully started to learn it. The Esoteric Buddhist school has hence been called a dominant force. The Exoteric teachings were overwhelmed and paralyzed by it, being as imperfect as a pearl of which one half is missing.

When a pair of phoenixes are seen flying in harmony, people secretly look forward to the appearance of a sage king such as Yao or Shun. Whether the Dharma appears or remains concealed in the world depends upon the trend of the times. I have now imported the teachings of the Diamond Vehicle (Vajrayāna) contained in more than one hundred texts and in the dual mandalas, the pictorial presentations of the sacred assembly that is extensive as the sea. I have crossed the sea abounding with whales, though the billows were high and the ship drifted about in storms, and have returned safely to the domain of His Majesty. This is due to the effect of His Majesty's influence.

[1] See Part Two, p. 95, for a discussion on the Esoteric Buddhist precepts.
[2] The teachings of Esoteric Buddhism in terms of the Diamond and Matrix Realms.
[3] Monks, nuns, laymen, and laywomen.

The highest virtue of His Imperial Majesty is like that of heaven; [the name of] the Buddha, who is analogous to the sun, will rise higher and higher.[4] His Majesty is like a father of the people and an incarnation of the Buddha. Out of compassion for his people, he dips his feet in water;[5] he calls together those who are committed to the Buddha[6] and bestows robes upon them. That newly translated sutras have recently arrived from afar may be due to the fact that the emperor had newly ascended the throne, the pivot which regulates the movements of the cosmos. Or it may be because of the way the emperor graciously nurtures the seagirt world that paintings of the oceanlike assembly [mandalas] have come here across the sea. There seems to be a mysterious coincidence here; who but a sage knows why?

Though I, Kūkai, may deserve to be punished by death because I did not arrive punctually,[7] yet I am secretly delighted with my good luck that I am alive and that I have imported the Dharma that is difficult to obtain. I can hardly bear the feelings of fear and joy which alternate in my heart. I respectfully submit this memorial to the throne and entrust it to Takashina Mahito Tōnari of the senior sixth rank, upper grade, judge and senior secretary of Dazaifu. Also attached to it is a list of newly imported sutras and other items. Dishonoring by my haste the dignity of His Majesty, I am increasingly struck with a sense of awe.

Most respectfully,
Monk Kūkai
Twenty-second Day of the Tenth Month,
Daidō 1 (806)

[4] The implication is that under the patronage of the emperor, the name of Mahāvairocana Buddha, the Great Sun Buddha, will be greatly enhanced.

[5] To share the sufferings of farmers who toil in the rice paddies.

[6] Serious and dedicated Buddhist clergymen.

[7] Three interpretations are possible: that Kūkai came back too late to report his return to Emperor Kammu who sent him to China, for the emperor died about a half year before his return; that he could not be in time for the enthronement of the new emperor to whom he wrote this memorial; or that he returned too soon, for his original plan was to stay in China for twenty years. The last interpretation seems to be nearest to the truth; if so, he spent within two years the government stipend allocated for twenty years.

NEWLY TRANSLATED SUTRAS

[The titles of 142 works, mainly of Esoteric Buddhism, in 247 fascicles, are listed in the original.]

The sea of Dharma is of one flavor but has deep and shallow aspects in accordance with the capacity of the believer. Five Vehicles [8] can be distinguished, sudden and gradual according to the vessel. Among the teachings of sudden enlightenment, some are Exoteric and some, Esoteric. In Esoteric Buddhism itself, some aspects represent the source, others, the tributary. The teachers of the Dharma of former times swam in the waters of the tributary and hung on to the leaves, but the teaching transmitted to me now uproots the enclosure which blocks the source and penetrates it through and through. Why?

In ancient times Vajrasattva personally received the teaching from Mahāvairocana. Several centuries later it was transmitted to the Bodhisattva Nāgārjuna, who transmitted it to the Acharya Vajrabodhi (670–741), the Tripiṭaka Master, who for the first time taught the fivefold Esoteric Buddhist doctrine [9] in China during the K'ai-yüan era (713–41). Although the emperor himself revered the doctrine, Vajrabodhi could not spread it widely. Only through my spiritual grandfather [Pu-k'ung], the Acharya of Broad Wisdom, did it become popular. Pu-k'ung first received the transmission from Vajrabodhi, the Tripiṭaka Master, and moreover visited the Acharya Nāgabodhi in southern India and acquired completely the *Vajraśekhara Sutra* comprising eighteen divisions. After having studied thoroughly the Esoteric Buddhist teachings consisting of the doctrines of the Matrix, etc., he returned to China during the T'ien-pao era (742–56). At this time Emperor Hsüan-tsung first received *abhiṣeka* from him; the emperor revered him as his teacher. Since then Emperors Su-tsung (r. 756–62)

---

[8] Vehicle (*yāna*) means the teachings that carry sentient beings to their respective goals. They are vehicles for common men, celestial beings, śrāvakas, pratyekabuddhas, and bodhisattvas.

[9] The fivefold Esoteric Buddhist doctrine means the teachings given in the *Vajraśekhara Sutra* in which the Buddhas, Bodhisattvas, and others are classified under the five divisions—Buddha, Vajra, Ratna (jewel), Padma (lotus), and Karma (action). Vajrabodhi, who came from India to China in 720, first introduced the Esoteric Buddhist teachings belonging to the Diamond Realm.

and Tai-tsung (r. 763–79) have received the Dharma. The Shen-lung
Monastery was built within the imperial palace and everywhere in the
capital the altars for *abhiṣeka* were set up. The emperor and the government officials went to the altars to receive *abhiṣeka;* the four classes
of believers and the populace reverently learned the Esoteric Buddhist
teachings. This was the period when the Esoteric Buddhist school began to flourish and from this time on the practice of *abhiṣeka* was
widely adopted.

According to Exoteric Buddhist doctrines, one must spend three
aeons to attain enlightenment, but according to the Esoteric doctrines
one can expect sixteen great spiritual rebirths [within this life].[10] In
speed and in excellence, the two doctrines differ as much as one endowed with supernatural power differs from a lame donkey. It is sincerely hoped that those who reverently look to the good will have a
clear understanding of its import. The superiority of the doctrines and
the origins of the Dharma are as explained comprehensively in the *Wu-
pi-mi-i-kuei*,[11] in the *Piao-chih chi* of Pu-k'ung,[12] etc.

WORKS IN SANSKRIT

[The titles of 42 works written in Sanskrit, in 44 fascicles, are listed.]

Buddhism originated in India. In India and China, however, circumstances are quite different. The sound system as well as the script is
dissimilar. As a result, only through translations can we savor the refreshing breeze of Indian spirituality. The mantras, however, are mysterious and each word is profound in meaning. When they are trans-
literated into Chinese, the original meanings are modified and the long
and short vowels confused. In the end we can get roughly similar
sounds but not precisely the same ones. Unless we use Sanskrit, it is
hardly possible to differentiate the long and short sounds. The purpose
of retaining the source materials, indeed, lies here.

[10] To experience the samadhi of sixteen Bodhisattvas in the mandala of the
Diamond Realm.

[11] An Esoteric Buddhist text on practice, translated by Pu-k'ung. T1125.

[12] A collection of memorials of Pu-k'ung. T2120.

TREATISES, COMMENTARIES, ETC.

[The titles of 32 works, in 170 fascicles, are listed.]

The three lines of the diagrams in the *Book of Changes* contain the principles; their significance is given in the commentaries (*Shih-i*). If the summary of the application of the diagrams in the *Book of Changes* and the commentaries were missing, of what use would be the signs that appear on the back of the tortoise shell? The principles of the One Vehicle [13] are profound and the real meanings are at times quite different from what we may imagine them to be from the writings. Their subtle expressions are of little value unless treatises and commentaries are used. Though these works are bulky and troublesome to transport, my earnest desire was to bring them back and to assist in the understanding of the sacred scriptures.

BUDDHIST ICONIC OBJECTS

[Three Matrix Mandalas, two Diamond Mandalas, and the portraits of Vajrabodhi, Śubhākarasimha, Pu-k'ung, Hui-kuo, and I-hsing [14] are listed.]

The Dharma is beyond speech, but without speech it cannot be revealed. Suchness transcends forms, but without depending on forms it cannot be realized. Though one may at times err by taking the finger pointing at the moon to be the moon itself, the Buddha's teachings which guide people are limitless. Extraordinary feats which may dazzle another's eyes, however, are not valued at all. The Buddha's teachings are indeed the treasures which help pacify the nation and bring benefit to people.

Since the Esoteric Buddhist teachings are so profound as to defy expression in writing, they are revealed through the medium of painting to those who are yet to be enlightened. The various postures and mudras [depicted in mandalas] are products of the great compassion of the Buddha; the sight of them may well enable one to attain Buddha-

[13] The One Great Vehicle of Mahayana Buddhism, the teaching which enables all beings to attain Buddhahood.
[14] These five portraits have been preserved at the Tōji in Kyoto.

hood. The secrets of the sutras and commentaries are for the most part depicted in the paintings, and all the essentials of the Esoteric Buddhist doctrines are, in reality, set forth therein. Neither masters nor students can dispense with them. They are indeed [the expressions of] the root and source of the oceanlike assembly [of the Enlightened Ones, that is, the world of enlightenment].

RITUAL IMPLEMENTS

[*Vajras* and other items, eighteen in all; nine kinds are listed.]

He whose wisdom is infinite and whose enlightenment is peerless is called the Buddha. Since his wisdom is infinite, he is all-knowing and since his enlightenment is peerless, his skillful means of guiding people are immeasurable. Thus, with various approaches, he is able to embrace and transform those who slumber in the darkness of the long night of ignorance. The *vajra* and other implements are the gates through which one approaches the Buddha's wisdom and his Dharma. If one accepts them with reverence one will derive from them benefits without end, in that they vanquish a host of tempters from without and subdue passions from within. They are the point of departure for the attainment of wisdom. Skeptics should bear this in mind.

OBJECTS BESTOWED BY THE ACHARYAS

[Listed here are eight objects—relics of the Buddha, a Buddhist sculpture made of white sandalwood, etc.]

The eight objects listed above are those which were originally brought back by the Acharya Vajrabodhi from southern India and handed down to the acharya of the Ch'ing-lung Temple [Hui-kuo]. The teacher of the Ch'ing-lung Temple further deigned to bestow them upon Kūkai. These are the tokens of the transmission of the Dharma, the refuge of all sentient beings.

[In addition, there are listed five items, a stole, etc., which were given by Hui-kuo.]

During the sixth month of Enryaku 23 (804), I, Kūkai, sailed for China aboard Ship One in the party of Lord Fujiwara, envoy to the

T'ang court. By the eighth month we reached the coast of Fukien and by the end of the twelfth month arrived at Ch'ang-an, where we lodged at the official guest residence. The envoy and his retinue started home for Japan on the eleventh day of the third month, Enryaku 24 (805), but in obedience to an imperial edict, I alone remained behind in the Hsi-ming Temple where our Eichū (d. 816) [15] formerly had resided.

One day, while calling on the eminent Buddhist teachers of the capital, I happened to meet the abbot of the East Pagoda Hall of the Ch'ing-lung Temple, whose Buddhist name was the Acharya Hui-kuo. This great priest was the disciple chosen to transmit the Dharma from the Tripiṭaka Master of Broad Wisdom [Pu-k'ung] of the Ta-hsing-shan Temple. His virtue aroused the reverence of his age; his teachings were lofty enough to guide emperors. Three sovereigns who revered him were initiated by receiving abhiṣeka. The four classes of believers looked up to him for instruction in the Esoteric Buddhist teachings.

I called on the abbot in the company of five or six monks from the Hsi-ming Temple. As soon as he saw me he smiled with pleasure and joyfully said, "I knew that you would come! I have waited for such a long time. What pleasure it gives me to look upon you today at last! My life is drawing to an end, and until you came there was no one to whom I could transmit the teachings. Go without delay to the altar of abhiṣeka with incense and a flower." I returned to the temple where I had been staying and got the things which were necessary for the ceremony. It was early in the sixth month [16] then that I entered the altar of abhiṣeka for primary initiation. I stood before the Matrix Mandala and cast my flower in the prescribed manner. By chance it fell on the Body of Mahāvairocana Tathagata in the center. The master exclaimed in delight, "How amazing! How perfectly amazing!" He repeated this three or four times in joy and wonder. I was then given the fivefold abhiṣeka and received instruction in the grace (kaji) of the Three Mysteries. Next I was taught the Sanskrit formulas and ritual manuals for the Matrix Realm and learned the yogic practices which use various sacred objects of concentration to gain transcendental insight.

Early in the seventh month I stood before the Diamond Mandala

[15] A Japanese monk who studied in China before Kūkai.
[16] To be exact, it was on the thirteenth of this month. Cf. K.Z., II, 157.

and I was given once more the fivefold *abhiṣeka*. When I cast my flower it again fell on Mahāvairocana, and the abbot marveled as he had before. Also, early in the following month I received the *abhiṣeka* for the ordination into the mastership of the transmission of the Dharma. On this day I provided a feast for five hundred monks and made wide offerings to the four classes of believers. The dignitaries of the Ch'ing-lung Temple, Ta-hsing-shan Temple, and others all attended the feast, and everyone was delighted for my sake.

Then I received instruction in the mantras and mudras of the five divisions of the *Vajraśekhara Sutra* and spent some time learning Sanskrit and the Sanskrit hymns. The abbot informed me that the Esoteric Buddhist scriptures are so abstruse that their meaning cannot be conveyed except through art. For this reason he ordered the court artist Li Chen and about a dozen other painters to execute ten scrolls of the Matrix and Diamond Mandalas and assembled more than twenty scribes to make copies of the *Vajraśekhara Sutra* and other important Esoteric Buddhist scriptures. He also ordered the bronzesmith Chao Wu to cast fifteen ritual implements. These orders for the painting of religious images and the copying of the sutras were issued at various times.

One day the abbot told me: "Long ago, when I was still young, I met the great Tripiṭaka Master [Pu-k'ung]. From the first moment he saw me he treated me like his son, and on his visit to the court and his return to the temple I was as inseparable from him as his shadow. He confided to me, 'You will be the receptacle of the Esoteric Buddhist teachings. Do your best! Do your best!' I was then initiated into the teachings of both the Matrix and the Diamond and into the secret mudras as well. The rest of his disciples, monks and laity alike, studied just one of the two great teachings [Diamond and Matrix] or a yogic practice on one sacred object of concentration with the use of one mudra, but not all of them as I did. How deeply I am indebted to him I shall never be able to express.

"Now my existence on earth approaches its term, and I cannot long remain. I urge you, therefore, to take the mandalas of both realms and the hundred volumes of the teachings of the Diamond Vehicle, together with the ritual implements and these objects which were left to me by my master. Return to your country and propagate the teachings there.

"When you first arrived, I feared I did not have enough time left to teach you everything, but now I have completed teaching you, and the work of copying the sutras and making the images has also been finished. Hasten back to your country, offer these things to the court, and spread the teachings throughout your country to increase the happiness of the people. Then the land will know peace, and people everywhere will be content. In that way you will return thanks to the Buddha and to your teacher. That is also the way to show your devotion to your country and to your family. My disciple I-ming will carry on the teachings here. Your task is to transmit them to the Eastern Land. Do your best! Do your best!" These were his final instructions to me, kind and patient as always. On the night of the full moon, in the twelfth month of the past year, he purified himself in a ritual bath and, lying on his right side and making the mudra of Mahāvairocana, he breathed his last.

That night, while I sat in meditation in the Hall, the abbot appeared to me in his usual form and said, "You and I have long been pledged to propagate the Esoteric Buddhist teachings. If I am reborn in Japan, this time I shall be your disciple."

I have not gone into the details of all that he said but have given the general import of the acharya's instructions.

THREE SANSKRIT MANUSCRIPTS

The Tripiṭaka Master Prajñā told me: "I was born in Kashmir and was initiated into Buddhism while still young and went on a pilgrimage all over India. With the pledge to transmit the torch of the Dharma, I came to China. I wish to sail for Japan, but circumstances do not allow me to fulfill my intention. Take with you the new *Avataṃsaka Sutra* [17] and the *Ṣaṭ-Pāramitā Sutra*,[18] both of which I have translated, and these Sanskrit manuscripts. I sincerely hope that these will help create conditions [in which to propagate Buddhism] so that people will be saved." I will not itemize them as it is tedious.

The teachings of Buddhism are extensive and know no limit. In short, their purport is to offer two benefits: benefit to oneself, such as attain-

[17] T293.   [18] T261.

ing the effect of eternity and bliss; and benefit to others, such as re-
lieving them from the causes of suffering and from meaninglessness. A
mere wish to attain eternity and bliss is futile. A random effort to eradi-
cate suffering likewise will have little chance of success. One must make
efforts to attain both bliss and knowledge and must practice samadhi
and prajna side by side. Then one can relieve others from their sufferings and enjoy bliss for one's own sake. Many methods of samadhi are
known: some are sudden and others, gradual. To play with the sharp
sword of One Mind [19] is the Exoteric Buddhist teaching; to brandish
the *vajra* of the Three Mysteries is the Esoteric Buddhist teaching. If a
man takes pleasure in the Exoteric Buddhist teachings, he is bound to
spend a period as long as three aeons before he attains enlightenment;
but, if he commits himself to the Esoteric Buddhist teaching, he may
attain enlightenment quickly by means of sixteen spiritual rebirths [in
this life]. The most sudden among the sudden approaches is the Esoteric
Buddhist teaching. This is the reason why the Tripiṭaka Master Śubhākarasiṃha renounced the throne and became absorbed in it, and why
Emperor Tai-tsung, making himself humble, learned it and never grew
tired of it. Master Nāgabodhi is said to have lived eight hundred years.
A master of meditation, Ch'ung-hui,[20] refuted heretics and saved the
teaching from decline. In its suprarational functions no other teaching
surpasses this Dharma. Students who yearn to be awakened, listen to
this hitherto unheard of teaching.

> The Dharma knows neither appearing nor concealing;
> Depending on the individual it becomes manifest or hidden,
> Like a gem hidden in the ground difficult to obtain.
> If a man attains it he will open his spiritual eyes;
> To gain even a half stanza of the Dharma, we are told,
> A prince sacrificed his body, not to mention his treasures.
> The scriptures of the Dharma I have diligently copied;
> They have been brought back here a long way.
> May this great source of blessing be instrumental
> In pacifying the nation and in bringing prosperity to the people;
> May each and all be freed from their anxieties
> By listening to the teaching and by seeing the mandalas.

[19] Synonym for Suchness.
[20] This monk is known to have defended Buddhism against the attack directed
by the Taoist Shih-hua in the reign of Tai-tsung (763–80).

3

THE DIFFERENCE BETWEEN EXOTERIC AND ESOTERIC BUDDHISM

(Benkenmitsu nikyō ron)

There are three bodies [1] of the Buddha and two forms of Buddhist doctrine. The doctrine revealed by the Nirmanakaya Buddha [Shakyamuni Buddha] is called Exoteric; it is apparent, simplified, and adapted to the needs of the time and to the capacity of the listeners. The doctrine expounded by the Dharmakaya Buddha [Mahāvairocana] is called Esoteric; it is secret and profound and contains the final truth.

The sutras used in Exoteric Buddhism number in the millions. The collection is divided by some into ten and by others into fifty-one parts.[2] They speak of One, Two, Three, Four, and Five Vehicles.[3] In

---

[1] Trikāya. See Part Two, p. 84, n. 17.

[2] This unusual classification is based on a description given in a commentary to The Awakening of Faith (Shih-mo-ho-yen lun). Authorship of the commentary is attributed to one Nāgārjuna, about whom nothing is known. Kūkai used this commentary extensively in writing the Difference as well as other works. The author of the commentary is not the founder of the Mādhyamika school of Buddhism of second-century India. T32, p. 593a.

[3] One Vehicle—the universal teaching which enables all sentient beings to attain enlightenment; Two Vehicles—Mahayana and Hinayana; Three Vehicles —Śrāvakayāna, Pratyekabuddhayāna, and Bodhisattvayāna; Four Vehicles—Three Vehicles and Buddhayāna; and Five Vehicles—Three Vehicles, Vehicle for men, and that for heavenly beings.

discussing practices, they believe that the Six Paramitas [4] are the most important and explain that in order to attain enlightenment a period of three aeons is needed. The great Sage has explained these matters clearly.

According to the Esoteric *Vajraśekhara Sutra,* the Buddha, manifested in human form, preached the doctrines of the Three Vehicles for the sake of bodhisattvas who were yet to advance to the Ten Stages of Bodhisattvahood, for the followers of Hinayana, and for ordinary people; the Sambhogakaya Buddha taught the doctrine of One Vehicle for the bodhisattvas in the Ten Stages of Bodhisattvahood. Both of these teachings are Exoteric. The Dharmakaya Buddha, for his own enjoyment, with his own retinue,[5] preached the doctrine of the Three Mysteries. This is Esoteric. This doctrine of the Three Mysteries is concerned with the innermost spiritual experience of the Dharmakaya Buddha, and the bodhisattvas in the Ten Stages of Bodhisattvahood or even those who are nearly equal to the Buddha cannot penetrate it, much less the Hinayanists and ordinary people, who cannot cross its threshold. It is thus said in the *Shih-ti-ching lun* [6] and in the *Shih-mo-ho-yen lun* [7] that this experience is beyond their capacity. Also the *Ch'eng-wei-shih lun* [8] and the *Mādhyamika-kārikās* [9] deplore that it transcends words and thought determinations. Its transcendence is spoken of, however, from the viewpoint of those who have not yet been enlightened and not from the viewpoint of the enlightened ones. I shall give clear evidence for this in the following pages, on the basis of sutras and commentaries. It is hoped that those who aspire to attain enlightenment will understand their meaning clearly.

Being entangled in the net of Exoteric Buddhism, people wear themselves out like male goats dashing themselves against fences; being

---

[4] See *Indications,* n. 115.

[5] His retinue consists of those surrounding him in the mandalas, who are manifestations of Mahāvairocana himself. Thus, dialogues between Mahāvairocana and his own manifestations—Buddhas, Bodhisattvas, Devas, and others—are none other than a monologue in the form of a dialogue carried on by Mahāvairocana himself for his own enjoyment (*jiju hōraku*).

[6] The commentary on the *Daśabhūmika Sutra,* written by Vasubandhu and translated by Bodhiruchi. T26, p. 132b.

[7] The commentary on *The Awakening of Faith* attributed to Nāgārjuna. T32, p. 601c. Cf. n. 2, above.

[8] The commentary on the *Triṃsikā* translated by Hsüan-tsang. T31, p. 57b.

[9] T30, p. 24a.

blocked by the barriers of the Mahayana teachings of provisional nature,[10] they give up advancing further. They are exactly like those
who, wishing to rest there, believe in an illusory city,[11] or like children
who take a yellow willow leaf to be gold.[12] How can they hope to
preserve the glorious treasures which lie within themselves, numberless
as the sands of the Ganges? It is as if they were to discard ghee and
look for milk, or to throw away precious pearls and pick up fish eyes.
They are cut off from their Buddha-seed; they are victims of a mortal
disease before which even the King of Medicine would fold his hands in
despair, a disease for which even a rain of nectar would be of no avail.

If men and women once grasp the fragrance of this [Esoteric Bud-
dhism], they will have in their minds a clear understanding, as things
are reflected in the magic mirror of the Emperor of Ch'in, and the
differences between the provisional and the real doctrines will naturally
be resolved. Evidence to this effect is abundant in the sutras and commentaries, and I will reveal part of it in the hope of assisting beginners.

QUESTION: The transmitters of the Dharma in ancient times composed
extensive discourses advocating the six schools [13] and expounded the
Tripiṭaka so abundantly that the texts could not be stored even in a
large library, and people grew tired of opening them. Why then do
you bother to write this book? What is its worth?

ANSWER: There is much to be expressed; therefore, it should be
written. Everything transmitted by former masters is Exoteric Buddhist
teachings. Here I am concerned with the Esoteric Buddhist teaching
about which people have not had an adequate understanding. I should
like to compile, therefore, a handy guide book for your reflection,
quoting pertinent passages from sutras and commentaries.

[10] According to the T'ien-t'ai and Hua-yen doctrines, Mahayana is divided
into two types: provisional and real. The provisional does not hold that all
sentient beings will attain enlightenment. Here reference is made to the doctrine
of Yogācāra which recognizes a group of sentient beings, icchantika, the cursed
ones, who will never attain enlightenment.

[11] The story of the illusory city appears in the Lotus Sutra. The Buddha
showed the illusory city to a traveler who was unwilling to go farther in order to
encourage him and to arouse in him the energy to pursue the final goal, Nirvana.
T9, p. 25c.

[12] In the Nirvana Sutra a man who attaches himself to any Mahayana teaching
of provisional type is compared to a child who stops crying when given a
withered yellow leaf by his parents, which he takes for genuine gold. T12, p. 485c.

[13] Kusha, Jōjitsu, Hossō, Sanron, Ritsu, and Kegon.

QUESTION: What are the differences between the Exoteric Buddhist teachings and the Esoteric Buddhist teaching?

ANSWER: The teachings expounded by the Nirmanakaya Buddha in order to help others, responding to the needs of the time, are called Exoteric. What was expounded by the Dharmakaya Buddha for his own enjoyment, on his innermost spiritual experience, is called Esoteric.

QUESTION: The fact that the Nirmanakaya Buddha preached is agreed upon by all schools. As to the Dharmakaya Buddha, however, we understand that he is formless and imageless, that he is totally beyond verbalization and conceptualization, and that therefore there is no way of explaining him or showing him. Sutras and commentaries describe him in this way. Why do you now assert that the Dharmakaya Buddha preaches? What is your evidence for this?

ANSWER: Now and again the sutras and commentaries refer to this preaching. Misled by their biased preconceptions, people overlook these pertinent passages. Indeed, their meanings will be revealed only in accordance with the capacity of the reader: the same water may be seen as emerald by heavenly beings and as burning fire by hungry ghosts; the same darkness may be seen as light by nocturnal birds and as darkness by men.

QUESTION: If what you have said is really true and is given in the teachings of the Buddha, why have the former transmitters of the Dharma not discussed it?

ANSWER: The sermons of the Tathagata were delivered in accordance with the particular diseases in the minds of his audience; manifold remedies were provided, depending on their varied capacities. The sermons thus adapted to the capacity of his listeners were in many cases provisional and seldom final. When the bodhisattvas composed the commentaries, they wrote faithfully on the basis of the sutras which were provisional in nature. It is therefore said in the commentary on the *Daśabhūmika Sutra* written by Vasubhandu that "only the way to enlightenment can be talked about [and not the enlightenment it-self]," [14] and also in the commentary on *The Awakening of Faith* written by Nāgārjuna that "the perfect sea of enlightenment cannot be talked about." [15] These works were based on the [provisional] sutras and were not intended to advocate the final truth.

[14] *Shih-ti-ching lun.* T26, p. 132b.   [15] *Shih-mo-ho-yen lun.* T32, p. 601c.

The masters of the Dharma who transmitted the Exoteric Buddhist teachings interpreted the [passages of] profound significance [appearing in the Exoteric Buddhist texts] in the light of their shallow doctrines and failed to find any Esoteric import in them. Faithfully transmitting the Exoteric Buddhist teachings from master to disciple, they discussed Buddhism according to the tenets of their particular schools. They so eagerly supported their beliefs that they found no time to meditate on those [passages] which might have been disadvantageous to their doctrines. In the meantime, Buddhism had spread eastward in China and gradually gained a significant role there. The Buddhist texts translated from the time of Emperor Ming of the Later Han Dynasty to that of Empress Wu of the T'ang Dynasty were all Exoteric. During the reigns of Emperors Hsüan-tsung and Tai-tsung, when Masters Vajrabodhi and Pu-k'ung were active, the Esoteric Buddhist teaching flourished and its profound meaning was discussed enthusiastically. The new medicine had not long been in use, and the old disease was not yet cured. [The Chinese masters of Exoteric Buddhism]—even when they came across passages [of Esoteric significance] such as the statement in the *Lankāvatāra Sutra* that "the Dharmakaya Buddha preaches," [16] or in the *Ta-chih-tu lun* that "the Dharmakaya Buddha is endowed with an exquisite form" [17]—interpreted them according to their imagination or were governed by the professed doctrines of their schools. It was indeed a pity that these wise masters of ancient times failed to appreciate the taste of ghee [the final truth].

QUESTION: If this is the case, in which sutras and commentaries are the differences between the Exoteric and the Esoteric Buddhist teachings given?

[To this question, Kūkai gives the titles of six sutras and three commentaries,[18] and then passages from these and other texts [19] with short remarks of his own at the end of a quotation or a group of quotations. These quotations occupy the major part of the work. In the last section, he remarks:]

The foregoing quotations from sutras and commentaries prove that

---

[16] T16, p. 525b.

[17] The commentary on the *Mahāprajñāpāramitā Sutra* attributed to Nāgārjuna and translated by Kumārajīva. T25, p. 13c.

[18] They are: T1125, T867, T870, T848, T671, T865, T1665, T1509, T1668.

[19] T261, T310, T997, T1566, T1861, T1866.

differences exist between Exoteric Buddhism and Esoteric Buddhism and that the latter was preached by the Dharmakaya Buddha himself. It is hoped that learned readers will deliberate on them and remove their misconceptions.

QUESTION: According to your assertion, what the Dharmakaya Buddha preached on his innermost spiritual experience is Esoteric, and all other Buddhist teachings are Exoteric. Then why is the word Esoteric applied to some sutras preached by the Shakyamuni Buddha [Nirmanakaya]? We also wonder in which group we should include the dharani teachings imparted by that Buddha?

ANSWER: The meanings of exoteric and esoteric are manifold. If the more profound is compared with the less profound, the former is to be called esoteric and the latter, exoteric. This is the reason why we often find the term esoteric introduced in non-Buddhist scriptures as well. Among the teachings given by the Tathagata, various distinctions between exoteric and esoteric have been made. The Hinayana doctrines explained by the Buddha can be called esoteric when compared to the doctrines given by non-Buddhist teachers. In the same way, when the Mahayana doctrines are compared with the Hinayana doctrines, the former are esoteric and the latter, exoteric. Even in the Mahayana itself, the teaching of the One Vehicle is esoteric in contrast to the teachings of the Three Vehicles. In order to distinguish the dharani section from other lengthy discourses, we call it esoteric. The teaching given by the Dharmakaya Buddha is the most profound, while the teachings of the Nirmanakaya are apparent and simplified; hence, the former is called esoteric.

The term esoteric is also used in the senses of "conceal" or "hidden," that is, "sentient beings conceal," and "hidden by the Tathagata." Since sentient beings conceal their original nature, that is, true enlightenment, they "conceal" themselves through illusions derived from ignorance. The doctrine revealed by the Nirmanakaya Buddha is adapted to the needs of the time and is, as it were, an effective medicine to cure the diseases of the mind. Thus the Buddha who preaches for the benefit of others keeps his innermost spiritual experience hidden and does not reveal it in his instructions. It is hidden even from those bodhisattvas who are nearly equal to the Buddha; it transcends the range of understanding of those who are in the Ten Stages of Bodhisattvahood. This is the so-called experience "hidden by the Tathagata."

In this way, the meanings of the term esoteric are many, but the term in its proper sense should be applied only to the secret teaching revealing the innermost experience of the ultimate Dharmakaya Buddha. The dharani section preached by the Nirmanakaya is also called esoteric, but when it is compared to the teaching of the Dharmakaya Buddha, it is not final. Among the teachings called esoteric, there are the provisional and the final; they should be classified properly according to the context.

4

THE PRECIOUS KEY TO THE SECRET TREASURY

(*Hizō hōyaku*)

INTRODUCTION

From the dim, remote, and immemorial past,
Texts are transmitted in a thousand and ten thousand tomes,
Elucidating Buddhist and non-Buddhist teachings.
Abstruse, obscure, and indistinct
Are a hundred opinions and theories,
Each claiming to be the final way.

Copying and reciting until one's death,
How can one penetrate into the ultimate Source?

I do not know, however I ponder.
The Buddha, I believe, had no mind for this.
He took pity on diseased minds
And taught them to take medicinal herbs as Shen Nung did.

> Out of compassion, he showed the direction to the lost,
> As did the Duke of Chou by making the compass-cart.
>
> But deranged men do not perceive their madness;
> The blind are unaware of their blindness.
> Born, reborn, and still born again,
> Whence they have come they do not know.
> Dying, dying, and dying yet again,
> Where they go in the end they do not know.

As those with imperfect sight may imagine that flowers blooming in the sky dazzle their eyes or that a turtle has hair, so deranged men wrongly believe in the notion of a permanent ego and are firmly attached to it. They rush around like thirsty deer seeking water in a dusty field, believing mirages to be real; or, infatuated, they act like mad elephants or angry monkeys. Thus, day and night, they take pleasure in committing the Ten Evils.[1] The teaching of the Six Paramitas[2] is disagreeable to their ears and does not penetrate their minds. They blame people and abuse the Dharma, little reflecting that these acts are evils that reduce the possibility of attaining enlightenment. They indulge in wine and lust, not being aware of the results in their future life. Yama, the king of hell, together with his retainers, builds hells and judges crimes. Some are transformed into hungry ghosts that spew flame from their mouths; others, into birds that will be trapped eventually, or into beasts that must carry heavy loads. Forever transmigrating in the triple world, they wander among sentient beings in the four types of birth.[3]

Seeing this, how can the great Enlightened One, the compassionate Father,[4] silently let it pass? It was for this reason indeed that he provided all kinds of medicine and pointed out their manifold illusions.

[1] See *Indications*, n. 108.   [2] See *Indications*, n. 115.
[3] See *Indications*, n. 85.

[4] Here "the great Enlightened One, the compassionate Father" stands for the Dharmakaya Mahāvairocana Buddha, not the historical Buddha Shakyamuni. In Kūkai's system, Esoteric Buddhism is derived directly from Mahāvairocana. All other teachings in the world, whatever they may be, regardless of their historical origins, are derived indirectly from Mahāvairocana through his manifestations, in order to meet the needs of the time and to suit the capacity of the recipients. Thus, it was possible for him to maintain in what follows that Confucianism and other beliefs were medicines provided by Mahāvairocana.

Thus, when they practice the Three Human Duties [5] and the Five Cardinal Virtues,[6] the relationships between prince and minister, between father and son will be in proper order and without confusion. [Confucianism]

When they perform the Six Practices [7] and the Four Mental Concentrations,[8] they increase their dislike for the world below and their longing for the world above and make progress toward gaining pleasure in heaven. [Popular Taoism and Hinduism]

When they recognize the Five Psychophysical Constituents [9] only and realize that the notion of a permanent ego is unreal, they gain the results of the Eightfold Emancipation [10] and Six Supernatural Powers. [11] [The Śrāvaka of Hinayana]

When they practice meditation on the [Twelve] Links of Causation,[12] they gain the knowledge of emptiness and uproot the seeds of karma. [Pratyekabuddha of Hinayana]

When they cherish unconditioned compassion for others and deny the existence of the world of objects with the view that what exists is mind only, they extirpate both affectional and intellectual impediments and transform [their Eightfold Consciousness] into the Fourfold Wisdom.[13] [Hossō or Yogācāra of Mahayana]

[5] The duties of a prince, a father, and a husband.   [6] See *Indications*, n. 4.

[7] To perceive in contemplation that the world below is painful, coarse, and full of impediments, and that the world above is pure, exquisite, and free from impediments.

[8] The four stages of meditation performed in the world of form, a world higher than that of desire, but lower than that of formlessness. The first stage is characterized by the powers of investigation, reflection, joyfulness, bliss, and samadhi; the second, by serenity, joyfulness, and samadhi; the third, by equanimity, remembrance, wisdom, bliss, and samadhi; and the fourth, by neither pain nor joy, equanimity, remembrance, and samadhi.

[9] See *Indications*, n. 87.

[10] The eight stages of meditation to gain mental liberation: to meditate that all things are impure; to reduce attachment to external objects; to meditate on pure forms but not to develop any attachment, on infinite space, on boundless consciousness, on the state of nonbeing, on the state of neither thought nor nonthought; and to attain the state of complete cessation of all mental activities.

[11] The six supernatural powers that can be obtained by the practice of yoga: supernatural action, vision, hearing; ability to read the minds of others; knowledge of former states of existence; and freedom from vexation.

[12] See Part Two, p. 70, n. 20.

[13] See discussion on the subject, Part Two, pp. 84–85.

When they realize [the essential nature of] mind by means of [the Eightfold Negation [14] beginning with] "unborn" and transcend all false predications through the insight of absolute emptiness, then they realize One Mind which is tranquil, without a second, and free from any specific marks. [Sanron or Mādhyamika of Mahayana]

When they observe the One Way [15] in its original purity, the Avalokiteśvara [16] softens his face in delight. [Tendai or T'ien-t'ai of Mahayana]

When they meditate on the World of Dharma in the first awakening of their religious mind, the Samantabhadra [17] smiles. [Kegon or Hua-yen of Mahayana]

Now, stains covering the mind have been completely removed; the glory of the [Diamond or Wisdom] Mandala has gradually become visible. The eye of wisdom of [Shingon students who visualize] the letter *Ma* [in the right eye] and *Ṭa* [in the left] dispels the darkness of ignorance. In the effulgence seen in the samadhi of [*Ma* and *Ṭa* transfigured mentally into] the sun and the moon, they see the Bodhisattvas and the Five Buddhas [18] majestically posed in their respective mudras of the Wisdom Realm. The Four Mandalas grounded in the Essence of Dharma pervade all things. Acala's glare stills the wind of karma that turns the wheel of samsara; the three roars [of the mantra *Hūṃ*] of Trailokyavijaya destroy the waves of ignorance.[19] The Eight

[14] The Eightfold Negation is found in the opening stanza of Nāgārjuna's *Mādhyamika-kārikās*, the major text of Sanron or Mādhyamika school of Buddhism: unborn, imperishable, unceasing, nonconstant, nonidentical, not different, not going away, and not coming.

[15] Synonym for One Vehicle. See *Difference*, n. 3.

[16] According to Kūkai (*K.Z.*, I, 365–67; *K.Z.*, II, 161), the teachings of T'ien-t'ai, primarily based on the doctrines given in the *Lotus Sutra*, are the expression of the experience of the samadhi of Avalokiteśvara (Kannon). The twenty-fifth chapter of the sutra translated by Kumārajīva deals with the supernatural saving power of this Bodhisattva.

[17] This Bodhisattva is active in the *Avataṃsaka Sutra*. Kūkai states that the doctrines given in the sutra are the expression of the experience of the samadhi of this Bodhisattva. Cf. *K.Z.*, I, 386; *K.Z.*, II, 161.

[18] See discussion on the Fivefold Wisdom and the Five Buddhas of the Diamond Realm, Part Two, pp. 83–84.

[19] Both Acala, the Immobile One (Fudō in Japanese), and Trailokyavijaya, the Conqueror of the Triple World (Gōsanze in Japanese), are guardians appearing in the Esoteric Buddhist sutras and in the mandalas. By introducing these guardians, fearsome representations of wrath and energy, Kūkai greatly enriched the spiritual life of the Japanese. Worship of Acala is still popular in Japan.

Celestial Maidens [20] make exquisite offerings as glorious as a sea of clouds [seen below from a high peak at daybreak]; the Four Pāramitā Bodhisattvas [21] delight in receiving the bliss of Dharma. Such is the vision that even those most advanced in the Ten Stages [of Exoteric Buddhism] are unable to glimpse and those who contemplate the essence, attributes, and functions of One Mind [22] cannot approach. It is the secret of all secrets, the enlightenment of all enlightenments. [Shingon]

Alas! Men, unaware of the treasures they possess, regard their deluded state of madness to be the state of enlightenment. How foolish they are! The Father's compassion is penetrating; if it were not for these teachings, how could they be saved? If they refuse to take the medicines that have been offered, how can they be cured? If they merely talk about them or recite them emptily, the King of Medicine [the Buddha] will certainly reprimand them for it.

Thus, the nine kinds of medicine for the diseases of the mind sweep away the dust covering the surface of the mind and dispel its delusions. Only in the Diamond Palace [Shingon] are men able to open the inner treasury and to receive the treasures therein. To gain or not to gain them, to enjoy or not to enjoy them is for everyone to decide; it is not for one's father or mother to decide; [the inner treasury] must be realized by oneself.

Those who seek enlightenment must know the difference between a gem and a stone resembling a gem, between cow's milk and the milk of an ass. They must discern them; they must distinguish them. The sutras and shastras clearly explain which religious mind is more pro-

[20] The Diamond or Wisdom Realm Mandala consists of a central circle, the *Vajradhātu-mahāmaṇḍala* (*Katsuma-e* or *Jōjin-ne*), and of eight circles surrounding it in the eight directions. In the center of the central circle is Mahāvairocana, surrounded by four Buddhas, each Buddha being surrounded by four Bodhisattvas. The central circle again consists of inner and outer circles. In the four corners of the inner circle four Bodhisattvas called Pūjābodhisattvas (offering bodhisattvas) are found. The Eight Celestial Maidens are these four Pūjābodhisattvas called Vajralāsī (smile), Vajramālā (tress), Vajragītī (song), and Vajranṛtā (dance), and the four other Pūjābodhisattvas found in the four corners of the outer circle called Vajradhūpā (incense), Vajrapuṣpā (flower), Vajrālokā (light), and Vajragandhā (ointment).

[21] The four Bodhisattvas surrounding Mahāvairocana in the center: Vajrapāramitā, Ratnapāramitā, Dharmapāramitā, and Karmapāramitā.

[22] The theme of *The Awakening of Faith*. Here the attainment of the religious mind in the ninth stage, i.e., the perfected one in Hua-yen Buddhism, is implied.

found or more superficial; a discussion on these problems will be presented subsequently.

Invocation

I take refuge in That One
Who is the adamantine Life of all beings,
Transcendental, immaculate, causeless, and infinite; [Mahāvairocana]

In the Silent One,
Ka [evolving], *Ca* [involving], *Ṭa* [majestic],
Ta [Suchness], *Pa* [Truth], and *Ya* [Vehicle]; 23   [Dharma-mandala]

In the Compassionate One,
Symbolized as a stupa [and whose attributes are]
Banner, brilliant jewel, lotus flower, and conch shell; 24
                                                                [Samaya-mandala]

In Mahāvairocana,
Ratnaketu, Saṃkusmita, Amitābha, Divyadundubhi;
In Vajra, Ratna, Dharma, Karma, Vajragītā, and Vajranṛtyā; 25
                                                                [Mahā-mandala]

And in all the Enlightened Ones,
Who engage in infinite free activities,
Suggested by works of clay, casting, and carving.   [Karma-mandala]

Now, by imperial order I am to write about the Ten Stages.
May we immediately leave behind the Three Delusions; 26
May we realize the truth of our religious mind.

By removing the mist we see the Light;
And we find the inexhaustible Treasury open to all to enjoy,
Shining forth ever more fresh day by day.

To the question of how many stages there are in man's quest for enlightenment until he reaches the original Ground [from which he has wandered], the Tathagata explains that man enters the adamantine

23 "The Silent One" stands for Mahāvairocana. *Ka* is *kārya* (action); *Ca, cyuti* (falling); *Ṭa, ṭaṅka* (pride); *Ta, tathatā* (Suchness); *Pa, paramārtha-satya* (the ultimate Truth); and *Ya, yāna* (vehicle—the absolute Vehicle on which all are being carried).

24 "The Compassionate One" is the Mahāvairocana of the Matrix Realm. The stupa represents Mahāvairocana in the center; the banner, Ratnaketu in the east; the brilliant jewel, Saṃkusumitarāja in the south; the lotus flower, Amitābha in the west; and the conch shell, Divyadundubhimeghanirghoṣa in the north.

25 The Five Buddhas and Bodhisattvas in the Matrix Realm.

26 Rudimentary, subtle, and extremely subtle delusions.

Ground in the tenth stage. The names and the characteristics of the ten stages of development of the religious mind are as follows. Read them and clear your doubts.

The First Stage: The Mind of Lowly Man, Goatish in Its Desires. The ignorant, ordinary man, in his madness, does not realize his faults. He thinks only of lust and hunger like a goat.

The Second Stage: The Mind That Is Ignorant and Childlike, Yet Abstemious. Influenced by external causes, a man suddenly thinks of moderation in eating. The will to perform charity sprouts, like a seed of grain which has encountered the proper conditions.

The Third Stage: The Mind That Is Infantlike and Fearless. A non-Buddhist hopes for rebirth in heaven, in order to gain peace there for a while. He is like an infant or a calf that follows its mother.

The Fourth Stage: The Mind That Recognizes the Existence of Psychophysical Constituents Only, Not That of a Permanent Ego. This mind recognizes the existence of components only and denies a permanent ego. The Tripiṭaka of the Goat-cart of Hinayana [27] is entirely included herein.

The Fifth Stage: The Mind Freed from the Seed of the Cause of Karma. Having mastered the Twelve Links of Causation, the mind extirpates the seed of ignorance. Rebirth necessitated by karma comes to an end; even though one does not preach, the fruit is obtained.

The Sixth Stage: The Mahayana Mind with Sympathetic Concern for Others. Compassion arises unconditionally; this is the first instance of great compassion. Recognizing phenomena as illusory shadows of mind, [a student of Yogācāra who believes that] what exists is mind only negates the validity of the world of objects.

The Seventh Stage: The Mind That Realizes that the Mind Is Unborn. By means of the Eightfold Negation, useless arguments are ended. When an insight into the truth of emptiness is gained in a moment of thought, the mind becomes serene and undefinably blissful.

The Eighth Stage: The Mind That Is Truly in Harmony with the One Way. He who knows that the nature of mind is one and originally pure and that both subject and object interpenetrate is called Vairocana.

The Ninth Stage: The Profoundest Exoteric Buddhist Mind That Is Aware of Its Nonimmutable Nature. Water has no immutable nature of its own. When it meets with the wind, waves appear. The World of

[27] See Part Two, p. 70, n. 18.

Dharma (*dharma-dhātu*) is not yet ultimate. One must proceed further by receiving revelation.

The Tenth Stage: The Glorious Mind, the Most Secret and Sacred. When the medicines of Exoteric Buddhism have cleared away the dust, Shingon opens the Treasury. Then the secret treasures are at once manifested and one realizes all values.

First: The Mind of Lowly Man, Goatish in Its Desires. What is meant by this mind? It is the name given to lowly man who, in his madness, does not distinguish between good and evil, and who, ignorant like a stupid child, does not believe in the law of cause and effect. Lowly man creates karma and receives its fruits; he receives ten thousand different forms of life in the process of transmigration. His ignorance, therefore, can be compared to that of a goat.

Man is not born out of his own desire; yet he dislikes death. Birth after birth he transmigrates in the Six Transmigratory Paths;[28] death after death he sinks into the Three Evil Paths.[29] The parents who begot him do not know the origin of life; he who came into existence does not know where he goes after death. The past is obscure to him when he looks back to the beginning, which is undiscernible. When he looks to the future, it appears vague, and the end of time is inconceivable.

The sun, the moon, and the stars shine above, yet this man's world is as dark as the one seen by the eyes of a dog. Even though he stands on the Five Mountains,[30] he is as perplexed as a sheep that has lost its way. Chained to the hell of food and clothes, he labors day and night, running around near and far, finally falling into the pit of fame and wealth.

Furthermore, a man and a woman hasten to be united, like iron particles attracted by a magnet. As a crystal attracts water [when exposed to the moonlight], so woman responds naturally to man and generates offspring, and thus parents and children live happily together. Although children and parents may love each other, they do not know the character of their love. Although man and wife may love each other, they do not know the nature of their love. Their love is like a flowing stream whose water changes perpetually, or like the sparks of

[28] Hell, world of hungry ghosts, of beasts, of *asuras* (fighting demons), of men, and of heaven.

[29] The first three of the Six Transmigratory Paths.

[30] The five sacred mountains of China: T'ai-shan in Shantung, Heng-shan in Hunan, Hua-shan in Shensi, Heng-shan in Hopei, and Sung-shan in Honan.

a flame. They are bound by the rope of deluded thoughts and are intoxicated by the wine of ignorance. Their union is comparable to someone meeting another in a dream, or to travelers meeting each other by chance at the same inn.

There are some who believe that from the *one* [*ch'i*: vital force] *two* [yin and yang] were produced; from these *two*, *three* [heaven, earth, and mankind]; and from these *three*, all the myriad things in the universe. There are others who believe that Maheśvara is the creator, or that Brahmā created all. Not yet knowing the origin of the living, how can they discuss the coming into being of the dead!

Ferocious wild beasts devour other hairy creatures; *garuḍa* birds eat serpents and *rakṣasa* demons, men. Men kill and eat animals. Sometimes they annihilate boars and deer in the fields with bow and arrow, or exterminate fishes and turtles in the streams with nets and traps. It is said that when hawks and falcons fly, golden pheasants and snow geese shed tears; when huge fierce dogs run, foxes and rabbits rend their hearts. Even though there should be no birds and beasts left, people would still be unsatisfied. Larders may be filled with food, but people will be greedier than ever. Thieves, deluded by treasures, are punished by death; those who, captivated by beautiful girls, commit adultery either by seduction or by violence kill themselves in the end. Random utterance of the four kinds of evil speech [31] is, as it were, an ax with which to slash at men. Indulgence in the three wrongs of the mind [32] is poison to harm others. Being shameless, men commit eighty thousand sins. Not only do they commit sins themselves, but they also teach others to do the same, thus always multiplying their sins which are as numerous as particles of sand. This is because they do not know that sin invites suffering in hell, in the realm of beasts, and in the realm of hungry ghosts, and that good conduct helps one to approach the pleasures of Eternity, of Bliss, of the Self, and of Purity. [33]

There are some who say that when a man dies he returns to the "vital force" and will never be given life again; this kind of view is called "nihilism." On the other hand, there are some who say that a man will always be a man and a beast, always a beast, and that to be noble or ignoble, to be rich or poor is always a matter of predestination; this

[31] Lying, exaggerated speech, equivocation, and slander.
[32] Greed, anger, and biased views.
[33] Attributes of Nirvana or of the Tathagata as conceived by Mahayanists.

kind of view is called "determinism." Those who imitate the manners of a cow or dog or those who drown themselves in the Ganges [34] are people who harbor wrong views. There are innumerable heretics who believe in wrong views and do not know how to attain liberation. All of the deluded views mentioned above are of the "goatish mind." A summary in verse:

> Lowly men are blind to the difference between good and evil;
> They do not believe in the law of cause and effect.
> Being tempted by the prospect of immediate gains,
> They are unaware of the blazing fire in hell.
> Shamelessly they commit the Ten Evils,
> Yet they argue in vain that a man has a permanent ego.
> Being firmly attached to the triple world,
> Who can expect to be freed from the chains of vexation!

QUESTION: Which sutra have you used to develop the foregoing discussion?

ANSWER: I have used the *Mahāvairocana Sutra*.

QUESTION: How is it explained in the sutra?

ANSWER: The sutra says it as follows: "O Lord of Mysteries, a lowly man, ignorant and childlike, repeating the cycle of birth and death from the beginningless beginning, attaches himself to the notion of a permanent ego and to his possessions. He makes numberless subjective speculations. O Lord of Mysteries, since he does not perceive the true nature of ego, he develops the notion of I and mine. There are some who believe that time is the prime cause or that all things are transformations of the elements earth, etc.; there are some who believe in the Yoga school's concept of *ātman*, or who maintain that the created is pure, or that the created is impure but that the uncreated is pure . . . and others who believe in the eternal nature of sound or who do not believe in it. O Lord of Mysteries, these subjective speculations, from ancient times, have been bound up with discriminations; yet these people seek after liberation in accordance with their respective guiding principles. O Lord of Mysteries, these lowly men, ignorant and childlike, are comparable to goats." [35] In Nāgārjuna's *Aspiration to Enlightenment*

---

[34] Refers to certain Hindu ascetics.

[35] In the *Mahāvairocana Sutra* thirty heretical views of the Hindus are listed, but Kūkai has omitted many of them in this quotation. T18, p. 2a.

(*P'u-t'i-hsin lun*) it is said: "Ordinary men are attached to fame, or to things which bring them profit or livelihood, and strive to improve their material life. They indulge in the Three Poisons [36] and in the Five Desires.[37] The student of Mantrayāna (Shingon), indeed, must loathe and forsake them." [38]

Second: The Mind That Is Ignorant and Childlike, Yet Abstemious. The withered trees of winter are not always to be leafless; once spring arrives, they bloom and flourish. Thick ice does not remain frozen forever; when summer comes, it melts and flows. Given ample moisture, seeds of grain sprout, and when the time comes, plants bear fruit.

Tai Yüan's change of heart and Chou Ch'u's reputation for loyalty and filial piety are likened to the transformation of an unpolished stone into a precious gem or of a whale's eye into a source of light that breaks darkness. As there is no immutable nature in things, how can a man remain bad always? When favorable conditions are provided, even a fool aspires to the great Way, and while he follows the teachings faithfully, he aspires to be equal to a sage. A goatish man has no immutable nature; an ignorant child likewise does not remain ignorant. When his intrinsically enlightened nature begins to permeate him within and when the light of the Buddha shines upon him from without, there suddenly emerges in him an instantaneous thought that he should moderate his intake of food and practice acts of charity. As a plant continually grows through the stages of seed, sprouting, flowering, and bearing fruit, so this man continually develops his mind for goodness, avoids wrong-doing, and is concerned lest his good acts should not be equal to those of others. He will study the Five Cardinal Virtues and earnestly follow the Ten Good Deeds.[39]

The Five Cardinal Virtues are benevolence, righteousness, propriety, wisdom, and sincerity. "Benevolence" corresponds to [the Buddhist

[36] Greed, hatred, and delusion.

[37] There are two sets: the desire for property, for sexual love, for eating and drinking, for fame, and for sleep; and the desire for the five sense-objects, i.e., form, sound, smell, taste, and touch.

[38] *Bodaishin ron* (see Introduction, n. 7). T32, p. 573a.

[39] Synonym for the Ten Precepts of Buddhism: not to kill, not to steal, not to commit adultery, not to lie, not to use exaggerated speech, not to slander, not to equivocate, not to covet, not to give way to anger, and not to hold biased views.

precept] "not to kill." It means to treat others as you would want others to treat you and to practice charity. "Righteousness" is the same as "not to steal" and means to save things and to share them with others. "Propriety" is the synonym for "not to commit adultery"; it is to observe the Five Ceremonies [40] in good order. "Wisdom" means "not to take intoxicating liquor"; by heeding this, one can discern and reason well. "Sincerity" is another way of saying "not to lie"; it is to act upon one's words. When men practice these five virtues, the four seasons come in order and the five primary elements [41] function harmoniously. If a country observes them, it will be peaceful and will flourish. If each family practices them, no one in the family will be obliged to collect things abandoned in the road. This is indeed an excellent art of living for a man who wishes to promote his fame and enhance his ancestors' name; it is an excellent social practice by which to maintain a country in peace and to give comfort to individuals. In Confucianism it is called the Five Cardinal Virtues; in Buddhism, the Five Precepts. Though the names differ, their meanings as well as their practices are identical. The result a man obtains differs depending on which of these two he practices; yet both are the basis for forsaking evil and for cultivating good, the practice of which is the beginning of freeing oneself from suffering and of gaining bliss.

It is therefore explained in a sutra that "if a less qualified man practices the Five Precepts, he is to be born on the Jambu continent; if an average man practices them, he is to be born on the Pūrvavideha continent; a better qualified man, on the Aparagodanīya continent; and the best qualified man, or a man who has realized selflessness, on the Uttarakuru continent." [42] On these four respective continents, there exist kings. Of these kings, there are five kinds; that is, a minor king and four great kings. These kings were born to be kings because they had practiced the Ten Good Deeds. Thus, in the *Jen-wang ching* it is said: "When the well-qualified bodhisattvas who have practiced the Ten Good Deeds give rise to great aspiration, they will be freed for all time from the sea of suffering in the triple world. When average or inferior men practice them, they will be born as minor kings; better men, as

[40] The ceremony of sacrifice to ancestors, funeral rites, ceremonial rules of hospitality, military rites, and initiation and marriage ceremonies.

[41] Metal, wood, water, fire, and earth.

[42] Source unknown. According to Indian cosmology, these four continents centered on Mt. Sumeru, respectively in the South, East, West, and North.

iron kings; superior men, as copper kings who govern two continents; still higher men, as silver kings who govern three continents; and the most virtuous men, as universal monarchs, golden kings with the seven kinds of gems who govern the four continents." [43]

In view of these lines, it could be concluded that the kings and their subjects were able to be born as human beings as the result of having practiced the Five Precepts or the Ten Good Deeds. There have never been those who were born as human beings who had not observed them. It is by virtue of having practiced good deeds in their previous lives that they were born as human beings. If they do not practice them in this life, they will fall into the Three Evil Paths. Without having sown in spring, how could one expect to harvest in autumn? Good men and women should without fail take the precepts into their hearts. As to the results of practicing either the Ten Good Deeds or the Ten Evil Deeds, and as to the rulership of the wise or the mediocre king, they are as discussed comprehensively in the *Ten Stages*.[44] A summary in verse:

> A man ignorant and childlike has come to know
> A little about the evils of greed and anger.
> Suddenly he thinks of the excellence of being abstemious.
> The seed germinated within grows into a desire to do good.
> As the bud progressively unfolds,
> He appreciates more and more the norms of good conduct.
> Practicing the Five Cardinal Virtues and the Ten Good Deeds,
> He will become the teacher of kings and universal monarchs.

QUESTION: On the basis of which sutra have you explained this mind?

ANSWER: The *Mahāvairocana Sutra*.

QUESTION: How is it explained in that sutra?

ANSWER: The sutra says it as follows: "An ignorant and childlike man momentarily conceives an idea and decides not to eat for a day in order to offer the spare food to the needy. Having experienced joy from this humble effort, he tries to practice it from time to time. O Lord of Mysteries, this is the first stage in which the seed of good action grows. Because of this cause, he offers the saved food to his parents and relatives six days out of a month.[45] This is the second stage, that is, the stage of the germination of the seed of good action. Then he

---

[43] T8, p. 837b.   [44] *K.Z.*, I, 187–219.

[45] The days of fasting are the 8th, 14th, 15th, 23d, 29th, and 30th of each month.

extends his offerings to strangers. This is the third stage, comparable to the bud of the seed. Then he offers it to capable and virtuous men. This is the fourth stage, in which the leaves sprout. Again, he gladly offers this saved food to musicians or to elderly noble leaders. This is the fifth stage of flowering. Then he offers it to them with loving heart and honors them. This is the sixth stage of the fruit of the development of his seed of good action." [46]

Third: The Mind That Is Infantlike and Fearless. This is the mind of non-Buddhists who loathe the human world and of ordinary men who aspire to be born in heaven. Even if they are born in the highest heaven, known as the Heaven of Neither Thought Nor Non-Thought, or in the lowest, in the Palace of the Immortals; even if they are endowed with a body 40,000 *yojanas* [mythological units of measure] in height and 80,000 aeons in life span; even if they detest the lower world as if it were a scab, regarding human beings as ephemeral existences; and even if the luster emitted by them darkens the sun and the moon, and the happiness with which they have been rewarded surpasses that of the universal monarch, they are as inferior and as ignorant as infants when compared to the great Enlightened One. Being somewhat freed from bondage, they are fearless; however, since they have not attained the bliss of Nirvana, they are comparable to an infant.

QUESTION: We have heard that Huai's dog rose to the sky [47] and that Fei's dragon flew up on high.[48] The former event was brought about by taking an elixir of life, the latter by the art of a [Taoist] master. We wonder now through which teaching and through which teacher these heavenly beings were able to acquire such a free and bright body, with the blessing of longevity. We should also like to know how many kinds of heaven there are and their names.

ANSWER: As a bell rings when struck and a valley echoes to sounds, so, having been asked, how can I remain silent? I shall try to answer your questions. Now, a madman cannot cure his own madness until he meets a master of medicine. A precious gem is not, of course, precious until it is polished by a skilled artisan. The master of medicine and the

---

[46] T18, p. 2b.   [47] See *Indications*, n. 64.

[48] It was said that, when Fei Ch'ang-fang rode on a bamboo stick given to him by an immortal, the stick turned into a dragon and flew high into the sky carrying him on its back.

skilled artisan are no other than my great teacher, the Lord Buddha. The Tathagata is endowed with all excellent attributes; each of his attributes is [personified as] the Lord of a particular approach, and each Lord reveals manifold doctrines in accordance with the capacity of his audience and liberates sentient beings. It is said in the *Mahāvairocana Sutra*, therefore, that "the Tathagata, Worthy of Being Honored, the Omniscient One, preaches widely to innumerable beings with his wisdom in applying the teaching and with manifold expedient means, in consonance with beings in the various states of existence and accommodating himself to their nature and their desires. He elucidates the doctrines which lead a sentient being to be born as a Hinayanist or a Mahayanist; as one with the five supernatural wisdoms; as a heavenly being, a man, a serpent, a *yakṣa*, a *gandharva*, or a *mahoraga*." [49] According to this passage, the teachings of the Hinayana, of the Mahayana, of being reborn as a man or as a heavenly being are all preached by the Tathagata. If a man practices according to the teaching, he will certainly be born in heaven.

QUESTION: Then, are the practices of the various heretics based on the teachings of the Buddha?

ANSWER: Both yes and no; yes because they once were, and no because they are not any longer. In the beginning they were the teachings of the Buddha, but during their transmission from the immemorial past, their original meaning became distorted and lost. Thus, there are some who observe the precept of acting like a cow or a dog in accordance with their own views, wishing as they do to be born in heaven. In such a practice, the original meaning is altogether lost.

QUESTION: Then if it was the Buddha who preached them, He should have immediately preached the doctrine by which all can attain Buddhahood. Why was it that He preached the doctrine of being born in heaven?

ANSWER: It was in order to accommodate his teaching to the capacity of sentient beings that He preached thus. Other methods would have been useless to them.

QUESTION: We have now heard about the teacher and his teachings. We beg you to inform us how many heavens there are.

ANSWER: There are three: the heavens of desire, of form, and of

[49] T18, p. 1b.

formlessness. . . . Among these three categories of heavens, twenty-eight heavens can be identified. For fear of complicating the issue, I shall not presently describe their distance, size, inhabitants, etc., for I have already done so in the Ten Stages.[50]

QUESTION: We have now learned the number of the heavens and their names; we beg you to show us again the conditions under which one is born there.

ANSWER: The heretics also use such terms as the "Three Treasures" or the "Three Items of Mastery." [51] They regard Brahmā, etc., as the "Buddha Treasure," the four Vedas as the "Dharma Treasure," and those who teach or practice their teachings as the "Sangha Treasure." They use the terms "Ten Good Deeds," etc., to designate their precepts and "Four Mental Concentrations," [52] to designate their method of yoga. They say that their method of yoga can be perfected by meditating upon the thought that the world should be loathed because it is filled with suffering, vileness, and obstacles, and that the heavens above should be sought after with pleasure because they are pure, exquisite, and free. By virtue of the practice of this yoga, they believe that they will be born first in the lower heavens, later in the higher ones, birth after birth. By meditating upon the thought that the creator alone is real and that all other things are empty, some heretics develop the wisdom of emptiness. Thus by making an effort to perfect the "Three Items of Mastery," they gain the joy of being born in the heavens. This approach, however, is not the ultimate, for they are unable to transcend birth and death and to attain Nirvana. Even if they reach the highest heaven, that of absence of thought, they will [eventually] fall into hell, as an arrow shot into the sky falls when its momentum runs out. For these reasons, you should not long for it.

QUESTION: Why is it that these heretics are unable to cleanse their defilements and to attain Nirvana, even though they practice the "Three Items of Mastery" and are to be born in the two worlds [53] after having realized a state beyond verbalization, through the practice of meditation on emptiness?

[50] *K.Z.*, I, 228–49.

[51] Observance of precepts, practice of meditation, and obtaining wisdom, i.e., the most comprehensive summary of the way of life and practice, and of the goal of Buddhists.

[52] See above, n. 8.   [53] The worlds of form and formlessness.

ANSWER: Because they are attached to the two extreme stands [54] and to the two wrong views.[55]

QUESTION: Like Buddhists they meditate on the state of neither being nor nonbeing; why should you say that they have fallen into the two extreme stands and into the two wrong views?

ANSWER: They believe that all things belong to the creator; thus they do not know the Middle Way of Dependent Origination.

QUESTION: What do you mean by the Middle Way of Dependent Origination?

ANSWER: A man will not fall into the extreme stand of nihilism if he understands that existence is causally conditioned; he will not fall into the extreme stand of eternalism [56] if he perceives the emptiness of the self-nature (*svabhāva*) of any individual being. If he perceives that the World of Dharma is that in which all beings are empty [of permanent ego], he obtains the right view of the Middle Way. Because of this right view, he can quickly attain Nirvana. The heretics with biased views are ignorant of this truth and are, therefore, unable to obtain perfect peace. If they hear this principle, they can attain Arhatship [sainthood].

QUESTION: How many types of beings are there who, by observing the precepts, are to be born in heaven?

ANSWER: There are four types. The first are the heretics as already discussed. The second are the followers of Hinayana; they too are to be born in heaven. The third are the bodhisattvas of Mahayana; they become kings in the ten heavens.[57] The fourth are the Buddhas and the bodhisattvas who assume different forms in order to save others; they transform themselves into kings of the heavens. These problems are as discussed in detail in the *Ten Stages*. A summary in verse:

> When non-Buddhists become religious, they long for joy in heaven.
> Piously observing their precepts, they seek after their refuge.
> Not having any knowledge of the perfectly Enlightened One,
> How can they know the wrongs of worshiping Brahmā and the
> serpent?
> They perform the Six Practices, wishing to be born in heaven.

54 Eternalism and nihilism.
55 The views that all beings are real or that they are unreal.
56 Belief in the existence of a permanent ego, soul, or self.
57 The six heavens of desire and the four dhyana heavens.

Scorched by the fivefold heat,[58] they torment their body and mind.
With pleasure as their aim, they believe in nihilism or eternalism.
If they meet the Buddha, they will realize their faults.

QUESTION: What scriptures are the basis for your discussion of this religious mind?

ANSWER: The *Mahāvairocana Sutra* and the *Aspiration to Enlightenment*.

QUESTION: How is it explained in the *Mahāvairocana Sutra?*

ANSWER: In that sutra it is said: "O Lord of Mysteries, he who observes the precepts and wishes to be born in heaven is at the seventh stage where he receives the seed [of being born in heaven]. O Lord, while he, with this mind, transmigrates, he will hear the following words at the place of his good spiritual friend: 'This is the deva (god), the great deva, who bestows all joys upon you. If you worship him with reverence, all your desires will be fulfilled. The deva can be Maheśvara, Brahmā, Nārāyana, Śaṅkhara (Śiva), Maheśvaraputra, Sūrya, Candra, Nāgarāja, Deva-ṛṣi, or Mahendra. Each of them should be worshiped.' Having heard this, the man, with joy in his heart, will salute the speaker politely, follow his instructions, and practice them. O Lord of Mysteries, this is the eighth stage in which an ignorant and childlike man obtains 'the mind that is infantlike and fearless' in the midst of samsara. Next, there is a still higher practice. That is, by selecting a superior teaching and by devoting himself to it, the man may give rise to knowledge which induces him to seek liberation. What he believes in is eternity [of the creator and] transitoriness and emptiness [of the created]. By following such a teaching, O Lord of Mysteries, he does not understand the meaning of emptiness or nonemptiness. What he believes in is eternity and nothingness. He conceptualizes what defies conceptualization, that is, what is neither being nor nonbeing. How is it possible to conceptualize what is empty? Since he does not understand that all phenomenal existences are empty, he is unable to realize Nirvana. Thus he should understand the meaning of emptiness and free himself from the views of eternalism and nihilism." [59]

[58] The heat of the sun from above and the heat from the four fires burning around a Hindu ascetic.

[59] T18, p. 2b.

Remarks: These non-Buddhists, hoping to be liberated, torture their body and mind. To seek liberation by means of their doctrines of nihilism, eternalism, nonbeing, and being is to seek milk by milking the cow's horns. Once they understand the emptiness of causally conditioned existences, they will immediately gain liberation.

It is also said in the sutra: "O Lord of Mysteries, people in the mundane world—believing that the appearance or the disappearance of causes, effects, and functions are in the hands of the creator—come to meditate upon the thought that all are empty. This we call the samadhi of the people of the mundane world." [60]

Again in the same sutra it is said: "The Buddha preached the teaching of Mantrayāna for heavenly beings and for worldly beings in order to benefit sentient beings." [61]

In Nāgārjuna's *Aspiration to Enlightenment* it is said: "Non-Buddhists are attached to their lives: some wish to live forever with the help of medicines; others think that to be born in heaven is the final goal. The devotees of Mantrayāna should observe them. Even if their force of karma is exhausted, the non-Buddhists, still not having been emancipated from the triple world nor having extinguished their defilements or their evils committed in the past, will entertain evil thoughts. They will then sink into the sea of suffering and find it hard to escape from it. The teachings of these non-Buddhists are like phantoms, dreams, or threads of gossamer." [62]

Fourth: The Mind That Recognizes the Existence of Psychophysical Constituents Only, Not That of a Permanent Ego. A sword of lead cannot cut, and a dragon of clay cannot fly. Pebbles scattered among precious stones are often mistaken for gems. The confusing fact which has always been true is that there are many homonyms, just as the dried corpse of a mouse and unpolished jade bear the same name. [63]

Both Vaiśeṣika and Sāṃkhya use the term "truth (*tai*)" and some use the name "Buddha" for Brahmā and Nārāyaṇa; Dīrghanakha uses the term "reality (*jissō*)" and Vāstīputrīya, "beyond verbalization (*zetsu*-

---

[60] T18, p. 9c.   [61] T18, p. 9c.   [62] T32, p. 573a.

[63] People of the state of Cheng call the dried corpse of a mouse *p'o*, whereas people of the state of Chou designate unpolished jade by that name.

gon)." However, none of them know the cause of attaining Nirvana, and they strive in vain to seek after the wisdom of deliverance.

The great Buddha, the World Honored One, therefore preached the Goat Vehicle [64] in order to save the people from the extreme suffering of falling into the Three Evil Paths [65] and to release them from the karmic fetters of the Eight Sufferings.[66] His teaching is to promote the study of the Tripiṭaka and to observe widely the Four Noble Truths. The Thirty-seven Items of Mastery [67] help śrāvakas to attain their goals. There are eight classes of śrāvakas.[68] The śrāvakas recognize the five sense perceptions and mind, but not the seventh or the eighth [consciousness].[69] As for the period required to achieve perfection, even the most qualified ones require three lives, the less qualified, sixty aeons. They observe 250 precepts in order to prevent wrongdoing, and they practice the Fourfold Meditation [70] and the Eightfold Emancipation.[71] Every fortnight they confess their sins, and at the end of their summer retreat they perform mutual criticism on moral matters. This practice allows the holy ones to be distinguished from ordinary men. They shave their heads, wear robes, and carry an iron begging bowl and a stick. They walk with care so as not to kill even an insect. Whenever they sit, they practice breath-counting meditation with lowered heads. This is their pattern of life. They use euphemisms for such words as "to kill" or "to collect [money]." Regarding a beautiful girl as a corpse, they try to cut off the evils which might be caused by thinking or speaking about her. Sitting in cemeteries with their eyes closed, they focus their minds on skeletons. They beg for food in

[64] In the parable of the Burning House in the *Lotus Sutra,* carts drawn by goats, deer, and oxen are compared to the Vehicles of the śrāvakas, of the pratyekabuddhas, and of the bodhisattvas respectively. т9, p. 12c.

[65] See n. 29.   [66] See *Indications,* n. 98.

[67] The fourfold meditation, fourfold detachment, fourfold supernatural power, fivefold basis of spiritual progress, fivefold controlling power, sevenfold constituent of enlightenment, and eightfold noble path.

[68] There are four categories in Hinayana sanctification: entrance into the stream of sanctification, one rebirth, no returning, and enlightenment. Each category is divided into two, i.e., those who are in the process of attaining and those who have already attained; thus, eight classes are identified.

[69] The seventh is ego-consciousness and the eighth, *ālaya*-consciousness.

[70] To meditate that the body is impure, that sensations lead to suffering, that the mind is impermanent, and that all things are devoid of permanent existence.

[71] See above, n. 10.

villages and are satisfied with whatever humble food they get. They avoid rain by standing under trees, not wishing to live in fine houses. Protecting themselves from the wind with robes made of rags, they do not yearn for beautiful clothes.

By practicing the samadhi of the realization of emptiness, they know that the permanent ego is nonexistent, like an illusion or a thread of gossamer. Gaining wisdom by extinguishing their defilements, they become free from further existence in samsara. Their supernatural powers enable them to cause the moon to wane or the sun to be covered, or to reverse the positions of heaven and earth. They can perceive the past, present, and future. With their eighteen supernatural powers, they can walk through stone walls without difficulty and can fly into the sky. Because of their virtues, universal monarchs bow down to the ground before them; Brahmā and Indra take refuge in them; the eight kinds of creatures [72] honor them; and the four classes of believers [73] look up to them with admiration. Loathing foamlike, dew-like phenomenal existence and detesting the tortures of the Three Evil Paths, they long for the refreshing state of concentration, a state characterized by a sense of vastness like infinite space, tranquil and unconditioned. This, they believe, is the highest state of bliss. Such is the outline of this Vehicle, which aims at complete cessation of the body and mind. As they recognize as real only the Psychophysical Constituents and deny the existence of a permanent ego, this approach is defined as "the mind that recognizes the existence of Psychophysical Constituents, not that of a permanent ego."

A certain patriot asked the monk Genkan: [74] "Now we have heard about the śrāvakas and their doctrines; we have come to know that their way is more exquisite than the ways of men or of heavenly beings, and that they are superior to either Indra or the universal monarch. They are endowed with the Six Supernatural Powers [75] and are in

[72] Nonhuman guardians of Buddhism: *devas, nāgas, yakṣas, gandharvas, asuras, garuḍas, kiṃnaras,* and *mahoragas.*

[73] See *Memorial,* n. 3.

[74] "Patriot" is literally "he who worries about the state." In what follows Kūkai defends the Buddhist clergy against the threat of excessive government control. The patriot represents Confucian government officials. The name of the Buddhist monk Genkan means "fortress defending the profound."

[75] See above, n. 11.

possession of the Three Perfect Knowledges.[76] It is quite reasonable that both men and heavenly beings regard them with reverence, trusting them as the source of blessings, and make offerings to them. The emperors of former times and wise subjects therefore built Buddhist temples and placed clergymen therein, allotting many thousands of households to cultivate immense lands for their subsistence. They trusted and revered them simply because they wanted them to pacify the nation and to benefit people. Priests and nuns nowadays, though they shave their heads, do not shed their greediness; though they wear dyed robes, their minds are not imbued [with the spirit of Buddhism]. Those who strive to perfect the observance of the precepts, meditation, and wisdom are as few as the horns of a unicorn, but those who misconduct themselves and are outrageous are as many as the scales of a dragon. They kowtow at the feet of officials and of concubines day and night and, kneeling on the ground, present gifts even to their maids and servants morning and evening. The tradition of Buddhism has thereby declined, and the way of Buddhism crumbled to the ground. Because of their degeneracy, there have frequently been droughts, floods, and epidemics year after year, the world has been without order and lax in observing regulations, and both officials and people have been suffering extremely. The best solution is to discourage men and women from becoming monks and nuns and not to offer anything to them. If, however, there are clergymen who are truly enlightened, we should respect them with the utmost reverence and make offerings to them even at the cost of a decline in the nation's wealth."

The master said: "Excellent! Your comment is pertinent and beneficial. Listen to me well with the ears of Ling Lun [77] and think over my answers with the alert mind of Yen Hui.[78] With a few examples I will remove your misunderstandings.

"An insect that is said to live in the eyebrows of a mosquito does not see the wings of the roc; how can a tiny lizard imagine the scales of a dragon? The horns of a snail cannot reach to the firmament, nor can the feet of a dwarf touch the bottom of the ocean. A person blind from

[76] Knowledge of former births; of the future destiny of all beings; of the origin of sufferings and the way to be free from suffering.

[77] A famous musician who lived during the reign of the Yellow Emperor.

[78] A disciple of Confucius known for his sagacity.

birth is unable to see the sun and the moon; the deaf cannot hear the rumbling of thunder. Such are the ranges of comprehension of men of little wit. Among people, differences exist between the good and the bad, the wise and the foolish. The good and wise are rare, the bad and foolish, abundant. As the unicorn and the phoenix are the most prominent among birds and beasts, and the *cintāmaṇi* gem and the diamond, the most exquisite among minerals and stones, so the most excellent among men are sages; the most honored among kings, Yao and Shun; the most beautiful among queens, the wife of King Wen; the most praised among ministers, the Eight Good Men and the Eight Wise Men.[79] It is said that once a unicorn or a phoenix is seen, the world becomes peaceful; that when a *cintāmaṇi* gem or a diamond is discovered, every wish is fulfilled; and that when a sage-king appears, the whole world becomes tranquil, and the king has nothing to do because his wise ministers assist him in governing the country. Be that as it may, it is extremely rare to meet a sage-king; he may appear once in a thousand years. To be able to see a wise minister is also rare; he may appear once in five hundred years. We have only heard the name of the *cintāmaṇi* gem, and who has ever seen a unicorn or a phoenix? We cannot, however, insist upon annihilating all birds and beasts because there is neither a phoenix nor a unicorn, nor can we dispose of all gold, jade, etc., because they are not *cintāmaṇi*. Nor can we say that we should do away with the rulers of the world because they are not sage-kings as were Yao and Shun, nor discharge all ministers because they are not equal to the Eight Good Men and the Eight Wise Men. Confucius passed away a long time ago, but each country is filled with his students; Lao Tzu is dead but each province is crowded with his followers. Even if we do not have excellent physicians comparable to Pien [Ch'üeh] or Hua [T'a], the practice of medical science should not come to an end. Who would give up the art of archery, just because there is no master like the ancient I [Yu-ch'iung] or Yang [Yu-chi]? The virtuosos of the harp, Shih [K'uang] and Chung [Tzu-ch'i], and the celebrated calligraphers, [Wang] Hsi[-chih] and [his son] Hsien[-chih], have long been dead. Who has equaled them? Yet the fact remains that the sounds of the harp continue to bother our ears and the works of calligraphy, to obstruct our eyes. The reason for this is that it

[79] Sixteen famous ministers in the reign of the sage-king Shun.

is nevertheless wiser to practice these arts than to abandon them altogether.

"It is difficult to obtain the holy fruit of Arhatship in one lifetime; it is said that in order to gain it an ignorant man must spend sixty aeons devoting himself to severe ascetic practices, and a man of high aptitude, three lives. Therefore, even if there is not a sage who is close to gaining the goal, there is no reason to abolish the Way."

The patriot asked: "The difficulty of meeting a sage may be as you have said, but why is it that we have not yet heard of anyone who has observed the precepts strictly and has been endowed with wisdom?"

The master replied: "It is because of the force of time. It is said that, when the time is favorable, men think of the Ten Good Deeds, and when unfavorable, they indulge in the Ten Evil Deeds. Within one thousand years after the Buddha passed away, there were many who observed the precepts and attained the Way, but in the next one thousand and subsequent years, there have been few who have observed the precepts and have practiced the virtues. Now we are in a period of degeneration when the people's aptitude is low. Men may resort to and seek after the Way, but they are haphazard about it; it is difficult for them to penetrate into the exquisite Way, just as it is difficult for a light feather to stand still in a wind. How can the stars move to the east, while the firmament declines to the west? How can the grass and trees stand still while heaven and earth quake violently?"

The patriot said: "If what you have said is correct, it would be difficult for those who were predestined to be born with a low aptitude in this period to go against the currents of the time. And if so, I suppose there will certainly be none in this degenerate period who can observe the precepts, practice meditation, and gain wisdom."

The master then said: "Why should it be so? Even if the firmament revolves to the west, the sun and the moon rise from the east; while the Great Bear moves southward, the pole star remains in the same position; while green leaves wither in winter, pine needles stay fresh; while waves of cold freeze water, salt water and wine remain unaffected. The people of Chou may have been worthy of being killed house by house, but the Three Men [80] have been praised as being benevolent. The peo-

---

[80] Under the rule of the tyrant king Chou people were cruel, but Wei Tzu, Chi Tzu, and Pi Kan are said to have been exceptions.

ple of King Yao might have deserved to be given into serfdom family by family, but the Four Criminals [81] received their penalties. Fire burns things, but it is said that a certain kind of rat plays in the fire; water causes man to drown, but dragons and turtles swim in it. We can see that some conform to the world in which they live, while others rebel against it. Therefore, although we live in a degenerate period, there is no reason to suppose that there are no worthy ones."

The patriot asked: "I understand that there are worthy ones; but where are they, if there are any?"

The master replied: "A huge square has no corners; a loud sound is silent; an intense white appears as if spotted; precise straightness gives the illusion of being crooked; great perfection seems imperfect; a tremendous bulge appears as if empty; a profound virtue effaces one's identity. [82] Who would be able to recognize such a person if not a sage? Even the sages of ancient times lamented the difficulty of discerning such a person."

The patriot said: "I have heard that a sage would live among ordinary people and conceal his virtue. On the other hand, it is said that when jade is hidden in a mountain, trees and grass on that mountain grow well; when a sword is buried under a lofty mountain, its luster shines forth. By measuring the footprints [of an animal], we learn its size; by spotting the smoke, we learn the whereabouts of the fire. If there are any endowed with wisdom and with virtuous acts, it should not be at all difficult to find them!"

The master said: "Things have no intention of hiding themselves, therefore they manifest their attributes; men conceal themselves intentionally, therefore it is difficult to perceive them."

The patriot asked: "I understand that it is difficult to discern whether a person is a sage. The fact remains that Buddhism squanders the wealth of the state, as bookworms destroy books; clergymen consume the nation's food, as silkworms do mulberry leaves. What value is there then in Buddhism?"

The master said: "Whether or not Buddhism is beneficial will be discussed later. Now, let me illustrate generally which of the ways of life—that of a clergyman or that of a government official—is more

[81] They are Kung Kung, T'ieh Tou, San Miao, and Kun.
[82] These clauses are quoted from the *Tao-te Ching*.

wasteful or more beneficial. According to your question, you are concerned about whether Buddhism is beneficial to the state or not, without even considering the reason why Buddhism has spread. For a loyal patriot, the question you have raised may indeed be of primary concern.

"Now, the reason for founding a state, for installing officials for establishing rulership, and for governing the people is not to offer the country to the ruler for his use and domination, nor is it to provide for the officials by exploiting the people. The reason is to remove all the people's sufferings, as do parents [their children's].

"As bit and whip are necessary to restrain a horse, so the teachings are indispensable to control the people. It is to this end that [Confucius] preached the Five Cardinal Virtues and guided the people in the world. The Five Classics and the Three Books of History point to the right path and the laws prevent people from falling into wickedness and idleness. When the ruler observes these teachings, the nation will be peaceful, and when the people follow them, the world will be without troubles; there will then be propriety and order between the ruler and his subjects, between father and son; a congenial atmosphere will never be lacking between them.

"Nowadays those who recite the *Book of Odes* do not possess a benevolent and congenial heart; those who read the *Book of Rites* forget to assume a humble and courteous attitude. The essence of the *Spring and Autumn Annals* lies in rewarding the good and punishing the wicked. What the *Book of Changes* praises the most are serenity and exactness. Many people read them eagerly, but who observes Confucius' instructions and who follows the Duke of Chou's admonitions? Even a parrot can recite and speak; what is the difference between an orangutan and a man if the latter does not practice what he maintains?

"Among the innumerable people high and low, from the top government officials who administer affairs of state in the emperor's stead down to the local officers of prefecture, county, and village, and the general public, I wonder how many really practice benevolence and righteousness, loyalty and filial piety, propriety and sincerity, and how many obey laws and regulations? The people, high and low alike, read books, but they do not strictly observe their conduct; both noble and humble say 'yes,' but their intentions and behavior are unlike their words. There is a proverb about a man striking his mother's head with the very *Book of Filial Piety* that he reverently upholds. This refers to the kind of people I have just described.

"Without reflecting upon their own violations of the laws and the teachings, such people sharply criticize others for transgressing the teachings given in the scriptures. This is like calling attention to another's swollen legs while hiding one's own legs from which pus is oozing. Applying your method of argument, I can say that there are too many corrupt central officials and local public servants who violate the laws, and that there are too few among the people, if any, who practice loyalty and filial piety. The three teachings are adopted and their propagation is encouraged by our emperors. Why is it that you are so critical of the Buddhist clergymen who transgress their precepts and try to uncover even their minutest defects by meticulous scrutiny, while you are so tolerant of the wrongdoing of Confucian students?

"In fact, the number of households allotted to support the Buddhist temples does not exceed ten thousand; the amount that a monk or nun eats a day is no more than a bowl of humble food. Besides, clergymen recite sutras and worship the Buddhas, thus paying back the state for the patronage that they have received, and they practice meditation to fulfill their Four Obligations.[83] On the other hand, the life of laymen is extravagant: some receive a stipend of ten thousand households; some, an allowance of rice from a hundred *ri* of land. Various high government officials occupy offices despite the fact that they are, as it were, living corpses, yet their greediness is utterly enormous; they receive their stipends for nothing and disgrace their offices. I have heard of none among them who could be compared to such ancient worthies as the Eight Excellent Ministers and the Five Virtuous Officials,[84] or to I Yin, Kung Wang, Chang Liang, and Ch'en P'ing,[85] who served their lords with distinction. If you must censure a monk or a nun for one bowlful of rice, why not investigate the waste caused by public servants?"

The patriot, perplexed, did not know what to say. A while later,

[83] See Part Two, p. 95, n. 34.

[84] It is said that there were eight good ministers and five famous ones in the court of the sage-king Shun.

[85] I Yin became a cook in order to approach King T'ang of Yin and to advise him. Kung Wang was a famous minister of King Wen of Chou. Chang Liang and Ch'en P'ing assisted the founder of the Former Han.

with a sigh, he said: "The stipend of a public servant is given in accordance with his rank. Public servants go to their offices early in the
morning when the stars can still be seen and return home after the
stars have appeared again. Rain or shine, they work hard at their duties
for the public. There is no reason for them to decline their stipend.
Those monks and nuns, on the other hand, recite sutras and pay homage
to the Buddhas, sitting together in a hall and practicing disciplines as
they please. How could they possibly fulfill their Four Obligations
merely by reciting a volume of the *Prajñāpāramitā Sutra* or by repeating the name of a Buddha?"

The master answered: "What you have said seems to be correct, but
is only superficially so. The Dharma is the guiding principle of the
Buddhas, and the Buddhas are those who transmit the Dharma. It is, in
fact, extremely rare to have an opportunity to hear even a clause that
reveals the excellent teaching, or to hear the name of a Buddha mentioned. Indeed, it was for this reason that a bodhisattva who was practicing discipline in the Himalayas cast himself down [86] and that another,
summoning his energy, stripped off his own skin.[87] It is better to gain
a clause that reveals the Dharma than to acquire the wealth of the
entire world. To gain the Four Clauses [88] is worthier than to repeat
innumerable lives. It was quite natural that a universal monarch offered
his own body as a seat,[89] or that Bodhisattva Priyadarśana burned himself.[90] By reciting the name of a Buddha, a man can free himself from
his immeasurable, heavy sins; and by uttering a mantra of one syllable,
a man can acquire endless merits. Why is it that those who are satisfied

[86] Shakyamuni Buddha in a previous birth as a bodhisattva cast himself down
a cliff, offering his body to appease the hunger of a rākṣasa demon—who was in
reality Śakra assuming the form of a rākṣasa to test the bodhisattva—in order to
hear a verse which contained the final truth of Buddhism. The story appears in
the *Nirvana Sutra*. T12, p. 450a.

[87] A bodhisattva wrote a clause that revealed the Dharma on his flayed skin,
using his blood for ink and his bones for a pen. The story is given in the *Ta-
chih-tu lun*. T25, p. 178c.

[88] The verse mentioned in note 86 consists of four clauses as follows: "All things
are impermanent; they appear and disappear. When an end is put to appearance
and disappearance, then the bliss of Nirvana will be realized."

[89] A universal monarch offering his body to be used as the seat of a sage to hear
about the Dharma appears in the *Lotus Sutra*. T19, p. 34c.

[90] See the *Lotus Sutra*. T19, p. 53c.

with a bowlful of humble food a day cannot fulfill their Four Obligations?"

The patriot retorted: "What you have said is a lie and is unworthy of belief. My teachers, Confucius and Lao Tzu, have never uttered such words. If merit could be gained by reciting the scriptures and worshiping the Buddhas, I would recite the Five Classics and the Three Books of History and worship the images of the Duke of Chou and Confucius. What is the difference? The lines of the Five Classics and those of the Buddhist scriptures are, after all, written in the same Chinese ideograms. What difference is there as far as their recitation is concerned?"

The master said: "Your argument may seem logical when heard carelessly, but when reflected upon well, it is far from being correct. You may find it hard to believe the deep meaning of what I have said; let me explain by giving a simile. In so far as the use of Chinese ideograms is concerned, there is little difference between an imperial edict and a personal letter written by a subject, but between them there is a great difference in power and effect. Once an imperial edict is issued, the whole world obeys it; depending on whether it is an edict of reward or of punishment, people will be filled with joy or fear. It is the same with the sutras and teachings of the Tathagata; is there anyone who does not believe in them, be he a bodhisattva, śrāvaka, deva, nāga, etc.? [91] Non-Buddhist texts are comparable to letters written by subjects; Buddhist sutras, to imperial edicts. It is therefore said that by reciting the sutras Indra destroyed the army of the asuras,[92] and that the King of Hell salutes on his knees one who has recited the sutras.[93] There has never been a man who removed his sins by reciting the Five Classics, or who escaped from calamity by reading the Three Books of History."

The patriot remarked: "The Shakyamuni Buddha was eloquent and talked much about merit, but Confucius was humble and did not boast about himself."

The master said: "Do not speak in that manner. Confucius himself praised and revered the Sage of the West [the Buddha], and Lao Tzu

[91] Deva is a heavenly being and nāga, a serpent.
[92] The story is given in the *Ta-chih-tu lun*. T25, p. 469a.
[93] The story appears in the *Fa-hua-ch'uan-chi*. T51, p. 88c.

has also said that He was his master.[94] The great sages do not lie. Slander may cause you to fall into hell."

The patriot then asked: "I can understand that those who commit the Ten Evil Deeds and the Five Deadly Sins [95] might fall into hell, but why would a man who slanders or abuses the teachings?"

The master replied: "You still have not heard how to cure a disease. In order to cure a physical disease, three things are necessary: a physician, a book of medicine, and the medicine. If the sick man respects the physician, believes in his diagnosis, and with a sincere attitude takes the medicine, then his disease will quickly be cured. On the other hand, if he abuses the physician or distrusts his diagnosis and disregards the medicine, how can he expect to recover soon from his illness? So it is with the Tathagata's curing of the diseases of peoples' minds. The Buddha is the king of medicine; his teachings are the book of medicine, and his guiding principles, the excellent medicines. To think in accordance with the principles given by the Buddha is like taking medicine. As the sick can be cured by taking medicine according to the physician's prescription, so a man can extinguish his sins and attain enlightenment. At present, sinful and ignorant men slander those [who promote Buddhism] and the teachings; how can they be free from committing deadly sins? The teachings are to be spread by men, and those men are to be elevated by the teachings; no discrepancy can be found between what they believe in and what they are. To slander those men is therefore to slander the teachings; to abuse the teachings is to abuse those men. Anyone who slanders those men and their teachings necessarily will fall into hell and may then have no chance of escape. Ignorant of this, people in the world talk wildly and are unaware of the ensuing grave results. Even if they commit the Ten Evil Deeds and the Five Deadly Sins day and night, they must not utter even a word of abuse about those men and the teachings. By killing and stealing, they can gain clothes or food, but they cannot gain anything at all by abusing those men and the teachings."

The patriot said: "I have taken your instruction to my heart and

[94] These accounts appear in the *P'o-hsieh lun* of Fa-lin (T52, p. 477a) and in the *Kuang-hung-ming-chi* of Tao-hsüan (T52, p. 7b).

[95] Killing one's father, mother, or an arhat (saint), injuring the body of a Buddha, and causing disunity in the Buddhist community.

will never transgress the teachings. Though I have now come to understand that we should not slander those men and the teachings, I still do
not know how many kinds of teaching or what kind of followers there
are, nor which teaching is more profound or more superficial than
the others."

The master explained: "There are two kinds of teaching: the Exoteric
and the Esoteric. In the Exoteric teaching, there are again two kinds:
the doctrine of the One Vehicle, and the doctrine of the Three Vehicles. The doctrine of the One Vehicle is that which was preached by
the Sambhogakaya Buddha for the bodhisattvas in the Ten Stages of
Bodhisattvahood. The doctrine of the Three Vehicles is that which
was preached by the Shakyamuni Buddha, the Incarnate Body, for
the bodhisattvas who have not yet reached the Ten Stages of Bodhisattvahood, for the śrāvakas, the pratyekabuddhas, and ordinary men.
The Esoteric teaching is that which was preached by Mahāvairocana
Tathagata, the Dharmakaya, the Essence, in order to enjoy the bliss of
Dharma with his subordinates. This is the doctrine of Shingon.

"Thus the manifold sutras and doctrines are excellent medicines if
each of them is applied appropriately in accordance with the capacity
and the nature of the recipient. The bodhisattvas have composed many
treatises based on certain sutras or doctrines, and masters have written
exegetic works. The disciples of generations remote from the time of
the Buddha should recite the respective sutras and treatises and discipline themselves. I have now clarified the basic differences in the doctrines and in the kinds of followers. As to the discussion of the pro-
fundity and superficiality of these doctrines, they are as explained in the
Ten Stages."

The patriot asked: "I know now the differences which exist among
the doctrines and the followers. In the treatises and exegetic works,
however, the authors assert their respective stands and refute the others.
Is this not a practice that slanders the doctrines?"

The master replied: "The ways of thinking of bodhisattvas all stem
from their compassion and are preceded by the motivation to benefit
others. In this frame of mind, they try to remove people's attachment
to superficial doctrines and to guide them toward profounder ones.
This practice is exceedingly beneficial. If, however, a man tries to
denounce the profound doctrines with the intention of acquiring per-

sonal gain and reputation and clings to superficial doctrines, then he cannot escape from the sin of slandering the doctrines."

The patriot said: "Your instructions have dispersed much of the mist that had covered my mind, but I still have a question that needs to be answered. I have already heard from you that, even though there is no one who has attained enlightenment, the way to enlightenment should not be disrupted; also that, even though there are some who are endowed with a high moral caliber and wisdom, they appear to be soiled or ignorant.[96] It seems that many have become clergymen simply in order to escape from their duties to the state, and that many of these are thieves. Observing these conditions, the emperors and the wise ministers who assist them are unable to keep silent. How can the Buddhist laws be consonant with the laws of state?"

The master answered: "Two categories can be distinguished: one is the principle of compassion and the other, that of wisdom. From the standpoint of the principle of compassion, tolerance and forgiveness should be emphasized, whereas from the standpoint of the principle of wisdom, restraint and strictness should be maintained. The former is explained in such sutras as *Ti-tsang-shih-lun*,[97] and the latter, in the *Nirvana* and *Sa-che*.[98] Common to the two categories is the system of giving and depriving or that of sure penalty and certain reward. In handling bribery cases this system should be kept in mind. The laws of the state and the precepts of the King of Dharma are different in form, but the tenor remains the same. If a man restrains himself in accordance with the laws, he will benefit greatly; if he perverts the law and acts from selfish motives, he will be extremely sinful. People in the world do not know these meanings; they do not know well the laws of the state, nor do they have any desire to follow the laws of the Buddha. They promote or demote people according to their feelings of love or hate; they administer punishment severely or lightly according to the social status of the criminal. If anyone governs the world with such practices, he will never be able to escape the consequences of his evil deeds. One should be restrained and careful.

"You have said before that drought, flood, epidemic, and social dis-

[96] Because they do not exhibit their purity and conceal their wisdom.

[97] *Ta-ch'eng-ta-chi-ti-tsang-shih-lun ching*. T13, pp. 736, 756.

[98] The *Nirvana Sutra*, T12, p. 365; *Ta-sa-che-ni-kan-tzu-so-shuo ching*, T9, p. 334.

order are caused by clergymen. This is not true. Not knowing the great principle, you speak at random. Now you must discern the real situation, just as King Ch'in discovered the hidden truth by looking into the mirror given him by a spirit.

"If the calamities in the world are due to the wrongdoing of monks and nuns, why did the flood continue for nine years in the rule of ancient King Yao, or the drought, for seven years in the reign of King T'ang? Which priests caused these calamities to occur? The fact is that the Buddhist priesthood did not exist in those times. That the state of Hsia was overthrown, that the dynasty of Yin perished, that the state of Chou declined at last, that the heir apparent of King Ch'in was killed while still young were all calamities caused by women. The fall of these dynasties was due to the mandate of heaven. In those days the Buddhist priesthood was nonexistent; so how could Buddhist clergymen have had anything to do with them?

"For these calamities, three causes can briefly be identified: the fatal moment, the punishment of heaven, and karma. The fatal moment: calamities which are destined to happen at a certain period in the cycle of time are those such as the Nine Calamities.[99] The flood in the period of King Yao and the drought in the time of King T'ang belong to this category. It is said that a king [Fu Hsi] had prepared for the calamity, having learned of its approach by omens. It is due to the fatal moment that in a degenerate period the five kinds of calamity [100] occur frequently. The punishment of heaven: when laws are not enforced on the basis of principle, heaven punishes men. For example, when a filial widow was sentenced to death, it did not rain,[101] and when a loyal minister was imprisoned, there was frost in midsummer.[102] Karma: people who have done evil in their previous lives are born in an evil period and confront such calamities as stated in the foregoing lines because of the forces resulting from their previous evil deeds. These

[99] The theory held in ancient China that there would be five famines and four floods in each cyclical period of 4,560 years.

[100] Wars, natural disasters, etc.; heresies flourish; passions are strong; people are weak physically and mentally; and the span of life is short.

[101] When a filial widow was sentenced to death without having committed any offense, it did not rain for three years. The example is given in the *Han Shu*.

[102] Tsou Yen, a loyal minister of King Hui of the state of Yen, was imprisoned without having committed any crime. Because of his cry, frost was seen in midsummer. The story is given in the *Huai-nan Tzu*.

topics are discussed in detail in *Wu-hsing chih* (Accounts of the working of the five primary elements), in the Dynastic Historical Records, *Shou-hu-kuo-chieh-chu ching*,[103] *Wang-fa-cheng-lun ching*,[104] etc. Without knowledge of these things, you uttered statements that were nonsensical and absolutely pointless.

"Now I will answer your question as to whether or not Buddhism is useful to the state. If there were no diseases at all, there would be no need for medicines. As long as mental and emotional disturbances exist, there is a need for teachings. As good medicines were discovered out of man's sympathy for the diseased, so Buddhism came into being from the Buddha's compassion for his suffering fellow beings. The Noble One appears in the world out of compassionate love in order to bestow comfort upon men and to remove their sufferings. Nothing is better than to defend the root [mind], to make people comfortable, and to remove their sufferings; and the basis of defending the root cannot be established in the absence of the teachings. As a strong or mild medicine is required depending upon the seriousness of the disease, so there are profound and superficial doctrines as needs arise, depending on how deep-rooted people's disturbances are. In a favorable period, a universal monarch is able to guide men because the diseases of the mind are light, but in an unfavorable period the Tathagata must expound the teaching because people are deeply troubled. In the present degenerate period the diseases of the mind are most serious, for men are overwhelmed by the Three Poisons and tormented by the Eight Sufferings. The people are less blessed, and many suffer from poverty and illness. These sufferings result from their evil deeds committed in previous births. Yet gluttons kill living beings and fill their stomachs with flesh; misers try to cheat others in securing their own food and clothing; lewd men finish their lives as do moths which fly into a flame at night; men who like to drink, like orangutans, are held to the place where wine bottles are found. Such perverse views and wicked deeds are too numerous to count. If anyone commits wrong acts in this life, he will necessarily fall into the Three Evil Paths in the next life and will be unable to escape suffering there for a period of aeons. The Buddha, the compassionate Father, witnessing this horrible state of suffering, has preached the doctrine of cause and effect. By preaching it in terms of a vicious

[103] T19, pp. 571c–574c.   [104] T14, p. 797.

cycle, he has taught men how to escape from suffering. He has preached the doctrine of cause and effect, guiding men toward the good, and thereby bestowing upon them the way to bliss. There are two kinds of people who practice his doctrine; that is, clergymen and laymen. The clergymen are the monks and nuns who shave their heads and wear Buddhist robes. The laymen are those who dress themselves in secular clothes. From the emperor down to the commoners, those who observe the Five Precepts or the Ten Precepts and take refuge in Buddhism are laymen. Both the laymen who observe the Ten Precepts and practice the Six Paramitas and the clergymen who cherish the great aspiration for enlightenment are called bodhisattvas. They will be freed from sufferings as they cut off evil; they will obtain bliss as they cultivate the good. The fruit of obtaining birth as a human being or a heavenly being or of obtaining the realization of Buddhahood will result from the practice of cutting off the evil and cultivating the good. In order to show how to practice these two aspects, the Noble One established his doctrines. Now that the doctrines of the Buddha are already in existence, it is up to men to practice and to propagate them. Those who know the doctrines renounce their family ties and transmit the torch of tradition, and those who aspire to enlightenment enter the priesthood and change their appearance. In a sutra it is said that if kings or parents permit men and women to become clergymen, the merit which they thereby gain is immeasurable.[105] It is owing to the existence of monks and nuns that Buddhism does not come to an end, and it is because of Buddhism that men can open their eye of wisdom. When their vision is clear, they can tread the right path, thus being able to attain Nirvana. Wherever the doctrines given in the sutras are practiced, there the Buddha defends men and the heavenly beings protect them. Thus the benefits which Buddhism gives to the state are incalculable."

The patriot asked: "It is evident that those who know the doctrines and who spread Buddhism are of great benefit to the state. However, why do so many clergymen who violate the precepts and behave contrary to the teachings given in the sutras fill the land?"

The master replied: "A great mountain is all embracing in that on it birds and beasts gather and both medicinal herbs and poisonous plants

---

[105] *Hsien-yü-yin-yüan ching* (adapted). т4, p. 376b.

grow there. The ocean is deep and vast; fishes and turtles swim in schools, but dragons and demons live in it as well. In the vicinity of the *cintāmaṇi* gem ogres flock together in a circle, and in the neighborhood of the treasure house thieves always await their chance. Even if a beautiful girl does not give a sign of invitation, both handsome and ugly men compete to pursue her. Sick people throng at the gate of a physician though they are not called. Ants swarm around bloody flesh; flies, on a foul-smelling corpse. All nations submit to a sage-king though he remains silent; rivers flow into the sea though it does not think of receiving them. Poor people gather around a rich man though he does not invite them; students come to a wise man though he does not speak out. In a clear mirror, both beautiful and unpleasant images are reflected; in serene water, both large and small objects are reflected. Vast space indiscriminately embraces all things within itself, and the great earth without conscious intentions grows a hundred kinds of grasses. Though his son was stupid, King Yao was praised as a sage-king; though his father made an attempt to kill his son King Shun, the son remained filial to his father. Confucius had three thousand disciples, but only seventy are said to have been well known; the rest were obscure. Among the innumerable disciples of the Shakyamuni Buddha, the wicked ones were the Six Monks, Devadatta, and Sunakṣatra.[106] Even in the days of the Buddha, not all monks were necessarily pure-hearted, so you can imagine that there are more wicked ones in this later degenerate period. Yet the compassion of the Buddha, the Father of all, pervades the triple world; both wise and foolish, good and wicked men should look up to Him. Such is the truth, therefore, it is not at all surprising [that there are some wicked clergymen]. Nevertheless, a poison can turn into medicine; iron, into gold.

"It was due to the influence of the ruler's virtue or to the fatal moment that the people under King Yao were all worthy of being appointed feudal lords, whereas the people under King Chieh all deserved to be sentenced to death. The Kāśyapa Tathagata has clearly preached the reasons for these matters in the *Shou-hu-kuo-chieh-chu ching*.[107]

---

[106] The six monks are the representatives of the wicked monks who acted in a group in the time of Shakyamuni Buddha; Devadatta is the Buddha's cousin who rebelled against the order; Sunakṣatra (Zensei) appears in the *Nirvana Sutra* as a notorious monk who entertained biased views and violated the precepts.

[107] T19, pp. 571c–573c.

Those who wish to know more should read the sutra; in order to avoid tediousness, I will not quote from it here."

A summary in verse:

> Eternalists and nihilists!
> They are confident that their dogmas are the profoundest,
> Yet they are not free from vexations!
> They argue in vain that the subject is real,
> Or that the objects are real.
> But they are in the cycle of birth and death.
> For them the Great Sage opened the doors of the Goat Vehicle,
> Advising them to ride it and meditate to gain Nirvana.
> By practicing for three lives or sixty aeons
> The Fivefold Concentration [108] and Fourfold Meditation,[109]
> And by observing two hundred fifty precepts,
> They will be freed from the Eightfold Suffering.
> The fire that burns the defilements of egoism,
> The wisdom of Nirvana, consumes their body and mind.
> But when they come across the Tathagata's warnings,
> They will be mindful of the broader Vehicle of the bodhisattvas.

QUESTION: What sutra and treatise have you used to develop the discussion on this mind?

ANSWER: The *Mahāvairocana Sutra* and the *Aspiration to Enlightenment*.

QUESTION: How is it explained in the sutra and in the treatise?

ANSWER: In the sutra it is said that "they thus recognize the existence of Psychophysical Constituents but not that of a permanent ego; they struggle, being arrested by the objects of senses and mind." [110] Also in the same sutra: "The śrāvakas, engaging in the practice of contemplation and knowing how beings come into existence and come to an end, transcend the two extremes [of eternalism and nihilism]; with the knowledge derived from their correct observation, they gain the point of departure of freeing themselves [from the cycle of samsara]. This is called the path of samadhi of the śrāvakas." [111] And in the same sutra: "The mantras preached by the śrāvakas are lengthy." [112] Evidence from

---

[108] Breath counting; to meditate that all things are impure; to extend the thought of loving kindness far and wide; to meditate on the primary cause and secondary causes of all conditioned things; and to differentiate effects.

[109] See above, n. 70.   [110] T18, p. 3b.   [111] T18, p. 9c.   [112] T18, p. 10a.

the *Aspiration to Enlightenment* will be given in the following section, since it is applicable to this and also to the next mind.

Fifth: The Mind Freed from the Seed of the Cause of Karma. This is the mind to be realized and held by the pratyekabuddhas who live alone or in a group among themselves. They meditate on the Twelve Links of Causation and have a strong aversion to the world of samsara. Falling flowers and leaves evoke in them a keen awareness of the transitory nature of the phenomenal world of birth, growth, change, and destruction. They live in forests or in villages, keeping strict silence and devoting themselves to the practice of concentration with the aim of uprooting the tree stump of ignorance, the seed of karmic force and defilements. The heretics cannot approach them nor have a glimpse of them because they are, as it were, swimming alone in an abyss of serenity or wandering in an abode of nonattachment. They observe the precepts without having been ordained officially and obtain wisdom without having been instructed by any teacher. They realize on their own the Thirty-seven Items of Mastery [113] and understand the doctrines of the Aggregates, Sense-fields, and Worlds.[114] They may lead others to salvation with their supernatural power of transformation but not by oral instruction. Since they lack a sense of great compassion toward others, they are not equipped with the knowledge of expedient means in guiding people; they are concerned about extinguishing their own sufferings and about realizing Nirvana. It is therefore said in a sutra: "[The pratyekabuddhas] extinguish the seed of ignorance, the tree stump of karma and of the defilements, which causes men to repeat the cycle of the Twelve Links of Causation." [115] . . . A summary in verse:

> The pratyekabuddhas riding on the Deer-cart are taciturn.[116]
> They live alone like the horn of rhinoceros, or in a group.

[113] See above, n. 67.

[114] The Five Aggregates are the Five Psychophysical Constituents—form (or matter), sensation, conception, volition, and consciousness. The Twelve Sense-fields are the six cognitive faculties (eye, nose, ear, tongue, body, and mind) and the six categories of corresponding objects of the six cognitive faculties. The Eighteen Worlds are the Twelve Sense-fields and the six kinds of awareness of the cognitive faculties.

[115] The *Mahāvairocana Sutra*. T18, p. 3b.   [116] See above, n. 64.

Meditating deeply on the Twelve Links of Causation,
They gain supernatural power by a hundred aeons' discipline.
Extinguishing their karma, actual and potential defilements,
They aim at complete cessation of their body and mind.
They abide quietly in samadhi, long, as though intoxicated;
But being awakened by the Buddha from their slumber,
They are to be directed to the palace of One Suchness.[117]

QUESTION: On the basis of which sutra and treatise are you explaining this mind?

ANSWER: On the basis of the *Mahāvairocana Sutra* and the *Aspiration to Enlightenment*.

QUESTION: How do they explain it?

ANSWER: In the sutra it is said: "The pratyekabuddhas extinguish the seed of ignorance, the tree stump of karma and of the defilements, which causes men to repeat the cycle of the Twelve Links of Causation. They are free from the influence of heretics who advocate eternalism, etc.; the tranquil state of mind which they obtain cannot be understood by any of the heretics. The Buddha therefore preached that the pratyekabuddhas are free from all faults." [118] Also that "the pratyekabuddhas observe deeply the law of cause and effect, abide firmly in the practice of silence, and experience the samadhi of indifference to all things, which words fail to explain. This is called the way of samadhi of the pratyekabuddhas." [119] Further, "O Lord of Mysteries, should anyone master the mantras of the pratyekabuddhas and the śrāvakas, he can destroy various faults." [120] And, "The mantras explained by the śrāvakas are lengthy. The pratyekabuddhas differ somewhat from the śrāvakas in that they extinguish karma more thoroughly than the latter because of their superior samadhi." [121]

In the *Aspiration to Enlightenment* of Nāgārjuna it is said: "Of the followers of Hinayana, the śrāvakas apply themselves earnestly to the doctrines of the Four Noble Truths, and the pratyekabuddhas, to the Twelve Links of Causation. Knowing that the composites of the Four Great Elements [122] and of the Five Psychophysical Constituents wear out in the end, they develop a deep sense of aversion and destroy their attachment to the idea of a permanent ego. Devoting themselves to the

---

[117] The One Vehicle of Mahayana is implied.   [118] T18, p. 3b.
[119] T18, p. 9c.   [120] T18, p. 9c.   [121] T18, p. 10a.
[122] Earth, water, fire, and wind.

realization of their respective doctrines, they regard as their final goal
the attainment of the Nirvana of complete cessation. The students of
Mantrayāna should meditate as follows: The followers of these Two
Vehicles, though they have destroyed their attachment to the idea of a
permanent ego, are not free from their attachment to dharma.[123] They
purify their [six categories of] consciousness but have no knowledge of
others.[124] After a long period of time they attain their goal; upon complete cessation of their body and mind, they believe they enter Nirvana,
a state likened to serene and tranquil space. For those who are destined
to be followers of Hinayana, it is difficult to develop a new way of
life; they may well have to wait for aeons before they develop it. On
the other hand, those who are not so destined will convert from Hinayana to Mahayana, whenever an opportunity presents itself and without
having to wait for aeons, and come to believe that they have tran-
scended the triple world arising from the illusory city. Because of their
previous faith in the Buddhas, because they have received the grace
of the Buddhas and the bodhisattvas, and because they have been
guided by skillful means, they finally develop their aspiration for
Mahayana. Starting from the stage of faith, they finally attain enlightenment after having spent countless aeons going through hardships and
ascetic practices. Now it is obvious that the śrāvakas and pratyekabuddhas are of small and inferior wisdom; they should not be longed
for." [125]

In the commentary on the *Daśabhūmika Sutra* [126] it is said: "Should
anyone fall into the stage of the śrāvakas or of the pratyekabuddhas, it
would mean a great decline and misfortune:

> To fall into the two stages of Hinayana
> Is called the death of a bodhisattva;
> He loses all of his gains.
> The fear he must experience in falling into hell
> Is no greater than this;
> To fall into these Two Vehicles is
> The greatest fear, indeed.
> Even if he falls into hell,

[123] The belief that the Five Psychophysical Constituents are real.

[124] Others are the ego-consciousness and the *ālaya*-consciousness of the Yogācāra
school of Mahayana.

[125] T32, p. 573a.   [126] *Shih-chu-p'i-p'o-sha lun.* T26, p. 41a.

He may in the end become a Buddha;
But if he falls into the Two Vehicles,
The path to Buddhahood is completely obstructed.
It was precisely for this reason
That the Buddha preached in his sutra:
As a man wishing to live long fears decapitation,
So a bodhisattva should fear
Falling into the stage of the śrāvakas and of the pratyekabuddhas."

Sixth: The Mahayana Mind with Sympathetic Concern for Others.
Here is a Dharma for bodhisattvas known as the Vehicle of sympathetic
concern for others. It rises far above the teachings of non-Buddhists
and widely leads others to salvation, being superior to the teachings of
the śrāvakas and of the pratyekabuddhas.

Bodhisattvas wipe away the dust of attachment by realizing the
Twofold Emptiness [127] and the Threefold Nature.[128] By practicing the
Four Boundless Frames of Mind [129] and the Four Embracing Acts,[130]
they benefit others equally. They meditate profoundly and meticu-
lously on the *ālaya*-consciousness and pay close attention to the data
of mind, which are nonsubstantial like phantoms or flames of fire. They
spend aeons repeating the cycle of birth and death, encouraging themselves not to retrogress from their original resolution, struggling with
the three kinds [of lassitude]; [131] and they hope to gain the excellent
result of attaining enlightenment in their devotion to the practice of
the Four Vows.[132]

---

[127] Realizing the nonsubstantial nature both of a permanent individual ego and
of the Psychophysical Constituents.

[128] The three kinds of existence are distinguished according to the nature of
each group: existences produced from imagination (*parikalpita*); existences
arising from dependent origination (*paratantra*), phenomenal existences which
lack immutable self-nature; and the perfect existence (*pariniṣpanna*), Suchness.

[129] Boundless loving kindness, compassion, joy at the sight of others' happiness,
and equanimity.

[130] Charity, kind speech, beneficial acts, and adapting oneself to others.

[131] In the Yogācāra school there are five stages of progress toward enlightenment. In the first stage the three kinds of lassitude have to be overcome. Lassitude
develops on hearing that enlightenment is profound and great, that it is difficult
to perfect the spirit of charity, and that to attain enlightenment is not easy.

[132] The four great vows of all bodhisattvas: however innumerable sentient
beings may be, I vow to save them; however inexhaustible the defilements may
be, I vow to extinguish them; however limitless Buddhist doctrines may be, I
vow to study all of them; and I vow to realize unsurpassed enlightenment.

They construct, as it were, the walls of the city of samadhi and install therein the general of "mind-only"; fighting victoriously against a host of tempters, they overcome the leader of the bandits which are the defilements. Marshaling the fighters of the eightfold army,[133] they bind [sentient beings who have lost their way] with the rope of adaptation; [134] riding on the steeds of the Six Supernatural Powers,[135] they exterminate [the evils of biased views] with the sword of wisdom. In the fifth [final] stage they are to be rewarded with the title of nobility and appointed to the office of King of Mind in the capital of the Four Attributes.[136]

The result thus attained is the ultimate state in which genuine peace can be found; any attempt at describing it is beyond verbalization. They are to stand peacefully on the platform of the absolute Truth, living spontaneously in the palace of the World of Dharma. An ordinary man, for aeons rewarded by his efforts, is now to be called a Lord and for the first time be given the name of King of Dharma with the Fourfold Wisdom.[137] Then in the sea of the *ālaya*-consciousness, the surging billows of the seven consciousnesses [138] become tranquil, and on realizing the nonsubstantiality of the Psychophysical Constituents, the ill resulting from the six bandits [139] is severed. Like a lid to a box, their nondiscriminating perfect wisdom will be in harmony with the eternal Truth. Their compassion, further intensified by attaining enlightenment, will pervade all sentient beings in all paths. By preaching the teachings of the Tripiṭaka, they lead the three types of being of different capacity [140] to salvation; with the instruction of the Ten Precepts, they lead the beings in the Six Transmigratory Paths to salvation. As to Vehicles, they maintain only three; and as to the number of consciousnesses, they discuss eight types. They divide sentient beings into five categories and think that some lack the potential to attain en-

133 The Eightfold Noble Path is to be perfected in the fourth stage.
134 "Adaptation" is an item of the Four Embracing Acts (see above, n. 130), which are also required to be perfected in the fourth stage.
135 See above, n. 11.
136 They are attributes of Nirvana: Eternity, Bliss, the Self, and Purity.
137 See Part Two, p. 84, for a discussion on the subject.
138 The ego-consciousness, the mind, and the five senses.
139 Objects of the five sense-organs and of mind.
140 Bodhisattva, śrāvaka, and pratyekabuddha.

lightenment.[141] They believe that among the Three Bodies of Buddha one is constant but the others are transient,[142] that a hundred million Nirmanakaya Buddhas lead sentient beings to salvation on the six boats,[143] and that one thousand Shakyamunis on one thousand lotus leaves preach the doctrines of the Three Vehicles.[144]

The reason why this religious mind is called the mind concerned with others is that it is concerned with the salvation of all sentient beings in the entire world. The term "Mahayana" is given because it is the One Great Vehicle in contrast to the Goat-vehicle and the Deer-vehicle.[145] This is a system of teaching which a worthy man should practice and on which any bodhisattva should set his heart. The foregoing is an outline of the doctrine of the school prevalent in the north [of the Yangtze River, that is, the Yogācāra school in China]. A summary in verse:

> The sea of Mind is forever tranquil
> Without even a single ripple;
> Stirred by the storm of discriminations,
> Billows rage to and fro.
>
> Men in the street are deluded;
> They are fascinated by phantomlike men and women.
> Heretics are crazed;
> They adhere to the grand tower of mirage.
>
> They do not know
> That heaven and hell are fabricated by their own minds.
> Do they come to realize
> That "mind-only" will free them from their tragedies?
>
> Be that as it may,
> By practicing the Six Paramitas for three aeons,
> By practicing the fifty-two stages for enlightenment,
> They will uncover One Mind.[146]

[141] Determined to be a bodhisattva, and one not determined; determined to be a śrāvaka, and a pratyekabuddha; and a sentient being who lacks the potentiality to attain enlightenment. The first two will attain enlightenment; the second two will also attain enlightenment but only if they convert to Mahayana; the last one has no chance.

[142] The belief that the Dharmakaya Buddha is eternal, but that the Sambhogakaya and Nirmanakaya Buddhas are transient.

[143] The Six Paramitas.

[144] This is based on the Buddhology given in the *Brahmajāla Sūtra* (т1484).

[145] See above, n. 64.   [146] A synonym for Suchness.

When they become purehearted,
Cutting off their emotional and mental obstacles,
They will find their own Treasury—
Enlightenment, or Nirvana.

Now they are fully endowed with
The Three Excellent Qualities and the Four Attributes.[147]
Unaware of their own possessions,
How long have they groped after them elsewhere!

That which is beyond speech and conception
Pervades the entire universe;
Alas, not knowing this,
A son drifts like duckweed in the water of samsara.

QUESTION: Which sutra and treatise have you consulted in order to define this mind?

ANSWER: The *Mahāvairocana Sutra*, the *Aspiration to Enlightenment*, and others.

QUESTION: How do they explain it?

ANSWER: In the *Mahāvairocana Sutra* it is said, "O Lord of Mysteries, the practice of Mahayana is to develop the intention unconditionally to help save others. Nothing has immutable self-nature. Why can this be said? Because he who in the distant past practiced in this way observed the nature of Psychophysical Constituents and that of *ālaya*-consciousness; he knew that what appeared to be self-nature was like an illusion, phantom, shadow, echo, circle of fire, or mirage." [148] In Nāgārjuna's *Aspiration to Enlightenment*, it is said: "There are also beings who develop the Mahayana mind and who practice the deeds of the bodhisattva; of various doctrines, they leave nothing unstudied. Three aeons are spent in practicing the Six Paramitas and ten thousand disciplines. Upon mastering them completely, they realize the fruit of Buddhahood. They spend a long time before they attain their aim because the doctrines which they study call for development in stages." [149]

QUESTION: As for the Enlightened Ones who have thus severed both emotional and mental obstacles and who have realized the Four Attributes, can they be regarded as having reached the ultimate?

ANSWER: No, they have not reached the original Source.

QUESTION: How does one know this?

---

[147] The Three Qualities are the Dharmakaya, transcendental wisdom, and liberation. As to the Four Attributes, see above, n. 136.

[148] T18, p. 3b.   [149] T32, p. 573a.

ANSWER: Nāgārjuna explains that "even if the devotees have uprooted all evils, practiced all good, reached the ultimate stage going beyond the Ten Stages of Bodhisattvahood, perfectly realized the Three Bodies of the Buddha, and have been endowed with the Four Attributes, they are still in the stage of ignorance, not in that of wisdom." [150]

According to this evidence, the enlightened ones in this mind have not reached the ultimate Source of Mind; they have merely blocked the illusions which exist outside of the Mind. They have not yet uncovered the jewels in the secret Treasury.

Seventh: The Mind That Realizes that the Mind Is Unborn. The great space, being vast and tranquil, embraces all phenomena within itself; the great ocean, being deep and serene, contains in a single drop of water a thousand beings. As the cardinal number one is the mother of one hundred and one thousand, so is voidness the root of all relative beings. These temporary beings are not beings; [151] yet the universe is filled with beings. That which is absolutely empty [Suchness] is not empty; yet it manifests itself as a variety of phenomena and is nowhere fixed. Matter, which is not different from emptiness, unfolds itself as all phenomenal existences; yet it is of the nature of emptiness. Emptiness, which is not different from matter, nullifies all marks of particularity; yet it is manifested as a variety of temporary beings. Thus, matter is none other than emptiness, and emptiness itself is none other than matter; all phenomenal existences are of the same structure. What can remain an exception? The relationship that exists between these two is comparable to the inseparable relationship that exists between water and its waves or between gold and gold ornaments. For this reason, the term "neither identical nor different" has been introduced, and the expressions "double standard of truth" [152] and "four kinds of Middle

---

[150] This is quoted from the commentary on *The Awakening of Faith* (*Shih-mo-ho-yen lun*) attributed to Nāgārjuna. T32, p. 637c.

[151] This line means that all existences in the phenomenal worlds, being causally conditioned, are temporary existences and are not immutable existences or real entities.

[152] The absolute truth and the relative truth. The former is the truth of the ultimately Real, i.e., Suchness. This is Nirvana, which may be experienced but which is devoid of any empirical determinations. The latter is the empirical truth accepted by people in the world which can be communicated by the use of language.

Way" [153] have become known. One must perceive emptiness freely and transcend groundless speculations by means of the Eightfold Negation.

This being done, the Four Tempters [154] will be subdued without fighting, and the Three Poisons [155] will be extinguished of themselves. Since samsara is none other than Nirvana, there should be no distinction of classes. Since the state of defilement is none other than the state of enlightenment, there is no need to cut off defilement and to attain enlightenment. The existence of classes is based on the classless class; the existence of fifty-two stages [156] does not need to be abolished. Since these stages are classless stages, the existence of stages does not obstruct the devotee's attaining enlightenment in an instant. He is to practice disciplines in an instant, the perfection of which may take three aeons; unfolding the doctrines of the Three Vehicles based on the tenets of the one [and the absolute Middle] Way, he labors to help save others. He grieves over those who, abiding in the fourth mind, do not understand that the Psychophysical Constituents are not real. He also deplores the fact that those who belong to the sixth mind differentiate subject from object.[157] Now, the King of Mind [158] is free and has realized its original nature, like water free of turbulence; defiled and perpetual activity at the surface of the Mind, comparable to the waves on the surface of water, will cease. Being provided with correct wisdom and with the wisdom of expedient means [to strengthen his insight], he experiences enlightenment in the essential unity of Suchness. On the basis of the absolute Middle Way, the double standard of truth

153 They are: 1) The Middle Way in contrast to the biased views of the extremes—eternalism and nihilism; 2) freedom from eternalism and nihilism, called the Middle Way of Extinction; 3) freedom from the notion of the Middle Way; and 4) the Middle Way in terms of "neither being nor nonbeing," regarding "being" and "nonbeing" as relative concepts.

154 The Four Tempters are those of evil desires that injure one's body and mind; of the Five Psychophysical Constituents which cause suffering; of death, and of heavenly beings. These try to prevent living beings from doing good.

155 See above, n. 36.

156 The fifty-two bodhisattva stages for attaining Buddhahood, i.e., fifty stages of discipline, the stage of approaching Buddhahood, and the stage of Buddhahood.

157 Those who belong to the sixth religious mind, the followers of the subjective idealism of Yogācāra, recognize the mind only and deny the validity of the objective world.

158 Here, a synonym for the ālaya-consciousness.

—relative and absolute—can be gained. He realizes that the essential nature of his own mind is originally unborn and that the subject and the object are nondual. Such are the main tenets of the Southern school.[159]

Mahāvairocana, therefore, said to the Lord of Mysteries: "O Lord of Mysteries, he has thus forsaken even the notion that the permanent ego is unreal. Because of the freedom of the Lord of Mind, he will become aware that his mind is originally unborn. Why? Because, O Lord of Mysteries, the mind is unobtainable in time."[160] The commentary[161] says: "The Lord of Mind is the King of Mind. Because the Mind is unobstructed by the dichotomy of being and nonbeing, it knows no hindrances. Because it can perfect its excellent functions as it wishes, the words 'the freedom of the Lord of Mind' are used. 'The freedom of the Lord of Mind' indicates clearly the state of the enlightened mind whose brightness has been uncovered even further and is far superior to that of the previous stage. The King of Mind is just like the water of a lake whose nature is originally clean and pure. The purity of its functions is just like that of the purified particles of dust in the water. Therefore, when one realizes the purity of this Mind, he is able to become aware that the Mind is originally unborn. Why? Because the Mind is unobtainable in time. Waves in the great ocean, because they come to be contingent upon causes [wind, etc.], have not existed before and will not exist later [in their identical forms]. But the nature of water is different. The water was not nonexistent when the waves came to be contingent upon their causes, and it will not be nonexistent when the waves will come to cease at the disappearance of these causes. The King of Mind is like this; it knows no distinction of before and after. Since it is free from the distinction of before and after, though its functions come to be or cease to be conditioned by the wind of the world of objects, the essential nature of the Mind is free from appearing and disappearing. If one realizes that this Mind is originally unborn, one gradually enters the gate of the letter A."[162]

Thus, the meanings of the Unconditioned and of its conditions and

[159] The school popular south of the Yangtze River, i.e., the San-lun or Mādhyamika school of Chinese Buddhism.

[160] The *Mahāvairocana Sutra*. T18, p. 3b.

[161] T1796. The commentary on the *Mahāvairocana Sutra* expounded by Śubhā-karasiṃha and edited by I-hsing.

[162] T39, p. 603a. Here the letter A stands for *anutpāda* (unborn or uncreated).

the cause of remaining in the samsaric order, of being freed from it, or otherwise, are extensively discussed in such texts as the *Sheng-man ching*,[163] *Pao-hsing lun*,[164] and *Fo-hsing lun*.[165] The expression "originally unborn" stands for the Eightfold Negation—unborn, imperishable, unceasing, nonconstant, nonidentical, not different, not going away, and not coming. The students of Mādhyamika regard this Eightfold Negation as the absolute Middle Way. For this reason, Master Chi-tsang (549–623) enthusiastically discussed its meanings in such writings as the *Erh-ti-fang-yen* and the *Fo-hsing-i*.[166] A summary in verse:

> Causally conditioned phenomena are devoid of immutable self-nature;
> They are empty, temporal, and yet ultimately real; all are unborn.
>
> Waves which no sooner appear than they disappear are none other than the water itself.
> The One Mind is like water; it is originally clean and serene.
>
> Man's wisdom is penetrating when he realizes the unity between being and nonbeing;
> Then he will see clearly the truthfulness of the double standard of truth.
>
> The sharp sword of the Eightfold Negation cuts off all idle speculations;
> The five one-sided views [167] will be resolved of themselves, and man can gain genuine peace.
>
> Thus he enters the Way of the Buddha, his mind being free and unobstructed;
> He is now ready to advance to the next station from this preliminary gate [of negation].

In the sutra it is said: "O Lord of Mysteries, he has thus forsaken even the notion that the permanent ego is unreal. Because of the free-

[163] *Śrīmālā Sutra*. T353.   [164] *Ratna-gotra śāstra*. T1611.

[165] The treatise on the Buddha-nature, attributed to Vasubandhu and translated by Paramārtha. T1610.

[166] The former seems to correspond to the *Erh-ti-i* of Chi-tsang (T1854) and the latter, to chap. 3 (*Fo-hsing-i*) of the *Ta-ch'eng hsüan-lun* of the same author (T1853).

[167] The theory of being (realism), the theory of nonbeing, the theory of both being and nonbeing, the theory of neither being nor nonbeing, and the theory of not neither being nor nonbeing.

dom of the Lord of Mind, he will become aware that his mind is originally unborn. Why? Because, O Lord of Mysteries, the mind is unobtainable in time. He who knows the essential nature of his mind in this way is a devotee of yoga who has gone beyond the second *kalpa*." [168] In the *Aspiration to Enlightenment* we find: "The devotee should know that all phenomena are empty. If he realizes that all phenomena are uncreated, in his realization of the unity of the essence of his mind and Suchness, he will see no distinction between body and mind. Abiding in the true ultimate wisdom of equality and quiescence, he will not be made to regress from it. If an illusion arises, he should be aware that it is an illusion; he should not follow it. When the illusion ceases, the Source of Mind will become tranquil." [169]

QUESTION: Can this mind, which is peaceful and unconditioned, transcending groundless speculations, be called the culmination of enlightenment?

ANSWER: Nāgārjuna Bodhisattva explained: "The pure state of enlightenment, from the beginningless beginning, is not something that can be acquired by discipline or by the aid of some other power. Intrinsically one is endowed with perfect attributes and with original wisdom. Original enlightenment is also beyond the four modes of description [170] and the five one-sided views. To define it as natural is not natural; to define it as pure mind is also not proper. It can only be expressed by negation. Such a state still belongs to the realm of ignorance and not to that of enlightenment." [171]

Eighth: The Mind That Is Truly in Harmony with the One Way.[172] Confucius, born in China, advocated the Five Cardinal Virtues throughout the land. The noblest of men appeared in India and preached the doctrine of the One Vehicle, unfolding it into the doctrines of the

[168] The *Mahāvairocana Sutra*. T18, p. 3b.   [169] T32, p. 573b.

[170] Being, nonbeing, both being and nonbeing, and neither being nor nonbeing.

[171] The commentary on *The Awakening of Faith*, attributed to Nāgārjuna. T32, p. 637c.

[172] This is the title (*Nyojitsu ichidōshin*) as it appears in the Introduction to the *Precious Key*. The original at this point words the title differently and adds two more subtitles (K.Z., I, 455): "The Unconditioned Mind of One Way (*Ichidō muishin*)," or "Knowing One's Own Mind As It Really Is (*Nyojitsu chijishin*)," or "The Mind of Emptiness Transcending the World of Objects (*Kūshō mukyōshin*)."

Three Vehicles. The infatuated populace remained at home and did not go out [to hear Confucius speak]; the ignorant people walked away [from the Buddha's assembly] and did not return.[173] Only the seventy outstanding students [of Confucius] went to the lecture hall, and eleven thousand enlightened disciples believed in the golden sermons of the Buddha. The teaching of the Five Cardinal Virtues failed to be adopted fully in China, just as a circle cannot be accommodated to a square; the Vehicle waiting outside the [burning] house failed to attract the Hinayanists and some Mahayanists.[174] Such being the mentality of people, the Buddha was inclined to sit undisturbed under the Bodhi tree for three weeks; [175] he also had to wait forty years.[176]

At first, the Buddha preached the doctrine of the Four Noble Truths and then the doctrines given in the *Vaipulya Sutra*, etc., in order to wash away the grime of the false view that man's permanent ego and the constituents of the world are real. Then he expounded the perfect teaching, just as heaven pours abundant rain upon the buds and leaves of plants.[177] [In expounding the *Lotus Sutra*], he first entered the Lotus samadhi and meditated that the essential nature [of all sentient beings] is unsoiled [as a lotus remains unsoiled by mud]. Then he shed a ray of light from the circle of white hair between his eyebrows, revealing his perfect and all penetrating wisdom. He eulogized the wisdom of the Enlightened Ones who have realized that the doctrine of the One Vehicle contains the doctrines of the Three Vehicles and discussed

[173] The reference is to the beginning of chap. 2 of the *Lotus Sutra* which states that stupid and arrogant people left the assembly before the Buddha started preaching. T9, p. 7a.

[174] The Vehicle waiting outside the [burning] house is drawn by white oxen, the symbol of the powerful message of universal salvation of the One Vehicle of the *Lotus Sutra*. The burning house is the world of suffering in which unenlightened beings live without knowing the impending danger. The story appears in chap. 3 of the sutra. T9, p. 12c.

[175] There is a story that the Buddha Shakyamuni, after attaining perfect enlightenment under the Bodhi tree and during the three weeks of bliss which he subsequently enjoyed, wondered whether he should in fact preach the truth to the world.

[176] According to the T'ien-t'ai school, after the Buddha started preaching he waited for forty years before proclaiming the doctrines given in the *Lotus Sutra*.

[177] The great rain of dharma, as explained in the *Lotus Sutra*, causes the Buddha nature of all beings to sprout as rain helps grass to sprout—there being three kinds of grass, analogous to the bodhisattvas, the śrāvakas, and the pratyekabuddhas, and two kinds of trees, comparable to the followers of Mahayana and Hinayana. See chap. 5 of the sutra. T9, p. 19b.

how his enlightenment had taken place in the immemorial past, indicating that the Buddha Shakyamuni was merely a temporary manifestation of the eternal Buddha. [It is told in the sutra] that a stupa, adorned with precious gems, in which the two Buddhas [178] shared a seat, arose from the ground into the air; that the world shook and that those who were led by the four leaders emerged from a crack and praised [the Buddha preaching the sutra]; [179] that He encouraged the seekers of truth by presenting them with the precious gem of the universal monarch hidden in his topknot; [180] and that a bodhisattva offered a string of pearls.[181] Śāriputra, though known for his wisdom, wondered whether or not the Buddha had turned into a tempter,[182] and the Bodhisattva Maitreya, virtually an enlightened one, was shocked that the Buddha had called the older bodhisattva his son.[183] It was indeed on this occasion that the final truth, the long cherished plan, was proclaimed; it was on this day that all gained completely the unsurpassed path. Thereupon, the goats and deer collapsed, and the white oxen waiting outside [the burning house] ran swiftly. When a Nāga girl appeared, the King of Elephants welcomed her.[184]

The Twofold Practice [185] is, as it were, an abode that gives shelter to

[178] Shakyamuni Buddha and Prabhūtaratna, the eternal Buddha. That these two Buddhas shared the seat shows the identity of the two. See chap. 11 of the *Lotus Sutra*. т9, p. 32c.

[179] See chap. 15 of the *Lotus Sutra*. The number of bodhisattvas who have emerged from the earth is incalculable, symbolizing all sentient beings living on earth. т9, pp. 39c–40a.

[180] The gem stands for the doctrine of universal salvation or the One Vehicle of the *Lotus Sutra*. See chap. 14 of the sutra. т9, pp. 38c–39b.

[181] In chap. 25 of the *Lotus Sutra*, the Bodhisattva Avalokiteśvara, dividing a string of pearls in half, offered it to Prabhūtaratna and Shakyamuni. т9, p. 57c.

[182] Śāriputra, a representative of the śrāvakas, was astounded when he heard the unprecedented sermon of the Buddha on the doctrine of One Vehicle and wondered whether the preacher was a tempter in disguise. See chap. 3 of the *Lotus Sutra*. т9, p. 11a.

[183] See chap. 15 of the *Lotus Sutra*. т9, p. 41c.

[184] In chap. 12 of the *Lotus Sutra* there is a story that when an eight-year-old Nāga (serpent) girl came out of her Nāga palace, the King of Elephants, i.e., the Bodhisattva Mañjuśrī, received her, and that the Buddha predicted that she would attain Buddhahood. т9, p. 35bc.

[185] To discipline oneself through one's own strength, and to approach the Buddha to receive spiritual guidance. This twofold practice gives a devotee comfort in body and mind. See chap. 14 entitled "The Comfortable Practices" of the *Lotus Sutra*. т9, p. 37b.

both mind and body, and the Ten Factors of Existence [186] are a palace where one can perfect at ease the Practices of Cessation and of Clear Observation.[187] The Buddha of quiescence and light [Prabhūtaratna, the eternal Buddha] perceives in the oneness of seeing and seen the nature of Mind; and his temporal manifestations, in view of the vows [of universal salvation of the eternal Buddha], engage in activities in agreement with the signs given by him.

It [the state of enlightenment] is quiescent, yet illuminating; though illuminating, it is forever quiescent. It is like serene water or a golden mirror that reflects images. No distinction can be made between water and gold, or in the reflecting function between the reflecting and the reflected. It is clear that the known is the knowing (*prajñā*) and the knowing is the known. This is the reason why it [this mind] is defined as "transcending the world of objects"; to attain enlightenment is, indeed, "to know one's own mind as it really is." [188]

Mahāvairocana Buddha, therefore, instructed the Lord of Mysteries: "To attain enlightenment is to know one's mind as it really is. O Lord of Mysteries, perfect enlightenment cannot, however, be obtained at all. Why? Because the characteristic of enlightenment is like that of empty space. There are none who understand it, and there are none who reveal it. Why? Because enlightenment is without any sign. O Lord of Mysteries, all dharmas are without signs and are like empty space.

"At that time Vajrapāni asked: 'Then, O Lord, who seeks after all-inclusive wisdom? Who attains perfect enlightenment? Who develops the knowledge that helps others to attain enlightenment?'

"The Buddha said: 'It is one's mind which seeks after enlightenment and all-inclusive wisdom. Why? The original nature of mind is pure and clean: it is neither within nor without; nor is it obtainable between them. O Lord of Mysteries, the perfect enlightenment of the Tathagata is neither blue, yellow, red, white, pink, purple, nor of crystal color; neither is it long, short, round, square, bright, dark; nor is it male,

---

[186] Form, nature, substance, power, functions, primary causes, coordinating causes, effects, rewards, and retributions, the totality of the previous nine factors. See chap. 2 of the *Lotus Sutra*. T9, p. 5c.

[187] A method of meditation emphasized by the T'ien-t'ai school: the practice of cessation is to free one's mind from thoughts (*śamatha*), and the practice of observation is to observe phenomena clearly and realistically (*vipaśyanā*).

[188] See above, n. 172.

female, or androgynous. O Lord of Mysteries, the mind is identical neither with the nature of the world of desire, nor with that of the world of forms, nor with that of the world of formlessness. . . . It does not rest upon the world of perceptions of the ear, of the tongue, or of the mind. There is in it neither seeing nor seen. Why? The mind, whose characteristic is like that of empty space, transcends both individuation and nonindividuation. The reason is that since the nature [of the mind] is identical with that of empty space, the nature is identical with the Mind; since the nature is identical with the Mind, it is identical with enlightenment. Thus, O Lord of Mysteries, these three—the mind, the characteristic of empty space, and enlightenment —are identical. They [the mind and enlightenment] are rooted in the spirit of compassion and are fully endowed with the wisdom of means. O Lord of Mysteries, I preach the doctrines in this way in order to make all bodhisattvas whose *bodhicitta* (enlightened mind) is pure and clean realize their mind. O Lord of Mysteries, if any man or woman wishes to realize it, he should realize his own mind in this way. O Lord of Mysteries, to realize one's own mind is to understand that the mind is unidentifiable in all causally conditioned phenomena, whether it is in colors, forms, objects, things, perceptions, conceptions, predispositions, mind, I, mine, subjects of clinging, objects of clinging, pure state, sense organs, sense data, etc. O Lord of Mysteries, this teaching of the pure *bodhicitta* of the bodhisattvas is called the preliminary way of clarifying the Dharma.' " 189

COMMENTS: Such words as "without signs," "like empty space," and "neither blue, yellow" clearly suggest the unconditioned Truth of the Dharmakaya, Suchness, or One Way. The Buddha explains this teaching as being "the preliminary way of clarifying the Dharma." In the *Ta-chih-tu lun* it is called "the first step to entering the Way of the Buddha." 190 The name of the Buddha here denotes the Buddha of the Mandala, the Mahāvairocana of the Diamond Realm. In Exoteric Buddhist teachings, this [the unconditioned Truth] is understood as the ultimate principle, the theoretically postulated Dharmakaya; but, seen from the point of view of the Shingon approach, this is an introduction. Mahāvairocana Buddha and Nāgārjuna have clearly explained this point; therefore, there should be no doubt about it.

The sutra continues: "That which is known as emptiness is free from

189 The *Mahāvairocana Sutra.* T18, p. 3b.   190 T25, p. 289a.

sense perceptions and their objects, without any sign and without any object; it is beyond the reach of groundless speculations and is like empty space; it is free from the world of being and nonbeing and from all conditioning; it is free from the perceptions of the five senses and the mind." [191] This passage also clarifies the nature of the theoretically postulated Dharmakaya. . . .

Master Chih-i (538–97) [192] of the Kuo-ch'ing Temple on Mt. T'ien-t'ai in Sui China practiced, on the basis of this approach, the Meditation of Cessation and Clear Observation and gained the Lotus samadhi. With the *Lotus Sutra*, the *Mādhyamika-kārikās*, and the *Ta-chih-tu lun* as sources, he systematized the tenets of the T'ien-t'ai school. The outline of this doctrine is as given in the foregoing presentation. A summary in verse:

> The bodhisattvas in the former stages engage in groundless speculations.
> The experience of enlightenment of this mind is not yet genuine.
> The One Way, unconditioned and signless, is spotless;
> It unfolds the teaching of nonduality of neither being nor nonbeing.
> When both the seeing and the seen are negated, the eternal ground of quiescence will be found;
> When all thought determinations are exhausted, one will meet with Mahāvairocana.
> He, like vast space, knows no duality of body and mind.
> Adapting himself freely to all beings, He manifests himself forever and ever.

QUESTION: Can the principle of Suchness, the One Way, or the One World of Dharma, be regarded as the ultimate Buddha?

ANSWER: Nāgārjuna said: "The One Mind, the World of Dharma, cannot be predicated by a hundred negative statements or by a thousand affirmative expressions. It defies the middle position [the synthetic view of affirmation and negation]. Since it defies the middle position, it is not identical with [the name of] a heaven [known as 'neither thought nor nonthought']. Not being identical even with [the name of] the heaven, it defies all predications; no matter how eloquent a man may be, his speech must come to an end and his speculation must cease. Such an understanding of the One Mind still belongs to the realm of

[191] The *Mahāvairocana Sutra*. T18, p. 3b.
[192] The founder of the T'ien-t'ai school of China.

ignorance and does not belong to the category of authentic enlightenment." [193]

Ninth: The Profoundest Exoteric Buddhist Mind That Is Aware of Its Nonimmutable Nature. In interpreting this mind two approaches can be identified: one is the Exoteric, the other is the Esoteric.

The Exoteric approach: That which is very deep is the ocean, and that which soars high is Mount Sumeru; that which is vast is space, and that which is long is the period of an aeon. The period of an aeon can be exhausted, space can be measured; it is known that the height of Mount Sumeru is 160,000 *yojanas,* and the depth of the ocean, eight million *yojanas.* That which is near us and yet difficult to perceive is our Mind. He who is infinitesimal and yet who pervades all space is our Buddha. Our Buddha is suprarational and our Mind is boundless. Renowned mathematicians such as Ch'iao Li and Chung I would be perplexed and would give up their attempts to measure them; sharp-eyed Li Chu and Aniroddha [194] would likewise become blind before them and would fail to see them. King Yü would hold his tongue in his attempt to identify them, and K'ua Fu [195] would be unable to catch up with them. Neither the knowledge of the Hinayanists nor the wisdom of the Mahayanists is adequate to understand them. What is really mysterious and unfathomable is the Buddha which is our Mind.

Having lost sight of their own Mind, sentient beings are constantly tossed by the waves of the Six Transmigratory Paths. Once awakened to the fountainhead of their Mind, however, they will find that the water of Mind is serene and tranquil. As limpid water reflects the undistorted images of all things, so does the Buddha, which is their Mind, know all things as they really are. Being at a loss with this principle, sentient beings are incapable of freeing themselves from the cycle of transmigration. They are madly intoxicated; they are unable to realize their Mind.

The compassionate Father of great enlightenment has therefore shown them the way to return. The way to return is five hundred

[193] The commentary on *The Awakening of Faith,* attributed to Nāgārjuna. т32, p. 637c.

[194] One of the ten great disciples of the Buddha, known for his supernatural sight.

[195] A famous walker of ancient China who is said to have raced the sun.

yojanas long; this mind [the ninth] is, as it were, an inn. No inn is a permanent abode. They must move on, responding to new conditions. Moving on and on, they have no permanent place; they are not immutable. All phenomena are, likewise, devoid of immutability; therefore, it is possible for a man to make progress, leaving behind what is ignoble and advancing to what is nobler. Because of this reason it is possible to advance such a culminating doctrine [in Hua-yen] as "Suchness permeates," [196] or to receive such an Esoteric instruction [in Shingon] as "Anyone can realize the ultimate Truth, since he is not immutable." [197] Having been awakened from their spiritual stagnation in the eighth mind and realizing that the eighth is not the highest, they develop for the first time this mind which is identical with the nature of space. Thus the culmination of the eighth mind, in turn, becomes the basis. Though this mind is the highest attainment when compared to the attainments of former stages, it is still the beginning when compared to the last secret mind.

That "the moment a man sets his mind on enlightenment he has attained enlightenment" [198] must be true. The excellent power of an aspirant's Buddhahood, the moment he sets his mind on enlightenment, is mysterious; all excellent qualities are made manifest for the first time, and the One Mind is unveiled. When he realizes this mind, he will come to the awareness that the threefold world [199] is his body and that the entire universe is also his Mind.

Vairocana Buddha [200] preached extensively for two weeks the meaning of this [mind], after having attained enlightenment for the first time, to the great Bodhisattva Samantabhadra and to others. His preaching is the contents of the so-called *Avataṃsaka Sutra*. He was residing, as it were, in a lotus-adorned abode of glorious enlightenment in a country called the World of Dharma. He manifested himself in seven

[196] See *The Awakening of Faith*, pp. 56–57, for an explanation of this doctrine.

[197] Kūkai seems to have summarized in this sentence the ideas given in the discussion of seeking the highest doctrine in the *Aspiration to Enlightenment*. T32, p. 573b.

[198] A famous line in the *Avataṃsaka Sutra*. T9, p. 449c.

[199] The world of sentient beings, the world of matter, and the world of perfectly enlightened Buddhas.

[200] The main Buddha in the *Avataṃsaka Sutra*. The main Buddha of Shingon is Mahāvairocana, though he often appears in the Esoteric Buddhist sutras without the prefix *mahā*.

places and held eight assemblies to unfold the *Avataṃsaka Sutra*. He first entered the concentration known as the *sāgaramudrā* samadhi [201] and meditated on the complete diffusion of the Nature of Dharma (*dharmatā*).

As the sun first shines upon the high peaks while the world is still lying in darkness, so He [the Buddha] illumined those whose aptitude was high with the doctrine of the nonduality of the mind and the Buddha. He taught that infinite time is in one moment and that one moment is in infinite time; that one is in many and that many is in one, that is, that the universal is in the particulars and that the particulars are in the universal. He illustrated this infinitely interdependent relationship of time and space with the simile of Indra's net [202] and with that of the interfusion of the rays of lighted lamps. He concluded the discourse with a story about a young devotee named Sudāna who was caused by him to set his mind on enlightenment under the guidance of Mañjuśrī, and who finally attained enlightenment with the instruction of Samantabhadra by making efforts to improve himself all the time and by visiting his spiritual friends in more than one hundred cities. He taught that to practice one action is to practice all actions; that to sever one evil is to sever all evils; that though one attains full enlightenment the moment one sets one's mind on enlightenment, or the moment one perfects one's faith, in practice one must ascend the Five Ranks of Development of Bodhisattvahood; [203] and that, since the attributes and the essence are nondual, the Ten Bodies of Buddha [204] are to be returned equally to the Origin [Vairocana Buddha]. These are the essentials of the *Avataṃsaka Sutra*.

[The Esoteric approach:] Mahāvairocana Tathagata instructed the Lord of Mysteries: "That which is known as emptiness is free from sense perceptions and their objects, without any sign and without any object; it is beyond the reach of groundless speculations and is like empty space; being freed from the world of being and nonbeing, from

[201] A samadhi in which one perceives all things as they really are, just as the surface of a vast and serene body of water reflects all things without any distortion. *Sāgaramudrā* can be translated literally as "the sea symbol."

[202] See explanation of Indra's net, Part Two, p. 92.

[203] The five categories of the fifty stages of discipline of a bodhisattva. Each category includes ten stages. See above, n. 156.

[204] Ten attributes of Vairocana Buddha personified.

all conditioning, and from the objects of the five senses and the mind, one is to develop the profoundest mind that is aware of its non-immutable nature." [205]

On the phrase, "the profoundest mind that is aware of its non-immutable nature," the master Śubhākarasiṃha said that it embraces the entire doctrine of the Hua-yen school. [206] The reason for this is that the purport of Hua-yen is to clarify, upon investigating the Origin and looking toward the end, that the World of Dharma of Suchness does not remain immutable but manifests itself in relative order.

On the basis of this doctrine, Master Tu-shun (557–640) composed such treatises as the *Hua-yen wu-chao chih-kuan* [207] and the *Fa-chieh-kuan*, [208] and his disciple Chih-yen (602–68) succeeded his master. Master Fa-tsang (643–712), a disciple of Chih-yen, wrote extensively on the five major doctrines of Buddhism, including the *Chih-kuei*, [209] the *Kuan-mu*, [210] the commentary on the *Avataṃsaka Sutra*, [211] etc. These are representative works which elucidate the meaning of the teachings of the Hua-yen school. A summary in verse:

> The wind and the water of the sea are one; the Dragon King gives them forth simultaneously. [212]
> Suchness and the realm of samsara are one; both belong to the summit of the one World of Reality.
>
> He who is like a bright *lun-to-li-hua* mirror [213] reveals his essence, functions, and attributes.

[205] From the commentary on the *Mahāvairocana Sutra*. T18, p. 3b.

[206] From the commentary on the *Mahāvairocana Sutra*. T39, p. 612b.

[207] This may well be the work of Fa-tsang. T1867.

[208] *Fa-chieh-kuan-men*. The work is quoted in its entirety in Fa-tsang's *Hua-yen fa-p'u-ti-hsin chang* (T1878) and is also commented on by Chih-yen (T1883) and by Tsung-mi (T1884). This work establishes Tu-shun as the first patriarch of the tradition.

[209] *Hua-yen-ching chih-kuei*. T1871.

[210] *Hua-yen-ching wen-i kuan-mu*. T1734.

[211] *Hua-yen-ching-t'an-hsüan-chi*. T1733.

[212] In chap. 2 of the commentary on *The Awakening of Faith* attributed to Nāgārjuna, there is a story about a dragon king named "Spewing forth wind and water," who is described as spewing forth water from his head and wind from his tail. The perpetual waves of the sea are due to the workings of this dragon. T32, pp. 603b, 621a.

[213] In chap. 3 of the same commentary, this mirror is compared to the pure and bright state of original enlightenment which is intrinsic to the worlds of

Great is He who embraces the Threefold world—the worlds of matter, sentient beings, and Buddhas.

The state of mutual dependence of phenomena is demonstrated by the Profound Tenfold View.[214]

The sounds of the tidal current of the *sāgaramudrā* samadhi swallow the five currents of teaching.[215]

All phenomenal existences are interrelated like the meshes of Indra's infinite net;

And that which is secretly and perfectly diffused like light rays is the Mind.

The practice of the Hua-yen samadhi is an act, the performance of which includes all acts.

Vairocana Buddha consisting of Ten Bodies manifests himself freely in all the worlds.

To enter into this sanctuary is to be regarded as the preliminary step to Buddhahood.

In order to gain perfection one has to seek the practice of the Five Series of Meditation.[216]

A sutra explains: "Being freed from the world of being and non-being, from all conditioning, and from the objects of the five senses and the mind, one is to develop the profoundest mind that is aware

---

matter, sentient beings, and Buddhas. Here the mirror is compared to the Vairocana Buddha of the *Avataṃsaka Sutra*. T32, p. 622a.

[214] The theory was formulated by the second patriarch of Hua-yen, Chih-yen, developing the ideas transmitted from Tu-shun. The state of interdependence of phenomena is analyzed from ten different points of view: 1) all are in a state of simultaneous coexistence; 2) all beings, small and large, influence each other without any obstacle; 3) one and many influence each other without losing their identities; 4) all things are interrelated so that one is in all and all is in one; 5) the hidden and the manifest constitute the whole; 6) the minute and the subtle matters influence each other in an orderly manner; 7) all things reflect and correspond mutually like the jeweled meshes of Indra's net; 8) all things are symbols standing for things other than themselves; 9) the ten divisions of time are mutually interrelated—each past, present, and future contains respectively its past, present, and future, thus making up the nine divisions of time, and the division of time which comprises the nine divisions; and 10) any one thing or event can be the center or pivot of all the rest.

[215] The entire Buddhist teaching according to the Hua-yen classification is Hinayana, the primary stage of Mahayana, the final stage of Mahayana; the teaching of sudden enlightenment; and the perfect teaching of Hua-yen.

[216] A method of meditation advocated in Shingon. It is discussed in the analysis of the tenth mind in the following section.

of its nonimmutable nature. It will continue to develop the state identical with all Buddhas who are like immeasurable space. O Lord of Mysteries, the Buddha preached that a preliminary mind like this is the cause of attaining Buddhahood. This mind is free from the defilements of karma but may be subject to them." [217] . . .

Nāgārjuna says in his *Aspiration to Enlightenment:* "The unenlightened states of existence come to be contingent upon deluded thinking; reinforcing each other, they develop boundless defilements, and a man yet to be enlightened wanders the Six Transmigratory Paths. Once he is enlightened, however, all deluded thoughts will cease to be and manifold deluded states of existence will disappear. Thus it can be concluded that any state of existence is devoid of its own immutable nature. The compassion of the Buddha, developing from the Truth, saves all sentient beings. As a certain medicine cures a certain type of illness, so various teachings of the Buddhas cure those who are in delusion because of certain types of defilement. As one must leave his raft when he has reached the other shore, so one must abandon the teaching. One is not of immutable nature. When deluded thoughts cease to be, the fountainhead of the Mind will be quiescent and will be endowed with all excellent attributes, and its excellent functions will be boundless. Anyone endowed with this Mind is capable of revolving the wheel of doctrine, benefiting both himself and others." [218] . . .

QUESTION: Is this state of mind (the ninth) rooted in the principle of One Mind to be considered the highest?

[ANSWER: The question is answered by] Nāgārjuna [who] said: "Of the principle of One Mind with essence, attributes, and functions, the term One [of One Mind] is used. This 'One,' however, is not 'the One [without a second, that is, the Absolute],' but it is merely a sign, so that a student can approximate himself to it. Likewise, 'Mind' [of One Mind] is not 'the Mind' [Suchness] itself, but it is merely a sign, so that a student can approximate himself to it. Such and such a name is not my [intrinsic] name, yet I am called so. Though I was not the first to use it, it stands for me. The name is given to me as if 'I really am' but that 'I' is not the 'real I.' Though I have used the term 'self' about myself as if 'myself really is,' that 'self' is not the 'real self.' [What is real is beyond thought determinations.] It is deep; it is far. Such a

217 The *Mahāvairocana Sutra.* T18, p. 3b.   218 T32, p. 573b.

height of spiritual attainment still belongs to the realm of non-enlightenment and not to that of enlightenment." [219]

Tenth: The Glorious Mind, the Most Secret and Sacred.

> The nine stages of development of the religious mind are not stationary;
> The deeper a man penetrates, the profounder his mind becomes, each stage being a stepping stone toward the higher one.

> Revealed by the Dharmakaya Buddha is Shingon Esoteric Buddhism;
> It is the supreme Truth, the most secret and imperishable, like a diamond.

> The Five Series of Meditation, the Fivefold Wisdom,[220] the Essence of the World of Dharma, and
> Its four expressions—the Four Mandalas [221]—are to be unfolded in this final stage of mind.

> Buddhas as numerous as particles of dust are the Buddhas of our Mind.
> He who is of the Diamond and Matrix Realms, and who is one and many at once like drops of sea water is our Body.

> Each of the syllabic mantras [222] represents ten thousand images in the universe.
> Each of the physical symbols like sword and *vajra* suggests the majestic power of the symbolized.

> In our own nature we are completely endowed with all excellent attributes;
> In this life we are able to realize the most sublime and glorious Buddhahood.

The *Mahāvairocana Sutra* states: "O Lord of Mysteries, the bodhisattvas who engage in the practices of Bodhisattvahood according to the Mantrayāna method are all those who are endowed with immeasur-

[219] From the commentary on *The Awakening of Faith*. T32, p. 637c.

[220] See discussion in Part Two, p. 83.   [221] See Part Two, p. 90.

[222] The fifty letters of the Sanskrit alphabet: *a ā, i ī, u ū, ka,* etc. The preceding stanza represents the Mahā-mandala; this sentence, the Dharma-mandala; the next sentence, the Samaya-mandala; and the following stanza, the Karma-mandala and the theme of Kūkai's Esoteric Buddhist thought that one can attain enlightenment here and now.

able merits and wisdom cultivated from the immemorial past and those
who have mastery over the wisdom of means by which they perfect
their practices." [223] This passage praises the excellent qualities of the
bodhisattvas who approach the Shingon teaching for the first time.

Also it is said in the same sutra: "At that time, the Lord Vairocana
entered the samadhi known as 'the oneness of all Tathagatas and the
swift power' and preached about the samadhi on 'the essential nature of
the World of Dharma' which he himself experienced as follows:

> I have realized that which is unborn;
> It is what language cannot communicate;
> It is free from all defilements;
> It transcends causality.
> I know that it is void like space,
> I have gained the wisdom to see things as they really are.
> I am free from all darkness;
> I am the ultimately real and immaculate." [224]

The lines are terse, but their meanings are comprehensive. The tone
of the words may seem to be light, but the thoughts are profound. It is
therefore difficult to explain except face to face.

There are Shingon methods of meditation, the teachings of samadhi,
such as the meditation on the Circle of One Hundred Syllabic Mantras,
on the Twelve Syllabic Mantras; [225] on the Thirty-seven Holy Ones and
on the Four Mandalas in the Diamond Realm.[226] All of these are the
most secret samadhi taught by Mahāvairocana Tathagata. The sources
of information are too extensive to quote here in detail.

In the *Aspiration to Enlightenment*, it is explained: "After having
observed thus, how can a student of Mantrayāna realize unsurpassed
enlightenment? He should know that by virtue of the Dharma he is
to abide in the all-pervading great enlightened Mind. All sentient beings
are innate bodhisattvas; but they have been bound by defilements of
greed, hatred, and delusion. The Buddhas of great compassion, there-

[223] T18, p. 3b.   [224] T18, p. 9b.

[225] These two methods are given in the *Mahāvairocana Sutra*. The first is the
circle of one hundred Sanskrit letters—each of the twenty-five consonants is
accompanied by *a*, *ā*, *aṃ*, and *aḥ*. The second is the circle of twelve Sanskrit
vowels—*a*, *ā*, *i*, *ī*, *u*, *ū*, *e*, *ai*, *o*, *au*, *aṃ*, and *aḥ*. T18, p.30bc.

[226] By listing the last two, Kūkai refers to the methods of meditation given in
the *Vajraśekhara Sutra*. The thirty-seven Holy Ones are the five Buddhas, the
sixteen Bodhisattvas of wisdom, and the sixteen Bodhisattvas of samadhi in the
central circle of the Diamond Mandala.

fore, with the wisdom of skillful means, taught them this profound
Esoteric Buddhist yoga and made each devotee visualize in his inner
mind the bright moon. By means of this practice each devotee will perceive his original Mind, which is serene and pure like the full moon
whose rays pervade space without any discrimination. This method
is also called the yoga 'free from the notion of enlightenment,' or that
of 'the pure World of Dharma,' or 'the sea of transcendental insight
(*prajñā-pāramitā*) into Reality.' It is the basis on which the devotee can
develop a variety of samadhi of great value. It [his original Mind]
is just like the full moon, spotless and bright. Why? Because all sentient
beings are endowed with the all-pervading Mind. We are to perceive
our own Mind in the form of the moon. The reason the image of the
moon is used is that the body of the bright moon is analogous to that
of the enlightened Mind. There are sixteen phases of the moon, which
are analogous to the sixteen great Bodhisattvas beginning with Vajra-
sattva and ending with Vajramuṣṭi as explained in the *Yoga* [*Sutra—
Vajraśekhara Sutra*].[227] . . .

"The sixteen meanings of emptiness, beginning with the 'emptiness
of inner soul (*adhyātma-śūnyatā*)' and ending with the 'emptiness of
both nonbeing and own-being (*abhāvasvabhāva-śūnyatā*)' as stated in
the *Mahāprajñā-pāramitā Sutra* [228] likewise correspond to this series of
sixteen. What is latent in the core of mind of all sentient beings is a
portion of the pure nature, which is perfect in itself, the essence of
which is subtle, bright, and changeless even if it goes through the Six
Transmigratory Paths of existence. It is just like the sixteenth-day moon
[in the darker half of the month] when it meets the sun and its brightness is erased by the rays of the sun. After the new moon, the moon
increases its brightness day by day until it finally reaches perfection
without any hindrance on the fifteenth day.

"The student of meditation, therefore, should first by means of meditation on the letter *A* bring forth the brightness of his original Mind
and then gradually make it distinct and brighter and realize his innate
wisdom. The letter *A* stands for the idea that all things are originally
unborn. According to the commentary on the *Mahāvairocana Sutra*,[229]
the letter *A* has the following five meanings: 1) *A* stands for the en-

[227] The sixteen Bodhisattvas are those surrounding the Four Buddhas in the
four directions in the inner circle of the Diamond Mandala, which is explained
in detail in the *Vajraśekhara Sutra*.
[228] T7, p. 454b.   [229] T39, p. 723b.

lightened mind (*bodhicitta*); 2) *A*, for practice to bring out enlightenment; 3) *Aṃ*, for realization of enlightenment; 4) *Aḥ*, for Nirvana; and
5) *Āḥ*, for wisdom perfectly provided with skillful means. . . .

"Here is a verse on the letter *A*, which stands for the enlightened
Mind:

> Visualize: a white lotus flower with eight petals,
> [above which is a full moon disc] the size of a forearm in diameter,
> [in which is] a radiant silvery letter *A*.
> Unite your *dhyāna* with *prajñā* in an adamantine binding; [230]
> Draw the quiescent *Prajñā* of the Tathagata in [your mind].

"Those who understand the meanings of the letter *A* are to meditate
on it resolutely; they should meditate on the perfect, luminous, and
Pure Consciousness. Those who have had a glimpse of it are called
those who have perceived the absolute truth (*paramārtha*). Those who
perceive it all the time enter the first stage of Bodhisattvahood. If they
gradually increase their competence in this meditation, they will finally
be able to magnify it [the moon] until its circumference encompasses
the entire universe and its magnitude becomes as inclusive as space.
Being able freely to magnify or to reduce it, they will surely come to
be in possession of the all-inclusive wisdom.

"The student of the yoga should devote himself to the mastery of
the Three Mysteries and the Five Series of Meditation. The Three
Mysteries are: the mystery of body—to make mudras and to invoke
the presence of the sacred object of meditation; the mystery of speech
—to recite the mantras in secret, pronouncing them distinctly without
making the slightest error; the mystery of mind—to be absorbed in
yoga, keeping one's mind in a wholesome state like that of the bright,
pure, and full moon, and to meditate on the enlightened Mind. The Five
Series of Meditation are: to have an insight into the Mind; to meditate
on the enlightened Mind; to visualize the enlightened Mind in the form
of a *vajra;* to transform one's body into a *vajra;* and to realize unsurpassed enlightenment and obtain an adamantine body like a *vajra.* When
the student becomes perfected in the Five Series of Meditation, then

---

[230] A twofold instruction can be identified: one teaches that a student of this
meditation should enter into the state of unshakable concentration in the oneness
of body (*dhyāna*) and mind (*prajñā*); the other concerns the types of mudra to
be used in this meditation: one should unite the right thumb (*dhyāna*) with the
left thumb (*prajñā*) and form the mudra called *vajrāñjali.*

and only then will he become the Body of the most sacred One. Then his luminous being will be the all-pervading Body and Mind, which are identical with that of the Buddhas in the ten directions. There are individual differences as to the ways of practice and the time required to obtain the final realization; however, once the student has attained enlightenment, he will be in an order where the time distinctions between past, present, and future are unknown. Indeed, the ordinary man's mind is like a lotus flower yet to open and the Enlightened One's Mind, like the full moon.

"When this meditation is perfected, visible to the devotee are the pure lands and the impure lands in the ten directions, all sentient beings in the Six Transmigratory Paths, the followers of the Three Vehicles, the creation and destruction of the worlds in the three periods of time, the distinctions of karma of all sentient beings, the acts of the bodhisattvas in their pre-enlightened stages, and the Buddhas in the three periods of time. Realizing the Body of the most sacred One, he will fulfill all the vows of the Bodhisattva Samantabhadra.[231] It is therefore said in the *Mahāvairocana Sutra* that 'it is on such a true Mind that the former Buddhas have preached.' [232]

"QUESTION: It is said previously that the followers of the Two Vehicles are, because of their attachment to the dharma [the belief that Psychophysical Constituents are real], unable to attain Buddhahood. Now the practice of the samadhi on the enlightened Mind is encouraged. [Is not the practice of this samadhi also a form of attachment?] What is the difference?

"ANSWER: The followers of the Two Vehicles are attached to the dharma; after having realized the principle [of nonexistence of a permanent ego], they sink into and indulge in the state of quiescence of emptiness for aeons. Even after they develop the aspiration for the Mahayana mind, they remain in a confused state for innumerable aeons. These teachings should therefore be detested and not relied upon. Now, the devotees of Mantrayāna have already done away with attachment to the belief in a permanent ego and dharma. Though they are able to perceive what is true wisdom, they are unable to realize the all-inclu-

[231] See the vows of the Bodhisattva Samantabhadra in *The Buddhist Tradition*, pp. 173–78.
[232] T18, p. 22a.

sive wisdom of the Tathagata because of their separation from Him since the beginningless beginning. For this reason they earnestly seek after the true way, practice series of meditations, and, from the category of ordinary men, enter that of the Buddhas. Namely, it is this samadhi that enables them to penetrate into the Essence of all Buddhas, to have insight into the Dharmakaya of all Buddhas, to realize Wisdom in harmony with the Essence of the World of Dharma, and to integrate themselves into the Bodies of Essence, of Bliss, of Manifestation, and of Transformation of Mahāvairocana Buddha. Since you have not yet realized this, the practice of this samadhi is highly recommended.

"It is said in the *Mahāvairocana Sutra* that 'the consummation of the devotee is born out of the Mind.' [233] According to the *Vajraśekhara Sutra*, it is said that 'when the Bodhisattva Sarvasiddhārtha sat on the adamantine seat for the first time and was about to realize the unsurpassed Way, he received from the Buddhas instructions on this Mind and was able to realize the final goal.' [234] People of the present, if they practice with resolve as instructed, can in equal measure experience samadhi at once while sitting in meditation and thus be able to integrate themselves into the Body of the most sacred One. Also it is said in the *Mahāvairocana Sutra:* 'If a man finds himself insufficiently equipped with the power to benefit others, he should, in accordance with the teaching, simply meditate on the enlightened Mind, for the Buddha preached that this practice contains the effects which will be acquired by practicing ten thousand acts, and suffices for all other holy practices.' [235] Since this enlightened Mind contains all the merits obtained by the Buddhas, if a man actualizes it by discipline and realization, he will be the leader of all. If he returns to the root, he will find himself in the secret and glorious Ground, and there he will be able to immediately engage in the activities of a Buddha. Here is a verse on the enlightened Mind:

> Seeking after the Buddha Wisdom,
> If a man penetrates into the enlightened Mind,
> With his very body as given by his parents,
> He will realize quickly the great Buddhahood." [236]

[233] T18, p. 19b.

[234] T18, p. 207c. Reference is made to the moment of realization of enlightenment of the prince Siddhārtha Gautama who became the founder of Buddhism.

[235] T18, p. 45bc.

[236] Up to here Kūkai has filled the major part of the discussion on the tenth

QUESTION: We should like to know the meanings of the lines of the verse given in the beginning.

ANSWER: The doctrines of Shingon are difficult to elucidate though one may spend much time on them, in that every sound, syllable, word, phrase, and clause of the mantras is pregnant with limitless meanings. Each syllable stands for three things: sound, word, and reality. It also has two aspects: form and meaning. Each phrase contains double sets of meanings: exoteric and esoteric. Thus it is difficult to explain them casually. If they are to be explained as they really were intended to be, men of small capacity may develop doubts or abuse them; as a result, they may be born among the cursed ones or they may fall into hell. Hence, the Nirmanakaya Buddha kept the doctrines secret and did not preach them, nor did the bodhisattvas who transmitted them discuss them openly. It is in this spirit that the *Vajraśekhara Sutra* says: "This doctrine of samadhi taught by Mahāvairocana Buddha should not be explained, not even a single word, to those who have not received *abhiṣeka*. As to the rituals and mantras to be used during meditation on sacred objects, the student should not talk about them even to his fellow students who have been initiated. If he does so, he may die while young or may invite calamities in this life and fall into hell in the next life, etc." [237]

QUESTION: We will take what you have said to our hearts and will not violate the regulations. We should again like to ask you to explain the verse given in the beginning.

ANSWER: The first two lines, "The nine stages of development of the religious mind are not stationary;/The deeper a man penetrates, the profounder his mind becomes, each stage being a stepping stone toward the higher one," show that the minds, from the first to the ninth, have not yet reached the final fruit of Buddhahood. The nine minds are those from "The Mind of Lowly Man, Goatish in Its Desires" to "The Profoundest Exoteric Buddhist Mind That Is Aware of Its Nonimmutable Nature." The first mind points to those who indulge in evil acts only and do not practice a bit of goodness. The second stands

---

mind by quoting from the section on samadhi in the *Aspiration to Enlightenment*, which he did not use in the corresponding section in the *Ten Stages*. Kūkai's emphasis on the importance of practice in the Esoteric Buddhist meditation can be seen from the nature of the quotation. T32, pp. 573c–574c.

[237] T19, p. 321a. Kūkai has adapted the original.

for ordinary human life; and the third, for the life of the followers of
non-Buddhist teachings, those who loathe this world and hope to be
born in heaven but who will eventually fall into hell while seeking
after deliverance. These three belong to the profane mind and are not
yet called the religious mind proper. The minds from the fourth on are
called "obtaining the holy fruit." Among these six, the fourth and the
fifth belong to the Hinayana; the sixth and following minds, to the
Mahayana. Among those belonging to the Mahayana, the sixth and the
seventh are the attainments of the Bodhisattva Vehicles; the eighth and
the ninth, those of the Buddha Vehicles. Each Vehicle, though it may
promise to provide the doctrine to attain Buddhahood, when compared
to the following Vehicle, turns out to be groundless speculation. None
of them is stationary; hence, the term nonimmutable is introduced. No
mind is to be taken as final, but each is to be regarded as the basis for
the succeeding higher one. Thus it is said that "The deeper a man
penetrates, the profounder his mind becomes." The following line,
"Revealed by the Dharmakaya Buddha is Shingon Esoteric Buddhism,"
indicates the revealer of Shingon Buddhism. The seven teachings from
the second to the eighth are taught by the Nirmanakaya Buddha for the
sake of benefiting others. The Esoteric Shingon doctrine, the secret
treasury given in the two sutras,[238] is unfolded by the Dharmakaya
Mahāvairocana Buddha for the sake of his own enjoyment, while He
resides in the sacred shrine of the adamantine World of Dharma, the
holy palace of Shingon, in the company of the four Dharmakaya Buddhas, his four attributes. This point is elucidated well in passages in the
Shih-pa-hui chih-kuei [239] and elsewhere. I shall quote no further sources.
The next line, "It is the supreme Truth, the most secret and imperishable, like a diamond," shows that the Shingon teaching is the ultimate
Truth, transcending all other teachings.

[238] The *Mahāvairocana Sutra* and the *Vajraśekhara Sutra*.

[239] T869. An outline of the entire *Vajraśekhara Sutra*. The work is known to
have been translated by Pu-k'ung, but it may well be that Pu-k'ung himself composed it.

5

ATTAINING ENLIGHTENMENT IN THIS VERY EXISTENCE

(*Sokushin jōbutsu gi*)

QUESTION: In sutras and shastras it is explained that after three aeons one can attain enlightenment. Is there evidence for the assertion that one can attain enlightenment in this very existence?

ANSWER: The Tathagata has explained it in the Esoteric Buddhist texts.

QUESTION: How is it explained?

ANSWER: It is said in the *Vajraśekhara Sutra* that "He who practices this samadhi can immediately realize the enlightenment of the Buddha." [1] Also: "If the sentient beings who have come across this teaching practice it diligently four times day and night, they will realize the stage of joy in this life and perfect enlightenment in their subsequent sixteen lives." [2]

REMARKS: "This teaching" in the foregoing quotation refers to the king of teachings, the teaching of samadhi realized by the Dharmakaya Buddha himself. "The stage of joy" is not the first stage of Bodhisattvahood as defined in the Exoteric Buddhist teachings, but the first stage of Buddhahood of our Buddha Vehicle, the details of which are ex-

---

[1] *Chin-kang-ting (vajraśekhara) i-tzu-ting-lun-wang-yü-ch'ieh i-kuei*, T19, p. 320c. After the quotation there is a parenthetic comment which reads, "This samadhi is the samadhi of Mahāvairocana Buddha in the form of a universal monarch, represented by a seed mantra [*bhrūṃ*]."

[2] *Chin-kang-ting-yü-ch'ieh-san-mo-ti-fa*. T18, p. 331b.

plained in the chapter discussing stages.[3] By "sixteen lives" is meant that one is to realize the attainments of the sixteen great Bodhisattvas,[4] the details of which are also explained in the chapter discussing the stages.[5]

Again it is said: "If a man disciplines himself according to this superior doctrine, he will be able to attain in this life unsurpassed enlightenment." [6] Furthermore: "It should be known that he himself turns into the Diamond Realm; since he becomes identical with the Diamond, he is firm and indestructible. An awareness will emerge that he is of the Diamond Body." [7] The *Mahāvairocana Sutra* states: "Without forsaking his body, he obtains supernatural power, wanders on the ground of great space, and perfects the Mystery of Body." [8] Also: "If he wishes to gain the perfection of religious discipline in his lifetime, he must select a certain method of meditation that suits his inclinations and concentrate on it. For this, he must personally receive instruction in mantra recitation from an authentic master. If he observes the mantras and masters yoga, he will gain perfection." [9]

REMARKS: "The perfection of religious discipline" mentioned in the sutra refers to the perfection of yoga which uses recitation of and meditation on mantras and to the perfection of yoga of the Dharmakaya Buddha. "The ground of great space" is the Dharmakaya Buddha. He is analogous to great space; he is eternal, being unobstructed, and embraces in himself all phenomena. That is why he is compared to great space. Grounded on him, all things exist; therefore, the term "ground" is used. The term "Mystery of Body" is introduced because the Three Mysteries of the Dharmakaya Buddha are imperceptible, even by the

---

[3] Kūkai seems to be referring to the discussion of the ten stages of the development of the religious mind in the first chapter of the *Mahāvairocana Sutra*. T18, p. 3b.

[4] Kūkai interprets "sixteen lives" as realizing the samadhi of the sixteen Bodhisattvas surrounding the Four Buddhas in the inner circle of the Diamond Mandala, not as repeating the cycle of birth and death sixteen times.

[5] This reference is ambiguous. Kūkai may well be referring to the section on the emergence of the sixteen Bodhisattvas of the Diamond Mandala in the Mind of Mahāvairocana while in samadhi. Cf. *Fen-pieh-sheng-wei ching*, T18, pp. 288c–290c.

[6] *Kuan-chih i-kuei*. T19, p. 594a.

[7] *Chin-kang-ting-yü-ch'ieh-san-mo-ti-fa*. T18, p. 329a.   [8] T18, p. 21a.

[9] T18, p. 45c.

bodhisattvas in the Ten Stages of Bodhisattvahood, let alone by other bodhisattvas lower than they.

In the *Aspiration to Enlightenment* of Nāgārjuna it is explained: "It is through the teachings of Mantrayāna that we can attain enlightenment in this very existence; this teaching explains the way of samadhi which is either neglected or totally ignored in other teachings." [10]

REMARKS: By "samadhi" in this quotation is meant the samadhi realized by the Dharmakaya Buddha himself. The "other teachings" designate the Exoteric Buddhist teachings expounded by the Buddha [Shakyamuni] for the sake of saving others.

It is also said: "If, seeking after the Buddha Wisdom, a man penetrates into the enlightened mind (*bodhicitta*), he will quickly realize great Buddhahood in the very body given him by his parents." [11] This doctrinal evidence establishes the assertion.

QUESTION: How do you analyze the meaning of the words [attaining enlightenment in this very existence] given in these sutras and shastras?

A summary in verse:

> The Six Great Elements are interfused and are in a state of eternal harmony;
> The Four Mandalas are inseparably related to one another:
> When the grace of the Three Mysteries is retained, [our inborn three mysteries will] quickly be manifested.
> Infinitely interrelated like the meshes of Indra's net are those which we call existences.
>
> There is the One who is naturally equipped with all-embracing wisdom.
> More numerous than particles of sand are those who have the King of Mind and the consciousnesses;
> Each of them is endowed with the Fivefold Wisdom, with infinite wisdom.
> All beings can truly attain enlightenment because of the force of mirrorlike wisdom.

Interpretation: These two stanzas consisting of eight lines express the concept of "attaining enlightenment in this very existence." These words contain infinite meanings. In fact, the goal of all the teachings of Buddhism is no more than what this one phrase represents. The two

[10] T32, p. 572c.   [11] T32, p. 574c.

stanzas were composed in an attempt to express concisely the immeasurable value of this concept.

The first stanza expresses the meaning of "in this very existence"; the second, of "attaining enlightenment." In the first stanza, the first line stands for the essence (*tai*); the second, for the attributes (*sō*); the third, for the functions (*yū*); and the fourth, for the state of interpenetration (*muge*). In the second stanza, the first line stands for the enlightenment of the Dharmakaya Buddha; the second, for the infinite number [of his attributes, that is, beings]; the third, for the perfect endowment [of the element of enlightenment in all beings]; and the fourth, for the reason [why any being can attain enlightenment].

As to the first line, "The Six Great Elements are interfused and are in a state of eternal harmony," the Six Great Elements are earth, water, fire, wind, space, and consciousness. The definition of these elements is contained in the following verse given in the *Mahāvairocana Sutra:*

> I have realized that which is unborn;
> It is that which language cannot communicate;
> It is free from all defilements;
> It transcends causality.
> I know that it is void like space.[12]

The seed (*bīja*) mantras for these words are: *A, Va, Ra, Ha, Kha, Hūṃ. A* stands for "that which is unborn (*anutpāda*)," which is the earth element; *Va*, for "that which language (*vāc*) cannot communicate," which is the water element; *Ra*, for "free from all defilements," which is the fire element (*rajas*); *Ha*, for "transcends causality (*hetva*)," which is the wind element; *Kha*, for "void like space (*kha*)," which is the space element; and *Hūṃ*, for "I have realized," which represents the consciousness element. As long as a man has not gained the Buddha Wisdom, he is called consciousness (*vijñāna*) being; but once he attains enlightenment, he is called wisdom (*jñāna*) being. The Sanskrit words *buddha* and *bodhi* are derived from the same root *budh; buddha* means the enlightened one, *bodhi* means wisdom. . . . The verse of the sutra was formed from the viewpoint of the samadhi of the Five Buddhas.[13]

---

[12] T18, p. 9b.

[13] The Five Buddhas are Mahāvairocana and the Four Buddhas surrounding him in the inner circle of the Diamond Mandala. The idea is that the seed mantras *A, Va, Ra, Ha, Kha* symbolize the state of samadhi of Mahāvairocana, Akṣobhya, Ratnasambhava, Amitābha, and Amoghasiddhi respectively.

In the *Vajraśekhara Sutra* it is said: "All things are originally unborn; their intrinsic nature is beyond any verbal expression; it is pure and clean, being free from defilements and causality; it is equal to empty space." [14] Again, in the *Mahāvairocana Sutra* it is said: "I am Consciousness. I am omnipresent. I pervade all among the myriad sentient and nonsentient beings. *A* is Life (earth); *Va*, water; *Ra*, fire; *Hūṃ*, the wind; and *Kha* is identical with space." [15] The first clause "I am Consciousness" stands for the Consciousness Element which is the [Fivefold] Wisdom [in the case of the Enlightened Ones]. The last five clauses stand for the Five Great Elements. The clauses located in the middle express the attributes of freedom and nonobstruction of the Six Great Elements. The meanings of the Six Great Elements are given in the *Mahāprajñāpāramitā Sutra*,[16] *Ying-lo ching*,[17] and other texts.

These Six Great Elements create all the Buddhas, all sentient beings, and the material worlds, that is, the Dharmakaya in Four Forms and the threefold world.[18] . . . The Six Great Elements are the creating; and the Dharmakaya in Four Forms and the threefold world are the created. The created ranges from the Dharmakaya Buddha to the beings in the Six Transmigratory Paths. Although there are differences such as coarse or subtle, large or small among the created, they are not external to the Six Great Elements. The Buddha [Mahāvairocana], therefore, preached that the Six Great Elements are the essence of the World of Dharma. In Exoteric Buddhist teachings, the four great elements [earth, water, fire, and wind] are considered to be nonsentient beings, but in Esoteric Buddhist teaching they are regarded as the *samaya*-body [19] of the Tathagata. The four great elements are not independent of the mind. Differences exist between matter and mind, but in their essential nature they remain the same. Matter is no other than mind; mind, no other than matter. Without any obstruction, they are interrelated. The subject is the object; the object, the subject. The seeing is the seen, and the seen is the seeing. Nothing differentiates

[14] *Chin-kang-ting-yü-ch'ieh-san-mo-ti-fa.* T18, p. 331a.   [15] T18, p. 38b.

[16] T5, p. 979c.   [17] T16, p. 19c.

[18] For the Dharmakaya in Four Forms, see discussion in Part Two, p. 83. The threefold world is the world of perfectly enlightened ones, that of sentient beings, and that of nonsentient beings.

[19] See Part Two, p. 89, n. 26.

them. Although we speak of the creating and the created, there is in reality neither the creating nor the created. What kind of intellectual determinations can be made of the eternal Order that is naturally so (*hōni no dōri*)? Such terms as the creating and the created are symbolic expressions of Esoteric Buddhism, and we should not indulge in senseless speculation while clinging to the ordinary and superficial meanings of these words. The Existence consisting of the Six Great Elements, the essence of the World of Dharma, is free without any obstacle and is in a state of eternal harmony. He is perpetual, immutable, and is equally abiding in the apex of Reality. In the verse, therefore, it is said, "The Six Great Elements are interfused and are in a state of eternal harmony."

Concerning "The Four Mandalas are inseparably related to one another," it is explained in the *Mahāvairocana Sutra* that "there are three esoteric forms of expression for all the Tathagatas. They are *akṣara* [Sanskrit letters], *mudrā* [signs], and *bimba* [images]." [20] By *akṣara* the Dharma-mandala is meant; by *mudrā*, various religious symbols, that is, the Samaya-mandala; and by *bimba*, the physical forms of Buddha with major and minor characteristic marks, that is, the Mahā-mandala. Implicit in each of these three kinds of mandala are the deportments and activities which we call the Karma-mandala. . . . The four kinds of mandala are numberless, and each of them can be as large as space. One is inseparably related to another, just as the sky and rays of light do not resist each other. Hence, "The Four Mandalas are inseparably related to one another."

Concerning the third line "When the grace of the Three Mysteries is retained, [our inborn three mysteries will] quickly be manifested," the Three Mysteries are the mysteries of body, speech, and mind. The Three Mysteries of the Dharmakaya Buddha are so profound and subtle that the bodhisattvas who are in the Ten Stages of Bodhisattvahood or even those who are nearly equal to the Buddha fail to see or hear them; this is the reason the term "mystery" is used. Each of His manifestations is equally endowed with the boundless Three Mysteries and is related and interfused with others so that they embrace and sustain each other. It is the same with respect to the three mysteries of all sentient beings. If there is a Shingon student who reflects well upon

[20] T18, p. 44a.

the meaning of the Three Mysteries, makes mudras, recites mantras, and allows his mind to abide in the state of samadhi, then, through grace, his three mysteries will be united with the Three Mysteries; thus, the great perfection of his religious discipline will be realized. A sutra therefore states: "The three mystic letters [*oṃ bhūḥ khaṃ*] of Mahāvairocana Buddha are, singly or collectively, of immeasurable effect. If [a student of samadhi] consecrates his heart with these mystic letters accompanied by proper mudras, he will perfect the mirrorlike wisdom and obtain quickly the enlightened Mind and the adamantine Body. If he thus consecrates his forehead, he will certainly perfect the wisdom of equality and quickly obtain the anointed, meritorious and glorified Body. If he consecrates his mouth with these mystic letters, he will perfect the wisdom of observation; then, he will be able to turn the wheel of the dharma and to gain the Body of Wisdom of the Buddha. If he consecrates the crown of his head, he will perfect the wisdom of actions, witness the transformed bodies of the Buddha, and be able to subdue those who are difficult to control. If he consecrates his entire body with these mystic letters accompanied by proper mudras, he will realize the wisdom that perceives the essential nature of the World of Dharma and the Body of Mahāvairocana, the World of Dharma whose infinity can be compared to space." [21]

Also it is stated: "If [a student of samadhi] enters the meditation called the 'observation of Suchness, the Dharmakaya,' he will have a vision that all is undifferentiated oneness like infinite space. If he concentrates on practicing this meditation continually, he will in his present life enter the first stage of Bodhisattvahood and quickly accumulate the merits and provisions which would otherwise take immeasurable aeons. Being embraced by the grace of all the Tathagatas, he will reach the final stage and be equipped with the all-embracing wisdom; then, he will realize the unity of himself and others and be integrated in the Dharmakaya of all the Tathagatas. With the great compassion that pours forth unconditionally, he will benefit limitless sentient beings and thus engage in the great activities of the Buddha." [22]

These Esoteric Buddhist texts explain the methods of the samadhi of swift effect and suprarational action. If there is a man who whole-

[21] *Chin-kang-ting i-tzu-ting-lun-wang-yü-ch'ieh i-kuei.* T19, p. 322c.
[22] *Kuan-chih i-kuei.* T19, p. 602a.

heartedly disciplines himself day and night according to the prescribed methods of discipline, he will obtain in his corporeal existence the Five Supernatural Powers.[23] And if he keeps training himself, he will, without abandoning his body, advance to the stage of the Buddha. The details are as explained in the sutras. For this reason it is said, "When the grace of the Three Mysteries is retained, [our inborn three mysteries will] quickly be manifested." The expression "the grace . . . is retained (*kaji; adhiṣṭhāna*)" indicates great compassion on the part of the Tathagata and faith (*shinjin*) on the part of sentient beings. The compassion of the Buddha pouring forth on the heart of sentient beings, like the rays of the sun on water, is called *ka* [adding], and the heart of sentient beings which keeps hold of the compassion of the Buddha, as water retains the rays of the sun, is called *ji* [retaining]. If the devotee understands this principle thoroughly and devotes himself to the practice of samadhi, his three mysteries will be united with the Three Mysteries, and therefore in his present existence, he will quickly manifest his inherent three mysteries. This is the meaning of the words, "[our inborn three mysteries will] quickly be manifested."

"Infinitely interrelated like the meshes of Indra's net are those which we call existences." This line explains in simile the state of perfect interfusion and interpenetration of the infinite Three Mysteries of the manifestations [of Mahāvairocana]. Existence is my existence, the existences of the Buddhas, and the existences of all sentient beings. Also designated by this word is the Mahāvairocana Buddha in Four Forms, which represent his absolute state, his state of bliss, his manifesting bodies, and his emanating bodies. The three kinds of symbol—letters, signs, and images—are also included in this category. All of these existences are interrelated horizontally and vertically without end, like images in mirrors, or like the rays of lamps. This existence is in that one, and that one is in this. The Existence of the Buddha [Mahāvairocana] is the existences of the sentient beings and vice versa. They are not identical but are nevertheless identical; they are not different but are nevertheless different. It is therefore said in a mantra: *Asame tri-same samaye svāhā.*[24] *Asame* means non-sameness; *tri-same,* sameness of

---

[23] Supernatural action, vision, hearing; ability to read the minds of others; and knowledge of former states of existences.

[24] This mantra appears in the *Mahāvairocana Sutra.* ᴛ18, pp. 12c, 24b.

the three; *samaye*, sameness. The three stand for Buddha, Dharma, and Sangha, and for the Mind, the Buddha, and sentient beings as well. These three are identical; they are identical and one. One is within many, and many are in one, yet no confusion arises. That is why the verse says: "Infinitely interrelated like the meshes of Indra's net are those which we call existences."

Concerning the line "There is the One who is naturally equipped with all-embracing wisdom," in the *Mahāvairocana Sutra* it is said: "I am the origin of all. I am called the One on whom the world depends. My teachings are peerless. I am in the state of quiescence, and there are none who surpass me." [25] "I" in the quotation refers to Mahāvairocana, and "all," to innumerable existences. "The origin" means the primary one who realized naturally from the very beginning all the states of being characterized by the great freedom as suggested above. The Dharmakaya of the Tathagatas and the essential nature of sentient beings are identical; both are in possession of the principle of primordial quiescence. Yet, sentient beings are unaware of this and remain ignorant. The Buddha preaches this message and causes sentient beings to awaken to enlightenment. . . . Each of the Buddhas [actual or potential Buddhas, that is, all sentient beings] is endowed with the Fivefold Wisdom, with the Thirty-sevenfold Wisdom,[26] with infinite wisdom. This meaning is expressed in the following two lines ["More numerous than particles of sand are those who have the King of Mind and the consciousnesses;/Each of them is endowed with the Fivefold Wisdom, with infinite wisdom"]. . . . "The King of Mind" is the Wisdom that perceives the essential nature of the World of Dharma, and "consciousness" is a collective name for the manifold levels of consciousness.[27] . . .

The last line ["All beings can truly attain enlightenment because of

[25] T18, p. 22b.

[26] The Thirty-sevenfold Wisdom stands for the Thirty-seven Buddhas and Bodhisattvas in the inner circle of the Diamond Mandala, of which the center is Mahāvairocana. Since the thirty-six deities represent aspects of Mahāvairocana, the Thirty-sevenfold Wisdom is a synonym for the Fivefold Wisdom and for infinite wisdom, which represent the totality and the parts of the wisdom of Mahāvairocana.

[27] The Wisdom that perceives the essential nature of the World of Dharma corresponds to Pure Consciousness (*amala-vijñāna*), and consciousnesses, to the eightfold consciousness (*ālaya*-consciousness, ego-consciousness, etc.).

the force of mirrorlike wisdom"] gives the reason why [one can attain enlightenment here and now]. The reason why all the Buddhas are said to have realized enlightenment is that their mirrorlike mind functions like a bright mirror set on a high stand, reflecting all images. The faultless, bright Mind-mirror [of Mahāvairocana], being placed on the summit of the World of Dharma, illumines calmly all beings without any distortion or error. Which Buddha [sentient being with Buddha nature] does not possess such perfect, mirrorlike wisdom? It is therefore said in the last line: "All beings can truly attain enlightenment because of the force of mirrorlike wisdom."

6

THE MEANINGS OF SOUND, WORD, AND REALITY

(Shōji jissō gi)

INTRODUCTION

The Tathagata reveals his teachings by means of expressive symbols.[1] These expressive symbols have their constituent elements in the six kinds of objects.[2] These objects have their origin in the Three Mys-

[1] Here the Tathagata is the Dharmakaya Mahāvairocana Buddha. The original of "expressive symbols" is *monji*, which normally means a letter, character, or ideograph. Kūkai's use of *monji* in this treatise is not restricted to these ordinary meanings; objects of sight, hearing, smell, touch, taste, and thought are regarded as *monji*.

[2] The totality of the world of objects—objects of sight, hearing, smell, taste, touch, and thought.

teries of the Dharmakaya Buddha.[3] The universal Three Mysteries pervade the World of Dharma and are perpetual. The Existence, with the Fivefold Wisdom and the Four Forms,[4] comprises the ten worlds[5] and misses nothing.

Those who have realized Him are called the Enlightened Ones and those who are lost, sentient beings. Sentient beings are infatuated and blind and know no way of attaining enlightenment on their own. Through grace (*kaji*), therefore, the Tathagata shows them the way to return. The basis of the way to return cannot be established in the absence of superior teachings. The superior teachings cannot arise in the absence of sound and word. When sound and word are distinct, reality [the symbolized] will be revealed clearly. So-called Sound-Word-Reality is, indeed, the universal Three Mysteries of the Dharmakaya Buddha,[6] the innate *maṇḍa* [essence] of all sentient beings. Mahāvairocana Tathagata, therefore, by revealing the import of Sound-Word-Reality, arouses sentient beings from their long slumber.

In expounding teachings, whatever they may be—Exoteric or Esoteric Buddhist teachings, or non-Buddhist teachings—who would not resort to this approach? Now, guided by the instructions of the Great Teacher [Mahāvairocana],[7] I should like to extract the meaning of

[3] The Mystery of Body includes the objects of sight, smell, taste, and touch; the Mystery of Speech, the objects of hearing; and the Mystery of Mind, the data of mind.

[4] The Dharmakaya Mahāvairocana Buddha. On the Fivefold Wisdom and the Four Forms, see discussion in Part Two, p. 83.

[5] All the realms of living beings: hell, and the worlds of hungry ghosts, beasts, asuras, men, heavenly beings, śrāvakas, pratyekabuddhas, bodhisattvas, and Buddhas.

[6] In Sound-Word-Reality, Sound corresponds to the Mystery of Speech; Word, to the Mystery of Mind; and Reality, to the Mystery of Body of Mahāvairocana Buddha. The term "reality (*jissō*)" is used in two senses: that of any denoted or symbolized object, and that of an existence or the Existence (Mahāvairocana).

[7] There are two more possibilities. One is to interpret the expression Great Teacher as referring to Kūkai's Chinese master Hui-kuo. In the *Record of the Secret Treasury (Hizōki)*, which has traditionally been believed to be Kūkai's notes recording Hui-kuo's oral instruction on the Esoteric Buddhist teachings, there are a few lines written on the meanings of "sound, word, and reality": "*A Vi Ra Hūṃ Khaṃ*. . . . Meditate on the sounds, words, and realities [contents] in order and in reverse order. Sound is to recite the words [syllables]; word is to visualize the forms of the words; and reality is to meditate on the meanings of these words." K.Z., II, 13. Another possibility is to regard the Great Teacher

this [triad]. It is hoped that students of later times will devote their utmost attention to this and deliberate over it.

ON THE TERMS USED IN
THE TITLE

No sooner does the breath issue forth and touch the air [in the mouth] than a vibration invariably arises; this we call a sound (*shō*). The vibration depends on the sound; a sound, therefore, is the essential element of vibration.[8] When a certain sound is uttered, it is not in vain; it invariably indicates a name of something; we call this a word (*ji*). A name invariably corresponds to an object standing for the name; we call this reality (*jissō*). To distinguish the three categories—sound, word, and reality—is called defining (*gi*).

The designation "sound" is also given to that which arises from the vibration produced through contacts between the four great elements.[9] The five or eight notes of the Chinese musical scale and the seven or eight declensions of Sanskrit have come to exist through sound. That a certain sound [or sounds] expresses a certain name always results from its being an expressive symbol. Any expressive symbol is rooted in the six kinds of objects. Interpretations of the six kinds of objects in terms of expressive symbols will be given later.

If we apply the methods of analysis of the six types of Sanskrit compounds, [the following analyses of the compounds, sound-word and sound-word-reality, can be made:]

1. Through sound, word comes to be; word, therefore, is that which depends on sound. [Analyzed this way,] we are taking [sound-word]

---

as Śubhākarasiṃha, or I-hsing, who compiled the commentary on the *Mahāvairocana Sutra*, for in this commentary the following explanation is found: "The sound, word, and reality of each samadhi gate [methods of meditation] of the Tathagata have been like this regardless of the Buddha's [Shakyamuni] appearance or nonappearance." τ39, p. 657ab.

[8] This ambiguous line may well mean that vibration becomes perceptible only when accompanied by an audible sound.

[9] The elements of earth, water, fire, and wind.

as a dependent compound.¹⁰ If we say that reality becomes manifest by sound-word and that, therefore, reality is dependent on sound-word, we are also taking [sound-word-reality] as a dependent compound.¹¹

2. If we say that sound invariably has word, that is, that sound is the possessing and word is the possessed and sound has the content of word, we are taking [sound-word] as a possessive compound.¹² Sound-word invariably has reality, and reality likewise has sound-word; both are mutually possessing and possessed. We are also taking [sound-word-reality] in this manner.

3. If we state that other than sound there is no word and that word, therefore, is sound, we are taking [sound-word] as an appositive compound.¹³ If we state that other than sound-word there is no reality and that sound-word, therefore, is reality, we are taking [sound-word-reality] also as above. On this point the commentary on the *Mahāvairo-cana Sutra* gives a detailed explanation.¹⁴ Refer to it directly.

4. If we say that sound, word, and reality are extremely close and inseparable, we are taking [sound-word-reality] as an unchangeable compound.¹⁵

5. If we say that sound-word is provisional and falls short of truth, while reality is profound and quiescent and transcends name; that sound vibrates in vain and does not indicate anything; or that word [whose written symbol] has a pattern of up and down and short and long is different from sound, we are taking [the two compounds] as compounds combining two different things.¹⁶ A compound whose first element is a numeral ¹⁷ is not applicable.

Among the five kinds discussed above, the fifth is superficial, the third and the fourth are profound, and the remaining two can be taken as either superficial or profound.

---

¹⁰ *Eshushaku* or *tatpuruṣa*, in which the first member, sound, modifies the second noun, word, i.e., "word of sound."

¹¹ In the case of sound-word-reality, the first compound, sound-word, modifies the second noun, reality: thus, sound-word-reality is literally "reality of sound-word."

¹² *Uzaishaku* or *bahuvrīhi*.

¹³ *Jigosshaku* or *karmadhāraya*.

¹⁴ *Ta-jih-ching su.* T39, pp. 650c, 657a, 658c.

¹⁵ *Ringonshaku* or *avyayībhāva*.

¹⁶ *Sōishaku* or *dvṃdva*.

¹⁷ *Taisūshaku* or *dvigu*.

THE MAIN DISCOURSE

The Main Discourse consists of two divisions. First, a scriptural source will be cited and then interpretations on it given.

A. SCRIPTURAL SOURCE

QUESTION: Now, through what sutra can the meanings of sound, word, and reality be established?

ANSWER: They can be established on the basis of the *Mahāvairocana Sutra,* which contains clear evidence.

QUESTION: How are they explained in that sutra?

ANSWER: In that sutra the Dharmakaya Tathagata preached the following verse:

> The perfectly Enlightened One's mantras
> Are made up of syllables, names, or clauses;
> Like the statements made by Indra,
> They are meaningful and effective.[18] . . .

QUESTION: What is the meaning of these lines?

ANSWER: There are exoteric and esoteric meanings. The exoteric meanings are as given by the commentator of the sutra.[19] The esoteric implications are profound and manifold. In the verse, therefore, it is explained in a simile, "Like the statements made by Indra,/They are meaningful and effective." Indra has also both exoteric and esoteric meanings. According to the exoteric meaning, Indra is a synonym of Śakra-deva. "They are meaningful and effective" means that "Śakra-deva composed the treatise on Sanskrit grammar in which he was able to embrace manifold meanings in one word. This is the reason why reference was made to [Indra]. Even with respect to secular knowledge it [Sanskrit grammar] is like this; how much more meaningful and effective are the words of the Tathagata who has a complete mastery

---

[18] T18, p. 9c.

[19] The commentator refers either to Śubhākarasimha, who taught orally, or to I-hsing, who wrote down the former's explanations and edited them. An explanation of the verse is found in T39, p. 649c.

over the Dharma!" [20] If interpreted in an esoteric sense, each of the syllables, names, and clauses of a mantra is pregnant with boundless meanings; numberless Buddhas and bodhisattvas, preaching the meanings of each word all the while in the three divisions of time, cannot possibly expound them all. How would it be possible for an ordinary man to explain them completely? Now, an effort will be made to reveal part of them.

The words "The perfectly Enlightened One," which appear in the beginning of the verse, indicate the universal Body of Mystery of the Dharmakaya Buddha. This Body of Mystery is immeasurable in extent, as was explained in *Attaining Enlightenment in This Very Existence*. This Body of Mystery is reality. The "mantras" are the sounds and are no other than the Speech of Mystery of the Buddha. The "syllables" and "names" are the words; through syllables, names are revealed because names are words. Thus we have identified the sounds, words, and reality in the verse.

If we take the *Mahāvairocana Sutra* as a whole, the following interpretation can be made. The mantras of various deities appearing in the sutra are the sounds; the chapter in which the meanings of the syllables beginning with *A* are explained and the chapter expounding the wheel of letters [21] have to do with the words; and the chapter on Nondifferentiation [22] and the passages explaining the characteristics of various deities have to do with reality.

Again, if we interpret "sound, word, and reality" on the basis of a syllable, we can make the following analysis. Take, for example, the first syllable of the Sanskrit alphabet *A*. When we open our mouth and simultaneously exhale, the sound *A* [ə] is produced. This is the sound. For what does the sound *A* stand? It denotes a name-word (*myōji*) of the Dharmakaya Buddha; namely, it is sound and word. What is the meaning of the Dharmakaya? The so-called Dharmakaya stands for that which is originally the uncreated [quality] of all dharmas [existences], namely, for reality.

[20] Quoted from the commentary on the *Mahāvairocana Sutra*. T39, p. 649c.
[21] The former refers to chap. 2 (T18, pp. 4–13) and the latter, to chap. 10 (T18, p. 30), of the *Mahāvairocana Sutra*.
[22] Chap. 29 (T18, p. 44) of the *Mahāvairocana Sutra*.

B. INTERPRETATIONS

A summary in verse:

> The five great elements have vibrations;
> Each of the ten worlds has its language;
> The six kinds of objects are expressive symbols;
> The Dharmakaya Buddha is the Reality.

The first line explains the substances from which the sounds originate; the second line allows us to differentiate between the true symbols
of verbal expression and the false; the third line clarifies the expressive
symbols of sentient beings and of the physical worlds; and the fourth
line brings forth reality.

The five great elements are earth, water, fire, wind, and space. They
have both exoteric and esoteric meanings. The exoteric meanings
are those of the ordinary interpretation.[23] In the esoteric sense, the
five great elements stand for the five syllables, the five Buddhas,[24] and
all other deities in the congregation as large as the ocean [mandala].
The details of the esoteric meanings of the five great elements are as
given in *Attaining Enlightenment in This Very Existence*. The five
great elements of sentient beings and nonsentient beings are endowed
with [the power of producing] vibrations and sounds, for no sounds
are independent of the five great elements; these are the original substance, and the sounds or vibrations are their functions. Thus it is said
in the verse, "The five great elements have vibrations."

"The ten worlds" are the worlds of Buddhas, of bodhisattvas, of

[23] Material elements.
[24] There are two traditions as to the correspondence of the five great elements,
the five syllables, and the five Buddhas. According to Śubhākarasiṃha, they are:

Earth	*A*	Akṣobhya
Water	*Vaṃ*	Amitābha
Fire	*Raṃ*	Ratnasambhava
Wind	*Haṃ*	Amoghasiddhi
Space	*Khaṃ*	Mahāvairocana

According to Pu-k'ung:

Earth	*A*	Mahāvairocana
Water	*Va*	Amoghasiddhi
Fire	*Ra*	Ratnasambhava
Wind	*Ha*	Amitābha
Space	*Kha*	Akṣobhya

pratyekabuddhas, of śrāvakas, of heavenly beings, of men, of asuras, of beasts, of hungry ghosts, and of the inhabitants of hell. Any of the other worlds not listed here can be included in the world of heavenly beings, of beasts, or of ghosts. The reference is to the ten worlds in the *Avataṃsaka Sutra* [25] and in the *Chin-kang-ting-li-ch'ü-shih ching*.[26] All the languages in these ten worlds are produced by means of sounds. In sounds there are long and short [vowels], high and low [pitches], and inflections. These characteristics of the sounds are called the intonation pattern (*mon*). The intonation pattern is made known through word, and word becomes distinct through its intonation. When commentators say that the intonation pattern is word, they mean to express the inseparable and interdependent relationships that exist between the word and its intonation. All of these belong to the vocal sounds of sentient beings. There are ten different systems in these symbols of verbal expression, for there are ten different worlds as mentioned above.

Of these ten kinds of verbal symbols of expression, the symbols of verbal expression in the world of Buddhas are true, whereas those in the other nine worlds are untrue. In a sutra, therefore, it is said: "[The Buddha is he] who speaks what is true and what is real, who tells things as they are, who utters neither deceitful words nor inconsistent words." [27] These five kinds of speech are called *mantra* in Sanskrit. Because the word *mantra* contains these five different meanings, Nāgārjuna defined it as "esoteric words." [28] "Esoteric words" are called "true words (*shingon*)" because the translators chose one meaning out of these five.

QUESTION: What do these mantras (*shingon*) denote?

ANSWER: They are capable of denoting the Reality of all dharmas without any error or falsehood; thus they are called true words.

QUESTION: How do those mantras denote the Name [the Reality] of all dharmas?

ANSWER: Though there are endless varieties of mantras [denoting Reality], if we trace them to their root and source, we find that the mantra preached by Mahāvairocana Buddha while absorbed in the great *sāgaramudrā* samadhi [29] includes all of them.

QUESTION: What is that king of mantras?

[25] T10, p. 205b.   [26] T19, p. 607a.
[27] The *Diamond Cutter (Vajracchedikā) Sutra*. T8, p. 750b.
[28] *Ta-chih-tu lun*. T25, p. 336c.   [29] See *Precious Key*, n. 201.

ANSWER: It is the wheel of letters or the syllabary given in the *Vajraśekhara Sutra* [30] and the *Mahāvairocana Sutra*.[31] By the syllabary is meant *A, Ha*, etc. in the Sanskrit alphabet. *A*, etc. are the name-words, secret designations, of the Dharmakaya Tathagata. Gods, serpents, demons, etc. also have their respective syllabary. Yet the root of them is in the fountainhead of [the king of mantras of] Mahāvairocana. Emanated from this and ramified on and on are the languages current in the world. If a man knows the true significance of this, we call him one who knows the true words. If he does not know the fountainhead, we call him one who uses false words. The use of false words makes one subject to sufferings in long nights of darkness. The mantra uproots sufferings and gives bliss. The differences are precisely those between medicine and poison, enlightenment and delusion, or gain and loss.

QUESTION: How are the five kinds of speech explained by Nāgārjuna [32] related to these two categories of speech discussed above?

ANSWER: [Among the five kinds of speech explained by Nāgārjuna,] discriminative words derived from wrong notions, words uttered in dreams, words that adhere to false statements, and words conditioned by beginningless [influences contingent upon false attachments to wrong assumptions] belong to the category of false words. Words that convey reality as it really is belong to the category of true words.

Next, the characteristics of the expressive symbols of sentient and nonsentient beings will be interpreted. In the verse "The six kinds of objects are expressive symbols," the six kinds of objects are the objects of sight, hearing, smell, taste, touch, and thought. Each of these six kinds of objects has the characteristics of an expressive symbol of expression.

QUESTION: What are the definitions and categories of the first words, the objects of sight?

In answer, a summary in verse:

> The objects of sight are colors, forms, and movements.
> Endowed with them are both sentient and nonsentient beings.
> Of them there are conditioned and unconditioned aspects.
> They delude some and induce others to attain enlightenment.

[30] T18, p. 338.   [31] T18, p. 30bc.
[32] The commentary on *The Awakening of Faith* attributed to Nāgārjuna. T32, p. 605c-6a.

The first line lists the categories of the objects of sight; the next line suggests mutual relationships that exist between the objects of sight of sentient beings and those of nonsentient beings; the third line reveals that there is a twofold structure of the conditioned and the unconditioned; and the fourth line explains that the various objects of sight are harmful like poison to the foolish, but beneficial like medicine to the man of wisdom.

The first line distinguishes the three categories of objects of sight, that is, colors, forms, and movements.

1. Colors. Colors are those of the five great elements. The students of the Yogācāra school of Buddhism discuss four colors but do not include black. In the *Mahāvairocana Sutra*,[33] the colors of the five great elements are identified as yellow [earth], white [water], red [fire], black [wind], and blue [space]. These colors of the five great elements are the [basic] colors. . . . All these colors may be classified under the categories of liking, disliking, and neutral. A passage in the *Mahāvairocana Sutra* to the effect that "the mind is not blue, yellow, red, white, crimson, purple, crystal, bright, or dark"[34] denies the identity of the mind with any color.

2. Forms. Forms are to be described in terms of length, size, shape, and height. Square, circle, triangle, demilune, and the like are also forms. Configurations of objects which can be differentiated in terms such as length are also forms. A passage in the *Mahāvairocana Sutra* to the effect that "the mind is not long, short, round, or square"[35] denies the identity of the mind with any form.

3. Movements. Movements stand for grasping, releasing, extending, contracting, walking, standing, sitting, lying, and so forth. That the objects of sight continue in their configuration, now appearing and now disappearing, is because they are undergoing constant transformation. The same movement cannot be repeated at the same place where the former movement has occurred. Any movement is repeated continuously or continually, nearby or far away. While in motion an object of sight is subject to transformation. Furthermore, it may rotate by its inertia. All these distinctions are to be classified under the category of movement. . . .

Thus all colors, forms, and movements having to do with the work-

[33] T18, pp. 9a, 22c–23a.   [34] T18, p. 1c.   [35] T18, p. 1c.

ing of the eyes are the objects of the eyes. Those having to do with the working of sight are the objects of sight and the objects that are related to sight. Those having to do with consciousness are the objects of consciousness and the objects related to consciousness. We call these the categories of differentiation. They are expressions of patterns (*monji*), for the characteristics [which differentiate one from another] are patterns (*mon*). Each pattern has its own designation. Thus, we call them expressions of patterns. . . . What we call the expressions of the patterns of the objects of sight also include the written forms of the Sanskrit syllabary, *A*, etc.; the five colors; and the painted pictures of sentient and nonsentient beings in colors, brocades, etc. In the *Lotus Sutra*,[36] the *Avataṃsaka Sutra*,[37] the *Ta-chih-tu lun*,[38] etc., various categories of differentiation of the objects of sight are explained in detail. They are not, however, outside of the context of the ten types of sentient beings and their ten realms of existence.

All these expressions of patterns induce the stupid to increase his attachment to them and to develop defilements such as greed, hatred, and delusion, causing him to commit the Ten Evils and the Five Deadly Sins.[39] It is therefore said in the verse, "They delude some." A man of insight is not attached to them nor does he avoid them, observing how they have come to be. Realizing manifold mandala of the World of Dharma, he participates in the great activities of the Buddha [Mahāvairocana]. He honors all the Buddhas and helps all sentient beings; thus, his goal of attaining enlightenment and his acts benefiting others will be perfectly realized. This is the meaning of the line "[They] induce others to attain enlightenment."

The second line, "Endowed with them are both sentient and nonsentient beings," is to be understood as containing the three ideas that sentient beings are endowed with colors, forms, and movements; that nonsentient beings are also provided with these three; and that both sentient beings and nonsentient beings are not independent but are interrelated. It is said in a sutra that "the Body of the Buddha is suprarational in that all lands are in it,"[40] or that "[the Buddha, of whom]

---

36 T9, p. 50a.   37 T10, p. 231ab.   38 T25, p. 324bc.

39 For the Ten Evils, see *Indications*, n. 108. The Five Deadly Sins: killing one's father, killing one's mother, killing a saint, injuring the body of a Buddha, and causing disunity in the community of monks.

40 The *Avataṃsaka Sutra*. T10, p. 32a.

each hair contains many lands as vast as oceans, pervades the entire World of Dharma," [41] or that "in a follicle of [the Buddha's] hair, there are unimaginable lands as many as particles of dust, in each of which Vairocana Buddha is present, revealing the sublime Dharma in the midst of an assembly; even in a particle of dust of each land there are many—small and large—lands as numerous as particles of dust, in all of which without exception Buddha resides." [42] It is evident from these passages that [the manifestations of] the Body of the Buddha and the bodies of sentient beings are manifold in size. The Body of the Buddha can be regarded as having the magnitude of the World of Dharma, as vast as infinite space, or as having ten Buddha lands or one Buddha land, or as having the size of a particle of dust. Thus the Body of the Buddha, the body of each sentient being, and each land, small and large, are interrelated and interdependent. All of these sentient beings and the worlds of nonsentient beings are provided with the objects of sight—colors, forms, and movements.

The third line, "Of them there are conditioned and unconditioned aspects," will now be commented upon. The objects of sight—colors, forms, or movements—which we have discussed above, are the products of the unconditioned; in other words, they are the manifestations of the Body and Mind of the Dharmakaya Buddha. . . . Seen from the relative point of view, the bodies of the Buddhas and their lands have distinctions of large or small, coarse or fine, but seen from the absolute point of view they are equally the undifferentiated One. Thus, the bodies of the Buddhas and their lands have two aspects, that is, the conditioned and the unconditioned. All of these objects of sight are provided with the three attributes—color, form, and movement—and are interrelated. This is an interpretation given from the point of view of the Enlightened One. Even if we interpret the objects of sight from the point of view of unenlightened sentient beings, the same can be said, for it can be inferred that any sentient being is the originally enlightened Dharmakaya and is identical to the Buddha. He and the land where he resides are the unconditioned. What have come to be conditioned by karma are these sentient beings in the triple world and Six Transmigratory Paths and their respective realms. . . .

The objects of sight in terms of sentient beings and nonsentient

[41] The *Avataṃsaka Sutra*. T10, p. 30a.   [42] The *Avataṃsaka Sutra*. T10, p. 36b.

beings are harmful as poison to the foolish, but beneficial as medicine
to the man of wisdom. Hence, in the fourth line, "They delude some
and induce others to attain enlightenment."

QUESTION: Of these conditioned and unconditioned objects of sight,
which are the creating and which are the created?

ANSWER: The creating are the five great elements and five colors;
the created, the threefold world.[43] The threefold world is of infinite
[marks of] distinction, which are called the expressions (*monji*) of the
conditioned and the unconditioned. Here ends the interpretation of the
objects of sight.[44]

7

THE MEANINGS OF
THE WORD HŪṂ

(*Ungi gi*)

The word *Hūṃ* has two sets of meanings. One is invariant, and the
other, ultimate. Part One consists of the analysis of invariant meanings,
and Part Two, the interpretation of ultimate meanings.

[43] See *Attaining Enlightenment*, n. 18.

[44] With this line Kūkai ends this work. So far he has discussed only the first
item of the six kinds of objects, i.e., the objects of sight, and has not touched upon
the remaining five kinds of objects. Whether the work is complete or incomplete
has been argued for centuries. That Kūkai required those of his students who
specialized in Sanskrit to study it may indicate that the work was not unfinished.
Cf. *K.Z.*, V., 445.

PART ONE: INVARIANT MEANINGS

The graphic form of the word *Hūṃ* can be divided into four components. In the *Vajraśekhara* [1] it is interpreted as consisting of four letters [*H A Ū M*].

1. The letter *H* [of *Hūṃ*, when written in the Siddhām script,] is located in the middle. "It stands for the Sanskrit word *hetva* which means 'cause.' There are six types of causes.[2] Among them five types of causes can be applied here.[3] These points are explained in the Abhidharma texts. If we see the letter *H*, we know that all things have come to be because of causes; 'cause' is the invariant meaning of the letter *H*." [4]

2. The sound *A* [ə] is inherent in the letter *H*. The sound *A* is the mother of all letters; it is the essence of all sounds; and it stands for the fountainhead of all-inclusive Reality. "The very act itself of opening the mouth in order to utter any sound is accompanied by the sound *A*; therefore, apart from the sound *A*, no sounds are possible. The sound *A* is the mother of all sounds." [5] If we see the letter *A*, we know that all things are empty and nil [as isolated individual entities apart from the all-inclusive Reality]. This is the invariant meaning of the letter *A*.

3. The letter *Ū* stands for [the Sanskrit *ūna*,] "wanting." If we see

---

[1] *Chin-kang-ting* (*vajraśekhara*)-*li-ch'ü-shih* (T1003), commentary on the *Prajñāpāramitā-naya Sutra* translated by Pu-k'ung. T19, p. 609c.

[2] 1) Coordinating cause (*kāraṇa* or *nōsa*) or indirect cause, such as the sun, soil, and water are for a growing plant; 2) coexisting cause (*sahabhū* or *ku-u*)—two or more elements exist together and are mutually dependent; 3) homologous cause (*sabhāga* or *dōrui*)—one dharma produces another dharma of homologous nature, as good produces good, evil produces evil; 4) corresponding cause (*samprayuktaka* or *sōō*)—the causal relationship that exists between the mind and the data of mind; 5) all-pervading cause (*sarvatraga* or *hengyō*)—twelve basic causes, such as basic blindness, adherence to perverse views, which cause man to remain unenlightened; 6) mutational cause (*vipāka* or *ijuku*)—causes effecting results which are not identical with themselves, i.e., evil producing suffering.

[3] The second to sixth types of causes given in n. 2.

[4] Quotation from the commentary on the *Mahāvairocana Sutra*. T39, p. 656a.

[5] T39, p. 656a.

the letter *Ū*, we know that all things are impermanent, that they induce suffering, that they are empty and without permanent entity, etc.;
in short, "wanting" is the invariant meaning of the letter *Ū*.

4. The letter *M* stands for the Sanskrit word *ātman*, which can be
translated as "entity." Of entity there are two kinds: one is the permanent self, and the other, the entity of a thing. The letter *M* reminds
us of [the perverse view] that all things pertain to permanent selves,
such as I, thou, they. We call this "augmentation" [of a false assump-
tion]. "Entity" is the invariant meaning of the letter *M*.

People in the world know only the invariant meanings and have
never come to understand the ultimate meanings; they therefore remain
in the cycle of samsara. Since Tathagatas know the ultimate meanings
as they really are, they are called the great Enlightened Ones.

PART TWO: ULTIMATE MEANINGS

The word *Hūṃ* consists of four letters: *H A Ū M;* accordingly, Part
Two will be divided into four sections.

1. The ultimate meaning of the letter *H*. The letter *H* connotes that
the first cause of all things is unobtainable. Why is the first cause unobtainable? All things have evolved contingent upon a series of causes;
we should therefore know that they have ultimately no point of departure on which to rely. Hence, we regard the absence of any particular cause as the origin of all things. The reason for this is that when
we observe in various ways the causes and conditions of arising of all
things, we see that all of them are of the uncreated. We should know
that [predications of] all things are of our mind only and that the real
feature of our mind is all-inclusive wisdom. Indeed, all things are of
the World of Dharma; that is, the World of Dharma is the essence of
all things, but cannot be regarded as the first cause [in contrast to the
notion of effect]. In other words, the first cause is of the World of
Dharma, the coordinating causes are of the World of Dharma, and the
causally conditioned phenomena are also of the World of Dharma. The
method of meditation on the letter *A* is to meditate from the source to
its offshoots and to arrive finally at the above conclusion. The method

of meditation on the letter *H* is to meditate from the offshoots to the source and to arrive finally at the above conclusion. On the letter *A* we should meditate that from the "originally uncreated" all things are derived; and on the letter *H*, that the causeless cause is the first cause of all things. The ultimate meaning of the beginning [letter *A* in the Sanskrit alphabet] and that of the last [letter *H*] coincide. The ultimate meanings of all the letters that lie between them can likewise be inferred.[6]

2. The ultimate meanings of the letter *A*. Three ultimate meanings of the letter *A* can be identified: a) being, b) empty, and c) uncreated.

a. The letter *A* in the Sanskrit alphabet represents the first sound. If it is the first [in contrast to others], it is relative. We therefore define it as "[relative] being."

b. *A* also has the meaning of non-arising. If anything arises in dependence, it does not have its own independent nature. We therefore define it as "empty."

c. By "uncreated" is meant the Realm which is one and real, that is, the Middle Way [Absolute]. Nāgārjuna said: "Phenomena are empty, temporal, and also middle."[7] . . . As the sound *A* is inherent in all other sounds, the mother of all as it were, so what is truly and ultimately meant by the letter *A* pervades all things. The reason for this is that there is not a single phenomenon that is not the product of co-ordinating causes. What is produced by coordinating causes necessarily has its beginning and root. We see that these coordinating causes that affect the development of a phenomenon have in turn their manifold causes. Which should we regard as the root? When we observe thus, we come to know that which is the limit, the "originally uncreated," which is the root of all phenomena. Just as we hear the sound *A* when we hear all sounds, so we perceive that which is the limit, the "originally uncreated," when we perceive the arising of all phenomena. He who perceives that which is the limit, the "originally uncreated," will come to know his mind as it really is. To know one's mind as it really is is [to gain] all-inclusive wisdom. Thus, this single letter is the mantra of Mahāvairocana.[8]

[6] The discussion on the ultimate meaning of the letter *H* is based on that given in the commentary on the *Mahāvairocana Sutra*. T39, p. 656a.

[7] From *Mādhyamika-kārikās*. T30, p. 33b.

[8] The seed mantra of the Mahāvairocana of the Matrix Realm is the letter *A*.

The common people in the world do not perceive the source of all phenomena. Therefore, they believe in their illusion that there is arising [and ceasing of particulars]. Thus, they follow the current of birth and death (samsara) and are unable to free themselves from it. They are like the ignorant painter who, having painted in various colors a dreadful picture of a *yakṣa* demon, looked at it and fell to the ground horrified. Assuming what they imagine to be the source of phenomena, they paint a picture of the triple world and submerge themselves in it, undergoing various sufferings by force of their heartaches. The Tathagata, a painter with insight and clear knowledge, can freely reveal the Mandala of Great Compassion.[9] In other words, as for that which is called the utmost secret treasury [the originally uncreated], sentient beings are the ones who conceal it, but the Buddha does not hide it from them.[10] Such is the ultimate meaning of the letter *A*.

A sutra states: "The letter *A* signifies 'the enlightened mind,' 'the gateway to all teachings,' 'nonduality,' 'the goal of all existences,' 'the nature of all existences,' 'freedom,' and 'the Dharmakaya.' " [11] These are the ultimate meanings of the letter *A*. The same sutra further elucidates the letter *A*.[12]

3. The ultimate meanings of the letter *Ū*. That no existence is found to be in want [of Buddhahood] is the ultimate meaning of the letter *Ū*.

Next, the World of Dharma of One Mind [13] is eternal, like infinite space which is one. The infinite wisdom [of One Mind] is like the sun, the moon, and the stars which have been shining there from the beginning. Even if Mount Sumeru blocks the sight of the Milky Way and buildings many stories high obstruct the sky, that space thereby is not decreased is an attribute of great space. Even if a flood in the age of universal destruction causes the earth to drift, or devouring flames burn

[9] The Matrix Mandala.

[10] The above discussion on the ultimate meanings of the letter *A* is based on the commentary on the *Mahāvairocana Sutra*. T39, pp. 649b, 651c.

[11] *Shou-hu-kuo-chieh-chu ching*. T19, p. 565c.

[12] One hundred meanings of the letter *A* are given in the sutra. See T19, p. 532a.

[13] One Mind is a synonym for the Dharmakaya or Mahāvairocana in Kūkai's terminology. When the Dharmakaya engages the realms of being, it is often expressed in terms of Mind. "The World of Dharma of One Mind" means "the World of Enlightenment of Mahāvairocana" or "the Diamond Mandala of Mahāvairocana."

the buildings, that space thereby is not decreased is an attribute of great space. The magnitude of One Mind is, indeed, like great space. Even if those who abide in the realm of ignorance are numberless and even if their arrogance is as lofty as Mount Sumeru, the One Mind comparable to space is not thereby increased or decreased, being perpetual from the beginning. Such is the ultimate meaning of the letter *Ū*.

Even if the six heretics[14] repudiate the law of cause and effect, the Three Mysteries [of Mahāvairocana] comparable to the attributes of space will remain in quiescence, just as they have been from the beginning. Such is the ultimate meaning of the letter *Ū*.

The Hinayanists may chop the fuel of body and mind with their sharp axes of negation of permanent self, but the original nature of One Mind will thereby neither increase nor decrease. This is the ultimate meaning of the letter *Ū*, signifying "non-decrease."

The raging flames of negation of the Mādhyamika of Mahayana may reduce to ashes, with nothing remaining, the dust of attachment to the belief in a permanent ego in man and in permanent existence in things; but the Three Mysteries are not thereby decreased. They are like a fabric made from the fur of a certain rat that lives in fire—they become pure as they burn, just as the fabric is cleansed of its dirt as it burns. Such is the ultimate meaning of the letter *Ū*.

Some [students of Yogācāra] may destroy the mansion of mirage conceived by the imagination or the city of illusion derived from relative knowledge, but the original nature of the Three Mysteries cannot thereby be harmed. Such is the ultimate meaning of the letter *Ū*.

There may be men [students of T'ien-t'ai] who detest the unreal state of the conditioned and who long for a state free from the falsehood of the unconditioned. They may attain a state of being beyond any description, in which the activities of their minds completely cease to be; yet the original nature of the Three Mysteries is never disrupted nor does it decline. Such is the ultimate meaning of the letter *Ū*.

All existences in samsara are characterized by the following six states

14 The six non-Buddhist philosophers active at the time of Shakyamuni Buddha in the Ganges area: 1) Pūraṇa-kassapa, a moral negativist who denied good and evil; 2) Makkali-gosāla, a fatalist; 3) Sañjaya-velaṭṭhiputta, a skeptic; 4) Ajita-kesakambarin, a materialist; 5) Pakuda-kacāyana, who explained the universe by seven elemental factors; and 6) Nigaṇṭha-nātaputta, the founder of Jainism.

of being: 1) subject to sorrow, empty, transient, and without a permanent self; 2) undergoing fourfold change; [15] 3) lacking freedom;
4) not abiding in their nature; 5) arising in dependence; 6) relative.
They are therefore spoken of as being in the state of wanting (*ūna*).
The ultimate meanings of the letter *Ū*, however, have nothing to do
with these six states. . . . Eternity, Bliss, the Self, and Purity are the
ultimate meanings of the letter *Ū*, for it stands for that which knows
no decrease [the Dharmakaya Mahāvairocana]; immutability in oneness of Suchness is the ultimate meaning of the letter *Ū*, for it stands
for that which is free from any alteration; having tenfold freedom [16]
is the ultimate meaning of the letter *Ū*, for it stands for that which
meets no obstacles; abiding in its essential nature is the ultimate meaning of the letter *Ū*, for it stands for that which is free from mutation;
independence from causality is the ultimate meaning of the letter *Ū*,
for it stands for that which is the "originally uncreated," like great
space; and transcendence of relativity is the ultimate meaning of the
letter *Ū*, for it stands for that which is the Self-identity. . . .

Those who are in the triple world, or in the Six Transmigratory
Paths, are long deviated from the truth of Suchness of Oneness and
are intoxicated by the poisonous wine of greed, hatred, and delusion.
Hunting game furiously in the field of illusion, they have no intention
of returning to their homes. [When tired,] they fall into a long slumber in the village of dream. When are they to awake?

Through the eyes of the Buddha, the truth can be perceived that
both the Buddhas and all sentient beings are abiding on the same ground
of deliverance. There is no distinction between this and that; they are
nondual and equal. No increase or decrease is called for; they are, like a
perfect circle, perfect in themselves [as to their intrinsic nature]. Since
among them there is no inferiority or superiority in classification, how

[15] The four characteristic states of existence in samsara: 1) arising—the coming
into existence analogous to the birth of a child; 2) abiding—the state of continu-
ity in growth analogous to the passage from childhood to manhood; 3) change—
the stage of change analogous to the period from the prime of life to old age;
and 4) stopping—the period of senility and death. These four characteristic states,
when used in a cosmic sense, designate one cosmic cycle that is repeated to
infinity.

[16] Freedom in longevity, mind, glory, action, birth, liberation, vow, supernatural power, doctrine, and wisdom. The *Avataṃsaka Sutra*. т9, p. 647bc.

can there be a distinction of high and low among men? This is the ultimate meaning of the letter *Ū.* . . .

> Those who are born in the triple world,
> Or suffering beings, fallen in the Six Transmigratory Paths,
> Appear here and disappear there in samsara
> Without stopping even for a moment.
> Sacrificing substance for shadow,
> They live in pursuit of illusions.
> Those who are subject to birth and death,
> Being produced in dependent origination,
> In one second undergo transformations
> Nine hundred times like a flame or running water.
> Yet the reservoir of their *ālaya*-consciousness is eternal,
> Though the waves of their sevenfold consciousness
> Are rippling and tossing constantly on its surface.
> Such transient states of their existence
> May appear to be devastating and injurious;
> Yet their intrinsic nature thereby is unaffected.
> Thus should be known the ultimate meaning of the letter *Ū.*

> The three luminous bodies—the sun, moon, and stars—
> Have been shining from the beginning in the sky.
> They may be hidden at times by mists and clouds
> Or veiled completely by smoke and dust.
> Ignorant people thereby may imagine
> That the sun and the moon come to cease to be.
> It is the same with the intrinsic Three Bodies; [17]
> From the beginningless beginning
> They have been living in the space of Mind.
> Yet being covered by their illusions
> And being entangled by their defilements,
> They are unmanifest like a mirror inside a box or a gem in ore.
> Deluded people thereby may imagine
> That they have no element of original enlightenment.
> What greater loss can be thought of
> Than this self-denunciation of the blind and stupid?
> Nonetheless, those intrinsic Three Bodies
> Are unperturbed without any gain or loss.
> Thus should be known the ultimate meaning of the letter *Ū.*

[17] Taken literally, the Three Bodies are the Trikaya—Dharmakaya, Sambhogakaya, and Nirmanakaya. The Three Bodies may be interpreted as indicating Buddhahood or as a synonym for the Three Mysteries.

The determined followers of Hinayana Buddhism
Erroneously give rise to the thought of extinction.
By annihilating the activities of their body and mind,
They try to realize the state of void like great space.
Heavily intoxicated by the wine of samadhi,
They are neither enlightened nor awakened.
Among them some are destined to be Hinayanists
And others turn to Mahayana Buddhism.
Either way, they must spend aeons until they reach Nirvana.
No loss indeed is greater than this.
Yet the intrinsic Three Bodies are firm and unmoved.
When the Buddhas omnipresent like space
Awaken them [Hinayanists] in alarm and reveal themselves,
They will move out of their magically conceived city
And direct themselves toward the Treasury.
If trees and plants are to attain enlightenment,
Why not those who are endowed with feelings?
By attaching themselves erroneously to imperfect teachings,
They must suffer a really great loss.
Thus should be known the ultimate meaning of the letter *Ū*.

Resulting from the correct causes of aeons' discipline
Are the Sambhogakaya Buddhas enjoying bliss,
Adorned with myriads of excellent virtues,
Whose Fourfold Wisdom is perfectly realized.
Yet they continue to be subject to the law of causality,
For indeed they are not immutable.
It is the iron law preached by the Buddha
That what is produced by causes has its end in time.
The sword of imperfect knowledge [of Yogācāra]
May kill or injure [the original Buddhahood].
Be that as it may, the intrinsic Three Mysteries in us
Are like the sun which shines gloriously in the sky.
The Fourfold Wisdom in us, boundless like space,
Is like gold buried under the ground.
A violent wind blowing the clouds away cannot create the sun,
Nor can a sharp hoe produce gold if it is not there.
Thus should be known the ultimate meaning of the letter *Ū*.

Suchness or the Nature of Dharma
Is the essence of our mind and is eternal.
What being with mind is wanting in this principle?
The wisdom of mind and the principle are identical;
The principle is not independent of the mind.
The mind and the principle are one.

Is the reflecting function of water [wisdom of mind]
Separable from the wet nature of water [principle]?
The Nature of Suchness equally pervades all beings.
For those whose ways of thinking are narrower and inferior,
A provisional teaching, a guide for beginners has been set.
Yet those deluded students [of Mādhyamika] do not know this.
By swinging the sharp halberd of negation of provisional means,
They are about to destroy that true Buddhahood.
We may call this a loss and decline.
Yet the eternally omnipresent original Buddha
Is not thereby to be lost or to wane.
Thus should be known the ultimate meaning of the letter *Ū*.

Waves do not exist apart from water;
Within the mind are the objects of mind.
If plants and trees were devoid of Buddhahood,
Waves then would be without humidity.
To teach that this possesses it while that does not
Is no more than a provisional doctrine [Yogācāra].[18]
To advocate nihilism refuting the theory of being
Is a partial and destructive approach [Mādhyamika].
The sharp, destructive ax of nihilism
May long crush the Buddhahood [of the ax-wielder].
Yet the original Buddhahood in all beings
Is neither harmed thereby nor decreased.
The threefold truth [of T'ien-t'ai] penetrates all; [19]
The ten divisions of time [of Hua-yen] are not obstructed.[20]
The threefold world is none other than the Body of Buddha,
Whose Four Mandalas reveal the true Buddha [of Shingon].
Thus should be studied the ultimate meaning of the letter *Ū*.

For the Hinayanists of inferior insight,
The existence of the sixfold consciousness is preached;
For the somewhat superior Mahayanists,

---

[18] In the Yogācāra or Hossō school, sentient beings are divided into the following five groups: śrāvakas, pratyekabuddhas, bodhisattvas, indeterminates, and *icchantikas*. The last group, according to the doctrine of the school, lacks any potentiality to attain enlightenment and repeats forever the cycle of samsara.

[19] The doctrine that all existences are empty, temporal, and yet real or absolute (the Middle Way).

[20] The ten divisions of time of Hua-yen consist of the following four categories: 1) past, present, and future in the past; 2) past, present, and future in the present; 3) past, present, and future in the future; and 4) the entirety of the above nine divisions of time.

The existence of eight- or ninefold consciousness [21] is shown.
Clinging to their respective tenets, they refuse to advance;
How can they know that consciousness is infinite?
They do not understand the esoteric import
And are satisfied with what little they have gained.
They are unaware of what they originally possess.
The sea of assembly of numberless Enlightened Ones [22]
Is the very treasure that belongs to them all.
Thus should be studied the ultimate meaning of the letter $\bar{U}$.

The universally identical One is Suchness of diversity;
Because of diversity Suchness remains Suchness.
The manifestations of this principle are infinite in number;
The functions of it are boundless in magnitude.
The particles of sand in the Ganges
And those of dust in the world are few
When compared to the number of that One's attributes.
Though raindrops are many, they are of the same water;
Though rays of light are not one, they are of the same body.
The form and mind of that One are immeasurable;
The ultimate Reality is vast and boundless.
The King of Mind and the attributes of the Mind are inexhaustible
And interrelated like the meshes of Indra's net;
Their manifold structure is difficult to conceive.
Each of the attributes is endowed with the Fivefold Wisdom.
The attributes are many, but they are one;
Though they are one, they are many at the same time.
Thus, the name "Suchness of Oneness" is called for.
The oneness here is the oneness of multiplicity;
Namely, the infinity [of Suchness] is the oneness.
Hence, Suchness does not stand for permanency;
It is the Self-identity of particulars of semblance.
Unless this principle is expounded,
Teachings are nothing but conventional ones.
Through conventional teachings people imagine
That the inexhaustible Treasury has been drained
And look upon the invaluable Vehicle of precious gems
As an article totally depreciated.

[21] The ninefold consciousness is the five sense perceptions, mind, ego-consciousness, *ālaya*-consciousness, and Pure Consciousness (*amala-vijñāna*). According to the *Ten Stages* (K.Z., I, 398), Kūkai maintains that Yogācāra and Mādhyamika recognize eight levels of consciousness; T'ien-t'ai and Hua-yen, nine levels of consciousness.

[22] The World of Enlightenment of the Matrix Mandala of Mahāvairocana.

This is what is called a great loss.
Yet the One with Four Forms and Three Mysteries,
The One too great to depict, even if we used
The earth for ink and Mount Sumeru for brush,
Is perfect and eternally present without alteration.
This is, indeed, the ultimate meaning of the letter *Ū*.

4. The ultimate meanings of the letter *M*. The ultimate meaning of the letter *M* is that nothing can be predicated as having permanent existence. Of existence two kinds can be identified. One is a permanent self in man, and the other is permanent existence in a thing. Here "man" stands for the Dharmakaya Buddha in Four Forms, and "thing," for all things, that is, the entire World of Dharma, Suchness, Enlightenment, and eighty-four thousand or an unspeakable number of things, comparable to particles of dust. The expressions of the Dharmakaya in Four Forms as described above are innumerable, but their essence is one and the same and there is no this or that. Since there is no this or that, how can there be permanent existence in each of them? This is the ultimate meaning of the letter *M* in terms of negation [of individual entity].

To such an understanding, the four types of devotee who have not yet returned to the Vajrayāna [Shingon] remain blind and deaf. It is completely beyond their reach. It cannot be predicated by the Four Clauses;[23] and it cannot be attained by those who have mastered the Six Supernatural Powers. This is the ultimate meaning of the letter *M* in terms of transcendence of conceptualization.

According to a sutra the letter *M* is a seed mantra of Mahāvairocana Buddha.[24] People in the world, though they speculate on the Self among selves, are yet to realize the ultimate meaning. Mahāvairocana Buddha is the sole great Self of selfless existences. While the Tathagata of the King of Mind exists as such, how can his innumerable attributes [existences] be outside of the Body of this great Self, just as the functions of our mind cannot be independent of our mind? Such is the ultimate meaning of the letter *M* in terms of affirmation [of the great Self].

According to a sutra the letter *M* has the meaning of "transforma-

---

[23] According to Nāgārjuna there are four alternative predications: 1) it is A; 2) it is non-A; 3) it is both A and non-A; and 4) it is neither A nor non-A.

[24] *Jen-wang-pan-jo-t'o-lo-ni-shih*. T19, p. 523c.

tion." [25] Mahāvairocana Tathagata, for his own enjoyment, exhibiting supernatural power, transforms himself into immeasurable existences and creates limitless exquisite lands. The ultimate meaning of the letter *M* is this marvelous function and suprarational transformation [of Mahāvairocana].

Also it is said that the letter *M* means "freedom in *samaya*" and "all-pervading." *Samaya* is translated into Chinese as "equally maintaining (*teng-ch'ih*)." [26] For the Three Mysteries of Dharmakaya a particle of fine dust is not narrow and great space is not broad. They do not discriminate [between] a tile, pebble, grass, or wood [and sentient beings], nor do they choose a man, god, demon, or beast [over nonsentient beings]. Where do they not pervade? Which object do they not embrace? "Equality" is the ultimate meaning of the letter *M*. . . .

If one enters the samadhi of the great Self, for which the letter *M* stands, one is led to understand that the great Self embraces in itself each and all existences. In a sutra, therefore, it is said: "The Self is the World of Dharma, the Self is the Dharmakaya, the Self is Mahāvairocana, the Self is the Vajrasattva, the Self is all the Buddhas, the Self is all the bodhisattvas, the Self is the pratyekabuddhas, the Self is the śrāvakas, the Self is Maheśvara, the Self is Brahmā, the Self is Indra, the Self is the gods, serpents, demons, the eight classes of supernatural beings, etc." [27] Among all sentient and nonsentient beings, there is none outside of what the letter stands for. Indeed, the great Self is one, yet can be many. It is small, yet contains that which is large. Thus, interpenetration of many in one and one in many is the ultimate meaning of the letter *M*.

PART THREE: SYNTHETIC
INTERPRETATION

The one word *Hūṃ* consists of four parts, that is, *A H Ū M*. The letter *A* symbolizes the Dharmakaya; the letter *H*, the aspect of his

[25] *Shou-hu-kuo-chieh-chu ching.* T19, p. 565c.

[26] *Teng-ch'ih*, "equally maintaining (tōji)," is normally a translation of samadhi.

[27] This passage is quoted from an unknown source in the commentary on the *Mahāvairocana Sutra.* T39, p. 788c.

bliss; the letter *Ū*, the aspect of his manifestation [in a human form]; and the letter *M*, the aspect of his emanation [in nonhuman forms]. Under these four categories, all the teachings can be summarized.

First, we will examine the specific feature symbolized by each letter. The letter *A* [standing for the Uncreated] summarizes completely the universal principle expressed in terms of Suchness, the World of Dharma, the Nature of Dharma, the Apex of Reality, etc. Symbolized by the letter *H* [standing for the cause of spiritual progress] are all the Buddhist and non-Buddhist teachings, that is, the Hinayana, Mahayana, Provisional, Real, Exoteric, Esoteric Buddhism, and so forth. The letter *Ū* [standing for decreasing defilements] embraces all the religious practices of the Three Vehicles, Five Vehicles, etc. The letter *M* [standing for the great Self] encompasses all religious attainments. The word symbolizes both the universal principle and all the particulars; therefore, it is called "that which contains all (*sōji* or *dharani*)."

Next, if interpreting from the point of view of their common features, it can be stated that each letter embraces the universal principle, all the teachings, religious practices, and attainments, just as [each word in the grammatical] statements made by Indra contains many meanings, or just as each of the hexagrams invented by Fu Hsi contains the signs of ten thousand phenomena.

In the word *Hūṃ* there is the letter *H* which stands for "cause." By "cause" is meant all existences of dependent origination. Among them there are phenomena known as religious teachings which are very chaotic, that is, the teachings of non-Buddhist religions, of Hinayana, of Mahayana, etc., each of which claims to be superior by clamorously denouncing other teachings as false. Summarized in the letter *M* are the false assertions of non-Buddhists, Hinayanists, or Mahayanists: that a permanent self is real; that the psychophysical constituents are real; that there is a first cause; that effects are real; that there is immortality; and that there is a permanent soul. All of these assertions belong to the extreme of the ungrounded affirmations of those who have yet to understand the Middle Way.[28] Summarized in the letter *Ū* are the false assertions that a permanent self, the psychophysical constituents, the

[28] The Mādhyamika terminology indicating that which is real or that which transcends the dichotomy of being and nonbeing. Kūkai uses the term here as a synonym for absolute truth or principle.

first cause, effects, immortality, and a permanent soul are unreal. All of these assertions belong to another extreme of ungrounded negation of those who have yet to comprehend the Middle Way. Summarized under the letter *A* as a negative prefix are the opinions that "it [Reality] is neither being nor nonbeing," "neither eternal nor momentary," or "neither one nor many," etc. Also symbolized in the letter *A* as a negative prefix is the Eightfold Negation beginning with "unborn, imperishable, unincreasing, undecreasing." Again, there is the opinion that the letter *A* implies that it [the Dharmakaya] is colorless, formless, voiceless, etc. All of these opinions result from not comprehending the ultimate truth and belong to the extreme of negation. All the statements, thoughts, and practices of those who do not understand the esoteric symbols, characteristics of expression, true significances, and real meanings of the various teachings are perverse and ungrounded, for these people do not know the true and ultimate principle. Nāgārjuna therefore said: "In Buddhism there are two standards of truth, that is, the conventional truth and the ultimate truth. For the conventional truth it is explained that there are sentient beings. For the ultimate truth it is explained that there are no sentient beings at all. But here again there are two standards. For those who do not know the characteristics of expression and esoteric symbols, it is explained that from the point of view of the ultimate truth there are no sentient beings; and for those who know the characteristics of expression and esoteric symbols, it is explained that from the point of view of the ultimate truth there are sentient beings." [29] Should there be a man capable of knowing the esoteric symbols and esoteric meanings of such a word as *Hūṃ*, he is to be called a perfectly knowing one. A passage such as "the moment one develops aspiration to attain enlightenment, one has realized perfect enlightenment and begun to turn the great wheel of dharma" [30] can, indeed, be understood only by knowing the ultimate true meaning.

Now, on the basis of the word *Hūṃ*, the causes, practices, and attainments of śrāvakas, pratyekabuddhas, and bodhisattvas will be disclosed.

[29] The *Ta-chih-tu lun*, T25, p. 336bc. Kūkai has adapted the original.

[30] This passage appears in the commentary on the *Mahāvairocana Sutra* (T39, p. 579c) as a quotation (adapted) from the *Mahāprajñāpāramitā Sutra* (T8, p. 226c).

On śrāvakas. In the word *Hūṃ*, there is the letter *H* standing for "cause." The *Yogācārabhūmi* [31] and others explain the special nature of being a śrāvaka, which corresponds to "cause." In the lower part [of the word written in the Siddhām script] the letter *Ū* is located; it stands for the "practices" of the śrāvakas. They are the Four Noble Truths, the Fivefold Meditation, the Sevenfold Skillful Means, [32] etc. These practices are designed to realize what the invariant meanings of the letter *Ū* suggest. A śrāvaka regards the complete annihilation of his body and mind as his final "attainment." The dot attached to the letter *M* in *Hūṃ* stands for "emptiness." The letter *M* indicates the ideas of emptiness of permanent self and existence in things. The principle of emptiness of permanent self is the principle that a śrāvaka is to realize. These are what we call the cause, practices, and attainment of a śrāvaka.

On pratyekabuddhas. The special nature of being a pratyekabuddha given in the *Yogācārabhūmi* and elsewhere corresponds to the "cause" which is indicated by the letter *H* in *Hūṃ*. A pratyekabuddha also practices meditation on the Twelve Links of Causation, the Four Noble Truths, Skillful Means, and others. These practices correspond to what the letter *Ū* in *Hūṃ* indicates. A pratyekabuddha also realizes the principle of emptiness of permanent self. This is his main "attainment."

On bodhisattvas. In the *Mahāvairocana Sutra*, the *Vajraśekhara Sutra*, and elsewhere it is explained that a bodhisattva regards "the enlightened mind as the cause, great compassion as the root, and the [use of] skillful means as the ultimate." [33] The essence of the word *Hūṃ* is the letter *H*, which stands for the "cause," that is, the enlightened mind of all the Tathagatas. The letter *Ū* that comes next stands for all the "practices" of great compassion. The dot signifying great emptiness symbolizes the "attainment" of the ultimate great enlightenment, Nirvana. This one word *Hūṃ* represents the religious persons, causes, practices, and attainments of the Three Vehicles with nothing left out.

[31] T30, p. 395c.

[32] The Fivefold Meditation: to get rid of greed by meditating that all is impure; to remove anger by meditating that all is pitiable; to stop remaining ignorant by meditating on the Twelve Links of Causation; to become free from the belief in the existence of a permanent individual self by meditating that all is a temporary combination of constituent elements; and to cause one's confused thoughts to cease by counting one's breath. The Sevenfold Means: the seven steps of spiritual progress or attainments of Hinayanists.

[33] The source is the first chapter of the *Mahāvairocana Sutra*. T18, p. 1bc.

Finally, that this single word embraces all the principles explained in various sutras and shastras will be elucidated. The essential purport of the *Mahāvairocana* and *Vajraśekhara Sutras* is no other than the three propositions that the enlightened mind is the cause, great compassion is the root, and the [use of] skillful means is the ultimate. If extensive discourses are reduced to their simplest expression and the branches, to their root, all the teachings will be summarized in these three propositions. The three propositions are contained in the single word *Hūṃ*. The contents of the word are broad, yet no confusion can be found; the form of the word is simple, yet nothing is missing. The word is, indeed, created by the suprarational power and the natural grace (*hōnen kaji*) of the Tathagata [Mahāvairocana]. . . .

8

THE SECRET KEY
TO THE HEART SUTRA

(*Hannya shingyō hiken*)

Invocation

The sharp sword of Mañjuśrī cuts off wild speculations;
The sacred words of Prajñā guide us to perfect self-control.
Dhiḥ and *Maṃ* are the seed mantras of these Bodhisattvas;
They are the dharanis which comprise manifold teachings.[1]

[1] The *Heart Sutra* or *Hannya shingyō* (*Prajñāpāramitāhṛdaya-sūtra*) is the shortest of all the *Prajñāpāramitā Sutras*, which expound the nature of transcendental wisdom (*prajñā*). The Bodhisattvas Mañjuśrī and Prajñā are the personifications of this wisdom. The former, riding on a lion, holds a sword that severs the root of ignorance, and the latter, a box containing the sutra. In this verse, Kūkai suggests the Four Mandalas of these two Bodhisattvas: 1) the images of the

From the endless cycle of samsara how can we be freed?
The only way is to practice meditation and correct thinking.
The samadhi of Prajñā is expounded by the Buddha himself; [2]
May His mercy be poured on me who am about to interpret it.

INTRODUCTION

The Buddha Dharma is nowhere remote. It is in our mind; it is close to us. Suchness is nowhere external. If not within our body, where can it be found? Since out of our own choice we either remain deluded or attain enlightenment, once we set our mind on enlightenment we will attain it. Since it is not by another's will that we see light or sink into darkness, if we establish our faith and devote ourselves to religious practice, we will at once realize enlightenment.[3]

Sad and lamentable are those who have never awakened from their long slumber in darkness. Bitter and painful are those who have been madly intoxicated. A drunkard scoffs at those who are sober. The ones in slumber mock the awakened. If they do not go seeking for the remedies of the King of Medicine, when will they ever be able to see the Light of the Great Sun? [4]

The intensity of hindrances and the duration of time necessary to attain enlightenment vary from person to person as do individual aptitude and inclination. This eventually calls for the Esoteric Buddhist teaching which consists of two aspects, as it were, two wheels [of a chariot] or two helping hands—the Diamond Realm and the Lotus Realm [5]—and the Five Vehicles which run abreast trampling down the barriers of delusion. As is necessary in counteracting poisons, the medi-

---

Bodhisattvas which the readers visualize upon reading the lines—Mahāmandalas; 2) "the sword" and "the sacred words (the box containing the sutra)"—the Samaya-mandalas; 3) the seed mantras, *Dhiḥ* and *Maṃ*—the Dharma-mandalas; and 4) the words "cut off" and "guide," i.e., their actions—the Karma-mandalas.

[2] Shakyamuni.

[3] This paragraph is a quotation from the commentary on the *Heart Sutra* written by Ming-k'uang. *Manji zokuzōkyō*, I, fascicle 41, p. 4. Cf. Katsumata, *Kōbō daishi chosaku zencho*, I, 109.

[4] Mahāvairocana Buddha, the Great Sun Buddha, is implied.

[5] The Lotus Realm is a synonym for the Matrix Realm.

cines provided differ from individual to individual. Such is the basic guiding principle taken by the compassionate Father when he leads his son.

The *Heart Sutra* expounds the great heart mantra and the samadhi of the great Bodhisattva Prajñā. All its words, consisting of fourteen lines, can be written on a sheet of paper. It is simple yet comprehensive; it is terse yet profound. The expositions on wisdom in the Five Collections [6] are contained in one clause without omission, and the goals of the seven Buddhist schools [7] are entered in one line without deletion.

"The Bodhisattva Avalokiteśvara [appearing in the beginning of the sutra]" represents the devotees of the various Vehicles. "Freedom from all suffering" or "Nirvana" indicates the state of bliss to be obtained by practicing the various teachings. "The Five Psychophysical Constituents" points to the world of objects seen in delusion, and "all the Buddhas in the three divisions of time" reveals the enlightened mind. When the Bodhisattva Samantabhadra [8] hears the words "Form is emptiness," he relaxes his jaw in a smile, understanding them to express the meaning of perfect interpenetration. When it comes to the discussion of "unborn," the Bodhisattva Mañjuśrī [9] breaks into a broad smile in view of the crushing effect it has in refuting all groundless speculations. At the expression "the world of consciousness," he who examines [the levels of consciousness] and maintains [subjective idealism] applauds.[10] He who advocates return to the oneness of the seeing and the seen [11] is delighted with the sentence, "There is no wisdom and no attainment since there is nothing to be attained." A mention of the Twelve Links of Causation [12] designates to the pratyekabuddhas the structure of samsara, and the doctrine of the Four Noble Truths indicated by the words "There is no suffering" surprises the riders of the Goat Vehicle [13] [be-

[6] Sutra, Vinaya, Shastra, Prajñā-pāramitā, and Dharani.

[7] Here Kūkai seems to have in mind the seven existing schools in Japan: Sanron, Jōjitsu, Hossō, Kusha, Ritsu, Kegon, and Tendai.

[8] Represents the Kegon or Hua-yen school.

[9] Represents the Mādhyamika or Sanron school.

[10] The Bodhisattva Maitreya, the representative of the Yogācāra or Hossō school.

[11] The Bodhisattva Avalokiteśvara, the representative of the T'ien-t'ai or Tendai school, is meant.

[12] Refers to the passage in the sutra, "There is no ignorance . . . no extinction of old age and death."

[13] The śrāvakas.

cause they encounter in this sutra their own basic tenet]. The two syllables *"gate"* symbolize the goals of all Hinayana teachings; the two words *"pāra"* and *"pārasaṃ"* comprise the doctrines of Exoteric Buddhism and those of Esoteric Buddhism. The significance of each sound and word [in the sutra] cannot be adequately expressed no matter how long one comments upon it. The content symbolized by each name defies verbal communication even though the attempt were made by numberless Enlightened Ones.

Such being the nature of the sutra, if anyone recites or holds fast to it, explains or respects it, he will be relieved from his suffering and granted bliss. If he practices the teachings and meditates upon them, he will attain enlightenment and develop supernatural power. It is indeed appropriate that the sutra be called an extremely profound one.

When instructing young novices, I abstract the essentials of the sutra and make an attempt to interpret the sutra by dividing it into five parts. Though there have been many commentators, there seem to be none who have ever detected its esoteric significance. Variations among the [Chinese] translations and differences of exoteric and esoteric significances will be discussed later.

QUESTION: The doctrine of wisdom belongs to the second category of sutras, in which the final truth is not revealed. How is it possible for the sutra to retain the contents of sutras belonging to the third category?

ANSWER: In the sermons delivered by the Buddha, a single word contains the teachings of the Five Vehicles; in a moment of thought, He preached the doctrines of the entire Buddhist scriptures. So what could be missing from this sutra, which consists of one volume containing one chapter? The words in it are comparable to the diagrams [manifested on the back] of a tortoise, the divination stalks which bear the signs of all phenomena, the endlessly interrelated meshes of Indra's net, or the words in the Sanskrit grammatical text composed by Indra which contain manifold meanings.

QUESTION: If so, why is it that the former masters have not uttered such words?

ANSWER: As a physician prescribes different kinds of medicine according to the nature of the disease, so the Sage gives teachings suitable to the aptitude of the recipients. Whether wise men speak out or keep silent depends on the character of the time and on the nature of the listeners. It is not clear to me whether they did not speak when they should have spoken, or whether they did not speak simply because it was not the time to speak. It may be that I am going to say what should not be said; if so, I prefer to leave it to men of wisdom to judge.

INTERPRETATION

The title of the sutra in Sanskrit is *Buddha-bhāṣa-mahā-prajñā-pāramitā-hṛidaya-sūtraṃ*. *Buddha* is the name of "the perfectly Enlightened One." *Bhāṣa* means that "by revealing the Esoteric Buddhist teaching, He bestows the nectar of immortality." *Mahā* is used to indicate "great, manifold, and excellent." The next word, *prajñā*, stands for "the wisdom gained by samadhi." The following *pāramitā* denotes that "what is to be done has been perfected." Next, *hṛidaya* (heart) means "the center." The last word, *sūtraṃ*, stands for "that which is held together by stringing like a garland of flowers."

In the title of the sutra as a whole, three elements can be identified: they are the elements of the religious person, letter symbols, and allusions. The title contains the name of the great Bodhisattva Prajñāpāramitā. This is the element of the religious person. This Bodhisattva is equipped with the method of samadhi of mantra recitation and visualization of the Dharma-mandala. Each letter in the title is a letter symbol (dharma). Though each word is conventional and simple, still it is a profound symbol standing for the nature of Dharma. This is what I mean by the element of allusion.

This teaching on samadhi was preached by the Buddha to Śāriputra and others while He resided on the Vulture Peak. There are many Chinese translations of this sutra. The version to which I am referring here is the one translated by Kumārajīva. . . .[14] There are critics who say that this sutra is a comprehensive summary of the *Mahāprajñā-pāramitā Sutra*, that it is for this reason that the term "heart" is intro-

[14] Here Kūkai lists variant readings found in four other renditions done by Hsüan-chuang (600–64), I-ching (635–713), Fa-yüeh (d. 741), and Prajñā, Kūkai's teacher in Ch'ang-an who came to China from India in 782. At the end of the list, he mentions that the explanations of the mantra found in the sutra are given in the *T'o-lo-ni-chi ching*. T18, pp. 804c–812b.

duced, and that it was not preached as an independent sutra on a different occasion. To this, I would say that a dragon has scales similar to those of a snake.[15]

The sutra contains five parts. Part One gives a general introduction to the religious person and the dharma, which corresponds to the lines, "When the Bodhisattva Avalokiteśvara . . . became free from all suffering." Part Two, which deals with the various Vehicles, corresponds to the lines, "form is emptiness . . . because there is no object to be attained." Part Three concerns the benefits that the devotee will receive and corresponds to the lines, "The Bodhisattva . . . perfect enlightenment." Part Four consists of the summary expressed in terms of a dharani which corresponds to the lines, "Therefore, one knows that the *prajñāpāramitā* . . . is true and not false." Part Five is the mantra, the secret treasury, which is "*gate gate . . . svāhā.*"

PART ONE: GENERAL INTRODUCTION:
THE RELIGIOUS PERSON
AND THE DHARMA

[The text: "When the Bodhisattva Avalokiteśvara was practicing profound Transcendental Wisdom (*prajñāpāramitā*), he discerned clearly that the Five Psychophysical Constituents are empty and thereby became free from all suffering."]

In this introductory section of the sutra, the five elements can be identified: that is, the primary cause, practice, realization, entering [into Nirvana], and time. "The Bodhisattva Avalokiteśvara" stands for anyone who engages in the practice. The element of intrinsic enlightenment of any religious person is the primary cause. "Transcendental Wisdom" is the dharma in which the seeing is the seen. By this the practice [of meditation] is implied. By the clause "he discerned clearly that the Five Psychophysical Constituents are empty," the state of realization of wisdom in terms of the seeing is identified. By the

---

[15] Kūkai seems to say that the *Heart Sutra* (dragon) contains some expressions similar to those found in the *Mahāprajñāpāramitā Sutra* (snake), but that the former is incomparably superior to the latter and cannot be regarded as a summary of the latter.

clause "[he] became free from all suffering," the effect of attainment is expressed. The effect is the entering [into Nirvana]. There is an infinite variety in attaining wisdom among those who practice the teaching. Because of the variety, the length of time required to arrive at this realization also differs from individual to individual—some must spend three lives, some three aeons, some sixty aeons, and others a hundred aeons,[16] contingent upon the intensity of their delusion and attachment. The variation in the time required is implied in the word "when."

> A man of meditation devotes himself to gain Transcendental Wisdom;
> He discerns that the Five Psychophysical Constituents are empty.
> Some students practicing contemplation may have to spend aeons,
> Yet they will be integrated into One Mind, which is free from defilement.

PART TWO: DISTINCTIONS OF VEHICLES

The Five Vehicles can be identified. They are Hua-yen, Mādhyamika, Yogācāra, Hinayana, and T'ien-t'ai.

1. By Hua-yen is meant the teaching of samadhi of the Tathagata who upholds [the tenet of interpenetration]. The corresponding passages in the sutra are from "form is emptiness" to "the same can be said."

[The text: "O Śāriputra, form is emptiness, emptiness is form; form is no other than emptiness, emptiness is no other than form. Of sensation, conception, predisposition, and consciousness the same can be said."]

"The Tathagata who upholds [the tenet of interpenetration]" is the esoteric name of the Bodhisattva Samantabhadra. This Bodhisattva's faultless cause [of attaining enlightenment] was primarily based on [his realization of] the Threefold Interpenetration;[17] hence, he is called by

---

[16] Three lives refers to the followers of Hua-yen; three aeons, to the followers of Mādhyamika and Yogācāra; sixty aeons, to the followers of the śrāvaka vehicle; and a hundred aeons, to those of the pratyekabuddha vehicle.

[17] One of the basic doctrines of Hua-yen: the perfect interpenetration of the universal and the particulars; of the universal and the universal; and of the particulars and particulars.

that esoteric name. He is also the embodiment of acts and vows flowing out of the enlightened mind of all the Tathagatas.

> Form and emptiness are nondual from the beginning;
> Particulars and the universal have always been identical.
> Without any obstacles the three are interfused.[18]
> The simile of water or gold explains the main tenet.[19]

2. By Mādhyamika is meant the teaching of samadhi of the Tathagata who is free from all groundless speculations. The corresponding passage in the sutra is from "all things are characterized by emptiness" to "neither do they increase nor decrease."

[The text: "O Śāriputra, all things are characterized by emptiness; they are neither born nor do they perish; they are neither tainted nor immaculate; neither do they increase nor decrease."]

"The Tathagata who is free from all groundless speculations" is the esoteric name for the Bodhisattva Mañjuśrī. The sharp sword of wisdom of Mañjuśrī can sever the deluded and attached mind with ruthless application of the Eightfold Negation;[20] hence, that esoteric name of the Tathagata.

> The Eightfold Negation stops all groundless speculations;
> Mañjuśrī is the very person who represents this approach.
> The principle of emptiness alone is the final truth;
> Its meanings and applications are abstruse and true.

3. By Yogācāra is meant the teaching of samadhi of the great Bodhisattva Maitreya. The corresponding passages in the sutra are from "Therefore, in emptiness there is no form" to "no realm of consciousness."

[The text: "Therefore, in emptiness there is no form, no sensation, no conception, no predisposition, no consciousness; no eye, ear, nose, tongue, body, mind; no form, sound, scent, physical sensation, objects of mind; no realm of vision . . . no realm of consciousness."]

[18] The Threefold Interpenetration. See the preceding note.

[19] Fa-ts'ang, the third patriarch and systematizer of the Hua-yen school, explained in his *Chin-shih-tzu-chang* or *Golden Lion* (T1880) the relationship between the universal (gold) and the particulars (the forms of the lion). The founder of Hua-yen, Tu-shun, expounded the theory of interpenetration of the universal and the particulars with the simile of water and its waves in his *Fa-chieh-kuan-men* (see *Precious Key*, n. 208).

[20] See *Precious Key*, n. 14.

The great Maitreya's samadhi is characterized by compassion; his guiding principle is to point out the law of cause and effect. Discussing the differences that exist between the essence and appearance, he denies the validity of the world of objects, declaring that what exists is mind only. All of this, of course, is motivated by his compassion.

> When can one sever the belief in a permanent self and in the existence of a thing?
> One may realize the Dharmakaya in three aeons of discipline.
> The *ālaya*-consciousness is the basic nature of all other consciousness;
> Phantomlike phenomena are name only and unreal.

4. Hinayana refers to two types: one is that which recognizes the Five Psychophysical Constituents only and not the permanent self (śrāvakas); and the other is that which is free from the seed of karma (pratyekabuddhas). In other words, these are the teachings of samadhi of the followers of the Hinayana.

[The text:] "There is no ignorance . . . no old age and death, no extinction of old age and death."

This passage corresponds to the samadhi of the pratyekabuddhas.

> Being reminded by falling leaves stirred by the wind,
> A man becomes aware of his existential situation.
> When can he, by attaining enlightenment,
> Be freed from the cycle of samsara?
> Being reminded by a fading flower in the dew,
> He hastens to uproot the seed of ignorance.
> Look, there pass the deer and goats running in rows, side by side! [21]

[The text:] "There is no suffering, no accumulation, no annihilation, no Noble Paths."

This clause reveals the samadhi attained by the way of the śrāvakas.

> Skeleton! Where is your eternal ego?
> Discolored corpse! You have never had one.
> My guru is the Fourfold Meditation.[22]
> What bliss to attain Arhatship! [23]

5. By T'ien-t'ai is meant the teaching of samadhi of the Bodhisattva Ārya-avalokiteśvara.

[21] The deer stand for the pratyekabuddhas and the goats, for the śrāvakas.
[22] See *Precious Key*, n. 70.
[23] The highest stage to be attained by the Hinayanists. Arhat means "the worthy one."

[The text:] "There is no wisdom and no attainment because there is no object to be attained."

This Bodhisattva, whose esoteric name is the "Tathagata whose own nature is pure," reveals to all sentient beings that the One Way [24] is unsoiled, as is a pure lotus flower in mud, and eliminates their fetters of suffering. The word "wisdom" in the text indicates the perceiving subject and "attainment," the object of realization. Since this samadhi is characterized by transcendence of both wisdom [subject] and principle [the object of realization], there is no way of predicating it except to describe it, if one is forced to, as being an experience of oneness. The doctrines given in the *Lotus Sutra, Nirvana Sutra,* and elsewhere, which emphasize the integration of the doctrines of the Three Vehicles into the One Vehicle,[25] are contained in this short line of the text. It is hoped that the readers themselves will observe the differences which exist among the doctrines of these Vehicles.

> Meditate on a lotus flower; be aware that your intrinsic nature is also pure!
> Behold the fruit in the lotus cup; realize that you too are endowed with excellence of mind!
> When the seeing and the seen are fused into one vision of Truth,
> The integration of the Three Vehicles into One Vehicle will take place quietly.

PART THREE: BENEFITS

[The text: "The bodhisattva has no obstacle in mind because of his dependence on Transcendental Wisdom; because he has no obstacles, he has no fear. Being free from all perverted views, he reaches ultimate Nirvana. All the Buddhas of the past, present, and future, depending on Transcendental Wisdom, attain perfect enlightenment."]

The section can be divided into two parts. One is on the religious person and the other on dharma. By the word "the bodhisattva," seven types of religious person are implied. Six types have appeared in the

---

[24] The identical Buddhahood in all sentient beings.

[25] The teaching of universal salvation advocated in these sutras. A synonym for the Buddha Vehicle. The Three Vehicles are the teachings of the śrāvakas, the pratyekabuddhas, and the bodhisattvas.

foregoing discussion; the seventh [Shingon] will be mentioned later. In accordance with the difference between Vehicles, there are differences in the mentality of sentient beings. They may be divided into four categories: ignorant beings, conscious beings, wisdom beings, and diamond beings.[26]

Four dharmas can also be identified: the primary cause, practice, realization, and entering [into Nirvana]. "Transcendental Wisdom" is "the primary cause" that enables one to attain [enlightenment] and inspires one to devote oneself to the "practice." Freedom from obstacles is the state of "entering" into Nirvana. The realization of enlightenment [of the Buddhas] is the effect of "realization" [of this wisdom]. Deliberate on the passages in the text as they are.

> The types of devotee number seven;
> Two repeated is the number of the dharma.
> All are in quiescence and enlightened intrinsically;
> Sentient beings and the world are deficient in nothing.

PART FOUR: SYNTHESIS
IN TERMS OF DHARANI

[The text: "Therefore, one knows that the *prajñāpāramitā* is the great mantra, the mantra of great wisdom, the highest mantra, the peerless mantra, which is capable of allaying all suffering; it is true and not false."]

Three elements can be pointed out. They are the names, essence, and function [of the mantra *prajñāpāramitā*]. "The great mantra, the mantra of great wisdom, the highest mantra, the peerless mantra" are the other names [of the same mantra]. "It is true and not false" indicates the essence, and "which is capable of allaying all suffering" reveals the function [of the mantra]. The first name, that is, "the great mantra," represents the mantra [*prajñāpāramitā*] of the śrāvakas; the second, of the pratyekabuddhas; the third, of the Mahayanists; and the fourth, of

[26] Ignorant beings—sentient beings in the Six Transmigratory Paths; conscious beings—followers of Hinayana; wisdom beings—followers of Mādhyamika, Yogācāra, T'ien-t'ai, and Hua-yen; and diamond beings (*vajra-sattva*)—followers of Shingon.

the Esoteric Buddhists. The same mantra has four different names. Here I have briefly pointed out to men of wisdom a portion of the implications. The first three will be integrated with the last one.

> *Prajñāpāramitā* is an all-embracing dharani;
> It contains the teachings and meanings,
> The insight into the Uncreated and supernatural power.
> The name dharani has been given to it,
> For it consists of sounds and words
> Symbolizing religious persons and their doctrines
> And stands for Reality itself.

PART FIVE: MANTRA, THE SECRET TREASURY

[The text: "*gate gate pāragate pārasaṃgate bodhi svāhā.*"]

There are five units in the mantra, the secret treasury. The first *gate* reveals the attainment of the śrāvakas. The second *gate* indicates the attainment of the pratyekabuddhas. The third, *pāragate*, points to the highest attainment of the various Mahayanists. The fourth, *pārasaṃgate*, clarifies the attainment in which the mandala [world of enlightenment] is fully realized by the Shingon [mantra] Buddhists. The fifth, *bodhi svāhā*, explains the ultimate realization of each of the foregoing approaches. These are the general meanings of the clause. If each word, however, should be interpreted from the point of view of its ultimate meanings, immeasurable significances—for example, that each word stands for certain Buddhas, certain doctrines, etc.—would be revealed. It is impossible to go into details. Those who wish to learn should ask [a Shingon master] in accordance with the prescribed regulations.

> A mantra is suprarational;
> It eliminates ignorance when meditated upon and recited.
> A single word contains a thousand truths;
> One can realize Suchness here and now.
> Walk on and on until perfect quiescence is reached;
> Go on and on until the primordial Source is penetrated.
> The triple world is like an inn;
> The One Mind is our original abode.

QUESTION: Dharanis are the secret words of the Tathagata. Old masters and commentators, therefore, kept silent and did not write on them. Now that you have made this interpretation, is it not against the intention of the Sage?

[ANSWER:] Among the sermons of the Tathagata, there are two kinds. One is the exoteric; the other, the esoteric. For those of exoteric caliber he preached lengthy sermons containing many clauses, but for those of esoteric caliber, he preached the dharanis, the words that embrace manifold meanings. It was for this reason that the Tathagata explained the various meanings of such words as *A* and *Oṃ*. These explanations were all made for the sake of men of esoteric caliber. Nāgārjuna, Śubhākarasiṃha, Amoghavajra (Pu-k'ung), and others also explained [the dharanis] to this effect. Whether the dharanis should be explained depends on the capacity of the recipient of the teachings. Therefore, either to explain or not to explain suits the intention of the Buddha.

QUESTION: Indeed there is a wide gap between the messages of the exoteric and the esoteric teachings. Yet it is not acceptable that the esoteric significances should be explained in this exoteric sutra.

[ANSWER:] The eyes of the King of Medicine never allow a medicinal herb on the roadside to pass unnoticed. An expert on gems detects a gem in ore. Who is to be blamed if one fails to see [the herb or the gem]? The mantra, ritualistic rules, and the method of meditation of this Noble One [the Bodhisattva Prajñā] are explained by the Buddha [Mahāvairocana] in the *Vajraśekhara Sutra*.[27] This is the secret among the secrets. What the Shakyamuni Buddha, the temporarily manifested body, preached while residing at Anāthapiṇḍada to the bodhisattvas and heavenly beings about pictorial images, the construction of mandalas, mantras, mudras, etc., is also esoteric. It is given in the *T'o-lo-ni-chi ching*, Vol. 3.[28] Regarding a sutra as exoteric or esoteric depends on the man who judges it and not on the sounds and words [of the sutra, for they remain the same]. Yet there is a distinction between the esotericism expressed in the exoteric teachings and that in the esoteric teachings: some are less profound, others are more profound.

[27] Kūkai apparently is referring to *Pan-jo-po-lo-mi-p'u-sa i-kuei*. T20, p. 610.
[28] T18, pp. 804c–808b.

On the basis of the Esoteric Shingon teaching,
I have briefly interpreted the five parts of the *Heart Sutra*.
The truth expressed in the sutra is everywhere to be seen;
It is in our mind, the beginning and end of which are unknown.
Yet blindfolded sentient beings fail to see it;
Mañjuśrī and Prajñā can dissolve their confusions.
May a shower of nectar be poured upon those lost on the Way;
May they equally be severed from ignorance, and may they vanquish
    hosts of tempters.

CHRONOLOGICAL TABLE

Year	Age	
774		Born to Saeki family on June 15 (according to traditional account) at Byōbugaura, Tado County, Sanuki (presently, Zentsūji, Kagawa-ken).
784	11	The capital is transferred from Nara to Nagaoka.
785	12	Saichō opens Mt. Hiei.
788	15	Goes to the capital; learns Chinese classics under Atō Ōtari.
790	17	Saeki Imaemishi, head of Saeki clan, dies at age 72. The government announces plan to send 100,000 soldiers to suppress the revolts in the northeast.
791	18	Enters the government college in the capital.
794	21	Heian (Kyoto) becomes the capital.
797	24	Writes the major part of the *Indications of the Goals of the Three Teachings* (*Sangō shiki*).
803	30	Discovers the *Mahāvairocana Sutra* at the Kume Temple, according to some accounts (*Kōbō daishi yuhō ki, Genkō shakusho*).
804	31	Ordained a monk, according to the official historical records (*Shoku Nihon kōki*, fascicle 4, *Kokushi taikei*, III, 38); leaves for China.
805	32	Meets Hui-kuo in Ch'ang-an and becomes master of the Esoteric Buddhist tradition. Saichō returns from China; conducts the first *abhiṣeka* ritual in Japan at the Takaosanji.
806	33	Writes the epitaph of Hui-kuo. Returns to Japan and presents *A Memorial Presenting a List of Newly Imported Sutras and Other Items* (*Shōrai mokuroku*) to the court. Saichō founds the Tendai sect with authorization to incorporate Esoteric

Buddhist elements (study of the *Mahāvairocana Sutra*) into its activities. Emperor Kammu dies.

807 34 In Kyushu awaiting orders from the court.

809 36 Emperor Heizei retires. Emperor Saga enthroned. Kūkai enters the Takaosanji. Emperor requests Kūkai to write calligraphy. Saichō writes a letter to Kūkai asking to borrow books.

810 37 Appointed administrative head of the Tōdaiji in Nara. Ex-emperor attempts to dethrone Emperor Saga. Kūkai prays for the state at the Takaosanji.

811 38 Appointed administrative head of the Otokunidera in the southern suburbs of Kyoto.

812 39 Conducts the *abhiṣeka* ritual for Saichō and others.

813 40 Outlines the aim of his order, the spirit of its observance of the precepts, and the principles of its meditation practice in *The Admonishments of Kōnin (Kōnin no goyuikai)*.

814 41 Around this time writes *The Difference between Exoteric and Esoteric Buddhism (Benkenmitsu nikyō ron)*.

816 43 Granted permission to build a monastic center on Mt. Kōya.

817 44 Writes *Attaining Enlightenment in This Very Existence (Sokushin jōbutsu gi)* and, in this or the following year, *The Meanings of Sound, Word, and Reality (Shōji jissō gi)*, followed by *The Meanings of the Word Hūṃ (Unji gi)*.

818 45 Stays on Mt. Kōya for about a year.

819 46 Conducts the consecration ceremony for Mt. Kōya. The central pillars of the Grand Pagoda of Mt. Kōya are cut. The temple is named Kongōbuji. Completes *The Secret Treasure-house of the Mirrors of Poetry (Bumkyō hifu ron)* on Mt. Kōya.

820 47 Writes *The Essentials of Poetry and Prose (Bunpitsu ganshin shō)*.

821 48 Reconstructs an artificial lake, Mannō no Ike, in his native locality. Writes *The Transmission of Shingon Dharma (Shingon fuhō den)*. Reproduces mandalas and other paintings brought back from China.

822 49 Builds a Shingon chapel in the Tōdaiji. Saichō dies.

823 50 Granted the Tōji. Emperor Saga retires.

824 51 Appointed junior director of monastic officials (*shōsōzu*).

825 52 Granted permission to construct the Lecture Hall (*Kōdō*) of the Tōji. Appointed tutor to the crown prince.

827	54	Appointed senior director of monastic officials (*daisōzu*).
828	55	Founds the School of Arts and Sciences (*Shugei shuchi-in*) for the general public near the Tōji.
829	56	Appointed administrative head of the Daianji in Nara.
830	57	Completes *The Ten Stages of the Development of Mind* (*Jūjūshin ron*) and, subsequently, *The Precious Key to the Secret Treasury* (*Hizō hōyaku*). Sometime between 830 and 835 compiles the dictionary *Tenrei banshō myōgi*.
831	58	Symptoms of his fatal disease appear.
832	59	Conducts the ceremony of Ten Thousand Flowers and Lights on Mt. Kōya. Stops eating grain. Seems to have left Kyoto for good to live on Mt. Kōya.
833	60	Emperor Nimmyō enthroned.
834	61	Initiates the Shingon ritual (*mishuhō*) in the palace. *The Secret Key to the Heart Sutra* (*Hannya shingyō hiken*) is probably written around this time.
835	62	Granted permission by the court to ordain three state-supported monks in the Shingon sect. Passes away on the twenty-first day of the third month on Mt. Kōya.

SELECTED BIBLIOGRAPHY

A. MAJOR WORKS OF KŪKAI

Sangō shīki (Indications of the Goals of the Three Teachings).

TEXT: *Kōbō daishi zenshū*, III, 324–56.

COMMENTARIES:

Fujiwara Tonkō (1063–1144). *Sangō kanchū shō. Shingonshū zensho*, Vol. XL.

Anonymous. *Sangō shīki chū. Shingonshū zensho*, Vol. XL.

Anonymous. *Sangō shīki chū shō. Shingonshū zensho*, Vol. XL.

Unshō (1614–93). *Sangō shīki chū sampo. Shingonshū zensho*, Vol. XL.

Katō Seishin. *Sangō shīki*. Tokyo, Iwanami shoten, 1935.

Watanabe Shōkō. *Sangō shīki. Koten Nihon bungaku zenshū*, Vol. XV. Tokyo, Chikuma shobō, 1964.

————, and Miyasaka Yūshō. *Sangō shīki: Seireishū. Nihon koten bungaku taikei*, Vol. LXXI. Tokyo, Iwanami shoten, 1965.

Shōrai mokuroku (A Memorial Presenting a List of Newly Imported Sutras and Other Items).

TEXT: *Kōbō daishi zenshū*, I, 69–102.

Benkenmitsu nikyō ron (The Difference between Exoteric and Esoteric Buddhism).

TEXT: *Kōbō daishi zenshū*, I, 474–505.

COMMENTARIES:

Seisen (1025–1115). *Benkenmitsu nikyō ron kenkyō shō*, T77.

Raiyu (1226–1304). *Benkenmitsu nikyō ron shikō shō. Shinkonshū zensho*, Vol. XXV.

Yūkai (1345–1416). *Benkenmitsu nikyō ron shō. Shingonshū zensho*, Vol. XXV.

Yūkai. *Benkenmitsu nikyō ron kōkoku shō. Shingonshū zensho,* Vol. XXV.

Kakugen (1643–1720). *Benkenmitsu nikyō ron satsugi shō. Chizan zensho,* Vol. VIII.

Ryōkai (1698–1755). *Benkenmitsu nikyō ron kōen. Chizan zensho,* Vol. VIII.

Kaijō (1750–1805). *Benkenmitsu nikyō ron chōhiroku. Buzan zensho,* Vol. VIII.

Kaijō. *Benkenmitsu nikyō ron kōroku zassō. Buzan zensho,* Vol. VIII.

Hizō hōyaku (The Precious Key to the Secret Treasury).

TEXT: *Kōbō daishi zenshū,* I, 417–73.

COMMENTARIES:
Fujiwara Tonkō. *Hizō hōyaku shō. Shingonshū zensho,* Vol. XI.
Raiyu. *Hizō hōyaku kanchū. Shingonshū zensho,* Vol. XI.
Seishuku (1366–1439). *Hizō hōyaku shiki. Shingonshū zensho,* Vol. XI.
Unshō. *Hizō hōyaku sange. Chizan zensho,* Vol. VII.
Kakugen. *Hizō hōyaku satsuyō shō. Chizan zensho,* Vol. VIII.
Ryōkai. *Hizō hōyaku kōen. Chizan zensho,* Vol. VIII.

Sokushin jōbutsu gi (Attaining Enlightenment in This Very Existence).

TEXT: *Kōbō daishi zenshū,* I, 506–18.

COMMENTARIES:
Kakuban (1095–1143). *Shingonshū sokushin jōbutsu gi shō. Kōgyō daishi zenshū,* Vol. I.
Raiyu. *Sokushin jōbutsu gi kentoku shō. Shingonshū zensho,* Vol. XIII.
Shōshin (1287–1357). *Sokushin jōbutsu gi shō. Shingonshū zensho,* Vol. XIII.
Yūkai. *Sokushin jōbutsu gi shō. Shingonshū zensho,* Vol. XIII.
Kakugen. *Sokushin jōbutsu gi satsugi shō. Chizan zensho,* Vol. VIII.
Donjaku (1674–1742). *Sokushin jōbutsu gi shiki. Shingonshū zensho,* Vol. XIII.
Ryōkai. *Sokushin jōbutsu gi kōen. Chizan zensho,* Vol. VIII.

Shōji jissō gi (The Meanings of Sound, Word, and Reality).

TEXT: *Kōbō daishi zenshū,* I, 521–34.

COMMENTARIES:
Dōhan (1178–1252). *Shōji jissō gi shō. Shingonshū zensho,* Vol. XIV.
Raiyu. *Shōji jissō gi kaihi shō. Shingonshū zensho,* Vol. XIV.
Kōhō (1306–62). *Shōji jissō gi kuhitsu* (recorded by Kembō). *Shingonshū zensho,* Vol. XIV.
Yūkai. *Shōji jissō gi shō. Shingonshū zensho,* Vol. XIV.
Kakugen. *Shōji jissō gi satsugi shō. Chizan zensho,* Vol. VIII.
Donjaku. *Shōji jissō gi shiki. Shingonshū zensho,* Vol. XIV.

Ryōkai. *Shōji jissō gi kōen. Chizan zensho*, Vol. VIII.

Shūkai (d. 1789). *Shōji jissō gi kiyō. Shingonshū zensho*, Vol. XIV.

Unji gi (The Meanings of the Word Hūṃ).

TEXT: *Kōbō daishi zenshū*, I, 535–53.

COMMENTARIES:

Raiyu. *Unji gi tanshū ki. Shingonshū zensho*, Vol. XV.

Ryūgen (1341–1426). *Unji gi shaku kanchū shō. Shingonshū zensho*, Vol. XV.

Yūkai. *Unji gi shō. Shingonshū zensho*, Vol. XV.

Raiyo (1455–1531). *Unji gi monsho. Shingonshū zensho*, Vol. XV.

Kakugen. *Unji gi satsugi shō. Chizan zensho*, Vol. VIII.

Donjaku. *Unji gi shiki. Shingonshū zensho*, Vol. XV.

Ryōkai. *Unji gi kōen. Chizan zensho*, Vol. VIII.

Shūkai. *Unji gi sanyō. Shingonshū zensho*, Vol. XV.

Hannya shingyō hiken (The Secret Key to the Heart Sutra).

TEXT: *Kōbō daishi zenshū*, I, 554–62.

COMMENTARIES:

Kakuban. *Hannya shingyō hiken ryakuchū. Kōgyō daishi zenshū*, Vol. I.

Raiyu. *Hannya shingyō hiken kaihō shō. Shingonshū zensho*, Vol. XVI.

Kōhō. *Hannya shingyō hiken monsho* (recorded by Kembō). *Shingonshū zensho*, Vol. XVI.

Yūkai. *Hannya shingyō hiken shō. Shingonshū zensho*, Vol. XVI.

Yūkai. *Hannya shingyō hiken shinriki shō. Shingonshū zensho*, Vol. XVI.

Kakugen. *Hannya shingyō hiken satsugi shō. Chizan zensho*, Vol. VIII.

Ryōkai. *Hannya shingyō hiken kōen. Chizan zensho*, Vol. VIII.

B. STUDIES ON THE LIFE AND THOUGHT OF KŪKAI

Akamatsu Toshihide. "Shoki no Tōji (The Tōji in its early period)," *Bukkyō Geijutsu: ARS Buddhica*, XLVII (1961), 1–12.

Battacharya, B. *An Introduction to Buddhist Esoterism*. London, Oxford University Press, 1932.

Bharati, Agehananda. *The Tantric Tradition*. London, Rider, 1965.

Ch'en, Kenneth. *Buddhism in China: A Historical Survey*. Princeton University Press, 1964.

Chou I-liang. "Tantrism in China," *Harvard Journal of Asiatic Studies*, VIII (1945), 241–332.

Das Gupta, S. B. *An Introduction to Tantric Buddhism*. University of Calcutta Press, 1950.

de Bary, Wm. Theodore, ed. *Sources of Japanese Tradition*. New York, Columbia University Press, 1958.

———, ed. *The Buddhist Tradition*. New York, Modern Library, 1969.

Dengyō daishi shōsoku (Letters of Dengyō daishi), Shakuka Section, *Zoku gunsho-ruijū*, Vol. XXVIII. Tokyo, Zoku gunsho-ruijū kanseikai, 1926.

Dengyō daishi zenshū (The collected works of Dengyō daishi). 5 vols. Tokyo, Tendaishū shūten kankōkai, 1912.

Eliot, Sir Charles. *Japanese Buddhism*. London, Arnold, 1935.

Glasenapp, H. V. *Buddhistische Mysterien*. Stuttgart, W. Spemann, 1940.

Gorai Shigeru. *Kōya-hijiri*. Tokyo, Kadokawa shoten, 1965.

Hakeda, Yoshito S., tr. *The Awakening of Faith*. New York, Columbia University Press, 1967.

Hase Hōshū, ed. *Kōbō daishiden zenshū* (The complete biographies of Kōbō daishi). Kyoto, Rokudai shimpōsha, 1935.

Hasumi Shigeyasu. "Tōji no chōkoku o chūshin toshite (Concerning the sculptures in the Tōji)," *Bukkyō Geijutsu: ARS Buddhica*, XLVII (1961), 27–40.

———, ed. *Kōnin Jōgan jidai no bijutsu* (Arts in the Kōnin Jōgan period). Tokyo University Press, 1962.

Ienaga Saburo, ed. *Nihon Bukkyōshi* (History of Japanese Buddhism), Vol. I. Kyoto, Hōzōkan, 1967.

———, ed. *Nihon Bukkyōshisō no tenkai* (Development of Japanese Buddhist thought). Kyoto, Heirakuji shoten, 1956.

Igarashi Tsutomu. *Heianchō bungakushi* (History of Heian literature), Vol. I. Tokyo, Tokyodō, 1937.

Ishida Mosaku, and Okazaki Jōji. *Himitsu hōgu* (Esoteric ritual implements). Tokyo, Kōdansha, 1965.

Kamei Katsuichirō. *Nihonjin no seishinshi* (Spiritual history of the Japanese), Vol. I. Tokyo, Bungeishunjūsha, 1967.

Kanayama Bokushō. *Kōbō daishi no shinkōkan* (The outlook of the faith of Kōbō daishi). Koyasan University Press, 1943.

———, and Yanagida Kenjūrō. *Nihon Shingon no tetsugaku* (The philosophy of Japanese Shingon). Tokyo, Kōbundō shobō, 1943.

Katsumata Shunkyō, ed. *Kōbō daishi chosaku zenshū* (The complete works of Kōbō daishi), Vol. I. Tokyo, Sankibō, 1968.

Katsuno Ryūshin. *Hieizan to Kōyasan* (Mt. Hiei and Mt. Kōya). Tokyo, Shibundō, 1959.

Kawaguchi Hisao. *Heianchō Nihon kambungakushi no kenkyū* (Studies in the history of Japanese kambun literature in the Heian period), Vol. I. Tokyo, Meiji shoin, 1960.

Kawasaki Yasuyuki. *Nihon bunkashi taikei* (History of Japanese culture), Vol. IV. Tokyo, Shōgakukan, 1958.

Kitayama Shigeo. *Heiankyō: Nihon no rekishi* (History of Japan: the Heian capital), Vol. VI. Tokyo, Chūōkōronsha, 1965.

Kobayashi Taichirō. "Tōji ni hayuru geijutsu no eikō (The glories of art at the Tōji)," *Bukkyō Geijutsu: ARS Buddhica*, XLVII (1961), 60–70.

Kōbō daishi shodeshi zenshū (The complete works of the disciples of Kōbō daishi). 3 vols. Kyoto, Rokudai shimpōsha, 1942.

Kojima Noriyuki. *Jōdai Nihon bungaku to Chūgoku bungaku* (Ancient Japanese and Chinese literature), Vol. III. Tokyo, Hanawa shobō, 1965.

Konishi Jin'ichi. *Bunkyō-hifuron-kō* (Examination of the *Bunkyō-hifuron*). 3 vols. Kyoto, Ōyashima shuppan, 1948 (vol. I). Tokyo, Kōdansha, 1951 (vol. II); 1952 (vol. III).

Kōyasan daigaku, ed. *Mikkyōgaku Mikkyōshi ronbunshū* (Studies of esoteric Buddhism and Tantrism, in commemoration of the 1,150th anniversary of the founding of Koyasan [sic]). Koyasan University Press, 1965.

Kurata Bunsaku. *Mikkyō jiin to Jōgan chōkoku* (Esoteric Buddhist temples and the sculpture of the Jōgan period). Tokyo, Shōgakukan, 1967.

Kushida Ryōkō. *Shingon Mikkyō seiritsukatei no kenkyū* (Studies in the process of establishment of Shingon Esoteric Buddhism). Tokyo, Sankibō, 1964.

Makino Shinnosuke. *Kōbō daishiden no kenkyū* (Study of the biographies of Kōbō daishi). Kyoto, Zenshōsha, 1921.

Matsunaga Yūkei. *Mikkyō no rekishi* (History of Esoteric Buddhism). Kyoto, Heirakuji shoten, 1969.

Miura Akio. *Kōbō daishi denki shūran* (Compendium of the biographies of Kōbō daishi). Tokyo, Morie shoten, 1934.

Miyasaka Yushō. *Ningen no shujusō: Hizō hōyaku* (The various aspects of man: the precious key to the secret treasury). Tokyo, Chikuma shobō, 1967.

Miyasaka Yūshō, and Umehara Takeshi. *Seimei no umi: Kūkai* (The sea of life: Kūkai). Tokyo, Kadokawa shoten, 1968.

Moriyama Shōshin, ed. *Bunkashijō yori mitaru Kōbō daishiden* (The life of Kōbō daishi seen from the standpoint of cultural history). Tokyo, Buzanha shūmusho, 1931.

———, ed. *Shingonshū nempyō* (Chronology of the Shingon sect). Tokyo, Buzanha shūmusho, 1934.

Naitō Torajirō. *Nihon bunkashi kenkyū* (Studies in Japanese cultural history). Tokyo, Kōbundō shobō, 1936.

Nakano Gishō. *Kūkai, gendai Bukkyō kōza*, Vol. V. Tokyo, Kadokawa shoten, 1955.

———. *Shingonshū, Bukkyō kōza*, Vol. VI. Tokyo, Daitō shuppansha, 1959.

———. *Kōyasan: hihō* (Mt. Kōya: secret treasures), Vol. VII. Tokyo, Kōdansha, 1968.

Nishida Naojirō. *Nihon bunkashi ronkō* (Examination of the cultural history of Japan). Tokyo, Yoshikawa kōbundō, 1963.

Okada Masayuki. *Nihon kambungakushi* (History of Japanese kambun literature). Rev. ed. Tokyo, Yoshikawa kōbundō, 1960.

Onozuka Kichō. "Kōbō daishi kyōgaku keisei no haikei (The background of the formation of the teachings of Kōbō daishi)," *Taishō Daigaku Kiyō*, LIV (1968).

Osabe Kazuo. *Ichigyō zenji no kenkyū* (Study of the master I-hsing). Kobe, Kobe shōka daigaku press, 1963.

Ōya Tokujō. "Sangō shīki sakusei no haikei toshiteno Naracho no shisō (Thought in the Nara period as the background to the composition of the Indications)," *Mikkyō Kenkyū*, LI (1934), 265–89.

Ōyama Kōjun. *Mikkyōshi gaisetsu to kyōgi* (An outline of the history of Esoteric Buddhism and its doctrine). Koyasan University Press, 1962.

———. *Kōbō daishi no shōgai to shisō* (The life and thought of Kōbō daishi). Koyasan University Press, 1965.

Saunders, E. Dale. *Mudra: A Study of Symbolic Gestures in Japanese Buddhist Sculpture*. New York, Bollingen Foundation, 1960.

Sawa Ryūken. *Mikkyō bijutsu ron* (On the Esoteric Buddhist arts). Kyoto, Benridō, 1955.

———. *Nihon no Mikkyō bitjutsu* (The Esoteric Buddhist arts of Japan). Kyoto, Benridō, 1961.

———. *Mikkyō no bijutsu* (The Esoteric Buddhist arts). Tokyo, Heibonsha, 1964.

Shimizu Zenzō. "Tōji kōdō shoson ni okeru kyōgi to sono hyōgen (Doctrines and expressions of the deities in the lecture hall of the Tōji)," *Bijutsushi*, XIV, No. 2 (1964).

Sonoda Kōyū. *Saichō to Kūkai* (Saichō and Kūkai). *Nihon rekishi*, Vol. IV. Tokyo, Iwanami shoten, 1962.

Tajima Ryūjun. *Etude sur le Mahāvairocana-sūtra (Dainichikyō), avec la traduction commentée du premier chapitre*. Paris, Maisonneuve, 1936.

———. *Les Deux Grands Maṇḍalas et la Doctrine de l'Esoterisme Shingon*. Tokyo, Maison Franco-Japonaise, 1959.

Takakusu Junjiro. *The Essentials of Buddhist Philosophy*. Honolulu, University of Hawaii Press, 1947.

Tamaki Kōshirō. *Shoki no Bukkyō* (Buddhism in its early period). *Nihon Bukkyō*, I. Tokyo, Chikuma shobō, 1968.

Tōji bunka hozonkai, ed. *Daishi no mitera: Tōji* (Daishi's temple: Tōji). Tokyo, Bijutsusha, 1965.

Toganoo Mitsudō, ed. *Kōbō daishi to Nihon bunka* (Kōbō daishi and Japanese culture). Kyoto, Rokudai shimpōsha, 1929.

Toganoo Shōun. *Himitsu jisō no kenkyū* (Study of Esoteric Buddhist praxis). Koyasan University Press, 1935.

———. *Mandala no kenkyū* (Study of mandalas). Koyasan University Press, 1937.

———. *Himitsu Bukkyōshi* (History of Esoteric Buddhism). Koyasan University Press, 1937.

Tsuji Zennosuke. *Nihon Bukkyōshi* (History of Japanese Buddhism), Vol. I. Tokyo, Iwanami shoten, 1944.

Tsunoda Bunei. *Saeki Imaemishi.* Tokyo, Yoshikawa kōbunkan, 1963.

Tucci, Giuseppe. *The Theory and Practice of the Mandala.* London, Rider, 1961.

Watanabe Shōkō. *Saichō to Kūkai* (Saichō and Kūkai). *Nihon bunka kenkyū,* Vol. II. Tokyo, Shinchōsha, 1955.

———. *Japanese Buddhism: A Critical Appraisal.* Tokyo, Kokusai Bunka Shinkōkai, 1968.

———, and Miyasaka Yūshō. *Shamon Kūkai* (Monk Kūkai). Tokyo, Chikuma shobō, 1967.

Suzuki, Beatrice Erskine Lane. *Impressions of Mahayana Buddhism.* London, Luzac, 1940.

Yoshioka Yoshitoyo. "Sangō shīki no seiritsu ni tsuite (On the organization of the introduction to the three teachings [sic])," *Indogaku Bukkyōgaku Kenkyū,* XV (1960), 114–18.

INDEX

A: as *anutpāda*, 80*n*, 203*n;* as seed mantra, 80*n;* in sound-word-reality, 239; meanings of, 219

Abhidharma, 247

Abhiṣeka: defined, 32*n;* 141 ff.; first in Japan, 36-37; fivefold, 147, 148; introductory (*kechien kanjō*), 44; of the Transmission of the Dharma (*dembō kanjō*), 45

Abishido, 121*n*

Acala (Fudō), 99, 160*n*

Ādi-anutpāda, 80*n*

Admonishments of Kōnin, The (Kōnin no goyuikai), 45, 94-95

Ākāśagarbha (Kokūzō), 16, 102*n;* mantra of, 22

Akṣara, 230

Akṣobhya (Ashuku), 83, 240*n*

Ālaya, defined, 71*n;* -consciousness, 71*n,* 197, 198, 200, 256*n,* 270

Amasake Kiyonari, 15

Amaterasu, 8, 81, 90

Amitābha (Amida), 84, 240*n*

Amoghasiddhi (Fukūjōju), 84, 240*n*

Amoghavajra, *see* Pu-k'ung

Analects, 15, 58, 104, 105, 113

Aniroddha, 211*n*

Annen, 5

Anutpāda, 203*n*

Arhatship, 173, 270*n*

Aspiration to Enlightenment (Bodaishin ron), 9, 75, 166-223 *passim,* especially 175, 195, 200, 205, 216, 218 ff., 227

Atō Ōtari, 14-15, 102

Attaining enlightenment in this very existence, 77 ff.; essence, 88

Attaining Enlightenment in This Very Existence (Sokushin jōbutsu gi): interpretation, 227-34; summary in verse, 227; verse on Six Great Elements, 228

Attributes (*sō*), 228

Avalokiteśvara (Kannon), 160*n,* 207*n,* 264, 267

Avataṃsaka Sutra, 23, 149, 241, 244, 245; essentials of, 212-13

Awakening of Faith, The, 23, 27, 137*n,* 196

Being: four modes of, 205*n;* six states of, 252; three types of, 198*n*

Bimba, 230

Biography of Kūkai Sōzu (Kūkai sōzu den), 15*n;* quoted, 14-16, 26-27, 59-60

Birth, four types of, 127*n,* 158

Bodaishin ron, see Aspiration to Enlightenment

Bodhicitta (bodaishin), 82, 96-97, 209, 227

Bodhisattvahood: Five Ranks of Development of, 213*n;* Ten Stages of, 152, 156, 187